Sarah Beelur

March 2077

D1596087

Eclipse of Action

Eclipse of Action

Tragedy and Political Economy

RICHARD HALPERN

The University of Chicago Press

CHICAGO AND LONDON

The University of Chicago Press, Chicago 60637
The University of Chicago Press, Ltd., London
© 2017 by The University of Chicago
Published 2017
Printed in the United States of America

26 25 24 23 22 21 20 19 18 17   1 2 3 4 5

ISBN-13: 978-0-226-43365-3 (cloth)
ISBN-13: 978-0-226-43379-0 (e-book)
DOI: 10.7208/chicago/9780226433790.001.0001

The University of Chicago Press gratefully acknowledges the generous support of
the Abraham and Rebecca Stein Faculty Publication Fund at New York University
toward the publication of this book.

Library of Congress Cataloging-in-Publication Data
Names: Halpern, Richard, 1954– author.
Title: Eclipse of action : tragedy and political economy / Richard Halpern.
Description: Chicago ; London : The University of Chicago Press, 2017. | Includes
bibliographical references and index.
Identifiers: LCCN 2016032545 | ISBN 9780226433653 (cloth : alk. paper) |
ISBN 9780226433790 (e-book)
Subjects: LCSH: Tragedy—History and criticism. | Tragedy—Themes, motives. |
Economics in literature.
Classification: LCC PN 1892 .H23 2017 | DDC 809.2/512—DC23 LC record
available at https://lccn.loc.gov/2016032545

♾ This paper meets the requirements of ANSI/NISO Z39.48-1992
(Permanence of Paper).

Contents

Acknowledgments

I am grateful to the John Simon Guggenheim Memorial Foundation for a fellowship that contributed significantly to the completion of this book. That fellowship was enhanced by the generosity of the Dean's Office at Johns Hopkins University. The Dean of Graduate Studies at New York University likewise provided much-needed relief from teaching.

My thanks to those who read and commented on chapters in various stages, some dating back twelve years: Crystal Bartolovich, Jonathan Goldberg, Martin Harries, Julia Jarcho, Victoria Kahn, Christopher Kendrick, Joseph Lowenstein, Julia Reinhard Lupton, Joanna Picciotto, Clifford Siskin, and Connie You. I wish in addition to thank the anonymous readers for the University of Chicago Press for their very helpful suggestions. Mark Griffith of the Classics Department at Berkeley deserves special mention here. I cold-called him years ago on the topic of Aeschylus, and he responded with a truly stunning and memorable display of intellectual generosity. He is a mensch. Dori Hale, Aaron Landsman, and Mary Poovey helped in their own ways.

Connie, Annie, and Beau were (and are) a continual source of delight and support.

*   *   *

Portions of chapters 1 and 4 originally appeared as "Eclipse of Action: *Hamlet* and the Political Economy of Playing," in *Shakespeare Quarterly* 59, no. 4 (2008): 450–82. Reprinted with permission by Johns Hopkins University Press. Copyright © 2008 Folger Shakespeare Library. An earlier version of chapter 3 appeared as "Marlowe's Theater of Night: *Doctor Faustus and Capital*," in *English Literary History* 71, no. 2 (2004): 455–95. Copyright © 2004 John Hopkins University Press. A portion of chapter 5 appeared as "Samson's Gospel of Sex: Failed Universals in Milton and Freud," in *Rethinking Feminism in Early Modern Studies: Gender, Race, and Sexuality*, ed. Ania Loomba and Melissa E. Sanchez (Burlington, VT: Ashgate, 2016), 187–94. Copyright © 2016. And a portion of chapter 7 originally appeared in *PMLA* 129, no. 4 (2014), published by the Modern Language Association of America, as "Beckett's Tragic Pantry: *Endgame* and the Deflation of the Act," 742–50. I thank the various publishers for permission to reproduce these materials here.

I

As an influential narrative has it, the history of tragedy is itself tragic. Following a miraculous birth in fifth-century Athens and an equally brilliant resurgence in the early modern period, tragic drama goes into an irremediable decline. Such is the argument of George Steiner's *The Death of Tragedy* (1961), perhaps the definitive statement of this position from within the field of literary criticism. But Steiner's claims would have been less influential had they not been backed up by a long pedigree. Much of the time, his imposing erudition merely fleshes out an intellectual scaffolding that can be traced back to Hegel and Nietzsche. Nietzsche pushes the decline of tragedy back to the Greeks themselves, where Euripides and then, definitively, Socrates kill the Dionysian spirit of music with their rationalism. In his 1693 volume, *A Short View of Tragedy: Its Original Excellence and Corruption*, Thomas Rymer blames everyone from the Romans to Shakespeare for defiling the Greek example. No matter the era, tragedy seems to be ailing.

Stories of cultural and artistic decline appeal particularly to conservative minds, an impression reinforced by the roster of names in the previous paragraph. It is perhaps telling that the most significant ripostes to Steiner came from Marxists: Raymond Williams's *Modern Tragedy* (1966) and Terry Eagleton's *Sweet Violence: The Idea of the Tragic* (2003). But lest the drawing up of political ranks seem too neat, a third Marxist, Alain Badiou, has more recently declared that "For the moment, there exists no modern tragedy.... Contemporary theatre desires the tragic, without for the moment disposing of the means necessary for it."[1] Badiou's repeated "for the moment" draws back from the definitive cadences of a Steiner, but the judgment is largely the same. Modernity and tragedy are somehow inimical.

Why? Steiner points to many causes, including the decay of a collective, ritual culture that bolstered premodern tragic drama. But for the most part, his diagnosis focuses on changes in thought and outlook. Christianity's promise of salvation is, in his view, profoundly untragic. But the main culprit for Steiner, as for Nietzsche, is rationalism: modernity's conviction that the world is ultimately knowable, and fixable, through the application of reason. "It is the triumph of rationalism and secular metaphysics which marks the point of no return."[2] Steiner defines "absolute tragedy" as "a view of reality in which man is taken to be an unwelcome guest in the world," and in which suffering is therefore both insupportable and inexplicable.[3] Such a worldview simply cannot thrive in the optimism of Enlightenment.

I do not believe that tragedy died, though it did go on extended vacation through the eighteenth and most of the nineteenth centuries, a fact that deserves continued attention. When significant tragedy does revive, it looks very different from what preceded it. Like Steiner, I think that modernity poses new (if not quite mortal) challenges for tragic drama, but I propose that we look for these in a counterintuitive place: the emergence of political economy in the eighteenth century. To be clear from the start: the discourse of political economy does not in any sense "cause" or provoke a difficult situation for tragedy. But it gives definitive intellectual form to conditions of capitalist modernity that do—conditions that cannot be reduced entirely to "worldviews" or cultural outlook, though they involve these as well. Specifically, capitalism induces a crisis of *action* that undercuts traditional conceptions of tragedy.[4]

Aristotle famously describes tragedy as "the imitation of an action."[5] The word for drama itself, as he points out, comes from the Greek verb *dran*, "to do."[6] Action is the very essence of tragedy; whatever view of the world arises from tragic drama depends entirely on the weightiness and intelligibility of the speech and action its characters perform. The centrality of action to Aristotle's poetics accords, moreover, with its centrality to his ethics, where it is primarily responsible for human happiness—or, conversely, the lack of it. Happiness is that which supervenes upon acting in a gracious, beautiful, and prudent fashion. It is less the goal of action than its side effect.

For Adam Smith in *The Wealth of Nations*, by contrast, "the public happiness" is secured not by action in an ethico-political sense but by production. Making, not doing, generates the wealth of nations and thus the very different conception of happiness pursued by modern, commercial societies.

But by demoting action from the summit of human activity, by canceling its privileged relation to human happiness or grief, Smith also, if only incidentally, degrades the very substance of tragedy as traditionally understood. This would be far less consequential for tragedy if political economy did not in this regard correctly diagnose the logic of capitalist culture. The crisis of modern tragedy is not, therefore, primarily a matter of worldview or outlook; it reflects a quite consequential crisis of action that afflicts modernity and is given its clearest intellectual form in political economy. In this sense Smith's views must be distinguished from those of earlier intellectual systems that likewise denigrated action to some degree. Stoicism and Protestantism are two conspicuous examples in the Western tradition. The difference between Smith's thought and those others is that the very structure of commercial society materially enforced his judgments. Smith's was a revolution in thought, but not in thought alone.

crisp "of" action not crisis in action

What I am calling a crisis *of* action must be distinguished first of all from the crisis *in* action that has always defined tragedy. Classical tragic drama portrays misguided or malign or unlucky actions and decisions that lead to catastrophic results. In this sense, crises within the realm of action are as old as tragic drama itself. What I am describing is something else: not particular actions that go awry but a crisis that afflicts the realm of action as such, and thereby threatens to render tragic drama's crises *in* action less meaningful and consequential.

In the theater of the late nineteenth and twentieth centuries, this crisis takes the form of a positive revolt against dramatic action in particular and Aristotelian dramaturgy in general. Edward Maeterlink, inventor of "static drama," asserted that, "Generally speaking, anybody is more interesting doing nothing than doing anything."[7] Gertrude Stein reconceived of drama as landscape in which a temporally unfolding action is replaced by spatial arrangements of characters and objects. Stein in turn directly influenced numerous postmodern or postdramatic playwrights, from Robert Wilson and Richard Foreman to Suzan-Lori Parks.[8] But the modernist revolt against dramatic action has antecedents that stretch back to eighteenth-century experiments in mono- and duo-drama, lyric drama, and melodrama. Just a few years before the publication of Smith's *Wealth of Nations*, the Swiss mathematician and aesthetic theorist Johann Georg Sulzer stated in his *Allgemeine Theorie des Schönen Künste* (1771–74): "The name of the lyric drama indicates that no gradually unfolding action takes place here, with plots, intrigues, and crisscrossing ventures, as in drama made for the theatre."[9] Describing the "aesthetic regime of art," which he traces from the mid-eighteenth to the early twentieth century, Jacques Rancière observes that "the theater itself, the ancient stage of 'active men,' in order to draw itself closer to art and life, comes to repudiate action and its agents by considering itself a choir, a pictorial fresco, or architecture in movement." He then goes on to coordinate this "tendency toward suspended action" in drama with a corresponding turn within the political itself. "Emancipated workers could not repudiate the hierarchical model governing the distribution of activities without taking their distance from the capacity to act which subjected them to it, and from the action plans of the engineers of the future. . . . The fullest expression of the fighting workers' collective was called the general strike, an exemplary equivalence of strategic action and radical inaction."[10] Without contesting Rancière's point about the withdrawal from action as a strategic form of resistance, I would merely point out that this strategy, along with its possibilities for success or failure, ought to be situated within the broader crisis of action I shall outline in this book. And that the turn from action in the theater should therefore be placed within this context as well.

The long, slow revolt against an Aristotelian plot that is the mimesis of action culminates in what Hans-Thies Lehmann has aptly dubbed "postdramatic theater," which decisively liberates itself from the dramatic text as masterpiece and from the fictional representation of action in order to become "more the presentation of an *atmosphere* and *state of things*."[11] "While for good reason no poetics of drama has ever abandoned the concept of action as the object of mimesis," states Lehmann, "the reality of the new theatre begins precisely with the taking away of this trinity of drama, imitation, and action."[12] Lehmann argues that postdramatic theater maintains some relation with drama even while representing an aesthetic advance beyond it that renders drama "obsolete" (a term he is fond of). Lehmann's brilliant treatment of postdramatic theater is mostly aesthetic and philosophical, though he does venture some social and political explanations in his book's epilogue. I would supplement these by suggesting that postdramatic theater can be understood with respect to the crisis of action I shall set forth in this book. But in making this diagnosis I am not, like some latter-day Lukács, arguing for the restoration of a healthier, more holistic, or more action-oriented form of dramatic art. Lehmann allows me to specify, in any case, that my own book is about drama and the dramatic tradition rather than about theater, although I shall offer some additional thoughts about postdramatic theater in my postscript. For that reason too I shall have little to say about performance theory, though I shall often place the plays I treat in theatrical context.

"Theatre without drama, we might suspect," writes Lehmann, "would be a theatre without the tragic."[13] He thus appears to align himself in some sense with Steiner, though without Steiner's mournful tones. But in fact, as Lehmann goes on to claim, postdramatic theater can deliver various forms of tragic affect and experience, though now detached from tragic plot. It might be argued, then, taking into account theatrical developments of which Steiner could be at best dimly aware in 1961, that the fate of tragedy precisely inverts that which he predicted. For Steiner, drama will go on, though now bereft of the resources of tragic vision. For Lehmann, by contrast, the tragic will go on, though now freed from the outmoded mechanisms of drama. In either case, tragedy, understood precisely as the generation of tragic feeling and experience *by way of tragic plot*, will have ended, decomposing into its constituent parts, which now go their separate ways. In this sense the two prognoses are complementary, though also exaggerated. But as I shall argue a bit further on, the separation of "the tragic" from tragedy is not without consequences.

I am not the first to suggest a link between the dilemmas of modern tragedy and a crisis of action. Although the name of Sigmund Freud is not immediately evocative of either, he does in fact advance notable views on the topic. Freud's best-known statement on tragedy occurs in *The Interpretation of Dreams* (1900), during the first public airing of his theory of the Oedipus complex, which he illustrates through readings of *Oedipus the King* and *Hamlet*. Both of these tragedies of fate, Freud claims, reveal "fate" to be the ineluctable prompting of Oedipal desire. In Sophocles's play, the Oedipal wish to kill one's father and marry one's mother is directly acted out. Things are different for Shakespeare:

> Another of the great creations of tragic poetry, Shakespeare's *Hamlet*, has its roots in the same soil as *Oedipus Rex*. But the changed treatment of the same material reveals the whole difference in the mental life of these two widely separated epochs of civilization: the secular advance of repression in the emotional life of mankind. In the *Oedipus* the child's wishful phantasy that underlies it is brought into the open and realized as it would be in a dream. In *Hamlet* it remains repressed; and—just as in the case of a neurosis—we only learn of its existence from its inhibiting consequences.[14]

For Freud, *Hamlet* is a play about *not* acting out the Oedipal wish—a play in which repression of that wish blocks Hamlet from acting at all in the one way that matters to him. Despite registering a kind of cultural illness suffered by the Elizabethan age compared to Sophoclean health, however, *Hamlet* is in no way artistically inferior to its Greek original.

Most readers of this well-known passage fail to recall, however, that

Freud does not stop there in his historical narrative. Discussing tragedies of fate, he remarks:

> The lesson which, it is said, the deeply moved spectator should learn from the tragedy is submission to the divine will and realization of his own impotence. Modern dramatists have accordingly tried to achieve a similar tragic effect by weaving the same contrast into a plot invented by themselves. But the spectators have looked on unmoved while a curse or an oracle was fulfilled in spite of all the efforts of some innocent man: later tragedies of destiny have failed in their effect. . . . There must be something which makes a voice within us ready to recognize the compelling force of destiny in the *Oedipus*, while we can dismiss as merely arbitrary such dispositions as are laid down in [Grillparzer's] *Die Ahnfrau* or other modern tragedies of destiny.[15]

Thus does Freud enlist himself in the "death of tragedy" camp. In attempting to depart from the primal sources of tragic power, embodied in the tale of Oedipus, modern playwrights go astray. Their failure is a miniature, dispiriting allegory of the modern—that is, of innovation separating itself from tradition and stumbling as a result. Just as Oedipus's active effort to free himself from the pronouncement of the oracle has tragic results, so the moderns wishing to depart from the immemorial Oedipal script find that their creative acts fall flat. Granted, were we to take Freud seriously, tragedies of fate would have precious few possibilities for plot. Moreover, the implication seems to be that the Oedipal ur-plot is not something intentionally chosen but rather something that must irrupt in the creative process itself. It is not as if consciously deciding to frame a surreptitiously Oedipal tragedy would work either. The modern tragic playwright truly has no options. Nor does Freud explain exactly why this should be so. But the arc of his narrative, in which civilization demands increasing levels of repression, implies that the movement from openly Oedipal plots in ancient Athens to hidden Oedipal plots in Elizabethan England eventually results in a state where the excessively civilized moderns are cut off from this energizing source entirely. Oedipus openly acts out Oedipal wishes; Hamlet finds himself unable to act because that wish has become repressed; and the characters in modern plays may act in any way they choose, but to no effect because the unconscious stakes of action have been withdrawn. For Freud, there is no point in even recounting the plot of *Die Ahnfrau*.

Freud's thesis that the progress of civilization entails increasing repression receives fuller treatment in his *Civilization and Its Discontents* (1931). There, the emphasis shifts from repressed sexual wishes to repressed aggression. Civilized behavior, Freud claims, cannot flourish unless our violent impulses toward our neighbor are repressed and turned inward, where they form the basis of the superego and engender conscience. Unfortunately, obeying the commands of the irrational superego simply makes it more insistent. Conscience punishes us for just wishing to do something wrong even if we don't actually do it. The result is a pervasive sense of guilt that Freud sees as modernity's distinctive affliction. But this is a guilty feeling in the absence of guilty *acts*. Not only do feelings of guilt pursue us if we don't do anything wrong; they will do so *especially* if we do nothing wrong—that is, if we follow the dictates of conscience and thus feed the superego's voracious demands. In modernity, guilt—the essentially tragic condition—has become definitively separated from the deed. It is not incidental that Freud quotes Hamlet's line "Thus conscience does make cowards of us all" at the beginning of his book's final chapter, which diagnoses guilt as the malaise of modern life.

Freud's understanding of modern tragedy and a crisis of action has some significant points of contact with my own. But for Freud, that to which action falls prey is inhibition or repression. Action retains its significance but becomes no longer available because still-stronger forces oppose it. This stance, and particularly the notion that guilty affect comes to replace action, obviously owes more than a little to Nietzsche. What I am describing is something different—a relative re-, or rather, de-valuation of action. For Freud, the act is—or would be, if allowed—still the means to achieve ancient forms of happiness that have become unavailable because proscribed. For Smith, or at least the Smith of *The Wealth of Nations*, a new form of happiness arises that requires not action but productive activity to achieve. People can act all they want, but this will merely distract them from what matters.

What I do share with Freud and most of the "death of tragedy" cohort is a conviction that the fate of tragic drama is entwined with larger civilizational processes, and that a long view is therefore required to assess what is happening. The fate of action demands an equally long view. As I shall argue, making and doing, *poiesis* and *praxis*, exist in a state of conceptual tension from the time of the Greeks. Political economy therefore brings into the open a long-simmering conflict. Drama stages this conflict in particularly vivid ways. As a literary form, drama has a privileged relation to action, since it involves actual bodies doing and speaking things onstage. At the same time, the theater is a made or manufactured world, from the play text to the stage itself, the costumes, the props. Drama brings the done and the made into an intimate adjacency wherein they, no less than the protagonists

the done and the made

onstage, play out their sometimes vexed relations, and do so in historically variable ways. To trace these shifting relations I shall look at select instances of canonical tragedy from the Greeks to the twentieth century. My book is in no sense a historical survey of tragedy in the vein of Steiner or Eagleton, however. Uncovering the themes and connections that interest me requires close, extended readings of individual texts. This would render a systematic survey through the centuries impractical even if I possessed the learning for it (which I do not). In addition, the crisis of action that I describe is as often as not a submerged problem for tragedy. It rises to the surface only on occasion, in works that display a particular kind of metatheatrical awareness. Not all tragic plays do this, but the ones that do provide important soundings for a more general problem.

In focusing upon tragedy as the imitation of an action, I am reducing Aristotle's definition to its barest bones. I'm happy to continue his sentence, at least, and specify that this action is "of stature and complete, with magnitude." But even saying this much tells us precious little about "the tragic" as it is usually conceived. None of Aristotle's subsequent determinations of what makes a dramatic plot tragic—the *hamartia*, the *peripeteia*, the *anagnoresis*—nor the kinds of characters, nor the cathartic effect of the whole, enter in here. I have clambered up to the very top of the definitional chain to grasp tragedy in the most abstract possible fashion as a making that imitates a doing. This is not because I am uninterested in "the tragic," as I hope my readings of individual plays will show. It is rather because in imitating action, tragedy also reflects on action in abstract as well as particular ways. What are action's conditions of possibility and of intelligibility, its efficacy and constraints, its fraught relation to production? All of these questions interest me, though the last in particular will be my focus here, since it is a pairing with both weighty Aristotelian origins and a portentous future in political economy. In meditating on the relation between action and production, tragedy does something akin to philosophical work. But as I hope to show, this intellectually abstract dimension redounds upon the very human concerns of tragedy as well, and ultimately inflects our very sense of "the tragic."

Still, I recognize that in adopting an Aristotelian perspective as my starting point, I am positing tragedy as a dramatic form rather than as a mode that might equally well instantiate itself in novels or films or even life itself. Isn't "the tragic" really of the essence here, the thing that deserves our continuing interest, and tragic drama merely the form that has historically attempted to embody something larger than itself? One might certainly think so from recent studies. Terry Eagleton's book on tragedy is subtitled "The Idea of the Tragic," and in this he follows Steiner, who pursues the tragic vein in various literary forms: the novel, poetry, epic, and so forth. For Steiner, tragedy is not primarily a form but a condition: that of feeling alienated from a world inhospitable to human life. Tragedy as a dramatic mode once expressed this condition, but never had a monopoly on it.

What matters about tragedy, then, is purportedly this thing or idea or condition or affect known as the tragic. But if one turns back to Aristotle on tragedy, the elements that count as tragic in the modern sense mostly come later on in the discussion, and even then they are treated in a fairly perfunctory, almost casual fashion compared with formal considerations of dramatic plot and action. Perhaps this merely speaks to certain limitations on Aristotle's part. And yet *The Poetics* stood as the premier statement on tragedy for two millennia, and this cannot be explained away as a mere blind attachment to authority. As late as the 1930s, Brecht was still struggling with Aristotle in formulating his notion of epic theater, and much of recent "postdramatic theater" is likewise reacting, if not against Aristotle per se, then against the dramatic form he canonized.[16] Aristotle lives on, if only as a target. The present study can be understood in part as a historical explanation of why the Aristotelian understanding of tragedy came to seem inadequate to modern sensibilities, and why a concept of "the tragic" eventually detached itself from tragic form. My argument holds that this has everything to do with the changing status of action.

If making and doing exist in a state of conceptual tension from the start, then by defining tragedy as a *poiesis* that imitates a *praxis*, Aristotle grants the tragic artwork the power to bring these potentially antithetical concepts into a tense and unprecedented intimacy. A kind of unease inhabits tragedy in its most abstract determinations, even before the specifically tragic accouterments of its *mythos* are named. It is important not to exaggerate: even though Aristotle applies this definition while discussing tragedy, it applies equally to comedy and epic. The conceptual friction at the heart of dramatic poetry is not necessarily tragic; *poiesis* and *praxis* are not Clytemnestra and Agamemnon in the bath. But a kind of conflict defines their relation—one that can assume tragic as well as comic form. Political economy will carry out a coup d'état on behalf of production against action, and, as we shall see in chapter 2, a strain of Greek political rhetoric attempted the reverse. Not just conceptual dissonance but repeated power struggles surround tragedy's constitutive elements.

For reasons that should be already apparent, my book's concerns play out across the fields of philosophy and theory as well as drama. Philosophers have long been fascinated by tragedy, which they regard not only as an aesthetic paragon but also as a way of thinking about action. Philosophy also absorbs the lessons of political economy with a perhaps surprising alacrity. It therefore provides a useful, supple language to describe the crisis of action in tragic plays, and sometimes even displays forms of response comparable to dramatic ones. For all these reasons (and at the risk of a facile formulation) my argument takes place "among" political economy, philosophy, and tragedy, my chapters shuttling back and forth from one to another—a practice additionally necessitated by the fact that philosophy is active (even especially active) during periods when tragedy goes dormant. Among the questions I hope to cast new light upon is why tragedy is so important to certain philosophers, especially those engaged in political philosophy and theory.

Indeed, if one looks to contemporary philosophy—and, more broadly, "theory"—one would be hard put to identify a crisis of tragedy, whatever may be happening on the stage. Among political philosophers and theorists in particular, tragedy is alive and well. *Antigone* commentary alone constitutes a minor industry. Judith Butler, Martha Nussbaum, Bonnie Honig, Peter Euben, Christopher Rocco, David Scott—these are just some of the illustrious names attracted to tragedy in an attempt to understand the modern condition.[17] It is striking, then, that in every instance these modern theorists turn to *ancient* tragedy. Even granted the power of the Hegelian example, which has congealed into a kind of disciplinary habit, how strange that Sophocles, rather than Ibsen or Beckett or Brecht, guides political philosophers in their attempts to grasp contemporary reality. Perhaps this is philosophy's implicit judgment on modern tragedy.

Without collapsing the sometimes significant differences among the thinkers listed above, I think it's a fair (and somewhat obvious) thing to say about them that the attraction of Greek tragedy derives largely from its intimate relation to the *polis*. Ancient drama poses the question of the political in its starkest and most searching form. In the age of political economy, however, the ideal of the *polis* as an organized public of political agents is increasingly challenged by a different and incommensurable social grouping: the *population* as a disorganized conglomeration of producers and consumers. The danger posed by the population is that it will render the notion of political action largely meaningless. As we shall see, Adam Smith actually celebrates something of this sort. And while a tradition of republicanist thinkers from Adam Ferguson to Hannah Arendt has tackled the threat

polis | population

of the population (or, as Arendt puts it, the "social") in their writings about tragedy and politics, this is a problem that has largely fallen out of more recent theorizing, and one aim of the present study is to remedy this deficiency. To try to analyze the problem of the political without accounting for the capacity of population to neutralize political agency is to turn to the past, not in order to think through the present, but in order to evade crucial aspects of it. As a result, while I admire the recent work on tragedy done by recent political philosophers and theorists, I myself shall set a somewhat different course here—in part by returning to Hegel and producing a rather different reading of his take on tragedy than the one that has inspired much subsequent theory. As I shall argue, Hegel's understanding of tragedy is bound up with his writings on civil society and its system of needs in the *Philosophy of Right,* and thus responds directly to the challenges posed by political economy. If it did not introduce this third element of civil society into the classical binary of *polis* and *oikos,* Hegelian thought would be unequipped to think through the problem of tragedy and modernity. Yet this third term is largely absent from recent theorizing on tragedy and the political.

I stated earlier that political economy as a discourse serves only as a screen on which a crisis of action can be traced. It does not initiate this crisis. And in particular, it has no direct effect on tragic theater. The same cannot be said with respect to philosophy. There political economy influences a number of eighteenth- and nineteenth-century thinkers, from Rousseau and Hume, to Hegel and Marx, to Mill and others. And when philosophy in turn begins to catch the ear of twentieth-century playwrights, then political economy does so indirectly as well. The most obvious instance would be the Marxism of Brecht. But as I shall argue in a later chapter, post-Hegelian thought responding to political economy plays a role in Beckett's early plays as well. In this sense political economy does make a somewhat circuitous appearance in the travails of twentieth-century tragedy. But this appearance is almost always mediated by philosophy, and I would continue to maintain that it has no significant causative force. Still, to trace these relations with the seriousness they deserve requires paying more than lip service to the discourses of philosophy and political economy. I shall spend about a third of my time discussing them, and any reader who expects this to be a book solely about tragic plays will therefore be disappointed. My book tracks a three-way conversation, and each participant will receive its due.

In this study I consider at length tragic plays by Aeschylus, Marlowe,

Shakespeare, Milton, Beckett (and, more briefly, Sarah Kane), as well as theoretical writings by Aristotle, Adam Smith, Adam Ferguson, Hegel, Marx, Hannah Arendt, Alexandre Kojève, and Georges Bataille. The sequence of plays in particular may elicit puzzlement. Four of the six predate the era of political economy, and three are clumped in the early modern period. Without denying that my own professional formation plays a role here, I would also point out that the modern crisis of action is just one episode—a particularly transformative one—in the longer history of *poiesis* and *praxis* that is the real topic of this book. The antecedents of the crisis are as important as its consequences. The early modern period, in particular, is of interest to me because it represents the beginning of a genuinely commercial theater, as well as the beginning of the commercial society Smith described. As we shall see, the three early modern plays I consider provide a theatrical "prehistory" for political economy. One of the major innovations of early modern tragedy is the addition of comic subplots. These generally involve "low" characters and thus bring the plebeian realm of production into a previously unimaginable contact with the aristocratic realm of tragic action (think Hamlet meeting the gravedigger). This mixing of makers and doers reworks the classical opposition between *praxis* and *poiesis* in ways that will prove telling for the era of political economy.

Another question that might reasonably be asked is: why *political* economy? To be sure, classical political economy, as inaugurated during the Scottish Enlightenment, held the field through the era of Ricardo, Marx, and Mill. But much of its underlying conceptual apparatus, in particular the labor theory of value, fell from prominence after the marginalist revolution of the late nineteenth century. Whatever challenge the discourse of political economy posed to tragic drama, did that not simply disappear when political economy itself did, replaced by the modern discipline of economics? Yes and no. As a system of thought, political economy enjoyed a vigorous afterlife in the culture at large via the continuing prestige of figures such as Smith, Hegel, and Marx. And of course, many of Smith's principles are still active in mainstream economics. But political economy is especially of interest because its economic theories still existed in solution with other discourses such as ethics and aesthetics. Adam Smith and Marx provide comparably impressive, if very different, examples of thinking that connects the economic to social, ethical, and cultural arenas. And finally, to repeat an earlier point: I maintain that the crisis of action diagnosed (and in the intellectual sphere, at least, set off) by political economy was a real one that was not resolved simply because the discipline of economics turned its attention to other matters. In any case, I shall touch upon selected later economic thinkers, of the early marginalist and Austrian schools, in context.

My own approach in this book is influenced by Smith, Marx, and Hannah Arendt to different degrees and in different ways. My long-standing intellectual commitments are Marxist, but in studying Smith I discovered far more than the precursor whose labor theory of value was later systematized and perfected by Marx. Smith's meditations on the market, labor, and action are highly generative. In posing Smith as a (sometimes unwitting) diagnostician of capitalism's crisis of action, I have therefore largely refrained from the criticisms that might justly be made of his work from a Marxist perspective, though I also read Smith through somewhat Marxist preoccupations.[18] To simplify, we might say that Smith painted a comic portrait of the capitalist marketplace, Marx a tragic one. Smith's vision of the market economy as a spontaneously organizing system guided by an invisible hand and producing ever-greater wealth proves influential for later thinkers, including Marx, but Marx, coming after and having the advantage of seeing the effects of industrial capitalism, adds an understanding of the market process as crisis-ridden, and of the capitalist system as alienating and exploitative.[19] Together, they can help illuminate the tragicomedy that is modern capitalist society. Arendt is someone whose treatment of labor, work, and action both sums up an entire philosophical tradition and subjects it to a striking new turn. While I, like some others, have doubts about the answers she proposes, her questions have proven invaluable. I take pleasure in thinking that the three guiding lights of this study, had they somehow found themselves in a room together, might have been vaguely uncomfortable in one another's company.

II

I want now to reapproach these issues in a way that will render their stakes more apparent. I shall do so in part by taking up figures—Bertolt Brecht and Arthur Miller—whose absence from this study might otherwise seem odd. When I speak of action in this book, what concerns me above all is *political* action. And when I speak of a challenge to modern tragedy, I do not mean to imply that modern tragedy either cannot or does not exist. I mean rather to raise questions regarding the political efficacy of tragic drama and of modern theater more generally.

The *polis* was always, in some sense, a contrivance for amplifying the possibilities of human action through the self-conscious cooperation of individual agents—cooperation necessarily achieved through processes of debate and negotiation. The *polis* is a people organized into a public, which can thereby collectively alter the conditions of its own existence in a way that no individual agent ever could. This was perhaps the major discovery of the Greeks, who established the institutions of democracy and tragedy in such a way as to reinforce each another. In his influential reading, Jean-Pierre Vernant argues that Greek tragedy transforms the mythic hero into a *problem* for himself and others and moreover sets competing notions of justice against one another. In so doing, tragedy encourages debate, and thereby sharpens the deliberative capacities of citizens who will then bring these to bear in the Assembly.[20] Theater and Assembly mirror and challenge each other in ways both formal and structural. But it should be kept in mind for what follows that the political efficacy of Greek tragedy depends not only on its formal and thematic resources but also on the placement of these within larger political structures. Tragedy is directly integrated with the religious and political life of the city, though as a questioning and prob-ing presence. Greek citizens do not attend the theater as isolated individuals but ranked into the political tribes founded by Cleisthenes. In their differ-entiated order they represent the *polis* as a consciously self-organized entity. Tragedy illuminates the nature (and problems) of the city but, conversely, the city is what allows tragedy's challenges to resonate and ramify rather than simply disperse after the performance. Action makes a different kind of difference when it is political.

The plot of Greek tragedy generally embraces the political dimensions of action in a straightforward way: the tragic protagonist is also a monarch, and thus directly embodies the state. Oedipus's guilt produces a miasma that physically sickens the people he rules. Antigone's decision to bury her brother directly challenges the kingship of Creon. In the actions of tragic protagonists, the fate of the state itself is at issue, and the individual deed has political consequence. If the disastrous decisions of these sovereigns convey an implicitly democratic message, the catastrophes they entail be-speak a dignity that attaches to action only in its political reach. This is a so-lution that will outlast the Greeks. The fall of Shakespearean kings produces disorders that are cosmic as well as dynastic.

Although modernist playwrights display a sometimes confounding nos-talgia for the figure of the sovereign, modern tragedy in general ejects the figure of the king, substituting middle-class protagonists for royal or aristo-cratic ones.[21] Arthur Miller's insistence that tragedy should depict the "com-mon man," and Linda Loman's famous cry that "attention must be paid" to people such her husband Willy, attest to the democratic impulse behind this transformation.[22] At the same time, modern tragedy tends to withdraw from the public realm into the confines of the bourgeois or petit bourgeois household. Greek tragedy invariably placed its characters outdoors, in the public realm, while modern tragedy occupies (often elaborately described or appointed) interiors. Miller subtitles *Death of a Salesman* "Certain Private Conversations in Two Acts and a Requiem." This withdrawal into the private has ambiguous effects. On the one hand, dramatic action loses its directly political reach. The decisions of characters rarely affect anyone beyond the confines of the household. If these characters continue to have political significance, it is rather as representative figures—as social specimens that exhibit or embody some larger problem, whether the suffocating confines of petit bourgeois domesticity for Hedda Gabler or the casual brutality of the commercial world for Willy Loman.

Insofar as he or she becomes a social specimen rather than a sovereign, the modern tragic protagonist does not embody the political order directly but is rather mediated by some larger entity: a gender, a social class, or often just "society" itself. Willy Loman stands for the implosion of a widely shared, middle-class, postwar "American dream." But this very form of representation speaks to an irreducible diffuseness that attaches to the nature of the social.[23] Hedda Gabler and Willy Loman instantiate, without quite locating, their respective problems. That is to say (to put the matter crudely), even if one could somehow "help" Willy Loman, or if someone in the play could help him, this would not matter because the apartment buildings that encroach on his home are filled with comparably tormented individuals. Willy embodies a problem in such a way that nothing he does, or nothing that could be done to him, could possibly make a difference. This is in one sense the tragic dilemma of the play.

Let us look more closely at those apartment buildings. The play opens with the following stage directions:

> *A melody is heard, played upon a flute. It is small and fine, telling of grass and trees and the horizon. The curtain rises.*
>
> *Before us is the Salesman's house. We are aware of towering angular shapes behind it, surrounding it on all sides. Only the blue light of the sky falls upon the house and forestage; the surrounding area shows an angry glow of orange. As more light appears, we see a solid vault of apartment houses around the small, fragile-seeming home.* (13)

The apartment houses, looming above and threatening the "fragile" home of the Lomans, symbolize (in somewhat heavy-handed fashion) the overwhelming social forces that will grind Willy and his family down. Modern embodiments of classical fate, they concretize (literally) the structures of the social order in which the characters of the play are trapped, brutally annihilating the suggestions of open space and flourishing nature conveyed by the flute's song. "Modern tragedy" is unmistakably announced here.

The apartment houses embody architectural structure, and that structure in turn suggests an immutable, implacable social order, yet the apartment house is not itself a social organization. Certainly it is not a *polis*, not a self-organized collective entity. It is rather a stacking of isolated producer/consumer families on top of one another—encroaching on the Lomans' space and blocking out their sunlight but not essentially different from them. Apartment buildings house, we might say, not a public but a population—the disorganized social agglomerate that was produced by capitalism and that formed the ultimate subject matter for political economy. And here they emit a foul Malthusian odor that informs the political vision of the play:

WILLY: There's more people! That's what's ruining this country! Population is getting out of control. The competition is maddening! Smell the stink from that apartment house! And another one on the other side . . . how can they whip cheese? (17)

Under such conditions, social solidarity with one's neighbors is unimaginable. Hence the prevalence of fantasized forms of escape in the play: to the countryside, to Alaska, to the jungle, to the world of dreams.

The audience experiences a related deadlock. As subjects of a democratic polity, they are in some sense sovereign and thus at least theoretically capable of bringing their collective powers to bear on the issues illuminated by the play. And yet their power of political decision is faced here with a "problem" and a (vividly individualized) specimen family that must evade their conceptual grasp, if not their empathy. Indeed, even that empathy will persist only so long as the Lomans are maintained in their distinctiveness and not allowed to recede into the Malthusian mass from which they emerge. But in any case, the problem they represent is posed in such a way as to be strictly speaking insoluble (hence tragedy). Attention must be paid, but it is not in the least clear what the next step after attention could possibly be. Political attention thus becomes a kind of purposiveness without purpose. What this deadlock bespeaks, on a theoretical level, is the contradiction between the people as politically sovereign and the people as population—between a people invested with the collective power to act and a mass of isolated consumer/producers that occupies a realm fundamentally alien to action. This public, after all, has poured out from the very kind of apartment houses depicted onstage. As isolated consumers they are fundamentally here for a night's entertainment—entertainment that might consist, in part, of the feelings of moral satisfaction that result from having paid attention to Willy Loman and his family. In any case, the consumption of the play as commodity further complicates the calling together of the audience as public. It extends to the audience the very contradiction embodied in the play.

Political drama attempts to call a public into being—to organize population *into* public by presenting them with a matter of shared concern or debate. This is perhaps political drama's—nay, drama's—fundamental vocation, regardless of its content. Yet it can also erode this project from within by presenting its audience with a cultural commodity or consumer good: by addressing it as population rather than as public. Miller's play at once gives voice to an ongoing unease in postwar culture and provides the satisfaction of knowing that attention *has been paid* and can henceforth go elsewhere. In a way, the insolubility of the social problem fits political attention to commodity consumption by assuring us that nothing further is in the end being asked of us.

The contradictory status of modern tragic drama results from the fact that it labors under an inherent disjunction between the social and the political, population and public. It could be argued, of course, that any human society displays a comparably double nature. The ancient Athenian was a member of an *oikos* (site of isolated production/consumption) as well as a *polis* (site of collective action). Capitalism, however, decisively shifts the balance in favor of the *oikos*. The world of *Death of a Salesman* is a world without a public arena—a world in which households fill all available space, stretching out indefinitely and filling the sky. The pressures of urban concentration generate a compulsion simply to flee from other people rather than cooperate with them—a tendency reinforced by the fact that everyone is competing for status. No longer a *polis*, the city is now just a looming population center. The closest thing to social solidarity is the private condition of being "well liked"—a pale substitute for the Aristotelian *philia* that binds the *polis* together. Under such conditions the calling-into-being of a public becomes increasingly difficult for theater, now stripped of any supportive political institutions or movements on which it might lean. Theater's public tends to disintegrate into population, its political attention to slip back into consumption. *Death of a Salesman*, I would argue, both depicts and symptomatically embodies the dilemma of modern tragic theater insofar as it aspires to political relevance.

In "Interview with an Exile" (1934), Bertolt Brecht appears to critique *Death of a Salesman* before it was even written.

> So the theater has outlived its usefulness; it is no more able to represent modern phenomena and processes with the means available to it than the traditional kind of novelist can describe such everyday occurrences as housing shortage, export of pigs or speculation in coffee. Seen through its eyes, a little middling business man who despite all his care and effort loses his money though an un- lucky stroke of business becomes a "speculator." He would "go bankrupt," just like that, without comment, and it would be a kind of inexplicable blow of fate, much as if a man had been struck down by pneumonia.[24]

Death of a Salesman does not correspond exactly to Brecht's imagined play. And yet it would seem to exemplify just about everything that Brecht found suspicious about tragedy, since the empathy it generates enervates the audi- ence rather than restores their capacity to act.

Brecht both does and does not merit a place in this book. No other modern playwright pondered the question of theater and political action as thoroughly and searchingly as he did. And yet both his theory and practice led him away from tragedy. For Brecht, tragic theater and political theater cannot coexist because of the problem of tragic empathy. It is on this basis that Brecht founds a nontragic, putatively non-Aristotelian drama. In his earlier writings, Brecht maintains that tragic empathy is a problem inher- ited from the Greeks. But in "A Short Organon for the Theatre," he appears to adjust this view: "And our enjoyment of the theatre must have become weaker than that of the ancients, even if our way of living together is still sufficiently like theirs for it to be felt at all. We grasp the old works by a comparatively new method—empathy—on which they rely little."[25] In this intriguingly vague remark, Brecht does not specify when the "comparatively new" method emerged or what historical forces might have prompted it. My treatment of Smithian sympathy in the first chapter of this book attempts to fill in these blanks.[26] As I claim, the rise of sympathy/empathy is both co- terminous with capitalism and an effect of the latter's crisis of action. I hope as well to give a more detailed explanation of why empathy tends, as Brecht believes, to rob spectators of their powers of action.[27]

Brecht's suspicions toward tragic empathy were anticipated in some respects by Adam Smith's contemporary, Immanuel Kant. The excess of "sympathetic grief" that finds pleasure in "maudlin plays," Kant declared, "creates a soul that is gentle but also weak" and "makes the heart languid and insensitive to the stern precepts of duty."[28] Comparing the "agreeable lassitude" induced by the "play of [sentimental] affects" to the relaxation of muscles effected by massage, Kant goes on to observe (in good Brechtian fashion) that "many people believe they are ... improved by the performance of a tragedy when in fact they are merely glad at having succeeded in routing boredom."[29]

The formal principles behind Brecht's antiempathetic dramaturgy are both clear enough on their own account and sufficiently commented upon that I feel no need to rehearse the alienation effect, the *gestus*, and so on. I would like to make two perhaps counterintuitive observations, however. First, while it has previously been observed that Brecht's dramaturgy may not be quite as non- or anti-Aristotelian as it seems, I think that this significantly understates the case.[30] In point of fact, under the guise of anti-Aristotelianism, Brecht is actually the most rigorously Aristotelian playwright of the twentieth century, above all through elevating plot and action above character and psychology. All of the alienation effects serve this end. And in devising a theater that aims to provoke debate, critical analysis, and decision, Brecht is likewise impeccably "Greek," at least according to the standards Vernant sets forth.

But what is most Greek about Brecht is his understanding that the relations between theater and politics must be institutional as well as formal. Epic theater "cannot by any means be practiced universally.... It demands not only a certain technological level but a powerful movement in society which is interested to see vital questions freely aired with a view to their solution, and can defend this interest against every contrary trend."[31] Brecht does not imagine that even the most politically advanced form of theater can radicalize a public on its own. To the contrary, it depends on an already-existing social movement, on a preexisting *demand* for radical thought. Moreover, theater must then be coordinated with other social institutions—the educational system and mass media—before it has a politically transformative role to play.[32] If Brechtian theater attempts to grasp the laws of society in their totality, it likewise aspires to become a total institution itself, or at least recognizes that it can find its true role only in a revolutionary (or postrevolutionary) situation. So thoroughgoing a materialist as Brecht would find laughable the idea that a Brechtian dramaturgy could achieve any meaningful political resonance when staged under capitalist conditions of production and for a quiescently bourgeois audience (even a "progressive" one). Great reckonings do not occur in little rooms. Or not only there.

As my reading of Adam Smith in the following chapter will proceed to argue, it is *political* action that political economy seeks above all to neutralize and disable. And this general problem therefore revisits tragedy precisely in its political dimension. It is not as if tragic drama can no longer be written or staged under capitalism. That is not my point. What tends to get hollowed out is the political reach and seriousness of action, and therefore of tragedy. It is not a question of whether tragedy continues to exist, but of how and whether tragedy matters. Oddly, if one's definition of tragedy comports with George Steiner's—if one sees it as depicting a world relentlessly and unchangeably inhospitable to man—then these would seem to be times as propitious as any for it. But if one understands tragedy as a genre devoted both to the depicting of action as significant and to engaging its audience's powers to act, then late capitalism does pose considerable challenges.[33] These attach to theater as such, not merely to tragedy. But since tragedy is a genre deeply invested in the dignity of human action, their consequences may be felt with greater seriousness there. It is not as if tragic theater is entirely bereft of resources for addressing them, but my project in this book has been confined to laying out the problem itself as clearly and extensively as I can.

Since the general problem I am addressing is not unfamiliar to Marxist thought, I am also not the first critic to ponder the fate of tragedy in its terms, at least as broadly construed. Of the Marxist critics to have examined tragedy, Raymond Williams is the one to whom I feel most indebted. His approach informs and, in some ways, challenges mine, and so I want to say something about it before proceeding. *Modern Tragedy* has a multifaceted political agenda, one element of which is to reconnect our understanding of dramatic tragedy to the term *tragedy* as commonly or informally employed—to designate situations of intense suffering, loss, or oppression. For Williams, academic discussions (such as my own) that try to separate tragedy from this popular nexus have the effect, and perhaps even the intent, of denying tragic dignity to the plight of ordinary people. Even more to the point, this aloofness of academic thought speaks to the central social fact that modern tragedy addresses: alienation, or the "terrifying loss of connection," among persons in our society.[34]

In rejecting a purely academic approach to tragedy, however, Williams does not rule out an Aristotelian definition—far from it. Central for Williams is action and the fact that tragedy presents a "whole" action. Wholeness means not just narrative completeness but—related to it and issuing from it—the fact that tragedy tries to grasp a social whole and indeed to construct such a whole via the sympathetic implication of its audience. Tragedy embraces its viewers in a shared experience of alienation and thereby, at least potentially, shows a way beyond it.

Tragedy is therefore not (as it is for Brecht) antithetical to revolution; indeed, revolution is for Williams the most fully tragic event. This is in part because revolution responds to tragic conditions and in part because revolution itself has an irreducibly tragic character. Tragic in the bad sense, in that it often involves mortal combat with those who are, in the end, fellow human beings. But tragic also in the more elevated, Aristotelian sense that revolution is a "whole" action:

> The tragic action, in its deepest sense, is not the confirmation of disorder, but its experience, its comprehension and its resolution. In our own time this action is general, and its common name is revolution. We have to see the evil and the suffering, in the factual disorder that makes revolution necessary, and in the disordered struggle against the disorder. We have to recognize this suffering in a close and immediate experience, and not cover it with names. But we follow the whole action: not only the evil, but the men who have fought against evil; not only the crisis, but the energy released by it, the spirit learned in it. We make the connections, because that is the action of tragedy, and what we learn in suffering is again revolution, because we acknowledge others as men and any such acknowledgement is the beginning of struggle, as the continuing reality of our lives. Then to see revolution in this tragic perspective is the only way to maintain it.[35]

While certain possible elements of tragedy—a sense that we are caught in an immutably tragic "condition," or a sense that human nature is essentially destructive—work against revolutionary hope, a tragic perspective must nevertheless be maintained so as to avoid the reemergence of alienation within the revolutionary process itself, either by dehumanizing the foe or by revolutionary leadership's reducing the "masses" to mere instrument of strategy. Only by maintaining the "whole action" of tragedy can the revolutionary overcoming of alienation be defended and advanced.

Such a perspective renders dramatic tragedy neither the enemy of revolution nor irrelevant to it, as it often is for Brecht. That being said, Williams's survey of modern tragic drama displays it as subject to a fundamental deadlock that inhibits its revolutionary potential. This emerges perhaps most clearly in what Williams calls "liberal tragedy," represented by Ibsen and Miller. Such tragedy achieves a conceptual milestone: "the increasingly confident identification of a false society as man's real enemy; the naming, in social terms, of the formerly nameless alienation."[36] But at the same time, the reversion to an *individual* liberator/victim renders this social problem intractable, even though, in Miller, society is shown to be both "false *and alterable*" (my emphasis).[37] Neither "liberal" nor the other forms of modern tragedy surveyed by Williams manage to overcome this deadlock. Indeed, despite an implicit anti-Brechtian lilt to much of his argument, among the plays that Williams surveys, only *Mother Courage* does overcome it. Modern tragedy is, for Williams, finally alienated from its own "whole story." It necessarily truncates and fragments that story in ways that block its political capacities, whatever its aesthetic and spiritual triumphs may be. For Brecht, the revolutionary task is to escape from tragedy; for Williams, to restore it to its full self. And he argues that even Brecht, in the best, maturest version, does the same.

Williams's reading of tragedy was, like any, a product of its moment. On the one hand, the failures of the "real socialist" societies revealed an undeniably tragic underside to revolution. On the other, this did not prevent a (highly guarded) sense of optimism from emerging, based on the ongoing revolutions in the so-called third world and the presence of a powerful, popular Labour Party in the United Kingdom. Williams could thus see revolution not as a distant goal but as an ongoing, if still incomplete, "activity immediately involving ourselves."[38]

Half a century later, the same can hardly be said. The structures of the present order seem more firmly cemented in place than ever, if simultaneously more fragile. The causes cannot be sought solely in the forms of unhappiness peculiar to capitalist society, I would argue, but rather in the relation between these and the forms of happiness promised by it as well— that is to say, the forms of happiness it affords to the ever-smaller minority who manage to enjoy a comfortable existence in the most advanced capitalist societies, including therefore most of the audience for its theater. Those forms of unhappiness and happiness are defined increasingly by production, not action, and thus render the reconstituting of tragedy's "whole action," as Williams saw it, ever more problematic. A politically effective form of tragic drama, if not impossible, nevertheless has high hurdles to surmount. Even if one finds persuasive (as I do), Nicholas Ridout's demonstration of a "communist potential" within theater, it is hard to imagine how this potential can realize and generalize itself—how it can become more than an appealing heterotopia—under current conditions.[39] Tracing the rise of those conditions is what I set out to do here.

It might be argued that in moving from Greek drama to figures such as Brecht and Williams I have stacked the deck against theater. In a Greek context, after all, theater's political role is merely to sustain and enrich the existing order, not to overthrow it or bring a new one into being. Positing theater, tragic or otherwise, as an agent of revolutionary change is to burden it with responsibilities its original inventors never envisioned. Isn't it enough that theater should contribute to serious democratic conversation? And mightn't arguments that theater has lost its political reach indicate not that something has changed in theater itself, but that new and inappropriately demanding criteria are being brought to bear upon it? Perhaps. But the demand for transformative change is not one imposed solely by critics but one made by political theater itself—certainly by playwrights such as Brecht and even in a self-defeating way by what Williams calls "liberal" tragedy. The demand for revolution arises from a deadlock within democratic conversation—the feeling that *it* has lost its political purchase, and that fundamental changes are needed to turn a population of consumers into a public that *can* discuss matters seriously and act upon them. Because it invokes a public from a population, theater finds itself burdened with the responsibility of bringing a political space into being. And it does so under increasingly difficult circumstances.

[margin annotation: a public from a population]

As I argue in my Beckett chapter, the modern crisis of action does not always induce a loss of interest in action, or a conviction of its futility; it can, by way of reaction formation, also provoke inflationary conceptions of the act that exaggerate its possibilities or reach. A good deal of modern political theory labors under such inflationary notions. It should therefore not be surprising that theater too might fall prey to chimerical ideas of its political vocation. Or that it might feel itself squeezed between massive responsibilities and limited effectiveness. Here I think tragedy serves as a particularly sensitive instrument for gauging the contemporary dilemma of theater. Because tragic action has an inherent grandeur or amplitude—what Aristotle called *megethos*—it occupies a delicate juncture. On the one hand it feels keenly any reduced conditions for the effectiveness or meaningfulness of action. But on the other it stands at the upper verge beyond which action becomes hyperbolic and loses its grounding in real conditions. For this reason, even in an era of postdramatic theater, the fate of tragedy is of more than merely antiquarian interest.

III

Chapter 1 of this book, "'Thy Bloody and Invisible Hand': Tragedy and Political Economy," begins by exploring the antitragic dimensions of *The Wealth of Nations*. By "antitragic," I mean not only that the Smithian market is essentially comic in its workings but also that Smith systematically invokes, and neutralizes, the resources of tragic drama in laying out his vision of a market economy. By so doing, he diminishes the status of action as well. Not only does Smith elevate production over action as the path to happiness, in a self-conscious revision of classical ethics; market mechanisms, which work only across vast aggregates or populations, also negate the ethical as well as the economic significance of the individual. Action in the heroic or tragic sense is either a distraction from, an unproductive cost added onto, or a statistically meaningless deviation from the market process. I then go on to argue that the same disregard for action informs *The Theory of Moral Sentiments*, which is more interested in moral psychology than in moral acts, and which bases its ethical theory on a figure—the impartial spectator—who by definition *does not act* but only judges. Smith frequently makes reference to tragic drama in *The Theory of Moral Sentiments*, but his readings of tragic playwrights from Sophocles to Shakespeare and Racine exemplify his lack of interest in dramatic action.

The chapter then turns to two figures from the classical republican tradition who attempt to defend political action from the threat posed by political economy. Adam Ferguson, a contemporary of Smith's, depicts the satisfactions of the market society as leading to a kind of animal complacency, and he extols the strenuousness of a tragic, agonistic brand of political action as the only truly human form of endeavor. Writing almost two centuries later, Hannah Arendt blames Smith and Marx for elevating labor over action and thus for contributing to the rise of the "social" and the erosion of politics as the sole meaningful arena for human action. While Arendt's vision of the *polis* attempts to maintain it at a distance from economic processes, however, the dynamics of political action as she depicts them are in fact modeled in large part on those of the Smithian marketplace. The contradictions in Arendt's and Ferguson's thinking show how difficult it can prove, in the wake of Smith, to rescue a viable concept of action from the challenge posed by political economy. Both figures battle mightily to surmount this challenge, however, and both invoke tragic drama in order to do so. For Arendt, in particular, tragedy may be the last remaining guarantor of the meaningfulness of political action.

In chapter 2, "Greek Tragedy and the Raptor Economy: The *Oresteia*," I lay out the classical conceptions of action that political economy overturns. Since economic production in ancient Greece was largely the province of women and slaves, it was, not surprisingly, denigrated—especially in comparison with political or military action. But a strain of Periclean political rhetoric took this view even further, claiming that Athens could provision itself entirely though imperial warfare, winning what it need not produce. Greek tragic theater is implicated in this "raptor economy" both financially and ideologically. Aeschylus's tragic trilogy *The Oresteia* critiques the dangerously hyperbolic conceptions of heroism such a rhetorical stance encourages and protests the conversion of human lives into expendable resources that it entails. In *Agamemnon*, Clytemnestra gives voice to the dignity of the household, viewed by Agamemnon as a standing reserve to be drawn on for heroic achievement. *The Libation Bearers* asks whether Orestes's revenge is an ethically justified form of action or a dangerous physiological reflex. *The Eumenides* attempts to separate justice and even warfare from the corrupting influences posed by the prospect of material gain, and offers an idyllic vision in which the city will be provisioned by justice, not war. Throughout, Aeschylus's trilogy is attentive to the rights of "mere life" as against the claims of heroic action, and to the importance of *poiesis* or making as that which nurtures life. Aeschylus works the seam between doing and making in order to find a proper place for tragic theater in the *polis*.

Chapter 3, "Marlowe's Theater of Night: *Doctor Faustus* and Capital," is the first of three chapters addressing tragedy in the early modern period, when theater first becomes a fully commercial enterprise. As an independent playwright, Marlowe produces works that cannot be artistically or financially realized without the stage as means of production, an apparatus over which Marlowe exerts no control. I argue that this alienated condition is reflected in Faustus's contract with Mephastophilis[40]—a contract that grants Faustus powers through an apparatus that he, too, can command but not ultimately manage. Essentially a source of special effects, Mephastophilis embodies the powers of theatrical capital, thereby allowing Marlowe to reflect upon both the futility of the dramatic text without theatrical embodiment, and, conversely, the finally disappointing resources that the theater can provide. The lack inherent to both parties opens up into a more general investigation by the play into a realm of the negative or void that manifests itself on ethical, aesthetic, theological, and ontological levels. Ultimately, the precocious modernity of *Doctor Faustus* involves envisioning a world in which action is impossible without dependence on some enabling apparatus or mechanism from which one is nevertheless alienated and over which one can therefore exert at best a provisional kind of control.

Chapter 4, "*Hamlet* and the Work of Death," attempts to recontextualize Hamlet's famous inability to avenge his father. What if, instead of understanding action as Hamlet does, as something opposed to inaction or delay, we instead contrast it with *poiesis* or production? Against Hamlet's crisis of the act, understood as punctual, decisive, and individualizing, the play presents an ongoing chorus of production, which is continual and anonymous. This is the work of death, figured as the worms dining on Polonius or Alexander being slowly transformed into a cork, but also given more substantial presence as the digging of the grave maker and the perpetual work of Danish armament makers described at the very beginning of the play. The encounter between Hamlet and the grave maker symbolizes a larger confrontation between the realms of action and production—one that informs the play's views of politics, the multitude, and dramatic creation. But above all, it allows us to see the ways in which Hamlet's *thought* gets trapped by the rhythms of production, making Hamlet into an anticipatory hero for the age of political economy.

Chapter 5, "The Same Old Grind: Milton's Samson as Subtragic Hero," looks at Milton's closet play *Samson Agonistes*—his final work, composed after the collapse of the Commonwealth and the Restoration of monarchy in England. If *Hamlet* stages an encounter between action and labor or production, *Samson Agonistes* takes this a step further by presenting something previously unexampled: a tragic hero who, himself, labors. His work at the mill is not merely something to which Samson has been confined; rather, Samson fuses with the mill, to such a degree that the play's violent conclusion—Samson's pulling down of the Philistine temple—is conceived as simply more milling. Trapped in a subheroic condition, Samson finds it impossible to make the transition from production back to action. Moreover, a universalizing logic in the play remakes Samson from exceptional hero to emblem of a more general condition, one that reflects the antipolitical conditions of post-Restoration England.

Tragic drama is eclipsed by the novel in the eighteenth and nineteenth centuries. It is not as if tragedies cease to be written. But the kind of literary talent the form attracts cannot compare with either the great novelists or the great lyric poets of the era. Moreover, when serious tragedy does return to the stage in the late nineteenth century, it has absorbed, and been transformed by, the characteristics of the novel. This is a well-known story, and I propose to tell it somewhat differently by looking to philosophy—tragedy's other "other" during this period. My sixth chapter, "Hegel, Marx, and the Novelization of Tragedy," attempts to place Hegel's treatment of tragedy in his *Lectures on Aesthetics* in relation to his depiction of civil society in the *Philosophy of Right*.[41] This latter work is deeply influenced by Hegel's reading of Adam Smith and other political economists. I show how the logic of political economy influences Hegel's treatment of tragedy, and particularly its metamorphosis into tragicomedy—a highly novelized form—in modern times. I then turn to Marx's *The Eighteenth Brumaire of Louis Bonaparte*, a work that employs the categories of tragedy and farce to analyze the revolution of 1848 in France. I examine the ways in which Marx's handling of these literary genres evinces a Hegelian influence, and how his depiction of class struggle in France likewise reworks Hegel's treatment of the *Pöbel* or rabble, the irreducibly tragic remainder of capitalism's "system of needs" in the *Philosophy of Right*. Against Marx's plot of crisply defined dramatic genres and a clear-cut historical dialectic, the "becoming-rabble" of both creates a counterplot in which tragedy cedes to novel, and imminent revolutionary triumph gives way to a seemingly interminable capitalist modernity.

The eclipse of action by production in the age of political economy does not necessarily result in reduced conceptions of action. On the contrary, one common response, especially in the realm of political theory, is a countermovement that gins up inflated accounts of action, often defined explicitly against the neutralizing powers of the marketplace. Hannah Arendt and Carl Schmitt are the prime suspects here. My seventh chapter, "Beckett's Tragic Pantry," tracks Samuel Beckett's response to two such inflationary theorists, Alexandre Kojève and Georges Bataille. Both were prominent figures on the Parisian intellectual scene, both took up the Hegelian legacy (though in very different ways), and both were writers with whose work Beckett was familiar. My chapter looks at Beckett's best-known early plays, *Waiting for Godot* and *Endgame*, as responses to the dilemmas of action in the twentieth century. *Waiting for Godot* situates itself at the Kojèvian "end of history," conceived explicitly as an end to possibilities for action. *Endgame* engages in a critical response to Bataille's notion of *dépense* in order to deflate the inflated notions of action then current. Beckett's aim is not therapeutic, however. He does not intend to restore action to an earlier condition of health, but rather to stage the contemporary impasse of action that inflationary theorists imagined they could surmount.

A postscript, "After Beckett," attempts to bring my long narrative up to something like the present day. In the material realm, post-Fordist production integrates the human capacities for judgment, decision making, and imagination—capacities that had formerly fueled political action—into the production process itself. Action is thus not merely eclipsed by production but, potentially, subsumed by it as well. This is one problem facing modern practitioners of tragic drama. Another, more literary, one is the burden of following Beckett, who self-consciously positioned himself as the "last" playwright. I consider Sarah Kane's *Blasted* as a play that, by taking on both of these challenges, reflects on the dilemmas and possibilities for contemporary tragedy. I also reflect upon the advent of postdramatic theater, which systematically dismantles the mechanisms of Aristotelian tragedy while enabling forms of tragic experience and affect to survive them.

CHAPTER ONE

"Thy Bloody and Invisible Hand"

Tragedy and Political Economy

"A public mourning raises the price of black cloth."[1] Adam Smith was so fond of this sentence that he used it twice within seventy pages of *The Wealth of Nations*. I want to employ it as an inroad into the thesis that the publication of Smith's great work on political economy was a significant event for the history of tragic drama. If the law of unintended consequences is the principal doctrine of *The Wealth of Nations*, this might well be the most unintended and unanticipated consequence of all.[2] Smith repeatedly invokes tragedy in *The Theory of Moral Sentiments* but has nothing to say about it directly in *The Wealth of Nations*. It is in the latter and later work, nevertheless, that Smith poses a fundamental problem for tragic drama by upending the classical conceptions of action that underwrote it.

"A public mourning raises the price of black cloth." Smith is discussing the question of how market prices—the amount actually paid for commodities—fluctuate above and below their "natural" prices as a result of shifting relations between supply and demand. A public mourning temporarily increases the market for black cloth and thereby its price. The example does not seem to be chosen at random. A tragic event of some kind has occurred, and of a magnitude that engulfs not just an individual or a family but the public as a whole. Quite possibly the death of a monarch or a great military leader—the quintessential occurrence of tragic drama. Indeed, classical tragedy can be understood as ritualized acts of public mourning. Yet the economic effect of this cataclysm is but a momentary blip in the price of a rather minor commodity. In the passage from the political sphere to the economic, the reverberations of public death have been both drastically reduced in magnitude and recoded into something purely numerical and thus without qualitative or affective resonance of any kind. Human significance is dipped into a strange bath that petrifies it and hollows it out. Whatever terrible thing happened, it is "outside" the marketplace, which registers only the relative prices of commodities and not their external causes. The death of a beloved public figure is thus indistinguishable from a bumper crop of cabbage or an unexpected shortage of candle wicks.

That Smith repeats the statement suggests he was proud of it. Yet while his formulation has a kind of aphoristic compactness, it lacks aphoristic wit. There is no striking rhetorical turn to underline the shocking disparity of magnitudes that the sentence yokes by violence together.[3] In its place is a flat neutrality that may be even more effective than rhetorical footwork in emphasizing the contrasts at work here. Through its deadpan tone, the sentence seems to be speaking not only of but also *from* the place of a market that is entirely unperturbed by events of tragic amplitude. It is as if the impartial spectator of *The Theory of Moral Sentiments* had been mortified into an insensible spectator, unmoved not only by public mourning but also by its disturbing conversion into minor price fluctuations. This is a rather naughty sentence after all, and Smith seems to enjoy the ethical fillip it delivers to the reader.

I am by no means claiming that *The Wealth of Nations* as a whole, or the voice that Smith adopts within it, is consistently or even predominantly amoral.[4] But in this one sentence, Smith memorably demonstrates that the market as such is buffered from human concerns, knowing nothing of mortality or loss in its abstract adjustments of pure quantities. By producing in the reader a slight frisson, however, the sentence reminds us that we are on the outside of this tragedy-free zone looking in. What we witness from without is the thoroughness with which economy neutralizes the tragic.

A not dissimilar process surrounds Smith's concept of the "invisible hand." The most obvious possible source for the phrase itself is *Macbeth* 3.2.49–53:

> Come, seeling night,
> Scarf up the tender eye of pitiful day,
> And with thy bloody and invisible hand
> Cancel and tear to pieces that great bond
> Which keeps me pale![5]

Macbeth invokes night's invisible hand not merely as something that is itself unseen but as something that blots out ethical vision in general, thus transferring its own invisibility to the human bond that ties him to Banquo. It thereby enables Macbeth to act "blindly" and without respect to the interests of Banquo as other. Not just a coincidence of phrasing, then, but the conceptual context that the passage generates would seem to confirm Shakespeare's status as inspiration for Smith's most famous term, and yet modern commentators can hardly be blamed for not making much of this fact. And that is because Smith's concept of the invisible hand manages to neutralize its tragic origins almost completely. This fact is all the stranger because the invisible hand is essentially a machine for producing irony, systematically inverting the intentions of economic agents and thus potentially resembling tragic Fate. Mercantilist efforts to intervene in the market through tariffs, regulations, or monopoly inevitably produce results both harmful and the exact opposite of those intended. For example: "Even the regulations by which each nation endeavors to secure to itself the exclusive trade of its own colonies, are frequently more hurtful to the countries in favor of which they are established. The unjust oppression of the industry of other countries falls back, if I may say so, upon the heads of the oppressors, and crushes their industry more than it does that of those other countries" (*Wealth of Nations*, 679). Reversals of this sort pepper *The Wealth of Nations*. I select this instance from among many simply because Smith's critical language rises to an unusual level of violence. An attentive reader can be forgiven for hearing echoes of Milton's *Samson Agonistes* and the collapse of the Philistine temple on the heads of Samson's captors. Yet the consequences of the policies Smith critiques here, while certainly unfortunate, fall far short of tragedy. And they do so because the more pervasive effect of the invisible hand, which is to turn the blind actions of self-interested agents into shared economic prosperity, invests the market with a resilient vitality that ultimately trumps misguided efforts to subject it to intentional manipulation.[6] The invisible hand is not the agent of tragic irony but rather of something that looks more like comic (or more properly, Stoic) Providence. Not only does Smith's market tend not to produce tragic outcomes, it also tends to buffer the populace as a whole from even the most ill-considered stratagems of statesmen and mercantile interests. If we don't hear Macbeth when we say "invisible hand," that is because Smith's invisible hand itself is not merely nontragic but profoundly antitragic in its workings. The Smithian market tends inexorably in the direction of increasing happiness. While this happiness is not yet evenly distributed and while its progress can be delayed through misguided policies, Smith insists, that progress cannot ultimately be derailed. But what kind of happiness is this?

I

The Wealth of Nations is a book concerned with "the public happiness" (447). Smith borrows this term from the theorists of police, that seventeenth- and eighteenth-century "science" of government that sought to provide for both the material and moral well-being of national populations.[7] If Smith's use of it retains a moral dimension (and I would argue that it does), this remains largely implicit.[8] For Smith, "public happiness" refers more explicitly to "subsistence, conveniences, and amusements" (311), those material means by which a people are enabled to live, and to live comfortably. For Smith, moreover, this form of happiness depends not only on an accumulation of material goods but also on the "flourishing" (374) condition of the economy—a dynamism that leads in the direction of increased production and prosperity.

One way to understand "the public happiness" is as the form of happiness that pertains to *populations* rather than persons. In this sense, material happiness is the only pertinent kind, since moral happiness as Smith understood it is experienced only by the individual. Nevertheless, Smith does not conceive material happiness as extravagant wealth. Vivienne Brown observes: "Although WN welcomes the better living standards made possible for the poor by rising annual revenue, it shows little sympathy for consumerism and a clear disdain for the new consumer goods such as 'trinkets and baubles' (WN V.i.b.7) and the 'diamond buckles' (WN III.iv.10) that provide consumption expenditure for the rich landlords."[9] Smith's paradigmatic figure for the commercial economy is not the dashing merchant adventurer who hazards all in pursuit of fabulous riches, but rather the frugal, industrious, and parsimonious laborer who exhibits "the uniform, constant, and uninterrupted effort of every man to better his condition" (*Wealth of Nations*, 373). Public happiness is a flourishing material condition that follows upon the incremental improvements made available by a commercial society.

I have been dwelling on the question of happiness in Smith because one's conception of happiness and of how to achieve it has an obvious bearing on one's conception of unhappiness, including those disastrous forms of unhappiness known as the tragic. Indeed, the phrase "public happiness" is the counterpart to the phrase "public mourning," with which I began. Adam Ferguson asked: "in what sense can a public enjoy any good, if its members, considered apart, be unhappy?"[10] This formulation suggests that private and public versions of happiness are inseparable; indeed, the second is merely the sum of the first. Yet there are readings of Smith that understand public happiness as not only consistent with, but in some sense as predicated on, individual unhappiness.[11] This would be a significant, perhaps tragic, irony endemic to public happiness from the start.[12] My concern in what follows, however, will not primarily be the relation between public and individual happiness, but rather the new concept of action entailed by a novel understanding of happiness as something experienced by populations or nations. What must be done to foster public happiness, and by whom?

For the theorists of police from whom Smith borrows the term, public happiness is ensured by the wise governing actions of the sovereign or state. Smith's great innovation is to argue that public happiness results not from action, and certainly not from sovereign action, but from production. Making, not doing, generates the revenues that support national wealth. Smith thereby both implicitly invokes and radically revises the classic philosophical distinction between *praxis* and *poiesis*. In the *Nicomachean Ethics*, Aristotle argues that happiness not merely results from but simply *is* action: "activity of soul in accordance with excellence" (1098a 16–17).[13] Aristotle's understanding of happiness makes it definitionally inaccessible by way of production, while Smith's understanding of public happiness makes it inaccessible by way of action as understood in an ethico-political sense. The attainment of public happiness rests on productivity, not active virtue. Indeed, any attempt to *act* virtuously in the context of the market generally produces harmful, unintended consequences. "I have never known much good done by those who affected to trade for the public good" (*Wealth of Nations*, 485).

Aristotle places making or *poiesis* on a lower rung than doing or *praxis* because the activity of making always aims at an end other than itself—the useful, made thing—while an excellent action is performed for its own sake (*Nicomachean Ethics*, 1140a1–1140b10). Action is autotelic while production is subordinated to external purposes. Yet the fact that Aristotle is so careful to distinguish production from action at all bespeaks the similarities that otherwise bind them. Both are practical activities that can be done well or badly and hence are subject to judgment. Both improve as the result of practice. And both are temporally bounded in a way that grants them narrative closure. Making a shoe, like performing a courageous or generous action, is something with a beginning, a middle, and an end.

For Aristotle, the thing that brings the distinct categories of making and doing into the most intimate propinquity is poetry. Tragic drama, in his famous definition, is a *poiesis* or making that imitates a *praxis* or action (119b24). Yet the tensions inherent to this formula should give us pause.

Neither common sense nor Aristotle's definitions make it at all obvious how a making *can* imitate a doing. How can something that serves another end imitate something done for its own sake? If the two can be brought into a tense relation, surely this relies in part on their temporal resemblance.

But Smith disarticulates precisely the narrative coherence of Aristotelian *poiesis*, which takes artisanal acts of making as its model. On the one hand, artisanal production is internally broken down by the division of labor, such that a worker no longer makes a finished shoe or nail, but only performs a component procedure that does not by itself directly result in a made thing. In addition, and more importantly, production is not governed by the temporal or utilitarian finality of the made object. Smith's emblematic pin-making factory churns out 48,000 pins a day, every day (*Wealth of Nations*, 5). While Aristotelian *poiesis* always has its end in the finished, useful object it crafts (though that end is merely a means), Smithian production is an endless, ongoing process. It thus loses the narrative and temporal structure that allowed Aristotelian *poiesis* at least to be discussed together with *praxis*. In the *Poetics*, Aristotle insists that the action imitated by a tragic play must be "complete" (*Poetics*, 1449b25).[14] But in the realm of Smithian production, not only has doing given way to making, but any notion of narrative completeness has also disappeared.

If the realm of the economic is immune to tragedy, we now see that this has to do with more than an absence of mournful affect. In addition, the achievement of happiness has been divorced from action, while the productive activity that takes action's place lacks its narrative coherence. I want now to look more closely at Smith's concept of productive labor, and particularly at his chapter "Of the Accumulation of Capital, or of Productive and Unproductive Labor." A good deal turns on the title's "or," as we shall see.

In that chapter Smith states: "There is one sort of labour which adds to the value of the subject upon which it is bestowed: there is another which has no such effect. The former, as it produces a value, may be called productive; the latter, unproductive labour. Thus the labour of a manufacturer [Smith means a factory worker] adds, generally, to the value of the materials he works upon, that of his own maintenance, and of his master's profit. The labour of a menial servant, to the contrary adds to the value of nothing" (360). Here Smith expounds not the famous labor theory of value but rather its usually silent counterpart: the value theory of labor. In other words, he claims that, among the great variety of human activities, the one that counts as true, that is, productive labor, is that which creates value. What makes labor productive is not primarily the creation of a thing but rather the transfer of value to that thing, which then serves as a kind of battery in which the labor expended in making it can be stored: "But the labour of the manufacturer fixes and realizes itself in some particular subject or vendible commodity, which lasts for some time at least after that labour is past. It is, as it were, a certain commodity of labour stacked and stored up to be employed, if necessary, upon some other occasion. . . . The labour of the menial servant, on the contrary, does not fix or realize itself in any particular subject or vendible commodity. His services generally perish in the very instant of their performance, and very seldom leave any trace or value behind them, for which an equal quantity or service could afterward be procured" (360–61). If your menial servant adjusts your tie, or cooks your dinner, or cleans your room, that effort imprints itself on nothing and so vanishes at the moment of its expenditure, while the labor of the factory worker fixes itself in a material substrate. It can then be both preserved and, thereby, accumulated—hence the crucial "or" in the chapter's title. Productive labor makes possible the accumulation of wealth or capital, while unproductive labor fritters it away. Therefore, productive labor, and only productive labor, contributes to the public happiness at which Smith aims.

Having set out the two species of productive and unproductive labor, Smith then provides a list of unproductive laborers, showing that their ranks include not only menial servants but also "some of the most respectable orders of the society" (361). "Such are the people who compose a numerous and splendid court, a great ecclesiastical establishment, great fleets and armies, who in a time of peace produce nothing, and in time of war acquire nothing which can compensate the expense of maintaining them, even while the war lasts" (372–73). Princes, courtiers, popes, generals: it is not difficult to recognize here the *dramatis personae* who populated tragic plays of the sixteenth and seventeenth centuries. What counts for Smith is not the political or ethical repercussions of their acts, but rather the fact that action as such, including heroic action, is unproductive. For the political economist, individual actions matter less than the fact that those elite social groups who have traditionally held a monopoly on heroic action now count uniformly as an expense. If the public happiness depends on increasing revenue, these people can contribute nothing to it, no matter how well or badly they perform their roles. Smith includes an entire chapter titled "Of the Expense of Supporting the Dignity of the Sovereign." In *The Theory of Moral Sentiments*, the dignity of sovereigns is held to make them the most proper subjects for tragedy.[15] Here that dignity registers only as public expense, in a conversion of affect into the quantitative rather like that which turns public mourning into a rise in the price of black cloth. Elsewhere, Smith adds the sovereign to a list that includes "churchmen, lawyers, physicians, men of letters of all kinds; players, buffoons, musicians, opera-singers, opera-dancers, &c. The labour of the meanest of these has a certain value, regulated by the very same principles which regulate that of every other sort of labour; and that of the noblest and most useful, produces nothing which could afterwards purchase or procure an equal quantity of labour. Like the declamation of the actor, the harangue of the orator, or the tune of the musician, the work of all of them perishes in the very instant of its production" (*Wealth of Nations*, 361). Including kings in the ranks of laborers, and unproductive ones at that, has a quietly iconoclastic force. The solemn edicts of the monarch, the glorious battles won by his generals, the stirring orations delivered in parliament, leave no more economic value behind than the efforts of the most menial servant or the exertions of the professional buffoon. This gleefully leveling roll call of the unproductive is, I would argue, Smith's version of an epic, or rather mock-epic catalog. Inverting the deeds of Homeric heroes, preserved by the muse for eternity, the acts of these workers disappear in the very moment of their occurrence. Whatever other forms of human interest the activities of lawyers, intellectuals, and doctors may hold, from the perspective of the political economist they vanish instantly, since they leave no lasting *economic* trace behind them. Smith's transvaluation of values appears in the fact that kings and warriors, the very stuff of epic and tragedy, head his list of the ephemeral, whose activities sap the economic resources of their countries rather than contributing to the wealth of nations. The heroes of the new era announced by political economy will be not vainglorious soldiers but quietly industrious workers—not Achilles but the anonymous craftsman who fashioned his shield. *The Wealth of Nations* is, in this sense, an antiepic for modern times, celebrating a world in which mass-produced pins have replaced bronze spears.

It is worth remarking here on the relation between value and memory. Smith's description of productive labor as "fixing" itself in the commodity, of leaving "traces" there, suggests that value is a kind of writing system, a mnemonic apparatus that records or remembers the expenditure of labor beyond the moment of production by preserving it in the commodity itself. Value is the economy's counterpart to the epic's muse, memorializing past acts of production. But its mode of remembering is simultaneously an act of forgetting or erasure. Labor can form the basis of exchange value only because the time spent making different kinds of commodities is comparable. In other words, shoes can be exchanged for coats only because the labor expended in making each counts as abstract labor, labor as such, and not the specific labor of shoemaker or tailor.[16] Value records *by* evaporating specificities; it is only thus that it is capable of numerical addition or accumulation. And just as it homogenizes production, so it homogenizes action into the general category of the unproductive. Actions do not count as good or evil, prudent or extravagant, heroic or debased, virtuous or depraved, but are simply lumped under the same rubric. Whatever bards or singers may think of heroic battles, to the economy they count only as another form of public expense.

While Smith degrades the figure of the sovereign in ways we have just seen, he also degrades sovereignty itself, or at least delimits it in a way that transforms its very nature. After describing the economy as a self-organizing system composed of innumerable acts of production and exchange, Smith declares it incapable of superintendence from above: "The sovereign is completely discharged from the duty, in the attempting to perform which he must always be exposed to innumerable delusions, and for the proper performance of which no human wisdom or knowledge could ever be sufficient; the duty of superintending the industry of private people, and of directing it towards the employments most suitable to the interest of society" (*Wealth of Nations*, 745). The ambiguous phrase "is completely discharged from" leaves undecided whether the sovereign is courteously relieved of a burden or summarily deprived of a privilege. Michel Foucault opts for the latter: "*Homo oeconomicus* strips the sovereign of power in as much as he reveals an essential, fundamental, and major incapacity of the sovereign, that is to say, an inability to master the totality of the economic field."[17] If the sovereign loses power over only one area, that of the economy, it should be remembered that this field is not equal to the others but the one primarily responsible for the public happiness. It is not as if the sovereign will be left with nothing to do. For Smith, the state appropriately provides for matters of defense, justice, and public works. But in essence, these other matters offer little more than a supporting framework that allows the economy to proceed undisturbed in its mission of advancing the public happiness. This reduction of sovereignty results in what Foucault has called "governmentality."[18] Henceforth it is not just that the state will abjure from trying to govern the economy; more fundamentally, the legitimacy and authority of the state are no longer even defined by specifically political criteria such as "right" but rather by efficacy and frugality—criteria the economy itself imposes.[19] It needs only be added that the diminishment of sovereignty in the age of political economy is not something that affects only the sovereign but also extends to the problem of agency as such.

Public happiness, for Smith, is not only something experienced by a population but also something produced by one as well. It is the creation of a great mass, though one that does not act collectively but rather atomizes into individual economic agents each blindly pursuing his own self-interest. The effects of the market are those of a self-organizing order that not only functions in ways unanticipated by its individual members but also can do so only if they continue to remain blind to these effects.[20] As a result, the law of unintended consequences is no longer the tragic exception, borne by doomed figures such as Oedipus, but rather the comic norm. Individuals are not sovereign subjects but rather unconscious ones. The Aristotelian model of action, in which deliberation leads to decision, thereby conferring ethical weight to the agent and his acts, simply cannot pertain here. The individual is both blind in his movements and reduced to an insignificant component of an overarching, spontaneous order that makes decisions for him. As Adam Ferguson states in *An Essay on the History of Civil Society*: "Every step and every movement of the multitude, even in what are termed enlightened ages, are made with equal blindness to the future; and nations stumble upon establishments, *which are indeed the result of human action, but not the execution of any human design*" (my emphasis).[21] Or again, Benjamin Constant (1819): "lost in the multitude, the individual can almost never perceive the influence he exercises. Never does his will impress itself upon the whole; nothing confirms in his eyes his own cooperation."[22] Under such circumstances, a turn from the public to the domestic sphere, where the individual retains some semblance of visible agency, is not surprising. Hence (to hazard a brute causality), the rise of domestic drama and the eclipse of the stage by the novel.

The self-organizing order of the market not only acts "for" the individual but also does so via slow, continuous process rather than punctual event. As a result, its effects are often so subdued and subtle that they become visible only over long periods of time. "The progress is frequently so gradual, that, at near periods, the improvement is not only not sensible, but from the declension of certain other branches of industry, or from certain districts of the country, ... there frequently arises a suspicion, that the riches and industry of the whole are decaying" (*Wealth of Nations*, 374). Economic progress can thus be assessed, claims Smith, only by spanning distant historical moments: from the Norman Conquest to the Wars of the Roses, or from there to the accession of Elizabeth, or from there to the Restoration (375). But this *longue durée* is one in which the individual act—indeed, the individual life, which served Aristotle as the narrative totality granting meaning to individual acts—would be swamped temporally, just as the individual person is swamped by the market that contains him. As Smith points, out, the effect of a few lazy or improvident people will be canceled out by a nation of industrious producers (371).

Smith invokes significant historical events only as temporal markers or mileposts for assessing the work of a marketplace that is fundamentally indifferent to the event. The Wars of the Roses and the Restoration have no intrinsic meaning but simply block out periods of homogenous time. "In each of those periods, however, there was, not only much private and public profusion, many expensive and unnecessary wars, great perversion of the annual produce from maintaining productive to maintaining unproductive hands; but sometimes, in the confusion of civil discord, such absolute waste and destruction of stock, as might be supposed, not only to retard, as it certainly did, the natural accumulation of riches, but to have left the country, at the end of the period, poorer than at the beginning" (375). Historical events of tragic amplitude—war, civil discord—register solely as unnecessary expense that retards or temporarily reverses economic progress but cannot ultimately halt it. More to the point, though, historical event as such is reduced to a kind of background noise or temporary fluctuation that can do no more than momentarily obscure the deeper and fundamentally unstoppable movement of the market. Events, and thus action, become mere epiphenomena or surface effects that will be canceled out over the longer term, just as the price of black cloth will eventually gravitate back to its norm. A long-term rise in the public happiness will eventually annihilate the tragic event.

The rhythm of economic history not only cancels out the effects of political history, it also imprints itself on the temporality of the individual economic agent, who aims at the "slow, gradual bettering of one's condition" rather than at the decisive economic coup. For this form of economic life, the prudential virtues of frugality, industry, and perseverance, celebrated in the later editions of *The Theory of Moral Sentiments*, are more pertinent than the noble and more volatile virtues.[23] Accordingly, the dangerous and potentially tragic passions are muted into interests.[24] Not only in the narrative of economic history but also in the narrative (if it can still be called that) of the individual economic life, ongoing process trumps event, and activity trumps action.

But it is not enough that the ethical range of the human should be confined (in the economic sphere, at least) to safe, prudential qualities that lack Aristotelian *megethos* or tragic amplitude. It turns out that even these reduced virtues are not the ethical achievements of the individuals who display them. Rather, they are bestowed by the economy itself: "The proportion between capital and revenue, therefore, seems everywhere to regulate the proportion between industry and idleness. Wherever capital predominates, industry prevails: wherever revenue, idleness. Every increase or diminution of capital, therefore, naturally tends to increase or diminish the real quantity of industry, the number of productive hands, and consequently the exchangeable value of the annual produce of the land and labour of the country, the real wealth and revenue of all its inhabitants" (*Wealth of Nations*, 367).

This passage has received almost no attention from commentators on Smith—not, I think, because it is uninteresting but because it is *too* interesting. What Smith is saying here is that the ratio in which a nation's economic resources are reinvested in productive capital as opposed to being spent as revenue will automatically regulate the levels of industry exhibited by the members of its population. Marx himself could not have formulated a stronger version of economic determinism. It is not that the possession of certain prudential virtues leads to economic success. Rather, the market selects for the virtues that reinforce it, implanting either industry or idleness depending on large-scale distributions of the national revenue. This, I would argue, is the real "Adam Smith problem," and it is also the final dismantling of any agential self. Not only has action been divorced from intention; not only has the individual agent been subsumed within a larger, spontaneous order that cannot be directed from within or without; not only has ongoing, prudential activity displaced the sovereign act; but even the virtues that enable that activity are, as it were, on loan from the economic mechanism itself.

Now, despite my tone, it is not self-evident to everyone that all these developments taken together are necessarily a bad thing. The liberal tradition of political thought tends to accept Smith's view that the workings of a commercial economy are essentially benign, both providing material prosperity and safeguarding human freedom. While I would dissent from this optimistic reading, my point is simply that the diminished conception of human agency and its relation to human happiness that emerges from *The Wealth of Nations* poses a significant challenge to classical notions of tragedy and to the ethical self that grants it meaning.

II

To all of which, the skeptical reader might reply: "So what? You've shown that the Smithian marketplace is not compatible with tragedy. Who ever thought that it would be?[25] Moreover, you began by depicting the economy as walled off from the rest of social reality—as a topsy-turvy kingdom that converts public mourning into a rise in the price of black cloth. But as you yourself insisted, we stand outside of that realm, and thus things such as public mourning continue to exist for us. In addition, Smith did not just author *The Wealth of Nations*. He also wrote *The Theory of Moral Sentiments*, in which he depicts a fully working ethical self, and moreover insists on the importance of action to one's moral constitution. He also frequently brings tragic drama into the discussion. And those are just the problems internal to Smith's thought. There's also the historical problem of how, or whether, any of this radiated beyond certain intellectual circles of the Scottish Enlightenment to affect the tragic stage, much less the ambient social and cultural world in which it operates."

These are all significant objections that deserve an answer. The historical ones can be addressed initially simply by noting that Smith was at least partly correct in his description of how a commercial economy works. While publication of *The Wealth of Nations* was an epochal intellectual event, it was so in part because it gave brilliant conceptual expression to certain fundamental realities of capitalist modernity—realities that would have made themselves felt, and indeed had been doing so for some time, even if Smith had never written. For this reason, too, in the following discussion I am not much worried about the fact that the first edition of *The Theory of Moral Sentiments* precedes *The Wealth of Nations* by some years. And as to the inside/outside problem: yes, I insisted that the marketplace as Smith describes it is in some sense walled off from its social surround. But this does not mean that the economy, though largely impervious to outside influence, cannot act upon its environment. The separating membrane, as I shall argue, is semipermeable, and so the treatment of action in *The Wealth of Nations* finds its corresponding symptoms in *The Theory of Moral Sentiments*, including the latter's understanding of tragic drama.

That the logic of the marketplace informs Smith's *Theory of Moral Sentiments* is an argument that others have already made for me. The most compelling and fully elaborated case is in James R. Otteson's important study, *Adam Smith's Marketplace of Life*.[26] Otteson claims that Smith's fundamental intellectual discovery was the principle of spontaneous systems of social order: that isolated actions of individuals in society will tend to self-organize into coherent structures. The economic marketplace is the most celebrated instance in which Smith explores this process, but Otteson shows it at work as well in Smith's studies of morality and the history of language. "Smith's analysis of human morality in TMS," states Otteson, adopts a "model . . . of a market in which free exchanges among participating people give rise, over time, to an unanticipated system of order."[27] The mechanism by which this occurs involves "everyone's employing the impartial spectator procedure and modifying his judgments and behavior in terms of it."[28] Unlike mine, Otteson's reading does not assume a causal or deterministic model in which the economy reshapes other areas of social life to accommodate it. Rather, the self-organizing system is a kind of abstract machine that instantiates itself repeatedly in varied social and cultural terrains, the economic marketplace among them. In my view, this approach produces results even more totalizing than my own. Nevertheless, I shall here follow Otteson's lead in elaborating the consequences for Smith's moral philosophy of the highly attenuated view of human action put forth in *The Wealth of Nations*.

This will not (I should state from the start) involve any claim that Smith explicitly adopts either a quietist or a fatalist position in *The Theory of Moral Sentiments*. Indeed, he offers a full-throated insistence on the importance of action to his system of ethics:

> Man was made for action, and to promote by the exertion of his faculties such changes in the external circumstances both of himself and others, as may seem most favourable to the happiness of all. He must not be satisfied with indolent benevolence, nor fancy himself a friend of mankind, because in his heart he wishes well to the prosperity of the world. That he may call forth the whole vigour of his soul, and strain every nerve, in order to produce those ends which it is the purpose of his being to advance, Nature has taught him, that neither himself nor mankind can be fully satisfied with his conduct, nor bestow upon it the full measure of applause, unless he has actually produced them. (*Theory of Moral Sentiments*, 153–54)

Without wishing to negate the force or clarity of this, I will point out that it is the only such statement to appear in the 500-plus pages of *The Theory of Moral Sentiments*, and moreover that what Smith means by the term "action" cannot be understood outside of the total intellectual context that work provides.[29] As Charles Griswold notes: "this is not a book whose primary focus is moral action; the sentiments point us in the direction of character, though not by any means to the exclusion of action." "Smith," he correctly insists, "has written a book on the moral *emotions*" (my emphasis).[30]

The basic arguments of *The Theory of Moral Sentiments* are so well known as to require only the briefest of summaries. Human beings, Smith claims, are endowed with both a spontaneous capacity to sympathize with the feelings of others and an innate desire to have others sympathize with our own feelings. But we cannot know directly what others feel; we can only imagine how we would feel in their situation, and this produces a lower level of affective response than if the situation actually were our own. If we want others' feelings to accord with ours when, for instance, we are suffering, we must therefore lower the intensity with which we express, and even allow ourselves to experience, that suffering to the level that another person would feel for us. Over time, individuals learn to modulate their affects by imagining how others would judge their feelings and the situation that produced them. Practice in this process installs within us the "impersonal spectator," an imagined observer whose perspective allows us to distance ourselves from our own self-partiality and thereby produce increasingly sophisticated judgments on the propriety of feelings and action, both our own and those of others.

The process of mutual correction and regulation of sentiments to an equilibrium level strikes Otteson (among others) as analogous to economic mechanisms whereby market prices gravitate toward what Smith calls "natural price."[31] As Otteson puts it, "because the desire for mutual sympathy is universal, meaning that all people have it, this process of alternately moderating and amplifying sentiments tends ultimately toward an equilibrium of sentiment. Individual acts of judgment and sympathy give rise to standards universally shared within a given culture without anyone's intending to do so—an instance of spontaneous order."[32]

When Otteson speaks of "this process of alternately moderating and amplifying sentiments," he makes the analogy with market mechanisms clear, but this analogy in turn tempts him into misrepresenting the process of adjustment described by Smith, which almost always involves diminishing rather than amplifying sentiment. The mourner who wishes others to sympathize with him "can only hope to obtain this by lowering his passions to that pitch, in which the spectators are capable of going along with him. He must flatten, if I may be allowed to say so, the sharpness of its natural tone, in order to reduce it to harmony and concord with the emotions of those who are about him" (*Theory of Moral Sentiments*, 23). Indeed, an entire genus of virtues defined by Smith involves the laboriously learned exertion of self-control, while Smith never seems to dwell on the possibility that training is required to work up needed levels of sympathy. The role of the impartial spectator in moral judgment therefore tends in general toward a muting of affect—something we have already seen at work in the economic sphere.

More fundamentally, Smith's analysis of moral virtue displays a focus on sentiment almost to the exclusion of action. Smith's premise is that learning

Sentiment not action

to feel and judge correctly will allow us to act correctly, but in practice his emphasis falls almost entirely on the sentiments and their regulation. "And hence it is," states Smith, "that to feel much for others, and little for ourselves, that to restrain our selfish, and to indulge our benevolent affections, constitutes the perfection of human nature" (27). Note that restraining feelings requires effort while "indulging" them implies simply not bothering to stop a spontaneous flow. Above all, human nature is "perfected" for Smith not through action but through achieving a proper proportion and attunement of feeling. The sentiments are not merely spurs to action, but ends in themselves. It is surely no coincidence that the imaginary figure who regulates Smith's entire moral system—the impartial spectator—is by definition someone *who does not act* but only sympathizes and judges.

Smith's analysis consistently privileges the intentions or sentiments that give rise to action over the effects of the action itself. Indeed, he insists that intention should be the sole basis for judgment, and while he recognizes that we generally take consequences into account, he ascribes this to an "irregularity of sentiments" (133-34, 152ff.). Smith's approach inverts Hume's emphasis on considerations of utility in judging action. Instead of seeing motive or intention as prelude to the act, Smith regards action primarily as an expression or signifier of intention. And while he insists in the passage quoted above that benevolent feelings without action are not granted full approbation of the spectator, this is not so much because of the objective consequences of action as, I would argue, because action qualifies the intention. In other words, feelings of benevolence that include a sincere intention to act are superior to feelings of benevolence that do not. Action matters because it indicates a more admirable brand of intention and sentiment, not because of its practical effects. And it is thus converted from a means of transforming the external world into a disclosure of subjective sentiment—a kind of theatrical performance.

We can begin to judge the distance between a Smithian ethics and an Aristotelian one by focusing on the role of habit in each. For Aristotle, acting virtuously involves applying practical reason to the specifics of a situation, but that reasoning will have no effect without an underlying disposition to act virtuously. And how is that disposition developed? Through what Aristotle calls habituation. In short, one evolves a disposition to virtue by habitually acting in a virtuous manner. We acquire the habit of doing well by repeatedly doing well. Action installs the disposition to act (*Nicomachean Ethics*, 1103a15-1103b26). While the behaviorist if not tautological quality of this notion bespeaks the relative thinness of Aristotle's moral psychology compared to Smith's, it also bespeaks Aristotle's commitment to *energeia* or actualization. What counts for Aristotle is the realization of the merely potential.

Habit plays an important role in Smith's moral theory as well. But for Smith, what we learn through "constant practice" (*Theory of Moral Sentiments*, 206) until it becomes "habitual" (209) is to see ourselves from the impartial spectator's standpoint. What we practice, in other words, is spectating, not acting—refining the judgment and regulation of our sympathies and sentiments, not actually doing anything. As a result of such training, action itself comes to seem passive—a matter of obeying the imperatives issued by the impartial spectator: "If we place ourselves completely in his situation, if we really view ourselves with his eyes and as he views us, and listen with diligent and reverential attention to what he suggests to us, his voice will never deceive us. We shall stand in need of no casuistic rules to direct our conduct" (333). Ideally, the viewpoint of the impartial spectator not merely informs and guides but entirely replaces our own. Although this spectator is created by our own practices of moral judgment, once formed he assumes an autonomous and even imperative status. We passively receive the messages he sends us and carry them out. Our actions are in some sense no longer our own. They are imparted to us by the self-organizing mechanisms of morality, just as the self-organizing mechanisms of the economy impart to us our industriousness or laziness.

And this brings me to a fundamental point of my argument: that action, as conceived by *The Theory of Moral Sentiments*, is at its core *not active* but *reactive*. It is a response to the prompting of the moral spectator—a form of obedience, not initiative. I borrow the term "reactive" from Friedrich Nietzsche, and here I wish to point out how perfectly Smith's moral system embodies the ethic of *ressentiment* dissected in *On the Genealogy of Morals*.[33] For Nietzsche, the problem with *ressentiment* is both that it is essentially reactive and that, in part as a symptom of this, it takes the form of feeling or sentiment rather than action, which is what allows it to pool or accumulate within the reactive subject rather than discharge itself in the act. The longer one looks, in fact, the closer the fit between Smith's celebration of moral sentiment and Nietzsche's critique of *ressentiment* becomes—to the degree that one begins to wonder whether a sentimental approach to morals is not one of Nietzsche's primary if unstated targets. If it is objected that Nietzsche is a rather far-flung and by no means impartial spectator of sentimental moralities such as Smith's, I would simply point out that Nietzsche is the nineteenth century's premier diagnostician of a crisis of action in modern culture. It is through Nietzsche's perspective that we can grasp how Smith's approach to morality is indeed a crisis—or rather will generate a crisis for others, though Smith himself does not perceive this.

Before proceeding to Smith's views on tragic drama, I want to look at one more passage on the impartial spectator:

> We must here, as in all other cases, view ourselves not so much according to that light in which we may naturally appear to ourselves, as that in which we naturally appear to others. Though every man may, according to the proverb, be the whole world to himself, to the rest of mankind he is the most insignificant part of it. . . . When he views himself in the light in which he is conscious that others will view him, he sees that to them he is but one of the multitude, in no respect better than any other in it. If he would act so as that the impartial spectator may enter into the principles of his conduct, which is what of all things he has the greatest desire to do, he must upon this, as upon all other occasions, humble the arrogance of his self-love, and bring it down to something which other men can go along with. (*Wealth of Nations*, 119-20)

Adopting the perspective of the impartial spectator involves not merely taking a distance on one's own actions (and Nietzsche—as well as Rousseau—would have a good deal to say about the self-division involved here) but seeing oneself as part of the "multitude." If this word gestures toward Stoic cosmopolitanism on the one hand, it invokes political economy on the other, and with it the recognition of oneself as an insignificant part of a population. Indeed, what this passage advocates in essence is placing the public happiness above individual happiness. One learns to privilege the general good over one's own by taking, as it were, an aerial view that locates one as a mere speck in the crowd. While *The Wealth of Nations* sees the public happiness as resulting from blind actions of self-interest, here Smith invokes the market regulation of sentiment as part of an intentional effort to achieve the same end. Ethics is, in this sense, the becoming-conscious of one's status as part of a population or mass. If this blunts naked self-interest and encourages public-mindedness, it is also potentially self-annihilating and has the capacity to make one's actions appear entirely inconsequential, in the way analyzed (as we have already seen) by Benjamin Constant: "lost in the multitude, the individual can almost never perceive the influence he exercises. Never does his will impress itself upon the whole; nothing confirms in his eyes his own cooperation."[34] Smith does not perceive this as a problem, but others will, up to and including Nietzsche, for whom consciousness of oneself as part of a mass can bode nothing good.

III

The essential theatricality of *The Theory of Moral Sentiments* has received extensive attention, and I have no interest in revisiting the matter.[35] My focus is rather on Smith's discussion of tragedy within the work. That Smith incorporates tragic drama into his discussion of moral philosophy is, among other things, a nod to Aristotle, who did the same thing in the *Nicomachean Ethics*. But just as Smith expounds a distinctly non-Aristotelian ethics, so he elaborates a correspondingly non-Aristotelian approach to the tragic.

For Smith, as for any number of eighteenth-century critics, tragic theater is an opportunity for the exercise of sympathy or compassion, and early on he distinguishes between forms of suffering that are appropriate and inappropriate for the theater. Mere physical pain, as embodied in the figure of Philoctetes and his wounded foot, makes a potentially ridiculous subject for tragedy, Smith claims, which Sophocles rescues only by focusing rather on the hero's solitude and by investing the scene with a romantic wildness (*Theory of Moral Sentiments*, 37).[36] By contrast, Racine's *Phèdre* attends appropriately to emotional and moral pain:

> We are charmed with the love of Phaedra, as it is expressed in the French tragedy of that name, notwithstanding all the extravagance and guilt which attend it. That very extravagance and guilt may be said, in some measure, to recommend it to us. Her fear, her shame, her remorse, her horror, her despair, become thereby more natural and interesting. All the secondary passions, if I may be allowed to call them so, which arise from the situation of love, become necessarily more furious and violent; and it is with these secondary passions only that we can properly be said to sympathize. (*Theory of Moral Sentiments*, 41–42)

In the theater of sympathy, tragic drama no longer imitates an *action* (as it had for Aristotle) but represents states of *suffering*. The stage is not a space for doing but one for feeling: shame, remorse, horror, despair, and so on. What holds the play together is no longer the narrative coherence of dramatic *mythos* but rather the sympathetic correspondence between the character's emotions and the spectator's reactions. Indeed, Smith gives no sense at all that anything *happens* on the Racinian stage; the play is rather dissolved into a series of affective tonalities within the title character. But this is the logical consequence of an ethics that regards action not with respect to its practical consequences but only insofar as it discloses the state of intentions and sentiments within the doer.[37]

In the encyclopedia article that inspired Rousseau's famous response, d'Alembert recommended that Geneva should welcome a theater because it would give the citizens "a fineness of tact, a delicacy of sentiment, which is very difficult to acquire without theatrical performances."[38] Given his approach, it is perhaps surprising that Smith never recommends tragic theater as a way of developing our capacities for sympathy or for refining our moral judgments. The first of these is unnecessary, since Smith regards us as invested with innate, fully loaded capacities for sympathizing that do not require artificial enlargement. And with regard to the second, tragedy apparently offers no greater opportunity to hone our skills of judgment than does everyday life. The impartial spectator finds situations to mull over in the tragic theater, but apparently none more challenging or edifying than those he regularly encounters.

Smith's focus on feeling rather than action, and on intention rather than effect, can produce some peculiar assessments:

> The distress which an innocent person feels, who, by some accident, has been led to do something which, if it had been done with knowledge and design, would have justly exposed him to the deepest reproach, has given occasion to some of the finest and most interesting scenes both of the ancient and of the modern drama. It is this fallacious sense of guilt, if I may call it so, which constitutes the whole distress of Œdipus and Jocasta upon the Greek, of Monimia and Isabella upon the English, theatre. They are all of them in the highest degree piacular, though not one of them is in the smallest degree guilty. (*Theory of Moral Sentiments*, 156)

Oedipus, as Smith sees it, feels subjectively guilty. But this feeling is fallacious. He does not incur objective guilt because he did not know he was killing his father or marrying his mother. Oedipus thus exhibits precisely that "irregularity in judgment" that causes people to take practical consequences into account, rather than intention alone, when judging actions. In Smith's reading, then, *Oedipus the King* does not conclude with an anagnorisis or recognition, as Aristotle held, but rather with an error or misrecognition. The tragedy of Oedipus is not the fact of having recognized what he had done but of having mistakenly assigned guilt to himself. Or, to invoke another Aristotelian term: according to Smith, Oedipus's *hamartia*, error, or "fallacious" act is not to have killed his father without recognizing him but to have incorrectly assumed a guilt that is not rightly his.

Now interestingly, Aristotle deals with the question of Oedipus's guilt in the *Nicomachean Ethics*. While discussing the ethical status of voluntary and involuntary actions (1135a), he takes up the hypothetical case of a man who accidentally kills his father without recognizing that it is his father. And as if to involve the reader in the game of recognition, Aristotle does not mention the name of Oedipus when discussing this man. Without analyzing his complex arguments in detail, I will at least note that the relevant distinction for Aristotle is one between an instance of the unjust (*to adikon*) and an unjust act (*adikéma kema*). Both are objective categories. Aristotle is uninterested in the question of subjective guilt or guilty feelings, and it is unlikely that he would even recognize any distinction between being and feeling guilty. Ethics is not, for Aristotle, a form of moral psychology. Likewise, for Oedipus, what matters is clearly what he has done, not what his intentions were when he did them. That he killed his father and married his mother trumps the fact that he was ignorant of doing so. His lack of awareness adds irony but does not subtract guilt. Indeed, Oedipus offers a kind of limit case for the independence of action from character and its priority over it, which may be yet another reason why Aristotle privileges Sophocles's play in a treatise on poetics that declares action the "soul" of tragedy.

Smith's most complex and provocative discussion of tragic drama occurs in an early discussion of sympathy:

> It is agreeable to sympathize with joy; and wherever envy does not oppose it, our heart abandons itself with satisfaction to the highest transports of that delightful sentiment. But it is painful to go along with grief, and we always enter into it with reluctance. When we attend to the representation of a tragedy, we struggle against that sympathetic sorrow which the entertainment inspires as long as we can, and we give way to it at last only when we can no longer avoid it: we even then endeavour to cover our concerns from the company. If we shed any tears, we carefully conceal them, and are afraid lest the spectators, not entering into this excessive tenderness, should regard it as effeminacy and weakness. (*Theory of Moral Sentiments*, 63–64)

The argument of the passage seems straightforward at first. It is easier to sympathize with joy than with pain, because sympathetic joy is itself pleasant to feel, and sympathetic grief is not. We are "reluctant" to sympathize with grief because if we do so, we must ourselves grieve, and we would just as soon avoid this unpleasing affect. Smith then turns to stage tragedy to illustrate his point, but the mechanism he describes there contradicts his initial premise. We resist sympathetic sorrow at a tragic play, apparently, not because the sorrow is unpleasant (if it were, why would we go in the first place?) but because our sorrow threatens to become "excessive." It is not that we have to laboriously gin up sorrowful affect against our will; rather,

the sweet force of it threatens to overwhelm us, and so we set up a secondary form of resistance to keep it in check. As I have argued, Smith never
sees any need to cultivate quantity or intensity of sympathetic response; the
trick is always to dampen it properly. (This is Smith's counterpart to Aristotelian catharsis.) The narrative here is of fighting off something dangerously
pleasurable, ultimately failing, and then shamefully attempting to hide the
evidence of what one has done. The appearance of the term "effeminacy"
at the end places the spectator in a female position and suggests a narrative of seduction and ruin (or is it rape?), with the tragic play as insistent
lover and the spectator as would-be virgin holding him off for as long as she
can but ultimately succumbing to his irresistible charms (or force), the tears
doubling as a kind of sexual effusion. If there is tragedy occurring onstage,
there is melodrama going on in the spectator's head.

Why exactly is the spectator's response shameful? Does not King Lear's
plight deserve our tears? Or is it the fact that this is "just a play," as Smith's
choice of the term "entertainment" may be intended to suggest? "These are
just fictional characters—why are you crying over them?" And what is the
force of the generalizing "we" Smith employs? Is everyone at the theater
undergoing an identical struggle, each fearing that he or she will become a
shameful spectacle to the others?

This passage is partly about how difficult it is to be an impartial spectator when attending a tragic play. Indeed, it throws the very concept of the
impartial spectator into some disarray. That spectator is supposedly the incarnation of generally shared ethical norms as these would be applied objectively by some other, uninvolved person to one's own situation. But if
everyone feels guiltily moved at a tragic play, then the "proper" response is
natural to no one, and the impartial spectator no longer embodies societal
norms. In this case the norm would rather be to sympathize with people's
difficulties in controlling their emotions at a tragic play, not to judge them
harshly. Indeed, one is struck by the disparity between the sympathetic response shown by spectators for the characters in the play and the resolute
lack of sympathy each shows for the emotional plight of his fellow the-
atergoers.[39] The impartial spectator now embodies a norm that *no one* can
live up to and so begins to look more like the Freudian superego that ir-
rationally punishes. But of course the main drama here is of the spectator's becoming a spectacle himself. What play is being performed, exactly?
What is happening onstage? Who knows? The Smithian spectator is too
busy struggling with his emotions and ashamedly hiding his own response
to notice. The play has triggered a reaction but then recedes into the back-

ground of this new struggle. The tragic agon has been transported from the stage, where characters are actually doing and saying things, to the spectator's own interior stage where gushing sympathy is in pitched battle with self-control. The actants are not ethically autonomous persons but internal psychic mechanisms operating a complicated sort of affective hydraulics. ("Open the valves to the tear glands!" "Never!")

In *The Theory of Moral Sentiments*, Smith divides the self into spectator and actor. He then urges his readers to identify with that spectator to the greatest extent possible and to act reactively only in response to the spectator's judgments. Given the fact that this division of roles is obviously based on a theatrical model, one would expect the literal act of theatrical spectating to be the most natural thing in the world, and yet it is unexpectedly fraught. It turns out that one can never coincide with the position of the impartial spectator; when you think you are there, he has retreated to a greater distance and is still judging you.

Rather than draw the obvious Lacanian moral here, I want to return to the problem of tragedy. The model theatrical audience one would expect to emerge from Smith's theory is a coolly Brechtian one, impartially assessing the actions onstage to determine which characters, if any, are worthy of sympathy. What one gets instead are trembling lips and wet eyes fearful of discovery by imagined dry eyes. Compare this with Jean-Pierre Vernant's treatment of Greek tragedy. For Vernant, the tragic play presents a conflict of incompatible versions of the good (in part the result of an incompletely unified Athenian legal system) that poses an intellectual *problem* for the audience and encourages them to exercise their deliberative faculties upon it. It thus sharpens the forms of judgment that are also brought to bear on political debate in the Assembly.[40] Tragedy is grasped as dramatic action, and the deliberative process to which it gives rise informs political action in turn. Without claiming that this model offers an exhaustive account of how Greek tragedy actually works, we can at least employ it to gain some perspective on Smith's account of tragedy, which he conceives as a presentation of emotional states that sets off an affective crisis in the viewer. Rather than deliberating or debating issues, the members of the Smithian audience are furtively scanning themselves and others.

Indeed, Smith's account of viewing stage tragedy begins to suggest a nightmare version of the invisible hand. In the *Wealth of Nations*, individual producers blindly make decisions based only on their own interests, yet these atomized decisions spontaneously organize into an overarching system that benefits all. At the Smithian theater, viewers are intensely aware of others yet isolated from them, absorbed in an internal drama of self-surveillance and self-control that everyone appears to be losing yet no one can abandon because the impartial spectator constructed out of each individual's judgments holds everyone in thrall. Not only is the theatrical spectator, as spectator, definitionally excluded from action, but also he cannot even give full range to his (now merely affective) response. Both paralyzed and emotionally constipated, what the Smithian spectator fears most is (ironically) publicly mourning, the very thing with which we began. He finds himself in an arena apparently designed for precisely that purpose, but the crisis of action precipitated by political economy returns there to snuff it out.

Otteson's reading of Smith tends to overlook an important difference between *The Wealth of Nations* and *The Theory of Moral Sentiments*, which is that the latter lacks the ironic structure of the former. Yes, individual moral judgments unintentionally organize into a moral system, but the process results in no reversal of aim comparable to those effected by economic markets. The impartial spectator perfects and completes, rather than inverts, the actions of individual moral agents. It is this relative absence of irony that allows the whole process to remain more closely coordinated with the conscious intentions of its participants. Only at the tragic theater does an overarching irony begin to reveal itself: that the result of apparently free moral judgments may detach itself from its moral agents and turn upon them with tyrannical force, converting the impartial spectator into something more like a Hobbesian sovereign. This time, however, the ironic reversal is not benign and begins to look rather more like tragic Fate. Or rather it would if the results were more than mere discomfort and embarrassment, in line with the muting of affect that marks Smith's discourse as a whole.

The invisible hand of *The Wealth of Nations* turns the bad (or at least self-interested) intentions of economic agents into good, but the invisible hand of *The Theory of Moral Sentiments* turns the good intentions of moral agents into a kind of ill. If the Smithian theater is a space of appearance or disclosure rather than action, what ultimately gets disclosed there is a problem that otherwise silently pervades *The Theory of Moral Sentiments* and becomes fully legible only to later figures such as Nietzsche.[41]

In the course of his play, Macbeth finds himself at a banquet where a tragic spectacle occurs. The bloody ghost of Banquo appears to him alone, and Macbeth's horrified reaction turns him into a spectacle that elicits embarrassment and dismay from those present. Macbeth thus anticipates the plight of the Smithian spectator, who likewise finds himself converted into helpless spectacle and wishes for night's invisible and bloody hand to cloak both him and his relation to others. His tragedy is that the invisible hand holding him in its grasp is in reality not Shakespeare's but Smith's.

IV

Responses to Smith were not long in coming. One of the first came from Smith himself. The 1790 edition of *The Theory of Moral Sentiments* included a new sixth part, titled "Of the Character of Virtue," which, it has been argued, attempts to ameliorate some of the ethical side effects of commerce.[42] "Of the Character of Virtue" adopts something that looks very much like an Aristotelian virtue ethics, and it endorses the "noble" virtues, such as magnanimity, as an antidote to the mediocrity fostered by polished, commercial society.[43] Of course, positing magnanimity as antidote places it in a reactive position; rather than simply affirming, it must now negate, and even define itself by way of that negation. But this is a fundamental contradiction of modernity from which not even Nietzsche's elevation of the noble virtues could extricate itself. In this one regard, at least, Smith is Nietzsche's precursor.[44]

An even earlier and, to my mind, more interesting "response" to Smith actually predates *The Wealth of Nations*. Adam Ferguson's *An Essay on the History of Civil Society* (1767) critiques numerous elements of commercial society that would find their way into Smith. For Ferguson, commercial society poses a challenge to action that manifests itself in both the political and dramatic realms. In a sense, he is the first to articulate the thesis that animates the present book, and he also serves as precursor to several of the nineteenth- and twentieth-century theorists (Hegel, Marx, Alexandre Kojève, Friedrich Hayek, and above all Hannah Arendt) with which this book will be concerned, while also providing a connection to a classical republican tradition of politics that stretches back to Aristotle. Ferguson counters Smith's economic optimism with a tragic vision of the political that also leads him to extol the genre of tragic drama. If political economy undermines tragedy, the republicanist tradition of political thinkers, from Ferguson to Arendt, becomes tragic drama's firm advocate and employs it as a wedge against the deleterious effects of a modern, commercial society. The rest of this chapter will be devoted to expounding a republicanist view of tragedy as antidote to political economy. In the case of both Ferguson and Arendt, however, the role of tragedy can be properly apprehended only within the broader context of their intellectual systems, and this will therefore require some prior groundwork.

For Ferguson, the human essence derives from action, and specifically action of a competitive, agonistic sort.[45] This fact is founded in the core of our animal natures:

> Every animal is made to delight in the exercise of his natural talents and forces: the lion and the Tyger sport with the paw; the horse delights to commit his mane to the wind, and forgets his pasture to try his speed in the field; the bull even before his brow is armed, and the lamb while yet an emblem of innocence, have a disposition to strike with the forehead, and anticipate, in play, the conflicts they are doomed to sustain. Man too is disposed to opposition, and to employ the forces of his nature against an equal antagonist; he loves to bring his reason, his eloquence, his courage, even his bodily strength, to the proof. His sports are frequently an image of war; sweat and blood are freely expended in play; and fractures of death are often made to terminate the pastimes of idleness and festivity. He was not made to live forever, and even his love of amusement has opened a path that leads to the grave.[46]

Ferguson regards mankind not in opposition to the animal but as a particular species of animal. And human pleasures are therefore forms of animal pleasure. These Ferguson divides into two kinds, without ever naming them as such. The higher or exertive pleasures as illustrated by the lion, horse, and bull push our innate capacities to their limits and allow us to rejoice in their active strength. Even as described above, they contain not only an agonistic but also a potentially tragic dimension, and are purchased at the cost of mortality. The lower or passive pleasures involve feeding, reproduction, and all forms of consumption that nourish and perpetuate life but do not raise it to a higher level. Ferguson describes both as animal pleasures but treats them very differently. The higher lead to politics, and the lower to political economy.

It is the higher or exertive pleasures, according to Ferguson, that produce specifically human forms of happiness: "The most animating occasions of human life, are calls to danger and hardship, not invitations to safety and ease: and man himself, in his excellence, is not an animal of pleasure, nor destined merely to enjoy what the elements bring to his use; but, like his associates, the dog and the horse, to follow the exercises of his nature, in preference to what are called its enjoyments; to pine in the lap of ease and of affluence, and to exult in the midst of alarms that seem to threaten his being" (*Essay on the History of Civil Society*, 47–48).

The human announces itself through its contempt for the merely passive sustenance of animal life and through its pursuit of exertive forms of pleasure: "In devising, or in executing a plan, in being carried on the tide of emotion and sentiment, the mind seems to unfold its being, and to enjoy itself. To a being of this description, therefore, it is a blessing to meet with incentives to action" (46). And of course, man exerts himself at the highest level in relation not to the rest of nature but to other men, and therefore political society is the only true setting for human happiness: "They are the most happy men, whose hearts are engaged to a community, in which they find every object of generosity and zeal, and a scope to the exercise of every talent, and of every virtuous disposition" (59). Here we return, in a sense, to the term *public happiness*, which sets Ferguson against Smith. For Smith, as we have seen, "public happiness" means the forms of happiness available to a population, which Ferguson would identify with the lower forms of animal being: "Because men, like other animals, are maintained in multitudes, where the necessaries of life are amassed, and the store of wealth is enlarged, we drop our regards for the happiness, the moral and political character of the people; and anxious for the herd we would propagate, carry our views no farther than the stall or the pasture" (*Essay on the History of Civil Society*, 140). Political economy provides sustenance for man as massed into a population or herd; the republic or political realm, by contrast, provides an organized context for the exercise of the active virtues, and thus for that form of happiness that Aristotle regards as supervenient to human activity. The happiness of populations requires their being provisioned with commodities; the happiness of citizens requires their active pursuit of virtue in the republic.

It is not just that these two forms of happiness are different or complementary. The active or strenuous form defines itself by its contempt for the other; it rejoices in depriving itself of lower bodily pleasures, in rejecting the dependence upon them. Ferguson's treatment of competitive or aggressive urges, for instance, which he sees as both innate to mankind and necessary for civic life, consistently emphasizes the way that they operate in defiance of material need or benefit. "We are fond of distinctions; we place ourselves in opposition, and quarrel under the denominations of faction and party, *without any material subject of controversy*" (27, my emphasis). For Ferguson, the best wars are those fought not for booty but for their own sake, as an end in themselves or a deadly game (26–27). And likewise, the political life involves the strenuous expression of republican virtue in complete disregard for the lower forms of pleasure catered to by political economy.

The originality of Ferguson's approach should not be overlooked here. The republic is being contrasted not with monarchy as a political form—the traditional dichotomy. The rule of the many is not defined against rule of the one, liberty is not set against tyranny. Indeed, it is not set against a form of rule at all but rather against a form of satisfaction: the pleasures of commercial society, something it cannot simply overthrow in a political revolution but with which it will rather have to coexist. Republicanism's other is not a rival form of government but its own socioeconomic context.

This theme informs Ferguson's one passing reference to a particular tragic drama: "The bosom kindles in company, while the point of interest in view has nothing to inflame; and a matter frivolous in itself, becomes important, when it serves to bring to light the intentions and characters of men. The foreigner, who believed that Othello, on the stage, was enraged for the loss of his handkerchief, was not more mistaken, than the reasoner who imputes any of the more vehement passions of men to the impressions of mere profit or loss" (36). The tragic passions, like the political ones, are distinguished by their transcendence of utility. But Ferguson's choice of reference seems overdetermined. Not only is Shakespeare's play set in Venice, renowned as the longest-enduring republic, but also Othello perfectly embodies Ferguson's ideal of active civic and military virtue exercised without respect for gain. Indeed, Shakespeare's play depicts the bringing down of that titanic virtue by a character who cares only for his purse and private ends regardless of their effect on the civic order. Read allegorically, *Othello* represents the very destruction of republican virtue by commercial selfishness that will occupy Ferguson throughout much of the *Essay*.

Nevertheless, even tragedy contains an element of hope, because the same sentiments that cause Othello to invest a handkerchief with meaning beyond its utility also cause the audiences of tragedy to take an interest in human affairs even when the issue at stake has no material bearing upon them. The very capacity to attend to a dramatic fiction, and one that is recognized as such, bespeaks a sociality that binds humans beyond their mutual dependence through the division of labor. Tragedy engages the passions that make a political life possible.

The antagonism between commercial society and civic virtue takes multiple forms. Excessive peace and tranquility (one of the primary blessings of commerce, according to Smith) dampen the competitive, aggressive impulses that feed civic life, while the pursuit of private gain distracts citizens from the public good. "The period is coming, when, no engagement remaining on the part of the public, private interest, and animal pleasure, become the sovereign objects of care" (*Essay on the History of Civil Society*, 242). Even the division of labor, which Smith extols as the primary means to enhancing the wealth of society, becomes destructive when applied to the political sphere: "The subdivision of arts and professions, in certain examples, tends to improve the practice of them, and to promote their ends. By having separated the arts of the clothier and the tanner, we are the better supplied with shoes and with cloth. But to separate the parts which form the citizen and the statesman, the arts of policy and war, is an attempt to dismember the human character, and to destroy those very arts we mean to improve" (218). Under the division of labor, "society is made to consist of parts, of which none is animated with the spirit of society itself" (207). Both the division of labor and the ascendance of private interests exert a centrifugal force that disperses the unity of the republic. "A change in national matters for the worse," warns Ferguson, "may arise from the discontinuance of the scenes in which the talents of men were happily cultivated, and brought them to exercise" (226). What makes Ferguson's illusion to "scenes" interesting is not merely the commonplace understanding of politics as theater, or even the notion that pursuit of private gain makes citizens into bad political actors. It is the possibility that dispersal into individual interest will cause the political "scene" as such to disappear, and with it the possibility of meaningful action. This is a concern that Hannah Arendt, among others, will take up in the twentieth century.

Ferguson is by no means unaware of the arguments made by proponents of *le doux commerce* that the interests it promotes are less dangerously harmful than the heroic passions they displace. Yes, he responds, the latter can lead to tragic outcomes. And yet:

> If men must go wrong, there is a choice of their very errors, as well as of their virtues. Ambition, the love of personal eminence, and the desire of fame, although they sometimes lead to the commission of crimes, yet always engage men in pursuits that require to be supported by some of the greatest qualities of the human soul; and if eminence is the principal object of pursuit, there is, at least, a probability, that those qualities may be studied on which a real elevation of mind is raised. But when public alarms have ceased, and contempt of glory is recommended as an article of wisdom, the sordid habits, and mercenary dispositions, to which, under a general indifference to national objects, the members of a polished or commercial state are exposed, must prove at once the most effectual suppression of every liberal sentiment, and the most fatal reverse of all those principles from which communities derive their hopes of preservation, and their strength. (*Essay on the History of Civil Society*, 244)

"Go wrong" invokes, indeed is almost a translation of, the Greek *hamartia*. Avoiding the grand errors of political life in favor of the security of the commercial one is not a way of avoiding tragedy, then, but simply the choice of a different form of tragic error, one that is mean and sordid as well as harmful. Commercial society has redoubled *hamartia* in that it chooses the wrong form of error, has been mistaken even in the kind of mistake it takes as its own.

Long before Ferguson, republican theory had been concerned with the difficulty of perpetuating civic virtue and thus the endurance of the republic itself against the tendency of its own success to spawn security and prosperity, then laxness and indifference, and finally decay and collapse. Polybius posited a kind of life cycle for the individual state, but with the assumption that when one republic dies, another is born elsewhere. Individual republics have histories, but the background conditions that make republican virtue possible do not change. Ferguson himself argues that the corruption and decay of the republic lays the basis for its eventual rebirth. But against this cyclical narrative stands the stadial theory of history entertained by Ferguson, Smith, and other members of the Scottish Enlightenment, which posited a more general historical evolution toward commercial society. If this is the case, and commercial society is destined to become the norm, then the conditions for republican rebirth—and with it, the possibility of active republic virtue—have gone into permanent decline.

This story of political decay in the age of commerce is, as it happens, also a story of literary decay, and thus a story of the decay of tragic drama. For Ferguson, the greatness of Greek letters was a direct efflux of Greek political turbulence: "Amidst the great occasions which put a free, and even a licentious, society in motion, its members become capable of every exertion; and the same scenes which gave employment to Themistocles and Thrasybulus, inspired, by contagion, the genius of Sophocles and Plato" (*Essay on the History of Civil Society*, 170). Conversely, as the "agitations of a free people" (210) are calmed and dampened by commercial society, so is the engine that powers literary greatness. The division of labor that encourages the growth of a separate literary *profession* encourages scholarship rather than vigorous invention: "After libraries are furnished, and every path of ingenuity is occupied, we are, in proportion to our admiration of what is already done, prepossessed against farther attempts. We become students and admirers, instead of rivals; and substitute the knowledge of books, instead of the inquisitive or animated spirit in which they were written" (206). For Ferguson, literary greatness depends on a republic of letters in which competition among authors imitates that among political actors in the actual republic. Once we admire the past instead of contending with it, we have lost all chance of challenging its eminence. Tragedy, among other genres, is therefore destined to wither along with the possibilities of political action, both victims of commercial society's triumph. The challenge to tragedy that tends to emerge only symptomatically in Smith, then, becomes an explicit warning in Ferguson—one that later thinkers will echo.

For Ferguson, literary questions are far from primary. Even Greek letters are merely the "inferior appendages of a genius otherwise excited, cultivated, and refined" (57). The decline of tragedy is little more than the sign of a more widespread and consequential crisis of action that centers on the *polis* itself. Given this, however, it is surprising how much attention Ferguson devotes to literary matters in the *Essay*. If Greek literature was not directly political, it derived its energies from political agitation and in turn supplied myths and stories that inspired political actors to still greater heights (77). And all this is aside from the purely literary rivalries that generate a quasi-political form of artistic greatness. Literature, including (perhaps, especially) drama, is fundamentally oriented by its relation to political action. It is certainly not a form of commercial activity, and, like the republic itself, it is threatened by the crisis of action that commercial society engenders.

My analysis opposes a republicanist Ferguson to a commercialist Smith, but the contrast isn't quite so simple, on either end. Although Ferguson deplores the effects of commerce on political virtue, he is not therefore opposed to commerce as such. And despite his emphasis on robust political action, he also inherits, somewhat contradictorily, an understanding of political institutions as complex mechanisms that can be thrown off-kilter if jostled excessively. He is thus committed to a principle of incremental change despite his republican, even somewhat Romantic, rhetoric of political action.[47] This principle is widespread in the Scottish Enlightenment and is something that Ferguson shares with Smith. Moreover, it connects with another important theme in Ferguson—the slow, unintended evolution of social and political institutions—that also, as we have seen, works as an impediment to any notion of purposive action.[48] If Ferguson opposes political economy, or at least insists that its principles do not make up "the sum of national felicity, or the principal object of any state" (*Essay on the History of Civil Society*, 140n), his thinking is nevertheless partially formed by its logic, which therefore constrains and limits his way of conceiving action. His situation in this regard is not a unique one; indeed, it becomes paradigmatic for all subsequent thinkers who attempt to reason their way past the impasse of action in Smith.

Finally, it is worth noting that Ferguson's defense of political action in the face of commercial society simultaneously defends a tragic view of life in the face of the historical optimism that pervades *The Wealth of Nations*. The possibility of action requires a political sphere founded on agonistic rivalries—a sphere that makes greatness possible but can do so only at the cost of risking deadly conflict and catastrophic error. Such a life must be lived in a constant state of agitation, uncertainty, and strenuous exertion: the very opposite of the tranquility, security, and material comfort offered by commercial society. The high tragedy of republican politics is, moreover, haunted by the low tragedy of commercial society's historical tendency to corrupt republican virtue and thus to replace heroic action with selfishness and mediocrity. Just as Ferguson speaks of a choice of errors, so he envisions a choice of tragedies—and this is something he will share with one of the heirs of his republican vision: Hannah Arendt.

V

Arendt may well be the twentieth century's most distinctive and controversial theorist of the act. Her insistence that action thrives only in the political sphere, her highly theatrical conception of politics and political action, and even her claim that drama is "the political art form par excellence," all place her squarely in the republicanist tradition of political thought occupied by Machiavelli, Montesquieu, and Adam Ferguson. Arendt's philosophical relation to figures such as Heidegger, Kant, and Aristotle has received extended and sensitive treatment.[49] Her indebtedness to political economy, by contrast, has attracted much less attention, in part because Arendt (like Ferguson) appears to treat this discourse solely as the enemy of politics, something that threatens to undermine the political sphere and therefore must be held at arm's length. Adam Smith and Karl Marx are, for Arendt, among the leading intellectual culprits behind the rise of "the social," that becoming-public of the properly private realm of labor that threatens to eradicate political action once and for all, replacing it with normalized, domesticated forms of activity that Arendt disparages as "behavior."[50] Both this conceptual opposition and the historical narrative of political decline it gives rise to place Arendt in a line of thought that includes Ferguson. Arendt's theory of action and its attendant theory of tragedy can therefore be seen as responses to the crisis of action Adam Smith initiated. And yet, as was also the case with Ferguson, Arendt's relation to political economy involves more than simply trying to negate it. Both classical political economy and modern economics play important if not always obvious roles in Arendt's thinking through of political action. Although the themes I intend to pursue here run throughout Arendt's work, I shall focus solely on *The Human Condition*, in part because it is Arendt's signature statement on the *vita activa*, in part because I will be concerned with the internal intellectual structure of that work, and in part because it is there that Arendt engages most fully with the traditions of political economy.

Before diving into the economic, however, I want to look briefly at a passage that will help orient discussion: "To live together in the world means essentially that the world of things is between those who have it in common, as a table is located between those who sit around it; the world, like every in-between, relates and separates men at the same time."[51] The word *between* can indicate connection (a secret shared between us) and separation (we were friends until she came between us). The table physically instantiates this ambiguity, gathering us around it yet maintaining us at a distance from one another. For Arendt, it represents the necessary structure of any human world, which requires things of shared concern in order to keep us from scattering yet also offers barriers to prevent us from colliding or collapsing into one another. A world can exist only when the centripetal and centrifugal forces of the "between" are in balance, sustaining both the plurality of differences and the shared focus of attention that allows a space for political action to form.

The "things" that compose the in-between of the human world are in part those durable structures, created by work, that provide the material setting for such a world. In this sense, the table is both a figure for such a thing and an example of it. But Arendt also appears to be playing with the Latin *res* or the German *Sache*, which can indicate a physical object and also a matter of discussion or contention, as in a legal trial or a political debate. Like a table, the objects of our political concern draw us together and keep us apart as our individual powers of judgment and action are brought to bear collectively upon them.

The image of the table, which holds the conflicting forces of the "between" in tension, offers, I suggest, a kind of master figure for the intellectual project of *The Human Condition*. The relate-and-separate is Arendt's counterpart to the Hegelian raise-and-cancel of the *Aufhebung*: a (not-quite, in Arendt's case) dialectical concept that organizes the intellectual structure of the book. It defines not just the structure of any world, but the proper relation between the public and private realms, and thus between the fundamental categories of labor, work, and action. It also happens to describe Arendt's relation to political economy more accurately than simple rejection does. The very fact that Arendt devotes roughly a third of the pages of *The Human Condition* to the categories of labor and work should make this obvious.

The problem of modernity, for Arendt, is largely the problem of what happens when our table disappears. The Greeks managed to maintain *polis* and *oikos* in productive tension, mutually dependent yet held carefully apart. But with the rise of the social, the private concerns of the household—labor, the body, material need, inequality, unfreedom—begin to obtrude upon the public realm, thus threatening the integrity of political space. Political economy is the intellectual vanguard of this movement. Its very name jams *polis* and *oikos* improperly together (*Human Condition*, 29). "The modern age," Arendt declares, "carried with it a theoretical glorification of labor and has resulted in a factual transformation of the whole of society into a laboring society" (4). By "theoretical glorification of labor," Arendt refers primarily to Smith's labor theory of value, and what seems to bother her about this theory is not the claim that labor is the source of all material goods (indeed, Arendt plainly accepts this, modifying it only through her distinction between labor and work) but rather the claim that labor is the source of all economic *value*. Like the twentieth-century economists with whose work she was at least somewhat conversant, Arendt rejects the labor theory of value. She regards it merely as emblematic of the way classical political economy injects labor's values (productivity in particular) into public intellectual space. Political economy is both symptom and cause of the rise of the social.

Not just classic political economy, however, but even modern economics is problematic for Arendt. Economics can become a science, in her view, only when human activity becomes statistically predictable—that is, when action, which is by definition unpredictable, has been replaced by behavior, which conforms to social norms (42). Economics is the science of behavior and hence the science of society, in which individuals no longer attempt to distinguish themselves and, if they occasionally do, their acts are statistically negligible and so can be discounted: "The unfortunate truth about behaviorism and the validity of its 'laws' is that the more people there are, the more likely they are to behave and the less likely to tolerate non-behavior. Statistically, this will be shown in the leveling out of fluctuation. In reality, deeds will have less and less chance to stem the tide of behavior, and events will more and more lose their significance, that is, their capacity to illuminate historical time" (43). The larger the group, Arendt holds, the more likely that the statistical norms of the social will dominate. Therefore the

action / behavior

proper object of economics is the population. The city provides the site of politics; the nation or population or society, the setting for economics. (The literary correlate of this, which will become important in a later chapter, is that the city is the site for drama and the nation or society is the setting for the novel.) Economics, predicated upon the disappearance of action, also reinforces the logic of the social that replaces action with behavior.

For this reason, Arendt's chapters on "Labor" and "Work" are pointedly *not* economic in approach, even when she turns to a consideration of the marketplace at the end of the "Work" chapter. Arendt treats labor and work strictly with respect to their end products, which she views as utilities or objects of use and not as exchange-values. Division of labor, prices, finance, entrepreneurial activity, capital, balance of trade, even money itself make no appearance in *The Human Condition*, and Arendt's representation of the market*place* bears little relation to the market process as conceived by modern economists. Labor simply supplies those consumables that support biological life while work crafts durable objects that constitute a human world. Arendt attends to these products only when they have already left the sphere of exchange. Nevertheless, the political sphere as Arendt describes it does have a complex if largely unstated relation to the economic, as we shall see.

Before turning to the category of political action, however, I want to remark briefly on the intellectual structure of *The Human Condition*—something that often gets lost given the tendency of commentators to isolate Arendt's theory of action from its context in the book as a whole. As is clear, in the progression from labor to work to action each subsequent category makes good the deficiencies of the prior one. Labor supports life but falls prey to futility because of life's transient nature. Work supplies permanence to combat futility as well as a shared, human world that makes up for the isolated existence of the *animal laborans*. And yet the world of work in turn succumbs to meaninglessness since its governing means-end rationality cannot find a final term. The realm of action remedies meaninglessness by producing stories and, in addition, provides a space of human freedom that separates itself from the necessity governing both labor and work. Action produces the problem of irrevocability, but manages to solve this on its own by way of forgiveness.

While each category corrects and in some sense transcends the prior one, however, it does not quite leave it behind. On the contrary, it leans back upon its predecessor for support. The world of work requires labor to maintain it (the city must be swept), and action leans back upon work because

the ways in which theatre is a polity

action and speech, themselves evanescent, require the durability of made things in order to persist through time. The categories are thus separated but remain in relation, as with Arendt's figure of the table. Action and work, in particular, entail complex ties that invite close investigation. The chapter titled "Work" ends with two sections, one on the exchange market and another on the artwork, that crucially prepare for the chapter on "Action."

The point of action, as Arendt formulates it, is not the end achieved but the disclosure of the agent. "In acting and speaking, men show who they are, reveal actively their unique personal identities and thus make their appearance in the human world" (*Human Condition*, 179). Disclosure is not the same as display because the agent cannot know who he or she truly is prior to committing the self to public exposure. Disclosure cannot be a willed or directed activity but rather something that is risked. Through disclosure, the natality of the individual, his or her inborn uniqueness, is made visible to others. The political sphere, which is founded on plurality and hence on the presence of formally equal yet individually different participants, thus provides the theatrical arena or space of appearance in which disclosure can most properly occur.

Action provides three attributes that work and labor cannot. One is freedom, which can happen only beyond the realm of necessity that governs labor's life-sustaining products and work's means-end rationality. The second is immortality, or at least the possibility of it for the superior few whose actions distinguish them from the many. And the third is meaning, which arises only from narrative accounts of action. All are exclusively human possibilities and make action a distinctively human endeavor. At the same time, however, political debate is obligated to be *about* something. It must therefore engage with worldly interests even as it rises above them. These latter are "overlaid and, as it were, overgrown with an altogether different in-between which consists of deed and words" (183). The realm of action supervenes upon questions of means and ends that necessarily form the topic of political debate. If political stakes were to disappear, disclosure would lose its existential gravity and become mere empty, narcissistic self-display. Some of the most controversial elements of Arendt's theories of action have to do with her insistence that social issues are not proper topics for political discussion. As I shall argue, this is a bit of a red herring, but the objection itself points to the fact that action, in its disclosive dimension, can never entirely separate itself from the worldly content of debate, which by definition belongs in some sense to the world of work (since it answers to the utilitarian logic of means and ends that governs any consideration of

freedom
immortality
meaning

what to *do* in a practical sense). This is the world of "things" (objects, matters) that, in Arendt's figure of the table, "is between those who have it in common," both dividing and relating them.

Action pushes against the set of things on which it rests by bringing to bear a set of criteria entirely alien to the world of work:

> The innermost meaning of the acted deed and the spoken word is independent of victory and defeat and must remained untouched by any eventual outcome, by their consequences for better or worse. Unlike human behavior—which the Greeks, like all civilized people, judged according to "moral standards," taking into account motives and intentions on the one hand and aims and consequences on the other—action can be judged only by the criterion of greatness because it is in its nature to break through the commonly accepted and reach into the extraordinary, where whatever is true in common and everyday life no longer applies because everything that exists is unique and *sui generis*. (*Human Condition*, 205)

This is the Aristotelian standard of *megethos* or amplitude, which, not incidentally, applies to the plot of tragedy as well. Action is judged not by whether it succeeds or fails (that is, not according to a means-end logic) but solely by the greatness of its extraordinary nature, which may be either constructive or catastrophic in its effects.[52] In either case it will be memorable and confer immortality on the doer. At the same time, presumably, standards of success and failure *are* being applied to the practical matters that form the subject of political debate and that occupy the physical space of action even while being held at arm's length from it conceptually. While Arendt depicts agora and assembly, marketplace and political space, as two separate entities (as indeed they were in fifth-century Athens), they are also in some sense the same space, which is defined by the tensions between them. The only thing that keeps one from taking the next step and saying that the political and the *economic* occupy the same space is that Arendt has carefully separated economics from work.

To complicate matters still more, Arendt states that "exchange itself already belongs in the field of action and is by no means a mere prolongation of production" and then goes on to discuss "free acts of exchange" (*Human Condition*, 209). According to the intellectual framework that she has established in *The Human Condition*, it is impossible (for me at least) to make sense of this claim. Exchange is a market activity, not a political one. It is governed by a means-end logic (one exchanges products in order to obtain one more useful to the purchaser, or else to make a profit). Moreover, the marketplace does not constitute a plurality as Arendt understands it, and it cannot serve as a site of disclosure, unless one were to regard one's purchases as effecting an unwitting disclosure of oneself comparable to speech and action—a consumerist idea that Arendt would clearly find horrifying. Exchange would seem to move in the direction of economy, not politics. How can it be assimilated to action?

Simply, I think it cannot. In these sentences, Arendt is not thinking as Arendt. Rather, she is ventriloquizing, and in a way that is revealingly symptomatic of a larger issue. The notion of exchange as action would have been readily available to Arendt, but by way of the liberal thinkers and economists who constitute her primary if implicit antagonists in *The Human Condition*. More specifically, it would have been associated with a book titled *Human Action: A Treatise on Economics* by the Austrian-school economist Ludwig von Mises. An English translation and augmenting of Mises's *Grundprobleme der Nationalökonomie* (1933), *Human Action* was published by Yale University Press in 1949, eight years prior to *The Human Condition*. The title alone, one imagines, would have rendered Mises's volume irresistible to Arendt, and yet it is not included in her library as preserved at Bard College, nor does she refer to Mises directly either in *The Human Condition* or, as far as I can tell, elsewhere. But it is hard to guess where else she would have picked up a notion of exchange as action.

For Mises, economic exchange is action because it involves a choice. In a world defined by scarcity (in the sense that there is not an infinitely available supply of everything) exchange involves sacrificing something in pursuit of something else—a choice among goods that will ideally benefit the chooser. In this sense, economics is just a subfield in a larger theory of action (or "praxeology," as Mises puts it). As his volume proceeds, however, it becomes clear that economic choice is not merely one kind among many but the paradigm for all choosing and hence for all action.[53] Not only is exchange a form of action, as Arendt asserts, but action is also always a form of exchange. What makes this exchange challenging—what makes, in other words, something that might seem a rather ordinary or even automatic form of economic behavior into something as elevated as "action"—is the radically subjective nature of economic value as Mises conceives it. Indeed, for Mises there is no objective or intrinsic "value" to a commodity on which exchangers can rely but merely the multiplicity of perspectives and valuations brought to bear upon it by different potential users. (In this sense there is a kind of "plurality" to the market.) Prices are not stabilized either by some underlying value (as in the labor theory of value) or by an equilibrium process but are moving constantly in an ungrounded flux: "Man himself changes from moment to moment and his valuations, volitions, and acts change with him. In the realm of action there is nothing perpetual but change. There is no fixed point in this ceaseless fluctuation other than the external aprioristic categories of action. It is vain to sever valuation and action from man's unsteadiness and the changeability of his conduct and to argue as if there were in the universe eternal values independent of human value judgments and suitable to serve as a yardstick for the appraisal of real action."[54] Because price is nothing other than the momentary juncture of two incommensurably subjective valuations, "there are in the sphere of values and valuations no arithmetical operations: there is no such thing as a calculation of values."[55] Values cannot be calculated; hence, exchange is never automatic or formulaic but the result of decisions that are at once a leap and a risk. And this noncalculability is what restores a kind of gravity to economic choice. The economic "hero" for Mises is the entrepreneur who launches himself upon this churning sea of values, undaunted by their flux, in pursuit of profit.

The ungroundedness of economic choice, for Mises, both confers freedom upon the chooser and entails an irreducible element of risk. Freedom and risk: for Arendt, the former is provided by, the latter demanded by, the political sphere. Indeed, her implicit argument with the liberal tradition is largely an attempt to recapture these things *for the political* and *from* the marketplace, where liberal theory had located them. This renders not more but less comprehensible her description of exchange as action, since it seems to concede too much to the enemy. Indeed, as I said, this description makes little or no sense in her own terms and strikes one rather as a momentary, inexplicable form of ventriloquism. The tenets of liberal thought somehow speak through her, against her intellectual will. I am interested in this not as a "symptom" of something in Arendt but as a symptom of something in *The Human Condition*. Just as the fields of action and work are drawn into tense propinquities, so is Arendt and the liberal tradition she rejects.

This will become clearer if we look more closely at the workings of the Arendtian *polis*. As we have already seen, the *polis* is a space of appearance in which participants disclose themselves to one another through their words and deeds, thereby achieving freedom and aiming at immortality. At the same time, if actions are not, as Arendt insists, to be judged by practical consequences, this is not simply because of external impediments but because of the inner nature of the *polis* itself—specifically, the way that individual acts of different participants interfere with one another and establish a "web" of relations in which every action becomes caught: "It is because of this already existing web of human relationships, with its innumerable, conflicting wills and intentions, that action almost never achieves its purpose; but it is also because of this medium, in which action alone is real, that it 'produces' stories with or without intention as naturally as fabrication produces natural things" (*Human Condition*, 184). This web "seems to entangle its producer to such an extent that he appears much more the victim and the sufferer than the author and doer of what he has done" (233–34). The *polis* is a field of irony in which acts are almost inevitably deflected from their original aims, usually in a way that appears tragic to the participants and turns them from doers into sufferers. Adam Ferguson's vision of the republic as tragic seems to find its echo here. At the same time, the sticky web of the *polis* also produces an unintended good: the stories of its participants, which invest their existences with meaning and presumably become more interesting (hence better) stories because of the ironic reversals their heroes are forced to undergo. These life stories "are not end products, properly speaking. Although everybody started his life by inserting himself into the human world through action and speech, nobody is the author or producer of his own life story. In other words, the stories, the results of action and speech, reveal an agent, but this agent is not an author or producer" (*Human Condition*, 184). Just as political actors cannot know beforehand (and therefore cannot "manage" or manipulate) the selves they disclose, so they cannot author the narratives of how their acts are deflected and inverted by the actions of others. Freedom (as Arendt makes clear) is therefore purchased at the cost of sovereignty, and the true "author" of the stories that impart meaning to our existences is not the individual political actor but rather the web in which he is caught.

As I hope this description already makes evident, the workings of the Arendtian *polis* are in some respects strikingly similar to those of the Smithian market. In both, a spontaneous order arises from the individual actions of participants; in both, that order ironically and systematically inverts intentions in ways that can be harmful but also provides a more global good: "public happiness" in the case of Smith and meaningfulness in the case of Arendt. Of course, Smith's invisible hand assumes economic agents working in isolation from one another, while Arendt's web takes form in a conscientiously shared world, care for which is what brings political actors together. That being said, and despite Arendt's disparaging (and oddly inaccurate) account of Smith's invisible hand, it nevertheless appears that her political realm is at least partly modeled on it.[56] If Ferguson's republic is the tragic antidote to a market economy, Arendt's *polis* is in some sense the tragic version *of* a market economy, the formal template of which has been absorbed, transmuted, and spun out like the spider's silk to form Arendt's web. What Arendt's figure of the table cannot account for, then, are other, more uncanny forms of intimacy that bind the political and economic together.

Insofar as the political web is an author, producing stories with ironic turns, it is also a ceaselessly revising author, since the colliding of actions never stops: "These consequences of action are boundless, because action, though it may proceed from nowhere, so to speak, acts into a medium where every action becomes a chain reaction and where every process is the cause of new processes" (*Human Condition*, 190). Not only is the life story refracted through the plurality of readers, then; it is always subject to retrospective revision in the light of subsequent events and in that sense never truly concludes. Moreover, while stories are, for Arendt, the sole carriers of meaning, the process that authors those stories—described both as a web and here, perhaps more tellingly, as particles colliding in a chain reaction—seems impersonal, aleatory, and meaningless. At the heart of the political lies something that is both unbounded and unnarratable. Moreover, the more Arendt's focus shifts from the individual actor to the process in which his actions are caught, the more not only sovereignty but agency as well threatens to evaporate. This is the price, I would argue, for importing Smith's model of the market into Arendt's theory of politics.

It is in the context of this dilemma that we can begin to assess the role of tragic drama in *The Human Condition*:[57]

> The specific content as well as the general meaning of action and speech may take various forms of reification in art works which glorify a deed or an accomplishment and, by transformation and condensation, show some extraordinary event in its full significance. However, the specific revelatory quality of action and speech, the implicit manifestation of the agent and speaker, is so indissolubly tied to the living flux of acting and speaking that it can be represented and "reified" only through a kind of repetition, the imitation or *mimēsis*, which according to Aristotle prevails in all arts but is actually appropriate only to the drama, whose very name (from the Greek verb *dran*, "act") indicates that playacting actually is an imitation of acting. But the imitative element lies not only in the art of the actor, but, as Aristotle rightly claims, in the making or writing of the play, at least to the extent that the drama comes fully to life only when it is enacted in the theater. Only the actors and speakers who reenact the story's

plot can convey the full meaning, not so much of the story itself, but of the "heroes" who reveal themselves in it. In terms of Greek tragedy, this would mean that the story's direct as well as its universal meaning is revealed by the chorus, which does not imitate, and whose comments are pure poetry, whereas the intangible identities of the agents in the story, since they escape all generalization and therefore all reification, can be conveyed only through an imitation of their acting. This is also why the theater is the political art par excellence; only there is the political sphere of human life transposed into art. By the same token, it is the only art whose sole subject is man in his relationship to others. (187–88)

Drama, like all art work, glorifies a deed and "by transformation and condensation, shows it in is full significance." One wonders what "full significance" can mean here, since the boundlessness of action subjects its import to endless reworking. But precisely because the poetic plot has, as Aristotle states, a beginning, middle, and end, it can grant action a seeming completeness unavailable in real life. Arendt stresses the need for artificial boundaries (private property, national territory, laws) to contain the boundlessness of political action (191), and the formal closure of art seems to provide an aesthetic correlate to this. Indeed, the belief that action *can* have a final reckoning or a definitively "full significance" might be necessary to induce political participation at all, and in this sense drama would be a necessary internal supplement to the *polis*—not something that merely imitates action but safeguards it.

Drama, however, distinguishes itself from other art forms—certainly from the epic, with which it is often paired—by the fact that its mimesis does not include a third-person, authorial voice whose perspective would ground judgment but only those of the characters themselves in their irreducible plurality. Drama thus presents speech and action in constant, unanchored flux, and is political in that sense as well. The Greek chorus seems to play a stabilizing role, though not quite a grounding one, since the chorus is still included in the fiction and is not a voice external to it. The separation of actor and spectator is one that Arendt cannot admit to the political realm, which depends on speakers also becoming listeners and vice versa, but perhaps here the division between actors and chorus represents not different groups but rather the split between action and judgment that every political participant must endure.

But the transformation of act into drama does more: it reifies the act, makes it into an object or "work," and thus connects it to the world of work that action otherwise transcends. As already noted, deed and speech disappear in the moment of their enactment and so require the durability of the made thing in order to persist. In the artwork, Arendt claims, this durability reaches a higher pitch. In part this is because artworks are not used for anything, and hence not used up. Their uselessness preserves them from the normal wear and tear that made objects are subject to (*Human Condition*, 167). Through them, as a result, the

> permanence, the very stability of the human artifice, which being inhabited and used by mortals, can never be absolute, achieves a representation of its own. Nowhere else does the sheer durability of the world of things appear in such purity and clarity, nowhere else therefore does this thing-world reveal itself so spectacularly as the non-mortal home for mortal beings. It is as though worldly stability had become transparent in the permanence of art, so that a premonition of immortality, not the immortality of the soul or of life but of something immortal achieved by mortal hands, has become tangibly present, to shine and to be seen, to sound and to be heard, to speak and to be read. (167–68)

The products of work are useful things that are also durable. Rescued from this usefulness, and hence from the means-end rationality of the *homo faber*, the work of art represents durability as such, its objectal permanence gesturing toward, and providing the appropriate worldly embodiment for, the immortality that only the deed can achieve. But this double status as both action and work, *praxis* and *poiesis*, means that drama has a structure similar to that of the *polis*, where the realm of action supervenes upon debate grounded in means and ends and hence the world of work. The political occurs when those means and ends are bracketed, just as the artwork suspends the means-end rationality of the useful object.

The status of the artwork thus relates the world of action to the world of work while also separating them: Arendt's table again. It is no coincidence that the section on the artwork concludes the "Work" chapter and thus provides both a transition to, and a buffer for, the "Action" chapter. The drama as art holds action and work in a healthy, related tension without allowing one to collapse into the other. But the section on the artwork is in turn preceded by one on "The Exchange Market," which is as close as Arendt gets to looking directly at the economic—or so at least the section's title would suggest. By "market," Arendt means market*place*: in classical times, the agora where manufactured items were set out on display. In the market, made things emerge from the privacy of the workshop into a shared, semipublic space: "Unlike the *animal laborans*, whose social life is worldless and herd-like and who therefore is incapable of building or inhabiting a public, worldly realm, *homo faber* is fully capable of having a public realm of his own, even though it may not be a political realm, properly speaking. His public realm is the exchange market, where he can show the product of his hand and receive the esteem which is due him" (160). The showmanship of the marketplace, its emphasis on *display*, is a shallower, almost typological prefiguration of the more profound *disclosure* that will occur only in the political realm. That display of craft must be both stripped of utility and sublimed into the pure appearance of the artwork before it can serve as material embodiment of the drama.

If Arendt's conception of politics strikes some as quaint, this is as nothing compared to her depiction of the "exchange market." Hers is a classical market *place* rather than a modern, unbounded market *process*. It involves a gathering together of producers into a delimited scene of shared display, which is what allows it to anticipate a political space. Such an exchange market is easily enough contained and ordered within Arendt's parade of categories. But it is hardly what her liberal antagonists understood by an "exchange market," and hence serves as something of a straw man for her argument. In effect, it is a way of avoiding an encounter with economic liberalism at its strongest points.

For a more challenging vision of a market society one might turn to Friedrich Hayek, whose work *The Constitution of Liberty* appeared in 1961, just three years after *The Human Condition*. Like Arendt (and his fellow Austrian-school economist Mises), Hayek is concerned with freedom, but he finds its most fundamental basis in a market society rather than the political sphere. Hayek is certainly a democratic thinker who joins Arendt in the denunciation of "totalitarian" societies. He also shares with her an interest in the new and unprecedented, though for Hayek this has less to do with human natality than with technological and commercial innovation. That being said, Hayek joins other post-Smithian liberals in supporting limited government and argues that the spontaneous order of the market does a better job of making decisions than does political deliberation. Simply put, the knowledge that undergirds a complex, modern society is so dispersed in separate practices and areas (this partly a result of the division of labor) that no deliberative body can possibly master it. Collective decision making, even of the most broadly democratic sort, cannot match the market's unconscious and spontaneous application of local knowledges. Indeed, the spontaneous order of the market can form *only* if economic agents pursue their aims blindly, without either trying to coordinate their efforts or confer upon their ultimate goals.

Hayek loves to quote Adam Ferguson on the workings of spontaneous order without ever acknowledging that his vision is anathema to Ferguson's highly politicized, republican ideals. In a way, we can see Hayek and Arendt as splitting Ferguson's conflicted vision between them. Hayek embodies Ferguson's "Smithian" side, Arendt his republican one, though this binary is too simple since a somewhat occulted version of the market's spontaneous order also informs Arendt's treatment of the *polis*.

Arendt's obsessive worry—for which she has been roundly and justly criticized—is that the socioeconomic will intrude as subject matter on the political space and ruin its integrity. But for economic liberals such as Hayek, the point is not to colonize the political but rather to free the market *from* the political. The world works better, in Hayek's view, the more people pursue their local interests in isolation, allowing the spontaneous order of the market to do the work of "deciding" in place of political deliberation. Such a world has no central public space, no arena for disclosure. It is not concerned with memorable deed or event but with the securing of public happiness.

Paul A. Kottman has aptly described Arendtian politics as a "politics of the scene," intimately connected with the dramatic.[58] The threat represented by Hayek's liberal vision is that such a scene can and to some degree should simply disperse. What I would like to suggest here is that tragic theater doesn't merely offer a model for politics in Arendt, a handy metaphor to describe its working, but rather a last desperate attempt to hold onto a conception of politics *as* scene in the face of the disintegrative critique waged by economic liberalism. Just as the narrative closure of tragic drama offers an antidote to the boundlessness of real action, so the theatrical "scene" offers an imagined antidote to the centrifugal force of liberal dispersal. I use the word "antidote" advisedly, because it is as if Arendt's ingestion of a market model into the *polis* is an attempt at a homeopathic cure, perhaps even an Aristotelian catharsis. In any case, it relies on intimacies well beyond those offered by the "table" model with which we began.

It is worth remarking that despite the largely pessimistic tone of *The Human Condition*—its running assumption that the advance of the social cannot on the whole be stemmed—Arendt never extends this history of decline to tragic drama. Not just the individual tragic artwork but the very category of tragedy seems immune to time. Nothing would be easier or more natural for Arendt than to follow Adam Ferguson's lead and suggest that the decay of political action impairs the art form that both depends on and perpetuates it. Yet she never hints at a death of tragedy. True, one is never certain that by "drama" she doesn't mean exclusively *Greek* drama. It may well be that, for Arendt, as long as *that* survives, all is well. Whether through embalming an ancient form or though aesthetic idealism or simple tact, the fact remains that Arendt exempts tragedy from the framing historical narrative of *The Human Condition.* What this suggests to me is that tragic drama carries a disproportionate burden of political hope for Arendt—hence hope for human action as well.

If Adam Smith's political economy poses a challenge to tragic drama by inhibiting classical notions of action, then tragic drama returns the favor almost two centuries later by helping Hannah Arendt defend political action against the depredations of the economic. What is surprising, perhaps, is how little the basic elements in this equation change over the course of almost two centuries. Even after the passing of classical political economy, its insights continue to haunt tragedy—and not only in the realm of theory, which has been the subject of this chapter, but on the stage as well. Moreover, the conflict between *praxis* and *poiesis* that political economy brings to a head also long predates it. Turning to Aeschylus, as we shall do next, we face a problem the exact inverse of that which troubled Arendt: the pretense on the part of Periclean politics that action can supplant production, something that in Aeschylus's view fosters dangerously hyperbolic forms of heroism. Once again tragic drama is the terrain over which this battle will be fought.

CHAPTER TWO

Greek Tragedy and the Raptor Economy

The Oresteia

Not many years after the *Oresteia* was staged in 458 BCE, a new and striking element was added to the pretheater festivities at the Greater Dionysia.
Silver ingots, tribute collected from allies, were piled onto the stage in a conspicuous display of Athenian wealth and imperial might.[1] Isocrates, writing
in the fourth century, described the spectacle with caustic disgust:

> For so exactly did they gauge the actions by which human beings incur the
> worst odium that they passed a decree to divide the surplus of the funds de-
> rived from the tributes of the allies into talents and to bring it all onto the
> stage, when the theater was full, at the festival of Dionysus; and not only was
> this done but at the same time they led in upon the stage the sons of those who
> had lost their lives in the war, seeking thus to display to our allies, on the one
> hand, the value of their own property which was brought in by hirelings, and
> to the rest of the Hellenes, on the other, the multitude of the fatherless and the
> misfortunes which resulted from this policy of aggression. And in so doing they
> themselves counted the city happy.[2]

Vulgar and undiplomatic it certainly was, yet heaping the Athenian stage
with extorted cash was not necessarily a mindless or even a simple-minded
gesture. This seemingly incongruous prelude to Greek tragedy may have
something important to tell us about Greek tragedy's central concerns—
particularly as these play out in the *Oresteia*. Teasing out the connections,
however, will require placing this ritual in military, economic, and even
philosophical contexts.

Isocrates provides the most immediate of these. Displaying the tribute
was annexed to an older rite: the parading of war orphans. Male children of

hoplite soldiers who died defending Athens became wards of the city, which raised and educated them and, when they reached ephebehood, presented them to the public at the Greater Dionysia, clad in the armor with which the state also equipped them. Even this simple dyad of rituals suggests a reciprocity: warriors enrich the city through imperial conquest, and the city in turn employs that wealth to support the offspring of its fallen soldiers.

Several of the other rituals at the Greater Dionysia invoked the distinctly military flavor of a *polis* in which service in the army or navy was a precondition for citizenship, influential politicians such as Pericles and Cleon were expected to have led military campaigns, Aeschylus himself fought at the Battle of Marathon, and Sophocles became a *strategos* or general. Aeschylus's earliest surviving tragedies—*The Persians* and *Seven against Thebes*—engage with military themes. And in Aristophanes's *The Frogs*, the character Aeschylus brags that his plays made their auditors into "noble six-footers ... men with an aura of spears, lances, white-crested helmets, green berets, greaves, and seven-ply oxhide hearts."[3]

In a suggestive if controversial essay, John Winkler extends the military dimension of Greek tragedy from content to form. The chorus, he claims, was comprised of ephebes undergoing military training, and their dancing echoed the military maneuvers they were expected to display on other occasions to the gathered populace: "Together these facts suggest that one might perceive the role and movement of the tragic chorus as an esthetically elevated version of close-order drill. The very persons (or rather a representative collection of them) who marched in rectangular rank and file in the orchestra as second-year cadets, performing for the assembled citizenry, also marched and danced in rectangular formation at the City Dionysia, but did so wearing masks and costumes."[4] In the movement of the tragic chorus, then, Athenian spectators witnessed a kinetic emblem of their city's military/civic cohesion.

The display of tribute, however, focused specifically on the economic benefits conveyed by military prowess. These were considerable, for the empire directly produced 60 percent of Athens' public revenue in the fifth century, and as an added bonus supplied slaves to work the silver mines at Laureion.[5] Limited to seasonal warfare by a citizen army comprised in large part of peasant farmers, Athens satisfied its imperial ambitions mostly through the collection of tribute rather than through the accumulation of territory, and the revenues yielded by empire were—or were at least felt to be—in many ways the lifeblood of the democratic *polis*.[6] They helped finance a massive building program in the fifth century, payments for public service such as jury duty and participation in the Council, subsidies for attendance at public festivals, and pensions for war orphans, injured soldiers, and Athenian refugees.[7] Imperial income also enabled Athens to avoid levying heavy taxes on its population, a consideration as important as direct payments in allowing poorer citizens the free time to participate in public life.[8] "Above all," notes M. I. Finley, "the naval force maintained largely by imperial tribute (as long as the empire lasted) guaranteed the supply of imperial grain," further contributing to social peace between rich and poor in the city. Aristotle claimed in *The Constitution of Athens* (24.3) that "more than 20,000 men earned their living as a result of the tribute, the taxation and the money the empire brought in."[9] Not surprisingly, such fiscal advantages served the Athenian *demos* as inducement to further imperial adventures.[10]

Its dependence on imperial revenues informed the economic life of Athens and, as a consequence, economic or protoeconomic thought there.[11] Finley endorses Max Weber's characterization of ancient cities as consumption centers, a status reinforced in Athens' case by the influx of wealth and commodities from the empire.[12] Urban manufacture took up part of the city's consumption fund but did not generate any notable wealth.[13] Under these conditions it is not surprising that economic production does not intrude significantly upon Greek consciousness—other than as something with which social elites sought to avoid association. Indeed, the provisioning of the city is attributed primarily to Athenian military prowess and democratic virtue by Pericles; in his Funeral Oration he brags that "because of its size, all sorts of merchandise comes into our city from all over the world, and foreign goods are no less ours to enjoy than those that are produced right here" (2.38).[14] And in a later speech, he declares: "Thus this sea power is a far greater thing than your lands and your farms, whose loss you think is so terrible. We ought not to trouble ourselves about them or take them any more seriously than gardens or the ornaments of wealth in comparison with this power" (2.62). In this view arms, not farms, feed the Athenian populace. Heroic action rather than productive activity supports the life of the city, and necessary commodities are therefore taken directly or purchased with booty, not made—a view expressed with both utopian glee and gentle mockery in Aristophanes's *Wasps*: "If they wanted to provide a living for the people, it would be easy. A thousand cities there are that now pay us tribute. If someone ordered each one to support twenty men, then twenty thousand loyal proles would be rolling in hare meat, every kind of garland, bee stings and eggnog, living it up as befits their country and their trophy at Marathon."[15]

This rather one-sided Periclean view contrasts with a more dialectical understanding that can sometimes be found in philosophical contexts. In Xenophon's *Oeconomicus*, Socrates reports that "when the King [of Persia] gives presents, he sends first for those who have proved themselves good in war, on the ground that there would be no benefit in plowing very much if there were no defenders; and that secondly he sends for those who cultivate their lands in the best manner and make them productive, saying that not even the brave could live if there were no workers."[16] Even here, though, it must be recognized that the Greeks set agricultural labor apart from other kinds of productive work.[17] Aristotle takes an only somewhat less balanced approach in the *Politics* (1329a 35-38): "We have shown what are the necessary conditions, and what the parts of the state: farmers, artisans, and labourers of all kinds are necessary to the existence of states, but the parts of the state are the warriors and councillors."[18] And in explaining why mechanics and lower-class persons should not be counted as citizens: "We cannot consider all those to be citizens who are necessary to the existence of the state" (1278a 3-4).[19] The *polis* depends for its material existence on the labor of farmers, artisans, and others, and Aristotle readily acknowledges this fact. But material dependence does not, in his view, justify the inclusion of such persons in the political life of the city. "As in other natural compounds the conditions of a composite are not necessarily organic parts of it, so in a state as in any other combination forming a unity not everything is a part which is a necessary condition" (1328a 22-26).[20]

The distinction between "parts" and "conditions" depends in turn on that between *zen* and *eu zen*, life and the good life, which defines the very essence of the political. "The state comes into existence, originating in the bare needs of life, and continuing its existence for the sake of a good life" (1252b 29-31).[21] While it is true that "mankind meet together and maintain the political community also for the sake of mere life" (1278b 24-25), yet "the state exists for the sake of a good life, and not for the sake of life only" (1280a 32).[22] As always in Aristotle, the *telos*, or final cause, takes precedence over preconditions. The political classes are thus to the producing classes as soul is to body: "And as the soul may be said to be more truly part of an animal than the body, so the higher parts of states, that is to say, the warrior class, the class engaged in the administration of justice, and that engaged in deliberation, which is the special business of political understanding—these are more essential to the state than the parts that minister to life" (1291a 24-29).[23] Farmers and artisans provision the bodily existence of the state, but the political classes embody that rational excellence that is the state's

very reason for existing. Even while privileging the political classes and indulging in the anti-banausic sentiment common among Greek intellectuals,
Aristotle nevertheless acknowledges the material dependence of the state
on its own producing classes.

Periclean political discourse, by contrast, denies this very dependence.
Pericles's funeral oration extols the Athenian "way of life" (*tropos*) at length,
just as Aristotle does the "good life" (*eu zen*). But rather than admit the reliance of democratic virtue and military valor on material preconditions,
Pericles claims that virtue and valor can supply those very preconditions
through imperial conquest. Athens does not require farms or workshops
or households so long as its empire can provide food and other goods. This
is "political economy" in quite another key: the *polis*'s dream of material
self-sufficiency that renders economics in the strict sense (management of
the *oikos*) unnecessary. A stage piled high with silver tribute, the fruits of
military action, will purchase what is needed to sustain mere bodily existence. Of course, these products must ultimately be made somewhere, by
someone. But their production falls outside of the *polis*—or at least, of its
ken. *Poiesis* is squirreled away in the household or the provinces, but silver
tribute is dazzlingly visible on stage to the assembled citizenry. Indeed, not
only is the *polis* now apparently independent of the *oikos*; it can even begin
to monopolize the latter's functions, which it demonstrates by raising war
orphans. As Simon Goldhill observes: "the city increasingly appropriated
the vocabulary of the family. For the city 'nourished'; the citizens were the
'children' of the laws; the city became a 'father,' a 'mother.' The term 'father-
land' was extended in its connotations."[24] The city as the sphere of action
and of excellence eclipses the household as the sphere of production and of
nurturing bodily life. The *eu zen* of the *polis* not merely completes and justifies mere life, as it does in Aristotle, but also appropriates the nurture of the
life-functions.

All of this has consequences for tragedy. As the Brazilian director and
dramatic theorist Augusto Boal observes: "Tragedy imitates human acts.
Human acts, not merely human activities. For Aristotle, man's soul was composed of a rational part and of another, irrational part. The irrational soul
could produce activities such as eating, walking or performing any physical
movement without greater significance than the physical act itself. Tragedy,
on the other hand, imitated solely man's actions, determined by his rational
soul."[25] Stephen Halliwell strikes a similar note in his commentary on Aristotle's *Poetics*: "Poetry should in some sense rise above mundane life (though
not with the necessarily optimistic import) and elevate human action to a

higher level of intelligibility, so that it requires something which even the philosopher might recognize as significant."[26] The mundane is the realm of the bodily, of "mere life"; the tragic, that of intelligible action, a zone in which excellence (*arete*) of an ethical or political sort can be achieved or disastrously missed. A distinction parallel to—and implicated with—that between *zen* and *eu zen* thus defines the very space of tragedy. The sacrifice of biological life (or at least its threat) is of course at the basis of tragic drama, but this is supposedly assimilated to the ethical sphere in which death assumes a more than bodily significance. In some sense tragedy sacrifices "mere life" *to* the ethico-political.

Here we may return to Winkler's thesis that the tragic chorus is composed of ephebes engaged in an aestheticized version of close-order drill. The ephebe is in a liminal or transitional state between childhood and adult male citizenship. He has up until now been "mere life," raised and nurtured in the safe confines of the household. Upon achieving ephebic status he leaves the *oikos* for a period of military training and possible service before being granted the privileges of male citizenship. In effect, the ephebe enters the field of death—as risk if not as actuality—in order to effect the transition from "mere life" to the higher "way of life" that constitutes the political existence of the citizen. The sacrifice of mere life to the ethico-political that constitutes the essence of the tragic fiction thus finds its visible social embodiment in the tragic chorus.

All of the above pertains to the reality of the tragic chorus—the fact that its dancers are ephebes. At the level of tragic fiction, as Mark Griffith nicely observes, things work rather differently:

> And from first to last, safe in his/her theater seat, every member of the audience knows that this "internal audience" of minor characters and chorus, will *survive*, to resume their lives after the drama has played itself out, just as they themselves (the theater audience) will resume their everyday lives upon leaving the theater. To that extent at least, these minor characters and this chorus are felt to be more *like* the theater audience, and closer to them, than are their leaders, upon whom so much attention (from both internal and theater audiences) is so firmly focused.[27]

If the actual members of the chorus are marked by their exposure to the field of death, their fictional personae enjoy an imperviousness to mortality. Leading tragic characters may die, but the chorus never. The fictional chorus bears an inexhaustible life that they, as a collective, share with the audience. This ongoing life is not attached or available to individual citizens, but only to the city as a whole, the shared existence of which transcends that of its perishable members. The Athenian "way of life" persists even if individual Athenians die—indeed, *because* individual Athenians die in defending it. But at the same time, the immortality of the fictional chorus evokes something independent of, and in some sense subtending, the city: an ongoing biological vitality, the endless continuity of the life process.[28] Indeed, the chorus generally does not represent the political class of the city but, as in the *Oresteia*, feeble old men or slave women or Furies whose coherence as a group has more to do with biological existence than with political solidarity. In this respect the chorus embodies a logic different from that of the civic sublimations I have been tracing, and points to a more difficult, dialectical tension between *zen* and *eu zen* (or, to invoke Giorgio Agamben's now influential opposition, *zoe* and *bios*) at the heart of tragic drama. This tension plays itself out with vivid intensity in the *Oresteia*.

Before turning to that work, however, I would briefly like to measure the distance that separates the worldview described here from that of political economy. The Periclean ideal in which action eclipses production reverses the Smithian one. (Pericles is rather a distant ancestor of Adam Ferguson's republicanism.) In describing Athenian culture I am setting a baseline from which the inversions effected by political economy can be grasped in their immensity. Like most dreams, the Periclean one is, of course, ultimately impracticable, but this might well have constituted one of its narcotic charms at the time. In the extreme form enunciated by Pericles, such a viewpoint was probably not shared by most Athenians. It bears, for one thing, the evident marks of an aristocratic outlook. And yet Pericles can use it to address and inspire the collected citizenry, which suggests that its underlying principles are not all that alien from those of Athenian culture at large. It assumes less stark form, for instance, in Aristotle's elevation of doing over making. And it clearly underwrites the exaltation of the act that suffuses Greek tragedy. What distinguishes the *Oresteia* from many other surviving examples of Greek drama is the intense scrutiny to which it subjects the Periclean dream, both exposing its fragility and laying out its costs.

I

The *Oresteia* concerns itself directly with the Athenian empire and its reliance on naval hegemony. Aeschylus's Agamemnon is described as the "*hegemon* of Achaean ships" (*Ag*. 184–85), a concept and reality that do not yet exist in Homer. David Rosenbloom compiles the topical evidence and argues that "the vision of [Aeschylus's] drama implies that naval hegemony, the form of war built upon it, the power derived from it, and most of all, the delusions of conquest and justice it supports, can be deleterious to the *polis*."[29] Here, though, I am interested less in empire as a direct topic of political celebration or critique than in the politico-economic vision (or fantasy) that empire encourages: a fantasy in which the *polis* is provisioned from without through heroic action rather than from within through labor.

Early in the *Choephoroi*, Orestes prays: "Zeus, Zeus, look down on these things! Behold the orphaned brood of the eagle father, of him who died in the twisting coils of the fearsome viper! The bereaved children are hard pressed by ravenous hunger, for they are not yet full grown so as to be able to bring home to the nest the prey their father hunted. So too you can see this woman, Electra, and me, children robbed of their father, both alike in banishment from their home."[30] These lines might well recall for Athenian audiences the presentation of the war orphans that preceded Aeschylus's trilogy. Of course, Agamemnon has died at the hands of his wife, not in battle, and the Homeric kingdom depicted here does not yet foster war orphans in any case. So much the worse for Orestes. Yet through its very absence, the figure of the eagle father embodies the Periclean vision of Athens as a city that provides for its members through martial violence. M. I. Finley has described Athens as a "conquest state," and Aeschylus seems to sharpen the image into one of a "raptor state" under the protective wing of its naval hegemon. Not surprisingly, given his circumstances, Orestes assigns the function of *trophe*, or provisioning, to the father, not the mother. Nourishment is provided not at home, either in the *oikos* or the farmlands that surround the city, but snatched from outside—a product of action, not labor.

Yet even in the context of the *oikos*, a similar logic prevails. Ischomachos's wife—the dialogue's embodiment of the perfect (or near-perfect) housewife[31]—in Xenophon's *Oeconomicus* declares to her husband: "I wonder whether the works of the leader are not rather yours than mine. For my guarding the distribution of the indoor things would look somewhat ridiculous, I suppose, if it weren't your concern to bring in something from outside" (VII.39). This statement occurs, interestingly, in a discussion about who is the leader or hegemon of the household. Ischomachos's wife assigns this role to the husband because he provisions the household from without, while the wife merely manages and distributes what he provides. Or as Socrates puts it in the same dialogue: "for while the possessions usually come into the house through the man's *actions* [my emphasis], they are expended for the most part in the course of the woman's housekeeping"

(III.15). Clytemnestra's housekeeping skills (as well as her claims to household hegemony) will of course come under scrutiny in *Agamemnon*. What interests me is the insistence that the house, like the city, is essentially provisioned from without by male action—a concept naturalized through the imagery of Orestes's prayer.

An earlier version of the eagle father appears in the first choral song of *Agamemnon*, where the chorus of elderly male citizens compares the grief of the Atreidae over the rape of Helen to the mourning of birds over lost offspring:

> like birds of prey who, crazed
> by grief for their children, wheel around
> high above their eyries,
> rowing with wings for oars,
> having seen the toil of watching
> over their nestlings' bed go for nothing;
> and some Apollo on high, or Pan,
> or Zeus, hearing the loud shrill wailing cries
> of the birds, exacts belated revenge
> on behalf of these denizens of his realm
> by sending a Fury against the transgressors.
>
> (*Ag.* 49–59)

Although the situation of Orestes's prayer is reversed, with avian parents of both sexes now mourning the loss of their children, we are still within the general space of a "raptor economy." But this version of the simile proffers intriguing complications, starting with the uncertain identity of the birds of prey. The Greek term *aigypios*, Alan H. Sommerstein helpfully informs us, "is usually rendered 'vulture,' but in Homer (esp. *Iliad* 17.460) they are raptors (like eagles), not scavengers; probably the lammergeyer or bearded vulture (*Gyptaeus barbatus*) is meant, since this bird was (wrongly) believed by the ancients to be a raptor."[32] This note is doubtless meant in part to calm the discomfort exhibited by earlier scholars such as Richmond Lattimore, who found the term "vulture" so unheroic that he opted for "eagle" in his translation (the Greek may allow for either).[33] But it seems to me that the ambiguity of the term is potentially meaningful, and should not so quickly be explained away. The Atreidae *are* raptors—at least, they like to think of themselves as such. But in truth they are also scavengers who sacrilegiously plunder the altars and pick over the corpses of defeated Troy. Perhaps the term *aigypios* is Aeschylus's way of allowing some moral ambiguity to seep into this otherwise heroicized vision of the raptor economy.

A related form of moral ambiguity stems from the fact that the specific kind of loss described by the chorus more closely resembles Clytemnestra's than Agamemnon's—an indirect way, perhaps, of condemning Agamemnon's unnatural sacrifice of his child. Even raptors care for their young more lovingly than does Agamemnon.[34]

But a still deeper uncertainty attaches to the level at which this simile should be understood. Animal nature offers a metaphor for human sociality while standing at a distance from it. This fact is made jarringly obvious when the *aigypioi* are described as "metics" or resident aliens of heaven—a political term whose obvious incongruity announces its status as mere conceit. But at another level, what is at stake is not so much similarity as continuity. As the chorus recounts, Zeus encourages the Atreidae to invade Troy by sending an omen in which two eagles attack and devour a pregnant hare and her unborn young (*Ag.* 104–21). Artemis, enraged that a wild animal in her care has been killed for this portent, demands Iphigenia as a counter-sacrifice before the Greeks can set sail to Troy, thus setting in motion the tragedy of *Agamemnon*.

This episode involving actual eagles has a complex relation to the other two invocations of raptors in simile and prayer. Here the eagles do not embody parental nurture but rather annihilate it in the pregnant hare. Indeed, their portent is ambiguous, pointing at once to the coming victory over Troy and to the violent assault on maternity (Clytemnestra's) that will be required to bring victory about. Most interesting, perhaps, the very event or occurrence of the portent (rather than its significance) engages the perspective of Artemis, that murderously maternal virgin—a perspective in which human and animal lives are not merely comparable but directly exchangeable. In Artemis's divinely indifferent gaze, Iphigenia is indistinguishable from a hare, both perfectly equivalent embodiments of "mere life."

At the same time, though, this omen points in very different directions. For the image of unborn young ripped violently from the hare's womb is echoed later in the play when the Achaean soldiers emerging at night from the Trojan horse are described as "offspring of the Horse" (825).[35] The violent caesarian performed upon the hare thus finds its response in an unnatural emergence of violent men from the womb of an artificial animal. In the first case the offspring are murdered, and in the second the "offspring" are murderers. The womb of the Trojan horse at once recalls and denatures that of the hare; its contents are united not by the bond of life but by military-political solidarity that aims at risking and yielding death. In other words, it once again gestures toward the *polis* as a raptor state defined by the transcendence/negation of "mere life" and maternal nurture. Indeed, I would go so far as to suggest that the ripping open of the hare's womb offers a nightmarishly condensed image of the transition undergone by Athenian ephebes as they leave the realm of the *oikos* and its nurture for the field of death and the political solidarity it underwrites—a symbolic transition cemented by the artificial, deadly "birth" of Achaean soldiers from the horse's "womb."

What I have been tracing through a close reading of the imagery of the *Oresteia* is a symbolic network in which the claims of mere life and those of political life tug insistently in opposite, and often contradictory, directions. In a sense, this exercise revisits the old opposition between *polis* and *oikos* enshrined in the Hegelian reading of tragedy, only here the competing ethical claims of each realm are underwritten by competing visions of material dependence in which the *oikos* supplies the state with its necessary "conditions" (as Aristotle would have it), and the state in turn protects the *oikos* even while forcefully repudiating its dependence upon it, claiming instead that it can provision itself. *Agamemnon*, in any case, obsessively replays the emergence of political life from mere life at the level of both symbol and plot. Agamemnon's sacrifice of Iphigenia is not merely done in the name of politico-military necessity, then; it is the very embodiment of the process by which the political and its field of action spring into existence in the first place by wrenching themselves violently free from the supporting matrix of "mere life." Of course, that matrix doesn't necessarily take all this lying down. Along with vulnerable hares and helpless daughters, the matrix of mere life also deploys the more formidable figures of Clytemnestra and Artemis to defend its interests, articulate its claims, and even initiate a deadly counterviolence. Mother-serpents can sometimes slay father-eagles, as Orestes's prayer puts it.

Clytemnestra is a famously unnurturing mother, but she is nevertheless careful to praise her own prowess in the field of home economics (*Ag.* 607–12). And while the watchman perched on Agamemnon's palace complains at the play's start that the house is "not now admirably managed as it used to be" (18–19), still, Clytemnestra is able to greet the news of her husband's return by lighting many lamps fed with "pure anointing oil, / a thick-flowing offering from the inner stores of the palace" (94–96). The implication is that Clytemnestra has expertly managed and conserved the resources of the *oikos* in her husband's absence. There is plenty with which to provision her family, to sustain its life—that is, if she had not exiled her son and planned to murder her husband.

In fact, Clytemnestra greets Agamemnon's return with a spectacular—and notorious—display of household wealth: the valuable tapestries spread on the ground for her husband to tread upon. While he is apprehensive about doing so, the same cannot be said for literary critics, who find these valuable textiles, "bought with silver" (949), an irresistible image of the economic in Aeschylus's trilogy.[36] I am less interested in questions such as whether the tapestries are commodities or not than I am in the symbolic and even rhetorical uses to which they are put.[37] It seems clear that the tapestries are intended in part to prevent Agamemnon's feet from touching Argive ground, thereby rendering his *nostos* forever incomplete. But even more fundamentally, in convincing Agamemnon to trample and soil the exquisite, delicate, and blood-red textiles, Clytemnestra is forcing him to reenact symbolically the sacrifice of Iphigenia. Agamemnon seems to intuit the sacrilegious dimension of defiling the tapestries: "For I feel a great sense of impropriety about despoiling this house under my feet, ruining its wealth and the woven work bought with its silver" (948-49). But Clytemnestra allays his misgivings: "There is a sea—who will ever dry it up?—which breeds an ever-renewed ooze of abundant purple, worth its weight in silver, to dye clothing with. So with the gods' help, my lord, we can remedy this loss; our house does not know what poverty is" (958-62). For Athens, the sea was in fact an apparently inexhaustible source of wealth—not only because of its natural fecundity but primarily because of the naval hegemony the city exerted over it and the commercial trade it conducted across it.[38] For Clytemnestra, by contrast, it is the sea's natural abundance, its ability to nurture or provision life within it, that matters, and she annexes this inexhaustible, maternal power to the *oikos*, which can in turn produce an endless flow of goods.

Simon Goldhill remarks of Clytemnestra's speech that "her faith in continuing prosperity seems more than somewhat hubristic."[39] But this, it seems to me, misses the point of Clytemnestra's scathing irony, for she is not expressing her own view of the *oikos* but rather ventriloquizing her husband's. Agamemnon's sacrifice of Iphigenia suggests that he regards the household as what Heidegger would call a "standing reserve," in a state of ever-readiness for instrumental exploitation.[40] And Clytemnestra's stratagem is meant both to display and trouble this fact. One doesn't quail at despoiling beautiful tapestries only if one regards the supply as infinite, and moreover if one sees a given tapestry as equivalent to all the others: simply another in a line of goods at one's disposal. But it is precisely in choosing beautiful objects that exceed mere utility of this sort that Clytemnestra manages to awaken a sense of vague unease in her husband. Maybe some things are too exquisite merely to be used up. And if this is the case with a tapestry (and here we come to the point of Clytemnestra's whole demonstration), how much more so in the case of the infinitely precious and irreplaceable life of Iphigenia?

Agamemnon's view of the household as a standing reserve remains merely implicit in the act of sacrificing his daughter. But in Thucydides, Pericles elevates it to an explicit principle. While discussing the losses of war, Pericles has this to say to Athenian parents: "Those who are still of childbearing age must endure their sorrow in the hope of other children. For them, personally, a new generation will be the way to forget those who are gone; and it will carry the two benefits for the city of preventing underpopulation and providing security" (2.44). For Pericles, a new child simply replaces the lost one—a perspective made possible only by viewing them not as unique lives but as perfectly fungible citizen-soldiers and thus as a standing reserve for the city. By contrast, the vision of tragedy is profoundly antipolitical insofar as it mourns the individual lives of its heroes and heroines as unique and irreplaceable and therefore not capable of sublation into a common good. In this sense it could be said to resist the conversion of mere life (which it invests with ethical value) into political life. By contrast, Periclean rhetoric knows only a generalized and denatured mourning. Pericles's famous funeral oration does not enumerate the precious dead but rather praises the city that shaped them. The internal logic of a raptor economy leads it finally to a willingness to plunder even its own—a characteristic that distinguishes it from the living, painfully mourning raptors depicted by Aeschylus.

What I am suggesting is that while Clytemnestra's performance with the tapestries may be a diabolical trap set for Agamemnon, it is based on underlying principles that carry real ethical weight. Tragedy as a form must take them seriously—despite the fact that Clytemnestra's adulterous entanglements may undercut the purity of her stated motives. It is true that just as Agamemnon errs in hardening his heart against Iphigenia once he has decided to sacrifice her, so Clytemnestra extracts excessive enjoyment from avenging her daughter. (Though even here we should be careful. How does the pleasure that Clytemnestra takes in this murder compare to the pleasure that we, the tragic spectators, take in it?) Nevertheless, Clytemnestra manages not only to exact justice upon Agamemnon but also to stage an ethically coherent, if perversely exaggerated, defense of the values of the *oikos* that her husband has violated. This demonstration reaches its conclusion in Clytemnestra's decision to murder Agamemnon in the bath—perhaps the ultimate embodiment of that tender care, that coddling of life, that is the business of the *oikos*. To turn just this place into a slaughterhouse is again to impart a final lesson to the dying Agamemnon. The bath is at once an externalized version of the maternal womb (in which he is now immersed) and a miniaturized version of the breeding sea that Clytemnestra invokes in her speech about the purple dye. Indeed, it could be said that the bloody murder of Agamemnon simply converts him into still more purple dye: part of the standing reserve that Agamemnon saw as the essence of the household.[41]

All of which would be easier to take seriously if not for the tones of gleeful mockery in which Clytemnestra describes the murder after the fact. And yet even here some pointed elements emerge. During her harangue to the chorus she boasts: "I staked out about him an endless net, as one does for fish" (1382–83). Invoking once more the abundance of the seas, Clytemnestra depicts herself again as provider, though now in a male role. Rather than dyeing nets, she casts them. A little further on she describes Agamemnon's exposed corpse as "the work of this right-hand of mine, an artificer of justice" (1405–6). The phrase *dikaias tektonos* means literally a "well-ordered woodworker (or builder)." Perhaps the ambiguity of the phrase can best be captured as "a just workman," where "just" indicates both technical proficiency and justice in the legal and even cosmic senses. In one regard Clytemnestra is asking: "Wasn't this well done? Is there anything to be complained of with regard to my *techne* or craftsmanship?" And in another, she is asking: "Have I not wrought justice?" Nor is it the case that the first of these meanings merely stands in for the second as metaphorical vehicle to tenor. Clytemnestra is just as proud of her cunning intelligence and her technical expertise (evident at the play's opening in the relay of torches she has arranged to provide advance notice of Agamemnon's return) as she is of her role as avenger. Earlier, when praising her performance as manager of the household, she states: "and I know no more of pleasure from another man, or of scandalous rumour, than I do of the tempering of steel" (611–12), thereby surreptitiously indicating that she does in fact understand this male craft. It is as if Clytemnestra not merely transgresses female modesty in taking on the role of avenger but transgresses both female modesty and aristocratic privilege in taking on the role of male artificer or craftsman. By blurring the lines between *techne* and *dike*, handicraft and justice, she constructs a demotic counterpart to Agamemnon's confusion of justice and warfare. It is as if she thrusts momentarily into public view not merely the murdered body of her husband but the productive activities of both household and workshop that the tragic stage—along with Periclean political rhetoric—is otherwise careful to occult. This human production is moreover aligned with the purely natural productivity of the ocean and its purple dye, or the mother hare and her (slaughtered) brood, as that which the raptor economy of Athens both violates and disavows. If this realm of nurture has now become perverted by the very violence it seemed to stand against, it should be kept in mind that the House of Atreus has been haunted from the very start by a monstrous deformation of household nurture in the banquet of Thyestes—a provisioning of "mere life" gone horribly awry.[42]

When Clytemnestra brags about her workmanlike accomplishments, she surely refers not just to the savage butchering of her husband's body. Nor can we necessarily assume that she produced either the tapestries on which Agamemnon tread or the netlike robe in which she entangled him. (Although we can't assume that she didn't produce them, either, especially given her systematic if implicit portrayal as an anti-Penelope.)[43] What Clytemnestra expresses artisanal pride in is rather a netlike *plot* in which she has captured her prey, a plot that required planning, rhetorical skill, and cunning as well as technical expertise.[44] Her "work" is thus rather like that of the playwright Aeschylus, himself a *dikaias tektonos* who weaves complex plots. I use this phrasing advisedly, since Aristotle's term for a "complex" plot in the *Poetics* is *peplegmene*, which means "plaited" or "woven." Indeed, Aristotle portrays the work of plot as essentially one of weaving and unweaving.[45]

What is theater's relation to the conflicting logics played out in *Agamemnon*? I suggested earlier an essential complicity between Greek drama's exclusive focus on action, as supposed to activity, and that strain of political rhetoric that saw the city as provisioning itself by means of military action rather than material production. At the same time, however, the tragic poet is himself essentially a maker or workman, though of a relatively distinguished sort. His fashioned products imitate actions and thus occupy the difficult boundary between *poiesis* and *praxis*.

This opposition, moreover, is in a sense mapped out across the theatrical space itself, divided as it is between the exteriority of the playing space and the interiority of the *skene*. As Ruth Padel points out, this is also a division between a public, political space and the hidden domain of the *oikos*.[46] Or, to vary the terms only slightly, between a public space in which political and military action occurs, and a veiled domestic one in which production and, more essentially still, the nurturance of life should take place (though, as here, it can spectacularly fail to do so). Moreover, the *skene* is "the factory of illusion where actors put on and exchange masks," and where props,

costumes, and the *ekkyklema* were stored. The *skene* thus not only represents the hidden interior where domestic production occurs but also contains the made things on which dramatic representation in part depends. It
both symbolizes and embodies the oppositions between *poiesis* and *praxis*,
oikos and *polis*.[47] Moreover, "The *skene* probably appeared only around 460
B.C.E., and the *Oresteia* (458) may well be the first drama to use this hidden interior, facade, and door."[48] The novel theatrical apparatus Aeschylus
is asked to wield maps out a set of symbolic spaces in which his own location as playwright is by no means clear. The stakes at play in the plot of
Agamemnon are redoubled in the material conditions of its staging and grant
a thematic urgency to its metadramatic dimension. Does theater symbolically underwrite the dream of a raptor economy? Does it, in fact, imagine
a world of pure action in which productive activity has no place, and in
which martial heroism transcends its own material preconditions? When
the *skene* disgorges the mutilated body of Agamemnon, we seem to have received our answer.

II

The action of the *Choephoroi* begins with Orestes cutting two locks from his
hair. The first signifies his attainment of ephebic status, and the second is
laid on Agamemnon's tomb as a funerary offering. Both together symbolize Orestes's attempt to sever relations with his mother and reinforce those
with his father. When the ephebe cuts his long, feminine hair, he makes the
transition from a boyhood spent in the maternal nurture of the *oikos* to the
adult male realms of military and political endeavor. In this context, however, the act also signifies a more general, thematic scission between the
second play of Aeschylus's trilogy and the first, and here too a rejection of
the maternal is at stake. For the *Choephoroi* does not so much renounce as
it simply forgets or represses the claims that *Agamemnon* makes on behalf
of Clytemnestra. Orestes and Electra are hardly mentioned in the earlier
play, thus placing the sacrifice of Iphigenia squarely at the center of its ethical vision. By contrast, apart from one brief reference by Electra (243), the
memory of Iphigenia seems to have evaporated in the *Choephoroi*, and with
it any conceivable legitimacy for Agamemnon's murder. It is particularly
perplexing that Orestes and Electra do not allow their sister's death to cloud
their devotion to their father. After all, if Artemis's capricious vengeance had
taken a slightly different tack, it might have been one of their throats that
Agamemnon had agreed to cut.

Complementing its erasure of Clytemnestra's claims, the *Choephoroi* reinstates the raptor economy that *Agamemnon* had called into question. Orestes admonishes Clytemnestra: "don't censure the man [Agamemnon] who toiled away while you were sitting at home" (919); and again, two lines later (in case we missed the point): "but it's the man's labor that feeds the women sitting at home" (921). This claim may not contradict Clytemnestra's role in the *Agamemnon* so much as it reflects her changed position after her husband's death. Once the conservator of his household, she now recklessly spends his accumulated wealth (135-37, 942-43). Domestic management is therefore reassigned to the chorus, those "servant women who keep the house in good order" (84). Since both the chorus and the nurse Cilissa are slaves from abroad provided by Agamemnon's martial conquests, the *Choephoroi* reestablishes the father/warrior as household provider—symbolized by the eagle simile in Orestes's prayer to Zeus (246-51). Even those things produced within the household are made by servant women fetched from without—and the play is careful to emphasize their foreignness. The chorus compares their mourning practices to those of Arian and Cissian women (423-24; both areas in Iran), and the nurse Cilissa's name identifies her origins in southeastern Asia Minor.[49] Complicating the topographical dichotomy of the *Agamemnon*, which plays the interiority of the *oikos* off against the exteriority of the *polis*, here the domestic space is comprehended by the *polis* and yet, by virtue of its foreign workforce, enfolds a geographical "beyond" or elsewhere with respect to it. That these female domestic servants play a small but decisive role in the assassination of their masters may have prompted a brief shudder of unease in an audience of Athenian homeowners, despite the women's allegiance to the "right" side.

In all of these ways, the *Choephoroi* detaches itself from the *Agamemnon*. And yet the preliminary symbol for this, Orestes's hair cutting, is only partly successful. When he finally encounters Electra, he meets with a female counterpart to himself whose pronounced physical resemblance may unsettle his wished-for masculine difference. The very lock he has cut off and laid on his father's tomb brings the pair together, and the role it plays in this reunion is potentially troubling. When she first spots the lock, Electra exclaims: "There is nobody who could have cut it except myself. . . . It greatly resembles my own" (172, 176). It is clear that Electra notices more than mere length, for in that case she could have attributed the lock to any woman (or boy, for that matter). No, the lock looks specifically like her hair. So far, so good. The thought then occurs to her that Clytemnestra might have cut the lock from *her* head, producing a momentary quandary about whether the hair is her mother's or her brother's: "Ah, if only it had a mind and voice like a messenger, so that I wouldn't be tossed about in two minds, but would know for sure that I should reject this lock, if it really was cut from the head of an enemy, or else, if it was my kin, it would be able to join in my mourning" (194–200). Since there is no reason to believe that Electra now suddenly brings a less discerning eye to the prospect that the lock is her mother's hair, it appears that this shared physical characteristic derives from Clytemnestra, not Agamemnon. Against their own wishes, Orestes and Electra are reunited by the mother's body, not the father's spirit. The cut lock, sign of Orestes's putative detachment from the maternal care of the *oikos*, actually points to a continuing, disquieting connection.

Of course, this reading cuts against Apollo's reproductive doctrine as stated in the *Eumenides*, 657–66. But Apollo's views are not necessarily Aeschylus's.[50] In fact, a number of pre-Socratic philosophers are reported to have held that women as well as men contribute seed to their offspring, and that resemblance in a given feature will depend on which parent has provided a greater quantity of sperm.[51] So Apollo's reproductive doctrine by no means represents a philosophical consensus. And frankly, Clytemnestra gives the general impression of being a gal equipped with a pretty ample and spunky batch of seed. One probably wouldn't want to go toe to toe with her, genetically speaking.

Physical resemblance to Clytemnestra through bodily connection raises the still more disturbing possibility of moral resemblance. When Electra first encounters Orestes and is uncertain of his identity, she asks: "Look here, sir, are you trying to weave some web of trickery around me?" (220), clearly recalling Clytemnestra's deadly stratagems in the *Agamemnon*. And later she observes: "for like a savage hearted wolf, we have a rage (*thymos*), caused by our mother, that is past fawning" (421–22). The word *thymos*, which can encompass life, appetite, temper, will, anger, and heart, points to a fundamental bond between corporeal and moral disposition. Through what means, then, has Clytemnestra "caused" the rage in her children? Moral affront at the injustice of her actions? Or by passing on her own intemperate physiology to her offspring?

This confusion presents us with two incompatible paradigms for understanding Orestes's act of matricide. On the one hand, both children cite the ideal of justice as underwriting their vengeance against Clytemnestra. Orestes invokes a whole array of converging ethical justifications for his act: "Many motives join together to point the same way: the command of the god, my great grief for my father, being deprived of my property weighs heavy on me, <and it is also my duty to liberate the city> so that its citizens, the most glorious people on earth, who overthrew Troy with resolute heart, should not remain, as they now are, subjected to a pair of women—for he [Aegisthus] will soon know whether he really has a woman's heart or not!" (299–305). In this paradigm, vengeance results from ethical deliberation, political reason, and religious propitiation. It is a considered and rational act. But in the paradigm invoked by Electra, it is rather a kind of physiological reflex or an expression of evil bodily humors—a case of "mere life" striking out blindly against its progenitor, and thus a repetition of Clytemnestra's violence rather than a remedy for it. Does action express reason, or does it surge up from the darkness of *physis*?

Perhaps it is partly in response to this quandary that Orestes must do the deed. He is, of course, the stronger of the two. And yet another woman, Clytemnestra, was capable of dispatching Agamemnon, a far more powerful warrior than the effeminate Aegisthus. It may not therefore be solely because of martial prowess that Orestes is the better choice but rather because, as a man, he is less subject than is Electra to "the reckless passion [or loveless eros] that overpowers the female" (600). And yet even in Orestes's case the mechanisms of revenge are not entirely clear. Shortly before murdering his mother, he states: "It is not I that will kill you: *you* will have killed yourself" (923). In one sense the statement means that the injustice perpetrated by Clytemnestra has returned to exact punishment. But in another, Orestes may be admitting that he is the physiological embodiment of Clytemnestra, her very substance, that has now turned its blind violence back on itself.

The question raised here is in some respects one of unmediated versus mediated acts. Action of the bad sort results from immediate (maternal) bodily impulse. Action of the good sort is mediated by way of paternal authorities that are both geographically and ethically removed: the gods in their heaven, or the spirit of Agamemnon in faraway Hades. Just acts must be routed through a distant outside before they return to the self. The *Choephoroi* thereby establishes conspicuously parallel circuits for ethics and economics. A raptor economy—exemplified by Agamemnon—provisions both household and city by plundering far-off lands and dragging the booty home. (Conversely, because the effeminate Aegisthus is a stay-at-home who does not sack other cities, the household of Agamemnon is being slowly depleted of its resources.) And Orestes must likewise gain ethical justification by appealing to the even further-removed realms of the gods and the dead. The chorus, it is true, insists that "it is the house that must provide the plug / for this wound, the cure cannot come from others / outside, but from members of the house itself" (470–72). And yet it is not Electra, "shut up within the bowels of the house" (447), who does the deed but rather Orestes, raised in distant Phocis, who returns to his homeland as an unrecognizable stranger. Indeed, the *Choephoroi* suggests at more than one point that Argos has now become the mirror image of Troy, sacked by avenging Orestes and Pylades who double for the earlier Atreidae (691, 935–41). By play's end, the very distinction between inside and outside has become somewhat muddled. This is both symptom of a bad maternal immediacy and the price that must be paid to undo it.

The very essence of that bad immediacy is found in Clytemnestra's dream of giving birth to a serpent that then draws blood from her breast. This is the final corruption of the nurture (*trophe*) that the *oikos* is supposed to provide. And yet the *Choephoroi* also offers a redeemed image of maternal care in the figure of the nurse Cilissa. Her memories of raising the infant Orestes provide one of the few tender moments in the play, and at the same time one of the most vividly detailed depictions of household labor in all of Greek tragedy:

> But dear Orestes, who wore away my life with toil, whom I reared after receiving him straight from his mother's womb! <Over and over again I heard> his shrill, imperative cries, which forced me to wander around at night <and perform> many disagreeable tasks which I had to endure and which did me no good. A child without intelligence must needs be reared like an animal— how could it be otherwise?—by the intelligence of his nurse; when he's still an infant in swaddling clothes he can't speak at all if he's in the grip of hunger or thirst, say, or of an urge to make water—and the immature bowel of small children is its own master. I had to divine these things in advance, and often, I fancy, I was mistaken, and as cleaner of the baby's wrappings—well, a launderer and a caterer were holding the same post. Practicing both these two crafts, I reared up Orestes for his father; and now, to my misery, I learn that he is dead! (749–63)

The notes of weariness and resentment that creep into Cilissa's narrative do not seriously compromise her affection for Orestes. Rather, the alienating effects of toil hold her at just enough emotional distance from the infant to prevent the kind of incestuous immediacy felt by Clytemnestra—an immediacy that in turn demands exile—and instead sustains a safe yet proximate interval for nurture. The object of that nurture, the infant Orestes, is not yet fully human. He is, rather, a demanding and often dirty bundle of animal needs and appetites: precisely the "mere life" that domestic care is meant to sustain and cosset.

But if Cilissa provides a redeemed image of maternal nurture, it is never-theless crucial that she is not actually Orestes's mother. She is, rather, for-eign slave labor imported by Agamemnon, and accordingly she "reared up Orestes for his father." Just as it is the eagle *father* who nourishes his off-spring in Orestes's prayer to Zeus, so even the maternal care provided to Orestes is ultimately supplied by Agamemnon. The proper form of nurture must be captured from without by the raptor economy, replacing the real mother with an improved, artificial one. That way there is no danger of stak-ing excessive maternal claims.

Simon Goldhill perceptively notes of this scene that "as well as being part of the justification for matricide, the splitting and metaphorising of the function of bringing up a child opens the way toward the development of the civic discourse, its appropriation of such language (in the claim that the city is the mother/father/educator/nourisher of its citizens)."[52] Ironi-cally, then, the play's most loving depiction of what we might call the labor of care, and hence the strongest claim for the dignity and rights of the *oikos*, is also the one most thoroughly appropriated by the *polis* and its dream of a raptor economy. Cilissa's remembrances of maternal care are the play's counterpart, in a way, to Clytemnestra's speech about the sea and its endless productivity in *Agamemnon*. Indeed, Cilissa provides a more direct and less hypocritical assertion of the dignity of the *oikos* than Clytemnestra can. It is as if Clytemnestra's deeply compromised claims find their truest embodi-ment only here. Yet now that they do, the space of domestic nurture no lon-ger offers a principal of opposition to the claims of the raptor economy but is a fully integrated part of it. Cilissa never strikes a blow, but her small yet crucial role in the death of Aegisthus (urged by the chorus, she changes Cly-temnestra's message and tells him to greet the stranger from Phocis alone, without his guard) is exerted entirely on behalf of Agamemnon and his off-spring, the foreign masters to whom she and the chorus show unwavering loyalty and love.[53] Subordinating the claims of domestic production and nurture to those of the *polis*—thus does the *Choephoroi* conduct its mediating work and prepare for the final, civic triumph of the *Eumenides*.

III

In order for that triumph to take place, however, a change of scene is needed. Argos is too tainted with blood and crime, too scarred by aristocratic in-fighting to resolve its own problems. It is for Athens and its modern demo-cratic institutions to set right the otherwise insoluble dilemmas of Homeric kingship. And it will do so in ways that fundamentally recast the conceptual categories I have been tracing in this chapter.

At the end of the *Choephoroi*, Orestes is seemingly on the verge of reclaiming his political rights. By the beginning of the *Eumenides* he is once again in exile, no longer concerned with his father's estate and his own kingly status but with saving his skin. When he arrives at the temple of Athena Polias he does not seek to be restored to office but simply to prevent the blood from being sucked out of his body by the avenging Furies. Stripped of both political status and heroic stature, Orestes reaches Athens as a half-mad, quivering supplicant. He has, somewhat like King Lear on the heath, been reduced to "mere life"—though in this case as prelude to being reconstituted as a new kind of political subject. Once rendered as defenseless as a child, Orestes must re-traverse the passage to male adulthood in a way that emphasizes civic rather than martial virtue.

This civic virtue is not his, exactly, but rather that of an institution: the Council of the Areopagus acting as anonymous jury. Orestes himself is not asked to do anything—indeed, is not in a position *to* do anything—other than submit to the decision of the court. He is not the subject of political deliberation but rather its conspicuously passive object. His life, formerly at the mercy of the gods, is now placed in the hands of the jury. In a sense, this is the civic counterpart to the ephebe's entry into the field of death, only now the wagering of life occurs not on the field of battle but in a court of law. Orestes must surrender his life to the state as a precondition of having it handed back to him. But what he receives is not the original, immediate, bodily life he relinquished; it is rather a life henceforth alienated in, and mediated by, the state. No longer a sovereign subject, Orestes is permanently attached to the city that grants him his life. And not only Orestes himself, but all of Argos is now bound in an unending alliance with Athens.

The trial scene in the *Eumenides* thus completes a movement that spans the length of the trilogy, from the bad immediacy of Clytemnestra's deadly motherhood, to the laborious nurture carried out by the nurse Cilissa (and provided indirectly by Agamemnon), to the jury vote that spares Orestes. The maintenance of life passes successively from mother to nurse/father to city, improving each time it is displaced. Yet when it reaches its final, political incarnation, sustenance has abandoned its originally material form. Here the state does not take over the function of *trophe*, or provisioning, as it did in the raptor economy. It does not supply food or other means of physical nurture. It delivers, rather, a finding of innocence that, in withholding the state's capacity to punish or execute, grants "mere" life only insofar as it happens to be comprehended within political life.

That the court exercises this function—and indeed, does so for a first and founding time—in a case involving Argives is surprising. The Council of the Areopagus tried cases of the willful murder of an Athenian citizen, a designation that on various grounds fails to include Clytemnestra. Both the perpetrator and the victim therefore fall outside of its jurisdiction. It is as if the court itself is "provisioned" from without in its inaugural session, in imitation of the raptor economy's essential movement.

The conversion of mere life into political life requires, as I have earlier stated, entry into the field of death. This is the passage that the ephebic soldier makes when he leaves the nurturing confines of the *oikos* for military training. It is also a passage made symbolically by initiates into the Eleusinian mysteries, a process that has been offered by critics as a paradigm for Orestes's symbolic death and rebirth in the *Oresteia*.[54] In fact, Orestes dies and is reborn twice. He undergoes a fictional death in the *Choephoroi* and what we might call a virtual death in the *Eumenides* by submitting himself to the vote of the jury. Nor is this passage through death on Orestes's part merely symbolic in the sense of leaving no effective traces behind. Before the trial, Orestes clings desperately to life; after it, he briefly mentions going home but then, instead of anticipating his days to come, promises only that he will enforce Argos's alliance with Athens when he is in the tomb (762–74). It is as if Orestes is already rendered somehow posthumous, saved only to contemplate his coming demise and its aftermath. Like the Furies, he is destined to a subterranean existence. All of this seems to mark political life or *bios* as a kind of afterlife with respect to a merely biological mode of being. Perhaps this is Aeschylus's reinterpretation of the Dionysian myth, which provides the occasion for tragic performance. Dionysos's death and rebirth are here refigured as the birth of political life or *bios* from the death of mere life or *zoe*.[55] If political life earlier posed as that which could secure its own provisioning, here it begins to look like something that doesn't require provisioning at all—a kind of abstract, bodiless life. It is not without reason that the motherless Athena, who herself required no *trophe* or infantile nurture, oversees the affairs of the *polis*.

The jury that effects this transition is likewise somewhat disembodied. Athena declares that "I shall choose for my city men without fault (*amomphous*) to be judges of homicide" (475–83). And later she refers to "this council, untouched by thought of gain" (704). This remark implicitly distinguishes the council members from Agamemnon, whose decision to avenge the rape of Helen, supposedly undertaken solely in pursuit of justice, ends with sacking the wealth of defeated Troy; from Clytemnestra, whose pursuit of justice is likewise contaminated by a desire to enjoy her husband's estate;

and even from Orestes, who while avenging his father likewise seeks that same estate. In the aristocratic/heroic world that provides matter for tragedy, justice appears inseparable from hope of gain. Only "faultless" men, untouched by these all too human passions, can deliberate disinterestedly about murder. This new civic type of man is therefore anonymous, purged of the corrupting desires that imprint tragic heroes with their oversized personalities. Like Orestes after the trial, the jurors too are in a certain sense posthumous. Theirs is a shadowy afterlife compared with the more visceral existence of tragic heroes. Such men are the very negation of "raptors."⁵⁶

And yet, oddly, their judicial activities have military consequences. "If," promises Athena, "you righteously fear an august body like this, you will have a bulwark to keep your land and city safe such as no one in the world has, neither among the Scythians nor in the land of Pelops" (700–703). Moreover, through their decision the jurors gain an important military ally for Athens. As he prepares to depart, Orestes promises that his countrymen will never attack Athens and in fact will always fight at its side (762–74). Indeed, Athens now has "a means to success that your enemies will be unable to escape, which will give you safety and make your wars victorious" (775–77). The sentiments expressed here are not very different from the Periclean claim that democratic virtue underwrites imperial conquest. And yet there is also a sense in which democratic institutions now seem to usurp, rather than merely bolster, military functions.

I am suggesting that the new civic institutions of Athens separate political from biological life even more radically than does the raptor economy. But then where does "mere life" and its claims (which Aeschylus has hitherto been careful to vocalize) go? In short: to the chorus of Furies. As already noted, the chorus always enjoys an inexhaustible life within the fictional world of tragedy. But in the case of the Furies, this quality becomes explicit. The Furies describe themselves at one point as "the everlasting children of Night" (*Nyktos aiane tekna*; 416). The word *aiane* ("everlasting") supposedly derives from *aei* ("always"). This is in turn connected to *aion*, which, according to Emile Benveniste, originally designates an ongoing life-force.⁵⁷ "Implying unceasing re-creation of the principle that nourishes life," he notes, *aion* "suggests to the mind a compelling image of something that maintains itself without end, in the freshness of the always new."⁵⁸ This ongoing life is not immune to death but rather includes death in its own self-propagation: it is "single and double . . . transitory and permanent, running out and being reborn in the course of generations, destroying itself in its renewal and subsisting forever in its endlessly beginning finitude."⁵⁹ The *aion* or ongoing life of the Furies feeds itself directly on death—a disturbing mixture of mortal violence and infantile nurture.

When the Furies declare that "We are many" (*pollai men esmen*, 585), they are not merely announcing the obvious fact that there is more than one of them but pointing to an internal multiplicity or heterogeneity. First spotting them, the priestess of Apollo is uncertain whether they are women or Gorgons or harpies (46–52), and they are in fact compounded by Aeschylus out of three related but distinct mythological species: Erinyes, Keres, and Semnai Theai.[60] In addition, the Furies enfold a number of paradoxical dichotomies: they are aged yet childlike, punishers of pollution yet polluted themselves (193–95), divine or superhuman yet animalistic and subhuman. They do not merely congregate but are essentially a congregation, likened at various points to packs of maenads (500) or wild dogs (130 and note in Sommerstein) and to a flock of sheep (196–97).[61]

It is the Furies' animalistic qualities that most conspicuously associate them with "mere" life, and thus with the propagation of a purely biological existence. Catching sight of Orestes, they insist: "No, you must give in return a thick red liquid from your limbs / for us to slurp from your living body: from you / may I draw the nourishment of a draught horrid to drink!" (264–66). The Furies fall beneath the level of human provisioning; they do not cultivate or cook their food but merely suck blood directly from their prey, like beasts. Here the word translated as "nourishment" is *boske*, which can indicate fodder or pasturage as well as food. The Furies suck, slurp, vomit, spew, and drip various forms of liquid, both nourishing and poisonous, and their circulation of fluids points to an absence of clearly defined corporeal boundaries. They are "many," but they are also fused into an indistinguishable mass of the living. As pack or flock they are an essentially animal, prepolitical collectivity, unable to generate the "plurality" of individual differences that for Aristotle constitutes the basis of any state.[62] Consequently, they always speak as one, and could never generate a split decision as the anonymous jurymen do, or momentarily fragment as the chorus of male citizens does in *Agamemnon* (1346–71).

This physiological fusion also associates them with the mother-child bond, which they defend at trial. When Orestes questions whether he really is blood kin to Clytemnestra, the Furies respond: "How else did she nourish you, you filthy murderer, beneath her girdle? Do you disallow your mother's blood, the nearest and dearest to your own?" (607–8). The blood fusion of mother and fetus (which provokes Apollo's rather tendentious speech on childbearing at 657–73 as an anxious riposte) is a paradigm for the Furies' own fused state—especially since, as "everlasting children," they are in need of perpetual nourishment. I would argue, in fact, that the "blood-dripping" (365) mass of Furies rework the image of the mother hare's fetal offspring consumed by the eagle at *Agamemnon* 119-20, as well as the morcellated children of Thyestes's banquet. The Furies, who require nourishment but do not themselves nourish, are the final, nightmare image of maternal nurture or *trophe* that the *Oresteia* has been reworking throughout.

The Furies' contaminating foulness, compounded of their association with animality, maternity, fluidity, and mixture in general, also includes a class element, as Mark Griffith acutely observes: "In addition to being female, ugly, and barbarous, the Erinyes are presented in this third play as socially disadvantaged, even déclassées: fatherless, and lacking connections in the dynastic network of divinities, they are unable to establish a reciprocal relationship with the patron goddess of Athens."[63] This "lower-class" characterization is clearly reinforced by the Furies' repeated association with labor. They themselves complain of the "man-wearying toil" (*mochthois androkmesi*, 248) involved in tracking Orestes, and the ghost of Clytemnestra, coming upon them passed out on chairs in Apollo's shrine, sarcastically observes: "Sleep and Toil-an appropriate pair of conspirators-have sapped the strength of the fearsome serpent" (127-28). In marked contrast, Zeus "disposes all . . . things, turning them this way and that, without any laborious effort [literally, 'not panting at all'; cf. the Furies' exhausted 'panting' at 248] by the sheer power of his will." Various mortal characters in the *Oresteia* complain of labor or toil, from the watchman on Clytemnestra's roof (*Ag.* 1, 20) to the soldiers sailing for Troy (*Ag.* 555). But given their (perverted) association with maternal nurture, when the Furies complain about their toil they most closely recall the nurse Cilissa, who emphasized the labor of nursing in the *Choephoroi* (749-63). And Cilissa's speech in turn reworked Clytemnestra's earlier amalgam of maternal nurture and artisanal labor. The Furies not only defend the ethical claims of the *oikos*, then; they also provide a nightmare image of the maternal care and domestic labor that in part underwrite those claims. Recall that Cilissa was able to redeem Clytemnestra's defense of these same values because her services were provided (and thus mediated) by the father, whereas Clytemnestra represented a bad maternal immediacy. The Furies drive this bad maternal immediacy to its final term, since they have a mother (Night) but no father. Without that paternal mediation, *trophe* devolves into a violent, merely animalistic feeding. Parent-child connection ramps up into utter collapse of boundaries and differences.

The bad maternal immediacy of the Furies is felt most acutely in their essential function, which is to prosecute murders within the family. The justice or *dike* that they represent has its own legitimacy, which the play respects even while overruling. Yet the mode in which they prosecute this justice disturbingly confuses principle with appetite. When the Furies say that "a mother's blood is drawing me on" (230), are they outraged by a crime or attracted like hounds to the kill? Are they disgusted, or allured? Is this a question of law, or of appetite? The Furies not only repeat the troubling zone of indistinction raised by Electra in the *Choephoroi* when she spoke of the savage *thymos* inherited by her and Orestes from their mother (421–22); they raise it to a higher level, since the *dike* they represent includes this indistinctness not as a possible space of perversion or miscarriage (wherein one might mistake bloodlust for justice) but in its very constitution. The Furies reveal that *no* prosecution of their *dike* is separable even *in principle* from animal appetite. When the ghost of Clytemnestra finds the Furies dreaming of their pursuit of Orestes, she remarks that "you are chasing a beast in your dreams, and giving tongue like a hound who can never desist from thinking of blood" (131–32). The Furies cannot not think of the chase, cannot detach themselves from the constant push of instinct, and therefore cannot clear a space for neutral deliberation. In this respect they offer an obvious contrast to Athena's chosen jurors, who are "untouched by thought of gain."

The *Eumenides*, I would argue, operates as a kind of conceptual centrifuge whose purpose is to separate out principles in solution. Of course, the *Oresteia* has been engaged in something similar from the very start. The dream of the raptor economy was intended to free the *polis* from its material dependence on the *oikos*, and thus liberate political life from mere life, action from production. And yet the conquest of Troy, while it prosecutes a kind of justice, is still contaminated by passions (thought of gain) as well as by the toil or labor of battle.[64] The *Eumenides* completes this merely partial separation, then, by relocating the essence of the city from warfare to a *dike* that is both dispassionate and, by virtue of being a purely mental act of judgment, definitively detached from bodily *ponos* or toil.[65] (The jurors, like Zeus—and unlike warrior heroes such as Agamemnon—make things happen without panting.) The rejected precipitate of this process is the Furies, who collect within themselves all of the maternal, animal, and banausic elements that this centrifuge is meant to extract. But more than this, they embody the collapse of boundaries and difference, the very principle of "holding in solution," that the conceptual centrifuge is intended to undo.[66] And the vileness of the precipitate serves in the end to justify the process by which it is separated out and excluded.

The phrase "in the end" introduces complications of its own, though. Because the jury trial of Orestes is not the end of the play, and once it has concluded, the Furies are transformed into benign *Semnai theai* and reintegrated into the city. Indeed, the opposition between *polis* and *oikos*, which the Aeschylean centrifuge was intended to enforce, gives way to a general reconciliation. As Simon Goldhill puts it: "The city is to be dwelt in together like an *oikos*; it is not merely the saving of Orestes' *oikos*, or of Athens, or simply the depiction of Athens as an *oikos*, but the interpenetration of vocabulary. The *polis* as *oikos* is also the relation of *oikos* to *polis*."[67] The trilogy ends on a note not of separation but of synthesis that may even look a bit like the category confusions originally engendered by the Furies. This reconciliation would be signaled by the fact that the final, Panathenatic procession includes not only male Areopagites but also female priestesses and attendants to Athena, all of whom together replace the Furies as chorus.[68]

The integration of the Furies into the *polis* simply involves rearticulating their two constitutive elements—life and justice—such that the former no longer interferes with or compromises the latter. In the Furies' bad incarnation, carnal appetites—the needs of life—become indistinguishable from the pursuit of the just. The new improved Furies will secure nurture not for themselves but for the city on behalf of its virtuous inhabitants. They will "cause blessings beneficial to [Athens'] life [*biou*] to burst forth in profusion from the earth" (924–26). These blessings include the fruitfulness of the citizens' land and livestock, and of the citizens themselves in bearing children (908–10). They also include (more on this later) stocking the soil with silver ore for mining (946–48). But while these riches will be enjoyed by all, they will flow with particular abundance to the righteous—or so, at least, urges Athena: "but may you give greater fertility to those who are pious; for like a shepherd of plants, I cherish the race to which these righteous men belong" (911–12). By "these righteous men," Athena is referring to the members of the Areopagite Council—the men who judge without thought of gain. What she asks for, in essence, is: give the greatest gains to those who don't care for gain. Nurture the life of those whose commitment to justice reflects indifference to bodily need. Foster those citizens whose political life is most definitively detached from mere life. Something like the raptor economy is at work here in that bodily needs are provisioned by political life—only here civic justice has taken over for military valor.

Indeed, as David Rosenbloom persuasively argues, "naval power was not only foreign to the civic tradition; the tradition of poetry Aeschylus inherited expressed the highest political values in the fertility of the *chora*: when the city is just, it 'blossoms' (*tethele polis*, Hes. *Op.* 227)."[69] Just as the Furies had earlier threatened to poison the *chora* by dripping venom onto the soil (478-79, 783-85), so now the blessings they bestow likewise arise from the soil. The new civic virtue does indeed seem, as Rosenbloom claims, to be attached to Athens as a self-sufficient, landed locality and not to imperial expansion. Perhaps nowhere is this more patent than in the implication that the city's silver reserves come entirely from the mines at Laureion—a gift of the gods in response to Athenian virtue—rather than from tribute. The raptor economy seems to be defunct by the end of the *Eumenides*.

Rosenbloom argues that the *Oresteia* rejects Athenian imperialism *tout court*, but this seems to me to go too far. Athena herself is certainly no pacifist: "Let there be external war," she declares, "and plenty of it, for him in whom there is a fierce desire for glory" (864-65). And later: "I would find it unendurable not to honour the city among men by making her a city of victory in glorious martial struggles" (913-15). The *Eumenides* by no means rejects imperial warfare, but, crucially, it strips it of its provisioning function. For Athena, warfare is undertaken solely for purposes of glory, not to supply a city for which the gods have already taken more than adequate care. In the same way that justice must be pursued "without thought of gain," so warfare is purged of base material motives. It now constitutes its own end. The raptor economy is undone, not by abandoning empire, but by detaching imperial warfare from its role in sustaining the city. It is as if the eagles were taught to hunt solely for sport.

As a result of all this, it is not the Furies who must be purged at the end of the *Eumenides*. They are rather refunctioned and reintegrated into the city as suppliers of material wealth. The figure who must ultimately be expelled is Orestes, who embodies everything against which the new civic order of Athens will define itself: kinship versus democracy, the mythic hero versus the anonymous citizen-juror, and above all the raptor economy versus a divinely fructified *chora*.

It is difficult to say whether the final social vision offered by the *Eumenides* is materialist or idealist. Certainly the rewards of justice are impeccably material: abundant crops and flocks, silver ore, and human offspring. But the mechanisms that provide these things seem rather magical. Silver does not, of course, remove itself from the ground; nor do crops plant, tend, and harvest themselves. But the idyllic vision of the *Eumenides* does not mention human labor. Rather, the gods provide a kind of Golden Age cornucopia in response to civic virtue. One may wonder, then: what becomes of the claims of domestic labor enunciated in different ways by Clytemnestra and Cilissa?

Has political life so fully subsumed mere life by the end of the *Eumenides* that the work of the *oikos* has simply disappeared?

The *oikos* has, to be sure, no independent representative or embodiment by the end of the trilogy. But it may manage to make itself felt indirectly through a different mechanism: a persistent, troubling ambiguity that haunts the close of the *Eumenides*. Commenting on the final procession, A. M. Bowie perceptively asks: "would not the Panathenaic robe, present or otherwise, with its depiction of the defeat of chaos, pick up the imagery of weaving and, with the red robe of the Eumenides, bring that symbolism, which has stood so long for entrapment and death, to an auspicious close?"[70] Bowie's question appears to be a rhetorical one, but I wonder whether it shouldn't be left open. In any case, he has correctly highlighted a striking similarity between the ending of the *Eumenides* and the climax of the *Agamemnon*. As the Panathenaic procession leads them to their new home in the underworld, the redeemed Furies are dressed in the red robes of metics—a reminder, surely, both of the red tapestries upon which Agamemnon walked on his way to slaughter and of the crimson robes in which he was entangled in the bath. Athena, moreover, has achieved her reconciliation with—or is it victory over?—the Furies by means of what she calls "the awesome power of Persuasion, the charm and enchantment of my tongue" (885-86; cf. 970-72). And this of course was the same means by which Clytemnestra achieved her victory over Agamemnon, in a play that describes Persuasion as "the unendurable child of scheming Ruin" (*Ag.* 386).

None of these parallels specify how we should read the ending of the *Eumenides* in relation to the *Agamemnon*. They could well serve, as Bowie suggests, to depict Athena as the redemption of Clytemnestra, thereby bringing the trilogy to a satisfying close. Alternatively, they could pose her as the repetition of Clytemnestra, in which case the Furies, inveigled by deceptive rhetoric, head as blindly toward the underworld (Agamemnon's current abode, by the way) as Agamemnon did toward his palace. The issue is further complicated by some unsettling aspects of Orestes's trial. Does the court established by Athena embody disinterested justice, or do jury intimidation and family connections fatally compromise the fairness of the proceedings?[71] Have the Furies succumbed to a higher *dike* or to yet another power play? And is Athens therefore the antitype of Argos, or its unwitting double? I do not raise these questions in order to supply an answer, but rather to limn alternatives that the play leaves in perfect balance. It is striking, in any case, that the material echo supplied by the Furies' red robes evokes the trilogy's initial symbol of domestic labor/nurture, and thus cuts against the sublimating rhetoric that otherwise marks the close of the *Eumenides*. The robes as made objects, rather than a particular character, may therefore be the play's last reminder of a realm it has otherwise forgotten or left behind. Costume's mute testimony is all that remains.

IV

What is the relation of Greek theater as an institution to the themes I have been exploring in the *Oresteia*? We may approach this question through one of the first metatheatrical moments in *Agamemnon*: the portent of the eagles and the mother hare. This performance resonates throughout the trilogy, since the slaughtered litter of fetal hares recalls the banquet of Thyestes and foreshadows (among other things) the mass of Furies in the *Oresteia*. I call the portent a "performance" because it may be seen as a playlet or microtragedy Zeus stages for the benefit of an Achaean audience. A signifying display composed of bodies in action, it is therefore theatrical, if not quite a "play," since its agonists are animals and its deadly violence takes place in earnest. But this confusion of levels is precisely the point, redoubled in the paradoxical consequences to which it gives rise. The portent not merely predicts the future but also affects it, since Artemis will react to the death of the hare by demanding Iphigenia's life in return. She thus reminds the others that the life subsumed within this pageant is real, and has its price. These consequences, moreover, retroactively color the meaning of the portent, which now prophecies not only the defeat of Troy but the sacrifice of Iphigenia as well. The portent thus establishes an actual and not merely symbolic circuit between the material realm of *zoe* or mere life and a signifying structure inaugurated by subjecting living bodies to a stroke of violence.

As an art form that arranges real, living bodies—and subjects them to the force of a signifying structure—Greek theater bears a certain resemblance to this portent. It also bears a resemblance to the institution of the ephebate, which takes the living bodies of boys and introduces them into the field of death as a way of producing political life from real life. Theater imposes a coercive discipline comparable—in its way—to that of the choral ephebes undergoing military training.[72] It not merely represents acts of violence but (like the portent) takes the actual living bodies of actors and twists them to its purposes. It encases those bodies not in armor but in costumes, high platform shoes, and masks, and it disciplines them not in close order drill but in the art of the dance. It is therefore complicit with the conversion of mere life into political life, though perhaps we can say that the task of its fictions is in part to render visible and unmistakable the violence involved in this conversion.

This dimension of theater is not political, exactly, since what it addresses is not the kind of issue that would come before the Council or the Assembly but what we might rather call the general metabolic conditions of the city—how it is supplied with fresh citizens, what the relation is between their political and bodily lives, what kinds of ethical or other costs attend these. This level of discourse does not preclude political commentary of a more direct sort, but it situates political commentary in a broad theoretical context. The kind of issues raised by Greek tragedy might well be called metapolitical, since they address the relation between the civic or political realm in the strict sense and nonpolitical spaces such as the *oikos*. The fact that tragedies are staged during the festival of Dionysos, when the political business of the city is temporarily suspended, clears a space for their metapolitical explorations. It is by shutting down the concrete, daily practice of politics that the *polis* as such can be brought into question.[73] Existing, as it were, on the edge of politics, tragedy is able to reflect on the life of the *polis* and its boundary conditions in a broadly encompassing way.

At the same time, Greek theater has an equally complex relation to the realm of *poiesis* or making. As I have already suggested, the physical structure of the Greek theater sets the enclosure of the *skene* off against the openness of the acting space in order to juxtapose household and city, made things and actions. But the play text is also, famously, a "made thing," though of a peculiar sort. Plays are built for collective, civic consumption, not for private use. They do not fulfill bodily or quotidian needs in the way that most manufactured objects do; indeed, the occasion of their staging involves a suspension of these needs, just as the festival of Dionysos suspends the daily business of politics. It is this suspension that allows theater to escape, at least in part, the contempt that could attach to manufacture of the more ordinary sort. Dramatic making is "free productive activity" (to borrow a phrase from Marx) that rises above the realm of need without quite forgetting it.

In fact, the realm of *poiesis* can be divided in a manner not only parallel to, but actually bound up with, the distinction between *zen* and *eu zen*, mere life and an excellent way of life. Insofar as its products fulfill quotidian need, the act of making provisions the space of mere life. But insofar as it exceeds mere utility and pursues its own standards of excellence—insofar, that is, as it becomes aesthetic—making begins to transcend bodily need and to look more and more "political" in the Arendtian sense of publicly disclosing its maker.[74] The competition for prizes that attends the presentation of plays at the Festival of Dionysos imparts to the proceedings a pursuit of individual excellence that is fully consonant with the conduct of Athenian politics. In this sense, poetics, the making that pursues excellence, is truly the counterpart to politics, the activity that pursues excellence.

And yet poetry cannot entirely escape from the social contempt that sometimes stains the production of the merely useful. Discussing poets and sculptors, Plutarch remarks that "it does not necessarily follow that, if the work delights you with its grace, the one who wrought it is worthy of your esteem."[75] He makes this assertion in the context of discussing how excellent actions spur emulation while excellent works do not. Young men of social stature should want to be like Pericles, not like a Phidias or an Aeschylus. Granted that poetical and political endeavors can incite comparable forms of competitive display, an impassible barrier nevertheless continues to separate them.

Dramatic poetry therefore occupies a kind of seam between the realms of *praxis* and *poiesis*, action and making. At this juncture resemblance and distinction compete to blur and reassert difference, respectively. Drama's function, I would argue, is in part to make this seam—its own distinctive location—"speak," and thus to articulate the vexed relations between action and making, political life and mere life. Another way to put this is that Greek theater's metapolitical vocation, its capacity to reflect upon the boundaries between the political and the non- (or sub-, or even anti-) political, is abetted by its own ambiguous location within the social order—a place that is neither that of the household nor that of the workshop nor that of the battlefield nor that of the courtroom, neither the place where tapestries are dyed nor that where infants are nursed nor that where empires are expanded nor that where justice is dispensed, but a place that nevertheless bears a strange and partial kinship to all of these.

CHAPTER THREE

Marlowe's Theater of Night

Doctor Faustus *and Capital*

The *Oresteia* appears to be something of an anomaly within Greek tragedy—though given how few tragic plays of the period survive, it is difficult to say exactly how anomalous. In any case, it shows at least one Greek tragic playwright reacting from the start against hyperbolic claims on behalf of action voiced in the political realm—claims that would later be echoed by some Greek philosophers as well. Yet it should not be surprising that tragic drama mounts a defense of *poiesis* against overweening *praxis*, since after all drama *is* itself *poiesis,* or rather a difficult hybrid compounded of making and doing. Aristotle's denigration of *opsis,* or the material elements of theatrical production, attempts to rescue drama as poetic invention from the merely mechanical realities of the stage, in a philosophical counterpart to Pericles's elevation of military action over production. But the *Oresteia* shows no interest in being so rescued, and instead gives a voice to the dignity of the made.

In modernity, as I have argued, the problem reverses. Political economy's claim that happiness depends on production rather than action threatens to devalue the latter and thereby tragedy's mythic substance as well. The early modern period, with which my middle chapters are concerned, precedes political economy. Yet early modern drama already plays out some of political economy's tensions. By mixing tragic with comic subplots, early modern drama brings an aristocratic realm of action in contact with a plebeian one of making. But the capacity to meditate on the dilemmas of commercial society has also to do with the fact that early modern drama became, for the first time in history, thoroughly commercialized. *excellent*

Both Greek and medieval drama were civic rather than commercial affairs. And as such, they were occasions for economic expenditure rather than profit. Roman theater was a more complicated matter.[1] For a time, at least, its business model anticipated that of the early modern period in some respects, with entrepreneurs purchasing play texts on behalf of actors' companies. Yet once a repertory of older plays had been established, the market for new work largely dried up. Moreover, Roman theater was always heavily dependent on patronage and public subsidies. The million sesterces awarded the Roman tragic playwright Lucius Varius Rufus by the Emperor Augustus for a performance of *Thyestes* easily dwarfed any profit the play could have earned its author on the market. Similar acts of political munificence, along with a daily honorarium of 4,000 sesterces, made the comic actor Roscius so wealthy he could afford to act without pay after 81 BCE. And the tragic actor Aesopus was able to leave his son an inheritance of 20 million sesterces. Not everyone in Roman theater enjoyed such posh circumstances, of course. My point is simply that while this theater was thoroughly monetized, its rewards were not exclusively or even predominantly distributed by the logic of the market, and in that sense it was not a genuinely commercial theater. That distinction goes first to the early modern period, when the direct economic advantages of patronage had largely dwindled into insignificance, and most companies were forced to survive solely on revenues gathered from patrons at the door. At the same time, theater achieved an unprecedented degree of autonomy from the political and religious institutions in which it had previously been embedded. It was freed, as a result, to respond to financial incentives alone. And finally, it demanded a division of labor that was relatively elaborate and sophisticated for the period.

As a result of all this, the early modern stage led a new kind of double life. It was a site of representation, on which Danish princes, Scythian warriors, alchemists, Egyptian queens, fairies, whores, shoemakers, caesars, shepherdesses, coney-catchers and gulls played out their imaginary stories. But it was, at the same time, what Marx would later come to call a means of production—something that generated not only use values (plays) but economic values as well. When combined with other such means, including stocks of costumes, stage properties, play texts, and so forth, and when set in motion by the human labor of actors, gatherers, prompters, playwrights, and stagehands of various kinds, the stage produced the cultural commodity known as the performance of a play, from which tidy profits could be made. The sum of these theatrical means of production thus constitutes a form of capital. This chapter explores the question of whether the stage's status as means of production can be brought into some meaningful relation with its status as site of dramatic representation. To put the matter more simply: what does the stage's somewhat abstract economic function have to do with what concretely transpired on it, in the production of a play? And how did play texts take cognizance of the structures necessary to their economic and artistic realization? Finally, what were the effects of all this on conceptions of tragic action?

Here I shall address one specific kind of labor associated with the early modern stage, that of playwriting. Christopher Marlowe's *Doctor Faustus* provides a particularly shrewd and penetrating commentary on the playwright's confrontation with theatrical capital. Although the story of Faustus is an old one, Marlowe reshapes it so as to comment on some very novel and historically pregnant developments. As my terminology thus far has suggested, addressing the modernity of *Doctor Faustus* will require us to overleap Adam Smith and call on the critical resources of a later thinker who both employs and critiques the resources of political economy: Karl Marx. Smith's understanding of the capitalist economy, with its comic emphasis on the providential role of the invisible hand providing ever-increasing prosperity, cannot accommodate the tragic facts of separation, alienation, and loss that pervade *Doctor Faustus*—facts that are at once economic, religious, and aesthetic in their reach. Faustus does, to be sure, procure for himself an endless supply of material goods, but the invisible hand that supplies them turns out to be anything but benign, and this material copiousness brings deadly forms of spiritual impoverishment in its wake. A different language is therefore required to excavate the logic of this play, one supplied by political economy's greatest critic. Because what Marlowe grasps in this play is not just that playwriting is a form of labor, and not just that it therefore creates economic value, but more fundamentally that this value is alienable and indeed necessarily alienated as a result of Marlowe's separation as direct producer from the means of theatrical production. As I shall argue, moreover, the alienation of labor provides a paradigm for the alienation of action as well, and indeed for the spectator's alienation from drama.

Separation/alienation is what constitutes the stage as theatrical capital, an abstraction that, for our purposes, will initially be personified by Philip Henslowe.

I

Henslowe, the well-known theatrical impresario, owned the Rose Theater and served as landlord to the Lord Admiral's Men, who gave the first recorded performances of *Doctor Faustus* in 1594. We know nothing about

Henslowe's business dealings with Marlowe, if any, and I want to explore his importance for *Doctor Faustus* more indirectly, by way of his relationship with the minor playwright Robert Daborne. Daborne was a competent but not brilliant professional writer who never achieved theatrical eminence. Only two of his plays have survived, and only one of these was published. He is best known to theater historians for his correspondence with Henslowe, beginning in April 1613. By this time Henslowe had moved his business from the Rose Theater to the Fortune, and he was in the (at least occasional) practice of buying plays directly from playwrights, either as a factor for an acting company or in order to resell them.

On April 17, 1613, Daborne contracts with Henslowe to write a tragedy called *Machiavel and the Devil*. Daborne will receive 20 pounds, to be paid in installments, and he promises to deliver the completed play by the end of Easter term. On the same day he signs a performance bond for 20 pounds with Henslowe, from which he will be released if he finishes the play by the promised date. At about the time he signs his contract, however, Daborne also becomes entangled in a lawsuit over his estate. The legal proceedings strain Daborne's savings and delay completion of the play until well past the promised date. Most of Daborne's subsequent correspondence with Henslowe consists of pleas for additional cash advances, along with protestations of his good faith and promises to deliver the completed play soon. Typical is a letter of June 10, 1613, in which Daborne writes: "I intended no other thing, god is my judge till this be finished: the necessity of term business exacts me beyond my custom to be troublesome unto you wherefore I pray send me the other 20 s. I desired."[2] By July 25, Daborne has still not completed the play. Upbraided by Henslowe for his tardiness, he responds with a combination of injured pride and abject submission: "before God I can have twenty-five pounds for it [the play] as some of the company know, but such is my debt to you that so long as my labors may pleasure them and you say the word I am wholly yours to be, ever commanded[,] Robert Daborne."[3] By July 30, Daborne's situation is more desperate still: "I pray Sir of your much friendship do me one courtesy more till Tuesday when we deliver in our play to you as to lend me 20 shillings and upon my faith and Christianity I will then or give you content or secure you to the utmost farthing you can desire of me, Sir I pray of all your gentleness deny not this courtesy to me and if you find me not just and honest to you may I want a friend in my extremity."[4] Daborne's troubles continue until November, at which point he has contracted to write additional plays for Henslowe. On November 5 he writes: "good Sir let me find you put some trust in me which when I deceive god forsake me and mine."[5]

What interests me about Daborne's correspondence is the fitful emer-
gence within it of what I would term a Faustian register. Having signed
a contract with Henslowe and become financially dependent upon him,
Daborne pledges his faith and Christianity against his obligations to his
worldly master, wishing that God may desert him if he proves false to
Henslowe. Such oathsmanship is not unusual in the Renaissance. But its
Faustian resonance is reinforced by its theatrical context. *Machiavel and the
Devil*, the play (now unfortunately lost) that Daborne was in the process of
writing for Henslowe, has a distinctly Marlovian title, evoking characters
from both *The Jew of Malta* and *Faustus*. In 1613, moreover, the same year in
which Daborne corresponded with Henslowe, Daborne's play *A Christian
Turned Turk* was published. The play's title refers to the conversion to Islam
of an English pirate named Ward, who finds himself unexpectedly among
the Ottoman Turks. In scene 7 of the play, Ward is seduced by a beautiful
Turkish woman named Voada. She promises to be his if he will turn Turk,
and Ward's defenses are overcome. This scene, in which Ward renounces
his Christian faith for sexual and worldly ends, has unmistakable Faustian
overtones. The beautiful Voada entices Ward in much the same way that
the phantasmagorical Helen of Troy seduces Faustus. Ward declares to her:
"There is no way so black I would not prove / That leads from heaven to
hell" (161–62).[6] He then celebrates his renouncing of Christianity in exchange for Faustian goods: "Beauty, command, and riches—these are the
three / the world pursues, and these follow me" (194–95). The Faustian resonance of this scene would be reinforced by the fact that in the *English Faust
Book*, Marlowe's principal literary source, Faustus visits the Grand Turk's ha-
rem and sleeps with six of his wives.[7] There is every reason to think, then,
that Faustus's pact with Mephistopheles was very much on Daborne's mind
during his correspondence with Henslowe.

I suggest that the Faustian register invoked by Daborne constitutes a
crude interpretation of Marlowe's play—or, if "interpretation" seems too
grandiose a term, then at least a practical application of it. Daborne implicitly casts himself in the role of Faustus and Henslowe in the role of
Mephastophilis.[8] This allegorical construction would be something of a
rhetorical embarrassment for Daborne, since it is generally inadvisable to
compare someone to the Devil when you're begging him for money. The
Faustian register emerges, therefore, not as a strategic intent but as an almost unavoidable structural necessity of the situation in which Daborne
finds himself.

An older tradition of scholarship, beginning with F. G. Fleay in 1890, saw in Henslowe the perfect image of Daborne's diabolical insinuations. Fleay's Henslowe was an illiterate philistine who exerted a ruinous financial grip on the acting companies under his command.[9] More recent scholarship has challenged this portrait, arguing for a more balanced view of Henslowe as businessman and for a more modest account of his dealings with the companies that performed in his theaters.[10] Rather than endlessly palpate Henslowe's moral fiber, we might do best to accept E. K. Chambers's shrewd judgment of some eighty years ago: "Whether Henslowe was a good man or a bad man seems to me a matter of indifference. He was a capitalist."[11]

We cannot, of course, know how sincere the pathetic, often fawning tone of Daborne's letters to Henslowe really was. As a playwright, Daborne was certainly capable of deploying the rhetoric of tragedy for instrumental purposes. He seems to have taken to heart Mephastophilis's advice to Faustus: "Hold, take this book, peruse it thoroughly: / The iterating of these lines brings gold" (5.156–57).[12] Iterating Marlowe's book had already brought gold to Daborne, contributing both to *A Christian Turned Turk* and, one surmises, to *Machiavel and the Devil*. In the correspondence with Henslowe, Daborne iterates the Faustian text once more, trying to squeeze additional shillings from his ambiguous benefactor. The title of Daborne's play in progress, *Machiavel and the Devil*, may therefore aptly describe both Henslowe's *and* his roles in the correspondence. In any case, Daborne's personal morality play seems to have ended happily. Sometime after 1614 he found preferment, abandoned the stage, and took holy orders, ending his life as Dean of Lismore.[13]

In what follows, I take Daborne's "interpretation" of *Doctor Faustus* seriously. By doing so I certainly do not mean to suggest that Marlowe wrote a *pièce clef* about his own relations with Henslowe. Indeed, there is no evidence that Marlowe had *any* relations with Henslowe, who seems not yet to have been in the practice of negotiating with playwrights or even serving as banker for the players during the period (1588–92) when *Doctor Faustus* was probably written. If W. W. Greg's surmise is correct, Marlowe didn't even write *Doctor Faustus* for the Admiral's Men, the company at the Rose Theater, but rather for Lord Pembroke's Men, who later resold it to the Admiral's Men.[14] There is therefore no reason to think that Marlowe had Henslowe at all in mind when composing his play.

Nevertheless, the first recorded performance of *Doctor Faustus*, in 1594, took place at Henslowe's Rose Theater. And Henslowe also fronted money for the 1602 "adicyons" to the play, by Bird and Rowley, that probably appear in the B-text.[15] More intriguing still is the fact that a list of costumes and stage properties among Henslowe's papers includes items, some of which are certainly, others possibly, meant for Marlowe's play: to wit, a "dragon in Fostes" a "sittie of Rome" a "Hell mought," and a "robe for to goo invisibell."[16] What interests me about this list is that it shows Henslowe as financial middleman (or more likely the Lord Admiral's Men directly) providing the very same things for the production of *Faustus* that, within the fiction of the play, Mephastophilis provides for the character Faustus: a dragon to pull Faustus's chariot through the sky,[17] invisible gowns, and so forth.[18] That is to say, a combination of Marlowe's play text and the material necessities of theatrical production somehow induct the source of theatrical capital into a Mephistophelean role. One could reverse this (and I intend to) to argue that Marlowe's Mephastophilis should be understood in the first instance as a purveyor of special effects. Mephastophilis, in other words, provides exactly those aspects of drama that do *not* flow from the pen of the playwright: the visual and spectacular apparatuses (including the stage itself) that Aristotle dismissed as *opsis* and that by the early modern period are the specific contribution of theatrical capital, whether furnished directly by an impresario such as Henslowe or by a joint stock company such as the Lord Admiral's Men. Indeed, "Henslowe" functions in my argument solely as a personification allegory—a kind of Vice figure in an economic morality play. What is at stake here is the playwright's relation to theatrical capital, not the specific form (individual or corporate) that the capital assumes.[19]

The pairing of Faustus and Mephastophilis establishes a primordial division and, at the same time, a primordial alienation of theatrical labor. Faustus's contractual dependence upon Mephastophilis, I would argue, reflects Marlowe's economic separation from the material apparatuses of theatrical production. Although Marlowe would not have signed the kind of contract that Daborne signed with Henslowe, his labor as playwright would operate under the same kind of structural embarrassment, an embarrassment at once financial and artistic. Simply put, a play text could not achieve either dramatic or economic realization except within a theatrical apparatus over which Marlowe as playwright could exert little or no control. Marlowe's learning, like Faustus's, is ineffectual without those forces of production that only capital could provide.

Such an interpretation places me, I recognize, within a tradition of biographical readings of *Doctor Faustus* that stretches back at least as far as Hazlett.[20] The kind of biography I submit, however, is of a rather abstract variety, since it battens not on the peculiarities of Marlowe's life but rather on a structural separation under which most early modern playwrights labored. What I propose is less autobiography than an extension of the play's well-known metatheatrical dimension to include the material conditions of its production. Nevertheless, such a reading will likely seem reductive. Can Faustus's metaphysical yearnings be reduced to Marlowe's wish to be adequately reimbursed for his labor? No, but those metaphysical yearnings are clearly haunted by such a wish. In his opening soliloquy, Faustus rejects the study of law because "This study fits a mercenary drudge / Who aims at nothing but external trash! / Too servile and illiberal for me" (1.34–36). But Faustus's rejection of dirty lucre is compromised almost immediately. In scene 5 of the A-text, before Faustus even signs a contract with Mephastophilis, the good and evil angels descend in the first of several battles for Faustus's soul. That battle ends when the evil angel admonishes Faustus to "think of honor and of wealth" (5. 21). "Of wealth!" (5.22), replies Faustus, and steels himself for the signing of the contract.

Even the play's moments of high tragic seriousness—and these are at best intermittent—are shadowed by the comic subplots, which invariably reduce spiritual matters to questions of cash flow. Take for instance the following exchange between Wagner and the clown in scene 4, the one immediately preceding the contract-signing scene:

WAGNER: Tell me, sirra, hast thou any comings in?
CLOWN: Ay, and goings out too; you may see else.
WAGNER: Alas poor slave, see how poverty jesteth in his nakedness! The villain is bare, and out of service, and so hungry, that I know he would give his soul to the devil for a shoulder of mutton, though it were blood raw.
CLOWN: How, my soul to the devil for shoulder of mutton though 'twere blood raw? Not so good friend; by'r lady, I had need have it well roasted, and good sauce to it, if I pay so dear. (4.4-12)

In the subplot, souls are placed on sale in response to physical hunger and financial indigence rather than, as in Faustus's case, grand but ill-defined aspirations to knowledge and power. I suspect that the clown's willingness to sell his soul for a shoulder of roasted mutton is meant to recall Esau's sale of his birthright to Jacob for a mess of pottage. In any case, this exchange merely renders explicit what Faustus's contract with Mephastophilis makes implicit: the reduction of soul to a commodity by means of its exchange for other material goods.[21] The materialization of soul is manifested by the ambiguous adjective "roasted" in the clown's phrase "I had need have it well roasted," which may modify either "mutton" or "soul." In its carnivalesque parody of Faustus's contract with Mephastophilis, this clownish exchange materially reduces it in a way that is also, simultaneously, a proto-Marxist interpretation of it.

In the contract-writing scene itself, Faustus puzzles over the commodification of soul in a more abstruse, metaphysical fashion. Two questions concern him. The first, posed to Mephastophilis, is: "what good will my soul do thy Lord?" (5. 39). In other words, what is the use value of my soul? Why does Lucifer wish to purchase it in the first place? The second question, posed by Faustus to himself on the verge of signing the contract, is: "Why should'st thou not [sell it]? Is not thy soul thine own?" (5.68). In order to become a commodity, soul must not only supply a use value to the purchaser but it must be alienable by the seller. It must, that is, be a form of property. In declaring ownership of his soul, and thereby the right to alienate it, Faustus expresses a primitive form of what C. B. Macpherson calls "possessive individualism."²² For Macpherson, such individualism originates in the capitalist wage contract, and the notion that one enjoys ownership in oneself is formulated only when that self becomes alienable through the sale of one's labor power. Faustus, of course, is not a wage laborer. And one would be tempted to argue that he does not have the right to sell his soul, since it is not his possession but rather a gift from God. Nevertheless, he appears to succeed in selling it, so we must assume that he does in some sense own it after all.

Faustus is not a wage laborer, but this cannot always be said with the same certainty of a playwright. Robert Daborne's contract with Henslowe for the writing of *Machiavel and the Devil* exchanges a certain amount of Daborne's intellectual labor—or rather, the material product of that labor—for a certain amount of money. This is not, to be sure, the same as the capitalist wage contract. Daborne is more akin to a late feudal petty producer than to a capitalist worker. And yet he is hardly an independent artisan; his contract with Henslowe is conditioned by his radical dependence on theatrical capital as the only means of realizing his intellectual labor, both artistically and economically. Daborne's dependence on Henslowe doesn't anticipate industrial capitalism (despite its superficial resemblance in some respects to piecework) so much as it reflects the structural subordination of petty production to merchant's capital in the late feudal and transitional economies. Marlowe no doubt sold his play directly to some company of players, but this act relies no less than Daborne's on alienating the product of his intellectual labor—an obscure process that Marlowe may be attempting to grasp poetically through Faustus's notorious contract with

Mephastophilis. It is telling that immediately after signing the contract with his blood, Faustus is given "crowns and rich apparel" (5.82.S.D.) by some subordinate devils. He is rewarded, in other words, with stage properties.

What I am arguing—to put the matter bluntly—is that *Doctor Faustus* constructs an implicit but carefully weighed parallel between Faustus's selling of his soul and Marlowe's selling of his play. This parallel may seem less extravagant if we keep in mind that similar if more general connections were frequently drawn from the opposite side. Thus in *The Magnificent Entertainment* (1603), Thomas Dekker writes that "the Soule that should give life, and a tongue" to a play is exhaled "out of Writer's Pens," while the stage and its properties are merely "the limnes of it."[23] In the introduction to *Hymenaei*, Ben Jonson invidiously compares the play text to immortal soul and Inigo Jones's stage machinery to ephemeral body.[24] I offer such expressions as a counterweight to the inevitable objection that my reading of *Doctor Faustus* relies on an anachronistic, "post-Romantic" concept of authorship. Many early modern playwrights cranked out their work at an industrial pace, and collaborative authorship was the norm. Indeed, there is some evidence that Marlowe worked with a collaborator on *Doctor Faustus*. Moreover, the penning of Marlowe's play is not an isolated, sublime event but a link in the chain of iterative production that leads from the German Faustbook to its English translation to Marlowe's play text to the performances of that text by various companies. Under such conditions, is not an equation between the commodified play text and the playwright's "soul" somewhat melodramatic?

No doubt many playwrights accommodated themselves comfortably to the pace and the division of labor that characterized early modern play production—most notably the exorbitantly prolific Thomas Heywood. But even Heywood, who boasted of writing or contributing to 220 plays, was also given to expressions of pride and proprietary interest in his work.[25] We may legitimately read comparisons between the play text and "soul" on the part of writers such as Dekker and Jonson as anxiously expressing a contradiction between the feudal artisan's pride in workmanship and an increasingly industrial regime, and, at the same time, an attempt to discriminate between intellectual or artistic labor and more vulgar, manual sorts. In any case, Marlowe's conspicuously sparse output, even given his short career, may suggest a proportionately large psychic investment in his plays.[26] I argue, therefore, playing on Joseph Loewenstein's suggestive phrase, that *Doctor Faustus* is in part an exploration of "dispossessive authorship."[27]

If *Doctor Faustus* reflects on the relation between Marlowe's poetic activity and the alienating institutions of theater, it does so largely through its repeated emphasis on the relative powerlessness of language relative to Mephastophilis's special effects. This is a lesson that Faustus learns the hard way. He begins the play convinced of the efficacy of magical language. After he conjures up the devil in scene 3, he declares: "I see there's virtue in my heavenly words!" (3.28). Earlier still, he tells Cornelius and Valdes that "your words have won me" to practice magic (1.101). Faustus's illusions about the power of language reach their highest pitch when he succeeds in summoning Mephastophilis himself, at which point Faustus declares himself "conjurer laureate" (3.33). But then Mephastophilis bursts his balloon by declaring that "I came now hither of mine own accord." "Did not my conjuring speeches raise thee? Speak!," demands Faustus (3.45–46). And he then learns the deflating news that Mephastophilis came not compelled by the power of Faustus's spells but simply because he spotted a vulnerable soul ripe for the picking. The theme of linguistic impotence is repeated again in scene 7, where Faustus and Mephistopheles make themselves invisible in order to play tricks on the Pope. When some outraged friars chant the *Maledicat* in order to banish these spirits, it only incites Faustus and Mephastophilis to give them a drubbing.

It seems to me that the play's repeated insistence on the powerlessness of language offers a pointed commentary on Marlowe's position as playwright. In scene 5, Mephastophilis gives Faustus a book and advises him: "The iterating of these lines brings gold" (5.157). For Marlowe, too, the iterating of these lines—that is, of the play text of *Doctor Faustus*—brings gold. But this is not an iterating that Marlowe himself can effect. The iteration must be made by paid actors, on a stage in a playhouse, with the appropriate costumes and other stage properties that only theatrical capital can provide. Just as Faustus's words are impotent unless supplemented by Mephastophilis's special effects, so Marlowe's words generate revenues only within a theatrical apparatus that Marlowe himself does not control. In light of this, I must revise my earlier assertion that the play text "inducts" theatrical capital into the Mephistophelean position. This would ascribe a magical efficacy to Marlowe's words. The play text of *Doctor Faustus* can no more "induct" capital than Faustus himself can conjure Mephastophilis. Capital approaches the play for the same reason that Mephastophilis approaches Faustus: because it sees a profitable opportunity there.

Nevertheless, the power relations both within the fiction of the play and within the reality of the playhouse are more balanced than this. Having won his soul, Mephastophilis finds himself subjected to Faustus's every whim for the next twenty-four years. And while the conjuring of an Alexander the Great or a Helen of Troy has a certain grave majesty, crossing the globe to fetch grapes for the Duke of Anholt's wife does not. Capital's profit motive likewise subjects it to a kind of quotidian drudgery—the furnishing of garments and stage properties—to which Marlowe need not descend.

Before concluding this section, I want to make a few general remarks about economic alienation and its relation to *Doctor Faustus*. The concept of economic alienation is elaborated largely in Karl Marx's early, Feuerbachian works—particularly the 1844 Manuscripts—where it is associated almost exclusively with capitalism. But for Marx, all historical modes of production involve the appropriation of an economic surplus from the direct producers and hence the alienation of labor or its products—although the modes and intensities of this alienation are historically variable, and the range of meanings associated with the word allow it to cover phenomena as disparate as the sale of his or her product by an independent, late feudal artisan and the forms of repetitive, wearisome, and overtly "alienating" labor introduced by the capitalist factory. The word *alienation* tends to take on psychological and even spiritual resonances that are perfectly appropriate as long as one keeps in mind that these are grounded in, and are the effect of, economic structures of surplus extraction based on class domination.

When I speak of the *alienation* of the playwright's labor, I too mean primarily economic alienation. Once the playwright sells his play, particularly in the era before copyright, it is no longer in any sense his, beyond the notoriety that may arise from having his name associated with it.[28] In this sense a play is like any other commodity. But plays are unlike other commodities in that they offer a particularly spectacular illustration of what this alienation entails. To see one's work repeatedly filling a large amphitheater with paying customers must have offered the early modern playwright a stark and unmistakable lesson in the fact that the profits produced by his labor were being appropriated elsewhere.[29] For a popular favorite such as Marlowe, the sight would likely have been gratifying and galling at once. But this economic alienation has an aesthetic dimension as well, since with the sale of a play went any right to influence the manner in which the play text was cut, altered, improvised upon, or staged. A playwright-shareholder-actor such as Shakespeare not only assured himself a percentage of the profits from his authorial labors but no doubt also had a greater say in its artistic realization than did Marlowe. Only a distinct minority of early modern playwrights were also shareholders in companies, however. For Marlowe, a play once sold would have been as irretrievable as Faustus's lost soul.

II

The kind of alienation I have been discussing thus far is something that happens to labor or production. Really, two interrelated species are at play. One is endemic to commodification as such: when a producer sells his product, he has alienated it to another, and no longer controls or enjoys it. The other, enabled but by no means reducible to commodification, is the separation of the worker from his or her means of production, a situation that introduces alienation into the very act of making itself and moreover distinguishes capitalism from prior modes of economic production. In both cases, though, alienation pertains to production—something that complicates the parallel I have been drawing between Marlowe and Faustus. And this is because Marlowe as playwright is a producer or maker, while Faustus, as a character in a tragedy, is someone who acts rather than makes. It is with Faustus's actions that the tragedy is concerned. But this apparent discrepancy is blunted from both directions. A play is a product, to be sure, but creating one is in some sense an act as well. Certainly it was so in the eyes of the law: the early modern playwright could be prosecuted for blasphemy against God or monarch. Conversely, Faustus's one real act in the play involves selling or commodification. *Doctor Faustus* creates a murky interzone where production and action converge, and this allows economic alienation to become a kind of controlling paradigm for action as well.

If one were to strip away its supernatural accoutrements, the play's action could be summarized as follows: "A man signs a contract to exchange goods for services." In order to account for a tragic dimension, we might add: "Subsequent to signing the contract, the man discovers that its terms are disadvantageous, but it is too late to change them. He considers breaking the contract but cannot bring himself to do so." It might be objected, of course, that the play's interest consists entirely in the supernatural accoutrements I have omitted: the fact that the "goods" in question are Faustus's immortal soul, and that the "services" provided—by the Devil, no less—consist of forbidden, necromantic arts. The fact remains, however, that the play's only real *act* is the signing of a contract—something we cannot imagine forming the center of a classical tragedy. Despite its medieval origins, this device imparts an irreducibly modern dimension to Faustus's story. Moreover, the signing of the contract occurs shortly after the play's beginning. What remains, then, is simply the expiration of the contract's term, which will occur regardless of what Faustus does or does not do during the interval. In this regard the play's *mythos* or plot does not encompass a unified action in the Aristotelian sense. Following the signing of the contract, the various scenes are episodic and mostly without consequence. One could easily switch their order with no real effect on the whole. Having signed the contract, Faustus becomes a spectator rather than an agent. One of the first things he views in this capacity is a pageant of the seven deadly sins, but one could argue that the entire play becomes a kind of pageant at this point, its disconnected episodes serving to fill the time between the signing of the contract and its consumption. In a sense, the irrevocability of the contract appears to alienate Faustus from his own capacity to act, thereby relegating himself to the position of audience to himself.

What dislocates a classical conception of the act in this play, however, is not so much the contract as the magical forces it unleashes. Once Faustus strikes his bargain with Mephastophilis, he has at his disposal a massive supernatural mechanism for the fulfillment of his every whim. From this point on, Faustus need not, strictly speaking, *do* anything. Rather, he needs only voice his wishes to Mephastophilis, who employs a vast, invisible network of spirits to serve him. What magic does is replace the act with the speech act, instantly accomplishing every verbal imperative.[30] Faustus soon discovers, however, that removing all effort or labor in the pursuit of one's ends renders those ends ultimately unsatisfying, with the result that his desire grows unanchored and aimless—another reason for the merely episodic nature of the plot. The play's aesthetics of disappointment (of which, more later) owes more than a little to the creeping sense of boredom that begins to infect Faustus's pointless adventures, none of which either costs him anything or accomplishes anything of importance. In becoming omnipotent, Faustus ironically finds himself trapped in complete passivity. Most of what happens in the play is powered by the infernal machine that only occasionally puts in a direct appearance. Faustus does no more than push its buttons. Another way of putting this is to say that Faustus has been converted from agent into *consumer*, and that this constitutes another aspect of the play's precocious modernity. Even Helen of Troy, ultimate prize of heroic effort and struggle, is simply delivered to Faustus's doorstep as if he had ordered her on Amazon.com.

Of course, the infernal mechanism is not the only one at work in the play. There is also the divine apparatus of salvation that presents itself through the Old Man, the Good Angel, and Faustus's irregular bouts of conscience. Here again no *action* is required; Protestantism had taken care of this by denying that one's deeds could contribute anything to being redeemed from sin. The question is only whether Faustus's infected will (assuming this to be a Lutheran world) will allow him to accept God's grace through faith.[31] If there is any drama to the play, it consists of Faustus's repeated, tortured, but ultimately failed attempts to turn toward God and renounce his pact with Mephastophilis. While the magical plot of the play grants Faustus an ultimately unsatisfying form of omnipotence, the spiritual plot finds him in a state of impotence—or rather, in a state of *akrasia*, since the problem is not that Faustus cannot accomplish his will to be saved but rather the fact that he cannot ultimately even will it. And of course even the Lutheran drama of faith is potentially undercut by the fact that this may be a Calvinist world in which Faustus's spiritual fate is doubly predestined, and what thus appears to be a genuine if failed struggle to be saved is merely the sign of his reprobate status.[32] It is under Calvinist presuppositions that the play's pageant-like quality assumes its fullest justification, since, deprived of salvific actions, the individual soul is left only with trying to decipher the ambiguous *signs* of salvation. In which case the Good Angel and Old Man would be nothing more than cruel jokes, proffering an empty form of hope. Faustus's status as theatrical spectator would thus accord with his spiritual status as mere spectator to his own salvation (or lack of it). Even the signing of the contract, his sole defining act, would be converted into just one more sign, which means that the play would be deprived of any meaningful action whatsoever.

Protestantism, we might say, confronts the individual with a spiritual mechanism from which he is fundamentally alienated, since he cannot set it into motion by his own efforts. It thus offers a pointed parallel to Marlowe's situation as playwright, faced with a theatrical mechanism that he likewise cannot operate or control. The genius of Marlowe's play, I would argue, consists largely of bringing these forms of material and spiritual alienation—Capital and Protestantism—into contact with each other. *Doctor Faustus* is a play in which action requires an immense apparatus, the capabilities of which far exceed those of any individual, and thus promise to extend human possibility beyond past limits. But at the same time, this mechanism cannot ultimately be controlled by the individual. Its actions are therefore its own, and we are (at best) along for the ride. Faustus's tragic error is to convince himself, for a time, that he *can* control it.

Is the story of Faustus that of a single act with overwhelming consequences, or of a world in which individual action has no consequences whatever? And is the tragedy of Faustus therefore that of the emptying out of action? Significantly, the play leaves this conundrum unresolved. But it is worth remarking that theater is the perfect medium for exploring it. Because real bodies actually move and speak and do things within it, theater offers a uniquely vivid depiction of the human act. But because these "actions" are parts of a fictional story, nothing really happens outside of that fiction. Theater, in other words, is a place where the most significant actions occur and one in which no actions occur. Here we might recall J. L. Austin's observation that theater neutralizes any performative speech act that takes place within it (actors who say "I do" in a play are not thereby really married—though their fictional characters really are).[33] Theater is in this sense the inverse of magic, which absolutizes the performative. But it is also in this sense the counterpart to Protestantism, which neutralizes the magical performatives of Catholicism (illustrated in Marlowe's play when Faustus proves invulnerable to the papal *Maledicat*). *Doctor Faustus* makes us aware of both of these facts.

Of course, Austin's claim that theater neutralizes the performative was less obvious in the early modern period than it would later become. The stories of an actual devil conjured by Faustus's invocations seem to attribute a perlocutionary force to the speech of players, as does the Act to Restrain the Abuses of Players (1606), which forbade them to "iestingly, and profanely speake, or use the holy Name of God, or of Christe Iesus."[34] If one could not really be married, one could at least really blaspheme within the context of a play. Or so the pious worried, though I find it highly doubtful than Marlowe shared these concerns. For him, I think, the theater is an apparatus for neutralizing the force of the divine performative in a transgressive fashion. The thrill of blaspheming onstage is for Marlowe precisely the fact that nothing happens as a result of it. His practice raises the question: did the authors of the Act Restraining the Abuse of Players pass it because they feared that the perlocutionary force of swearing on stage would invoke the wrath of God? Or did they rather fear that it wouldn't, and that this fact would erode the majesty of God's name? Marlowe, I believe, attempts to realize both forms of anxiety. Faustus's frightful invocations and damnation were doubtless intended to raise the hairs on the necks of the audience, but I think also, ultimately, to compromise belief. On most occasions, the actor playing Faustus could summon only other actors, not devils.

To stage the failure of the performative, however, requires an actual performance. No one worried that unholy incantations uttered by a fictional character in a book could conjure a demon in real life. An actor would have to actually say the words. Which means that, once again, only the theater as institution, not Marlowe as writer, can produce the effect. Marlowe can latch onto it and thematize it, render it powerfully visible, but he cannot himself produce it. Marlowe can achieve great things with theater but he re-mains economically and aesthetically both dependent upon it and alienated from it. Which returns us—and him—to our opening conundrum. If one can act only by way of a mechanism, then perhaps only mechanisms can truly act. This is one of the matters that *Doctor Faustus* darkly meditates.

III

One way to think of alienation is as an emptying or hollowing out. The alienated subject is deprived of some capacity or attribute or product that would otherwise constitute part of his being and is thus afflicted with lack. I have thus far considered both economic alienation and alienation from the capacity to act: two species that *Doctor Faustus* juxtaposes. Alienation from the capacity to act, I have argued, places the subject in the position of spectator. In a sense, theater is founded on alienation insofar as it presents a spectacle with which the spectator cannot, by definition, engage in any prac-tical way. The Brechtian *Verfremdungseffekt* in some sense merely reminds the spectator of an existing alienation about which he has forgotten.

By definition, alienation would seem to pertain only to subjects. And yet it can attach to objects as well. The alienated object, which is no longer available for practical interaction, can itself come to seem hollowed out or empty as it recedes into the state of mere visual datum. In the famous story of the Greek painter Zeuxis, he paints grapes so realistic that birds come to peck at them. The grapes, as aesthetic objects, prove "empty" in a practical sense when the birds make the mistake of trying to consume them. But the "emptiness" of the grapes (which, as images, are perfectly self-sufficient) merely projects the emptiness—the hunger—of the birds as subjects.[35] This story is, I think, directly relevant to the episode in *Doctor Faustus* in which Mephastophilis fetches grapes for the Duke of Anholt's wife. Within the fic-tion of the tale, the grapes are real, and the Duke of Anholt's wife eats them with satisfaction. The audience, by contrast, is alienated from the grapes. They may (or may not) look tempting, but we are unable even to attempt to eat them. Fake grapes would serve perfectly well for purposes of staging. These grapes serve as a synecdoche for theater as such and its capacities for both satisfaction and disappointment. One can imagine an audience mem-ber actually reminded by this scene that he or she is hungry—reminded, that is, of the subjective emptiness that constitutes the "objective" emptiness of the grapes onstage. This is a rather primitive—indeed, animal—form of alienation, admittedly. The episode of Zeuxis is embedded in the story of his painting competition with Parrhasius. When the birds peck at his painted grapes, Zeuxis declares that he has won the competition. Then Parrhasius invites Zeuxis to part the curtains covering his painting, and when Zeuxis attempts to do so he discovers that the curtains are painted—*are* the painting. The painted curtains produce both disappointment and wonder—disappointment that they are not really curtains and cannot therefore be opened, and wonder at the mastery that produces such a satisfying illusion. This is a human as opposed to animal form of alienation. Let us take the curtain in this story as the curtain of theater (admittedly, not yet in use during Marlowe's day), which can never be parted since the theatrical or aesthetic object can never be encountered directly.

In *Doctor Faustus*, alienation assumes the form of emptiness. For the aesthetic realm, this is an emptiness of the object that elicits a corresponding emptiness of the subject and thereby produces disappointment. In the theological and ethical realms, emptiness is evil. Through its pursuit of alienation, *Doctor Faustus* is led into the land of emptiness, which it calls home. Its land of milk and honey is the desert.

Marlowe's strategy in *Doctor Faustus* is to take the disappointment endemic to theater and inject it into the tragic plot. We have already encountered this disappointment with respect to language: Faustus's "magical" incantations prove to be utterly powerless, except in the incidental sense of alerting Mephastophilis to a potential victim. More striking still, however, is the fact that language's other in the play—the special effects Mephastophilis produces—are in the end no more impressive. As Harry Levin put it: "We ought to feel some incongruity between the . . . seemingly unlimited possibilities envisioned by Faustus' speeches and their all too concretely vulgar realization in the stage business."[36] In the end, the play's spectacular devices are rather minor, compared both with the visionary episodes of the *English Faust Book* and with such contemporary magician plays as Robert Greene's *Friar Bacon and Friar Bungay* (another Henslowe production). The A-text is especially restrained in this regard. Unlike the B-text, it explicitly requires neither a "robe for to goo invisibell," nor a hell mouth, nor a descending throne of God, nor even an elevated space from which characters can watch the action from above. The extreme theatrical austerity of the A-text was one of the grounds that led W. W. Greg to regard it as an abbreviated version produced by a touring company, which would have to make do without the more sumptuous resources of a London playhouse.[37] I think, in any case, that the play's paltriness of theatrical effect is thematically congruent with its repeated failure of language—not so much its contradiction as its complement and indeed its product, since, as Levin implies, what is in itself a mere spareness comes to seem a form of poverty only by contrast with the vast spaces opened up by Faustus's language. Marlowe's mighty line operates as a kind of inverted telescope, reducing and denigrating the material resources of theater by contrast. If Marlowe reflects sardonically on the ineffectual nature of verse—the play text's radical dependence on theatrical capital—he also reveals his discontent with the artistic means that his Faustian bargain procures, since the material apparatuses of theater, however necessary to realizing his labor economically, inevitably fall short of realizing it artistically.[38] *Doctor Faustus* divides theater into two components, each of which comes to seem insufficient when reflected back by its other. Moreover, this insufficiency cannot be made good by adding the two halves together, since each reveals a lack of that which its other cannot supply. The result is what one might call an aesthetics of disappointment in which promises are never quite kept, desires never quite fulfilled.

The question of whether dramatic spectacle is satisfying or disappointing necessarily engages the question of the degree to which it strikes the spectator as real, and this is something that Marlowe likewise explores. Faustus's magical effects repeatedly trouble the boundaries between the corporeal and the incorporeal. When asked by the Emperor to conjure up Alexander the Great and his paramour, Faustus demurs: "It is not in my ability to present before your eyes the true substantial bodies of those two deceased princes which long since are consumed to dust" (9.42–44). And yet, having examined the neck of Alexander's mistress for a mole, the Emperor insists: "Sure, these are no spirits, but the true substantial bodies of those two deceased princes" (9.66–67).[39] (Unlike the Emperor, however, the theatrical audience is unable to touch the image that remains at an irreducible distance.) Conversely, the horse that Faustus sells to the horse-courser seems real enough until the horse-courser rides it into the water and it melts away. These corporeal equivocations emerge most crucially in the first clause of Faustus's contract with the devil: "*First, that Faustus may be a spirit in form and substance*" (5.96). The clause would seem to stipulate that Faustus henceforth will no longer possess a human body but a spiritual, immaterial one—that he will, for instance, be able to appear and disappear at will, like Mephastophilis, or transport himself across the globe. And yet Faustus never demonstrates such a spiritual body. Thus he must, for instance, be carted to Rome in a chariot drawn by dragons. And in scene 12, Mephastophilis laments: "His faith is great, I cannot touch his soul, / But what I may afflict his body with, / I will attempt—which is but little worth" (12.69–71). Mephastophilis here seems to believe that Faustus does possess a body. Per-

haps he intends to afflict Faustus's spiritual body, but I think he rather inten-
sifies the nagging doubts about whether Faustus is still embodied or not. The
question is answered no more certainly of him than of Alexander the Great.

Doctor Faustus imagines two different but complementary solutions to
theater's constitutive condition of poverty or lack. The first, which I'll call
"the quality of hey ding ding," emerges in a speech of the horse-courser,
when he boasts of the horse he has purchased from Faustus for forty dol-
lars: "Well sir. Now am I made man for ever: I'll not leave my horse for
forty! If he had but the quality of hey ding ding, hey ding ding, I'd make
a brave living on him! He has a buttock as slick as an eel" (10.17–20). The
"quality of hey ding ding" seems to be the ability to procreate or multiply. If
the horse were a stallion rather than a gelding, muses the horse-courser, he
could make a fortune putting him out to stud. The theme of procreation re-
appears in the Duke of Anholt's "great-bellied" wife (11.5) and, more parodi-
cally, in the phallic stag's antlers stuck on the head of the abusive knight. It
appears as well in contemporary anecdotes about extra, unaccountable devils appearing in productions of *Doctor Faustus* and terrifying both actors and
audience.[40] In the case of the horse-courser, however, this magical, procre-
ative power is merely a wish. Not only does his horse lack the phallus, but
when the horse-courser rides him into the water he dissolves completely,
turning quite literally into liquid assets. The dream of self-multiplication
gives way to the reality of emptiness or sterility.

In the absence of a magical supplement that might make up for theater's
internal lack, *Doctor Faustus* adopts a radically different strategy toward this
lack by turning it into a positive force. This emerges indirectly in scene 3,
where Faustus first meets Mephastophilis and where the play's most famous
exchange takes place:

> FAUSTUS: How comes it then that thou art out of hell?
> MEPHASTOPHILIS: Why this is hell, nor am I out of it.
> Think'st that thou that I, who saw the face of God,
> And tasted the eternal joys of Heaven,
> Am not tormented with ten thousand hells
> In being deprived of everlasting bliss!
> O Faustus, leave these frivolous demands,
> Which strike a terror to my fainting soul.
>
> (3.76–83)

The metaphysical horror of Mephastophilis's response resides in the fact
that hell is conceived not as a place of active torment but merely as privation. Having once seen the face of God, Mephastophilis experiences the

everyday world as an unendurable void. But I think that the word "this" in the line "Why this is hell, nor am I out of it" can be taken to refer not only to terrestrial existence in the broadest sense but also more specifically to the stage, the place on which Mephastophilis actually stands as he says these words. Antitheatrical writers often described the stage as a devilish place— "the chapel of Satan," as Anthony Munday put it.[41] Defining the theater as a space in which visionary fullness *cannot* be achieved, Mephastophilis is the play's supremely disappointed spectator, the one for whom every sight is the crushing negation of what he once saw. Here disappointment results from theological, not aesthetic, alienation. And yet his case would be shared, if only by analogy, with the play's original audiences, whose hopes to view the more visionary episodes in the *English Faust Book*—such as Faustus's phantasmagorical, rollercoaster tour through the underworld—would remain unfulfilled. For them, too, "this is hell," or at least as close to its secrets as the playhouse will take them. Similarly, hell is for Marlowe the discrepancy between what the mind of the playwright can conceive and what the stage can afford.

The theme of privation, voiced so plangently by Mephastophilis, is introduced at the very beginning of the scene, as Faustus prepares to conjure.

> FAUSTUS: Now that the gloomy shadow of the earth,
> Longing to view Orion's drizzling look,
> Leaps from th'antarctic world unto the sky,
> And dims the welkin with her pitchy breath:
> Now Faustus, begin thy incantations . . .
>
> (3.1-5)

Night, here conceived as the shadow of the earth, a darkness produced by blocking the sun's radiance, is nature's counterpart to Mephastophilis's field of vision, defined by the absence of God's dazzling face. This parallel establishes Faustus at the center of two symmetrical obstructions. Between Faustus and the sun stands the body of the earth, casting him in physical shadow. And between Faustus and God stands the figure of Mephastophilis, casting him in spiritual shadow. And yet this double darkness is conceived not solely as that which prevents vision but also as that which enables another kind of vision, a crepuscular sight that can emerge only in shade. "Orion's drizzling look," like that of the other stars, shines forth in blackness. And Mephastophilis can appear only in the spiritual darkness created by the blocking off of God. Just as Marlowe's transgressive heroes flourish in a space that obscures or inverts society's dominant values, so Marlowe recasts the theater itself as a camera obscura in which visionary experience

takes the form of the photographic negative, its light reversed into darkness. Building with the very substance of privation, Marlowe constructs in *Doctor Faustus* a theater of night.[42]

IV

Both the material economies of theater and the logic of its own argument place *Doctor Faustus* in the space of the negative, the empty, the void, and thus in what I have called a theater of night. I want now to situate the play within a very brief and partial history of the negative, which will, among other things, open up onto a view of the play's ethical dimension and so approach the crucial problem of good and evil.[43] This will allow us to grasp the play's political dimension, and Marlowe's capacity for action, from a different angle. The foundational figure for any such investigation must of course be Saint Augustine, whose famous attempt to define evil as the privation of good conjoins ethical and ontological lack.[44] According to Augustine, and as further elaborated by Thomas Aquinas, evil is not simply privation as such but one that inhibits the specific nature of a given entity, constraining its *potentia* from realization.[45] Hence, blindness in a human being is an evil, but blindness in a stone is not. In a sense, evil is that which inhibits an entity from *acting* in the manner for which its nature should fit it. Evil corrupts or constrains the good, but it simultaneously depends on the good, since "unless [evil things] exist in good things they do not exist at all."[46] Augustine suggestively compares evil to a disease or wound that afflicts a body but that, when it is cured, does not take up its abode elsewhere but simply ceases to exist.[47]

For Augustine, evil does not entail a regression to absolute nothingness (indeed, he doesn't believe in absolute nothingness), but rather a turn from a higher and fuller form of being that is inherently good to a less substantial one—a turn that then manifests an underlying lack. His conception of evil as privation thus conforms in some respects to the concept of alienation as emptiness I have been pursuing. Here is what he has to say about the fallen angels: "Accordingly, the truest reason for the happiness of good angels is found in their clinging to him who has supreme being. And when we inquire into the reason for the unhappiness of bad angels, we are right in thinking that it is this: that, after turning away from him who has supreme being, they turn wholly to themselves, who do not have supreme being."[48] And having fallen, "they are no longer light in the Lord but darkness in themselves, since they have lost their participation in the eternal light. For evil in itself has no substance; rather, the loss of what is good has received the name evil."[49] What I have been calling the "aesthetics of disappointment" in *Doctor Faustus* is thus closely entwined with the play's ethico-religious dimension. Mephastophilis's loss of the sight of God scoops out the space of nothingness that is both his evil and the inadequacy of theatrical representation. And this nothingness is a state of alienation from the fullness of God.

The same negativity attaches itself to human as well as angelic evil. Augustine insists that there can be "no natural, or if the term is permissible, substantial efficient cause of an evil will."[50] Since evil is a lack of being, nothing that is in being can cause it, and evil thus falls outside of the chain of causes that rule natural things. "It will then be discovered that the evil will derives not from the fact that [man] is a natural creature, but from the fact that he is a natural being created out of nothing."[51] What evil manifests is the originary void or *nihil* that precedes creation, and even this nothingness is not evil in itself but only insofar as it comes to afflict creation.[52]

I find Augustine's thought particularly illuminating for the character of Faustus, who strikes me as unusual among Marlovian hero-villains. Like Marlowe's "mighty line," his protagonists are typically possessed of an unstoppable will, be it for imperial conquest in the case of Tamburlaine, wealth and vengeance in the case of Barabas, persecution and intrigue in the case of Guise, or proscribed love in the case of Edward II. The Marlovian hero is in some conventional sense evil, but he pursues his evil so doggedly—usually to the point of his own destruction—that his actions assume a kind of ethical consistency, even if of a negative sort. Marlowe's protagonists are not "good" in a Christian sense, but they display a Lacanian ethic of "not giving way on one's desire," an ethic that has received further elaboration by figures such as Slavoj Žižek and Alain Badiou. This Lacanian ethic, especially as developed by Badiou, founds ethical consistency on the void (*le vide*), on the element that is *subtracted* from a given conjunction and only made manifest by the ethical act.[53] At their best (or worst), Marlowe's protagonists display an unswerving commitment to evil in which the good finds its inverted reflection, much as Marlovian night is inverted day.

Faustus, however, is unlike his brethren hero-villains. In one sense his act is more daring than any of theirs, since it engages not merely with evil but also with Evil—the Devil himself. And yet Faustus never embraces this evil with any consistency. At the very moment of signing the contract he is not only terrified and afflicted with doubt but also incompletely convinced that the whole business really means anything—that he is seriously and irrevocably signing over his soul. And for the rest of the play he is a mass of indecision, sometimes wanting to repent but finding himself too intimidated or irresolute to do so, and on the other side unwilling to accomplish anything really dastardly or glorious with his powers. Above all he is repeatedly subject to a kind of *fear* that is utterly alien to the Marlovian hero. Faustus simply cannot create anything consistent out of his originary void and hence he remains this void. He begins the play with a powerful but undefined sense of lack and ends it in a state of spiritual paralysis. His evil is privation in the Thomist-Augustinian sense in that it inhibits his *potentia*, prevents him from acting to realize the limits of his being. But it is also Augustinian in suggesting that (for Faustus at least) the full potential of being can be achieved only by clinging to God. Hence Faustus does not provoke a sense of wonder and ambivalent admiration in the viewer but rather a combination of pity and contempt.

To put this problem another way, Faustus cannot forge the negative into anything positive or consistent. He cannot create from the void. In this sense he is not the counterpart of Marlowe as playwright but rather his opposite, since, as we have seen, Marlowe's genius in *Doctor Faustus* is to harness the negative, to convert darkness into vision and lack into substance.

He does this most memorably, perhaps, in Faustus's address to Helen of Troy:

> Was this the face that launch'd a thousand ships
> And burnt the topless towers of Ilium?
> Sweet Helen, make me immortal with a kiss;
> Her lips suck forth my soul, see where it flies!
> Come, Helen, come, give me my soul again;
> Here will I dwell, for heaven lies in those lips,
> And all is dross that is not Helena.
> I will be Paris, and for love of thee
> Instead of Troy shall Wittenberg be sack'd,
> And I will combat with weak Menelaus
> And wear thy colors on my plumed crest;
> Yea, I will wound Achilles in the heel
> And then return to Helen for a kiss.
> O, thou art fairer than the evening air
> Clad in the beauty of a thousand stars;
> Brighter art thou than flaming Jupiter
> When he appeared to hapless Semele,
> More lovely than the monarch of the sky
> In wanton Aretheusa's azured arms,
> And none but thou shall be my paramour.
> (11:81–100)

Faustus's speech to Helen might seem a strange place to seek out the negative, since this is the one moment in which illusion seems utterly satisfying, both to Faustus and (I assume) to the play's audience as well. For a brief space the play's incessant privation gives way to radiant fullness. This is probably also Marlowe's single most famous and frequently quoted passage of verse. At least, the first two lines are. I want to unpack Faustus's initial question slowly, because it opens up onto at least three readings, which point in different (though ultimately reconcilable) directions.

In the first and most obvious reading, Faustus poses what we might crudely call a "rhetorical question." Here, "Was this the face?" means roughly "This was the face!" A less crude way of putting it would be to say that Faustus's utterance is a declarative wrested by wonder into the form of an interrogative. Faced with the splendor of a beauty he dare not yet name or even address directly, Faustus hesitates, and the form his hesitation assumes is a question without any clear purpose or addressee. What is in danger of being "negated" here would then be Faustus himself, overwhelmed as he seems to be by the sight of Helen. Admittedly, this moment of self-loss is rather fleeting, for by the very next line Faustus has summoned up the courage not only to name Helen but to demand a kiss.

Another way of inflecting the question would be to place emphasis on the first word: "*Was* this the face?" Now Faustus's question becomes one of identity, and it asks: "Is this really Helen of Troy? Is the face that sank a thousand ships the same as the face I see before me now?" Use of the past tense, "was," seems to imply possible doubt about the correspondence between what Faustus beholds and the woman about whom Homer wrote. And the question of identity indirectly invokes the myth of the phantom Helen, the eidolon or false image that, according to the poet Stesichorus, was substituted for Helen and taken to Troy. What is in danger of being negated here is the reality of Helen herself.

A third way of inflecting the question would be to emphasize the word "this": "Was *this* the face"? Now the question expresses incredulity, even disappointment. All that fuss over *this* face? Such a reading, I admit, goes against the grain of the speech as a whole, yet it is awkwardly embedded there. And it threatens to drag the aesthetic of disappointment into the one image that might seem to have transcended it. What is in danger of being negated is not so much the reality of Helen as her ineffable singularity, and with it the consummate nature of Faustus's experience.

I want to begin with this third reading. The echo of disappointment that haunts Faustus's question does not, I think, seriously undermine the visionary fullness of this moment. Its purpose, rather, is to recall the play's origi-nary and paradigmatic moment of loss: Mephastophilis's banishment from heaven. The radiant face of Helen offers a sight that both mirrors and com-pensates for the face of God, privation of which proves an endless torment for Mephastophilis. This parallel will seem less strange if we keep in mind the intimations of divinity that surround Helen from the start. Daughter of Zeus (though she is also reported to have an earthly father, Tyndareus), Helen is celebrated as a goddess in Stesichorus's lost *Palinode*, and Herodo-tus records a Helen-cult (a nurse, he writes, even takes a baby to Helen's shrine in order to cure it of ugliness).[54] Even more pertinent is Helen's very first public appearance in literature, in Book III of the *Iliad* when she is spotted walking on the walls of Troy. "Terrible is the likeness of her face to immortal goddesses," sings Homer.[55]

The divinity of Helen's face leads Faustus to hope for eternal life from her: "Sweet Helen, make me immortal with a kiss: / Her lips suck forth my soul, see where it flies! / Come Helen, come, give me my soul again" (83–85). Faustus's wish, though delusional, also has Homeric precedent. In the *Odyssey*, Helen does grant immortality to her husband Menelaus, who, we are told, "will be exempt from death and transferred to the Islands of the Blest as his privilege for being Helen's husband."[56] For Faustus, who knows that death means also the consummation of his contract with Mephastophilis and the loss of his soul, Helen offers a last, desperate bid for a way out. Indeed, Faustus's description of the kiss as sucking forth his soul, and his request for another that would restore it, offers both a swift reminder of the alienation that follows upon his pact with Mephastophilis *and* a comic resolution of it.

At the same time (or just a little later), a very different kind of wish emerges in Faustus's address to Helen: "Brighter art thou than flaming Jupiter / When he appeared to hapless Semele" (96–97). The gender rever-sal in this simile is striking and, as has been persuasively argued, invokes sodomitical themes that run throughout the play.[57] It also, I think, reveals a deep wish on Faustus's part to be annihilated, and moreover through a con-suming sexual conflagration. The image of Helen as Jupiter in his full, flam-ing godhead invokes the terrible aspect of divine beauty noted by Homer. It also looks forward to Faustus's final speech, when the face of God will in-deed be revealed to him, and he will find it unbearable in its anger:

> [A]nd see where God
> Now stretcheth out his arm, and bends his ireful brows!
> Mountains and hills, come, come and fall on me,

> And hide me from the heavy wrath of God.
> No, no?
> Then will I headlong run into the earth:
> Earth, gape! O no, it will not harbor me.
> You stars that reigned at my nativity,
> Whose influence hath allotted death and hell,
> Now draw up Faustus like a foggy mist
> Into the entrails of yon labouring cloud,
> That when you vomit forth into the air
> My limbs may issue from your smoky mouths,
> So that my soul may but ascend to heaven.
>   (13:76–89)

Once more, as in the presence of Helen, the sight of a divine visage prompts in Faustus a desire to be rent apart, to suffer a consummative annihilation that would also, strangely, be a form of violent birth as his limbs emerge from the "laboring cloud." A few lines later, Faustus wishes: "O soul, be changed to little water drops, / And fall into the ocean, ne'er be found. / My God, my God, look not so fierce on me!" (13:110–12). Here Faustus confronts the true face of the ireful Christian God, as opposed to its more pleasant, pagan simulacrum in Helen. And yet this contrast also evokes the consistency of Faustus's desire, which is of a masochistic, self-destructive kind. Faustus finally gets what he has wanted all along; his pact with the Devil was always intended to deliver him to this place. In this sense the play really *is* a comedy, though an infernal one.

But let us return to Helen. The second of our readings construed "Was this the face?" as a question of identity, one alluding indirectly to the myth of the phantom Helen that was given to the Trojans in place of the true Helen. By asking "was this the face that sank a thousand ships[?]," Faustus may be asking whether he sees the actual Helen or an eidolon. Is he, like Paris, being fobbed off with a simulacrum? His puzzlement is not, in certain respects, very different from that of the Duke of Vanholt when he viewed Alexander the Great and wondered whether he was seeing a spirit or a true body. And yet Helen raises the question of appearance and reality with heightened urgency and depth.

The story of the phantom Helen is, according to Plato, first told by Stesichorus in his now-lost *Palinode*. It is elaborated by Euripides in his *Helen*, which combines Stesichorus's tale of the eidolon with Herodotus's claim that Helen was whisked off to Egypt. As Socrates relates in the *Phaedrus* (243a-b), Stesichorus was stricken blind for writing a poem that blasphemed against Helen but had his sight restored when he composed a palinode claiming that the real Helen was blameless, and that the Helen of whom Homer sang was merely a phantom given to Paris in her place. The effect of this tale is to resolve the ambiguities that surround Helen, dividing her neatly into a loyal and virtuous wife and a lustful, deceitful simulacrum— into, that is, morally and ontologically "full" and "empty" Helens.

For Marlowe, and for Faustus as well, the problem of the phantom Helen is at one level the problem of classical culture as such, which appears both as a source of beauteous splendor and as dangerous, pagan delusion. To some degree, Faustus is charmed less by Helen than he is by Homer, and he sees in her physical beauty the power of the Greek ideal. (In this sense, Helen is a figure of the Renaissance itself in *Doctor Faustus*'s Reformation world.) At the same time, we know that what Mephastophilis has conjured up is probably not Helen at all but a demon in disguise.[58] The distinction between the true and phantom Helens is thus the difference between classical culture taken on its own terms and that same culture as condemned by Christianity. Helen's eidolon invokes Helen as *idol*, the bugbear of Reformed theology.

The contradiction between being and seeming raised by the tale of the phantom Helen provoked interest from Greek philosophers as well as poets. In the *Republic* (586b–c), Plato compares the way that the ignorant masses fight over false pleasures with the way that the Greeks and Trojans fought over the phantom Helen. In both cases, what is pursued is a mere eidolon or empty image. Plato thus associates Helen with the seductive power of mimesis and with a kind of ontological vacuity. People who pursue false pleasure, Socrates asserts, "aren't filled with that which really is" (586a).[59] The sophist Gorgias, who wrote a celebrated encomium to Helen, also composed a short tract titled "On Not Being" (*Peri tou me ontos*).[60] Conversely, in *his* encomium on Helen, Isocrates writes that the real Helen "possessed the greatest share of beauty [*kallos*] which of things that exist [*ta onta*] is the most venerated, most honored, and most godly."[61] Euripides's *Helen* selfconsciously places its heroine "at the center of philosophical debates on Being and Seeming, Meaning and Being (*onoma/soma, onoma/pragma, ta onta/dokesis*, etc.) which were then current when the play was produced."[62] In her prologue, Helen declares that Paris "thinks he holds me now / But holds a vanity [*kenen*, 'emptiness']" (35–36), which is nothing more than a "name" [*onoma*] (43).[63] The phantom Helen thus returns us to the ontological dilemma of the *on kai me on*, being and not-being, that occupied Faustus in his opening monologue.[64] As phantom (or rather, if she is phantom), Helen represents pure seeming without being, and she is therefore the privileged embodiment of the void, the negative, privation, that we have been exploring in this section. In the Augustinian sense (and in a Platonic sense as well), the eidolon is "evil," which is to say, nonbeing. In cleaving unto her, Faustus abandons the fullness of God for an emptiness.

And yet these theological and moral misgivings are momentarily eclipsed by the dazzling spectacle that is Helen. Even her ontological emptiness presents itself in a uniquely satisfying mode. Elsewhere in the play, the vacuity of dramatic spectacle provokes disappointment. Objects are *perceived as* empty; everything that Mephastophilis conjures up has the feel of a mere prank to it. But here, the sheer force of Marlovian verse, combined with the accumulated aura of Helen's name, produces an aesthetic fullness. We thus arrive at a final set of associations annexed to the figure of Helen: the spell cast by her beauty is akin to that produced by the work of art. It is not by accident that Gorgias employs his *Encomium on Helen* to reflect on the power of art, and especially of poetry.[65] For Helen has, since Homer, been associated with aesthetic production. When we first see her in the *Iliad*, she is weaving a tapestry depicting the Trojan War, and thereby stands as a double for Homer. And in the *Odyssey*, she "tests" the Trojan horse by calling out the name of each Greek hero in the voice of his wife, thus displaying her uncanny powers of imitation. The eidolon or phantom Helen is pure, attractive mimesis without substance, and is in this respect the very embodiment of the work of art.

We may by now seem to have strayed far from the social concerns with which this chapter began. To the contrary: *Doctor Faustus*'s articulation of the aesthetic is intimately if at times antagonistically entwined with its social content. For what Helen of Troy conjures up is what Theodor Adorno calls the "semblance character" of art, and which is of a piece with its capacity for social protest. In his *Aesthetic Theory*, Adorno defines the difference between natural beauty and art beauty thus: "Nature is beautiful in that it appears to say more than it is. To wrest this more from that more's contingency, to gain control of its semblance, to determine it as semblance as well as to negate it as unreal: This is the idea of art. This artifactual more does not in itself guarantee the metaphysical substance of art. That substance could be totally null, and still the artworks could posit a more as what appears."[66] For Adorno, the ontological nullity of art's semblance character is fundamental to its capacity for denunciation: were the artwork to invest its *promesse du bonheur* with a substantial existence, it would reconcile itself with a world marked by domination, and thus lose its utopian character. Likewise, if it were to gesture toward some purely transcendental or other-worldly source of metaphysical solace. Faustus's Helen does neither of these things: as phantom or eidolon she lacks substance, and as representative of a culture "canceled" by Christianity she cannot serve as the repository of transcendent values. Her function is to produce the same effect on us that the face of God produced in Mephastophilis: dissatisfaction with the world as it is. "For all is dross that is not Helena."

For Adorno, moreover, the semblance character of the artwork is both the double and the negation of its commodity character. For the commodity too is "pure semblance" in that exchange value or sign function has eclipsed use value and thus the object's particularity. But the semblance character of the commodity is purely immanent—it does not seek or even imagine a form of satisfaction outside of that offered by the world of commodities. By contrast, the autonomous semblance of the artwork points beyond the reified world, functioning as an "apparition" that speaks from a just if nonexistent plane and promises "a blocked or denied sensuality."[67] Helen embodies this very dichotomy. Commonly denounced as whore, and hence as commodity, she nevertheless "transcends economic categories. . . . Helen, like Aphrodite, may be wounded but never bought, sold, or killed."[68] For Faustus she is kissable but not, ultimately, graspable, and she is the play's most compelling image of the beyond that Faustus desires but never quite manages to compass.

It is fitting that our "brief history of the negative" should end with Adorno, probably the twentieth century's most rigorously negative thinker. Adorno is doubly relevant to the current context since his work was an important inspiration for Thomas Mann's *Doctor Faustus*, and Adorno himself may even have served as a model for one of Mann's devils.[69] This choice would be, I hope we can now see, fully Marlovian in spirit. Just as Faustus embraces the empty but beautiful semblance of the eidolon, so Marlowe embraces an art that is, he recognizes, ultimately vacuous, but, precisely on that basis, a utopian denunciation of the given. Or to put it differently: Marlowe's material alienation from the product of his labor produces both an aesthetic of disappointment and, as its obverse, the artwork as pure semblance, whose very lack gestures beyond Marlowe's particular situation (while still preserving it) to constitute a form of artistic critique. Marlowe's theater of night makes something out of the void and thus turns the negative to account, but what it makes is a repository of emptiness—one that refuses to affirm the world of day.

CHAPTER FOUR

Hamlet and the Work of Death

If any play in the Western canon can lay claim to depicting a crisis of action, that play is *Hamlet*. Its title character has become a byword for indecision and delay. Having sworn to avenge his father's death, Hamlet then finds himself inexplicably unwilling or unable to carry out his promise, and his paralysis provides an interval in which he scrutinizes the very nature of action and, in the course of so doing, lays bare a consciousness as rich and enigmatic as any depicted onstage. Indeed, *Hamlet* is often regarded by critics as a kind of historical watershed in which dramatic character takes precedence over action. Hamlet's crisis of the act is not just one for him personally, then, but perhaps one for tragedy as such. Adam Smith's description of Racine's *Phèdre*, as I noted in chapter 1, dissolves the plot of that play into a series of affective tonalities in its title character. But if Smith's approach bespeaks an ethics that elevates character over action, it finds its dramatic correlate in the kind of play that *Hamlet* is. Tragedy and the aesthetic presuppositions encouraged by political economy meet halfway.

Critics have generally followed Hamlet's lead in interpreting his problem as one of delay, thereby defining action against inaction. But what if we define action or *praxis* against making or *poiesis* instead? What if the counterpart to action is not doing nothing but rather making something? The latter option has a long philosophical precedent in its favor, though it may not be immediately obvious where such activity is to be found in *Hamlet*. My answer would be: everywhere. In fact, the play's action is conducted against an ongoing choral backdrop of production. One need only prick up one's ears to hear it. Doing so will also enable us to note the play's anticipatory echoes of political economy.

Production turns out to be a not unimportant issue for Shakespearean theater. True, the early modern era precedes Adam Smith's distinction between productive and unproductive labor. Service to a lord was in its way just as respectable as practicing a craft. And yet the institution of professional theater caused economic, along with theological and social, unease among its critics. A 1597 petition from the Lord Mayor and Aldermen to the Privy Council complained that public playhouses "maintaine idlenes in such persons as have no vocation & draw apprentices and other servauntes from theire ordinary workes."[1] While professional acting companies aped some of the structures of craft guilds (apprenticeship, in particular), acting was not regarded as a legitimate craft—in part, no doubt, for reasons similar to those adduced by Smith. Playing, like any craft, required effort, training, practice, and skill. Nevertheless, players did not *make* anything; they did not produce material, durable commodities. Hence their endeavors elicited the kind of economic hostility that, for instance, the work of printers printing a play did not. And not only was playing itself dismissed as a form of "idleness," it also drew apprentices away from their work and thus interfered with industry far beyond the bounds of the theater. Playing was not only seen as nonproductive; it was, in the eyes of its critics, also antiproductive.

As its very name suggests, "playing" was associated with holiday, not work. It participated in the traditional and immemorial alternation of holiday and workday on which medieval and early modern economies relied. Yet professional theater violated this ancient rhythm. Open air structures such as the Globe Theater could operate only during daytime hours. Theater thus represented a kind of continuous carnival or holiday transposed to the heart of the working day. It embodied what Giorgio Agamben would call a "permanent state of exception" to the productive regime of early modern London, an ongoing amusement camp that scooped out a space and time of idleness, a permanent void or crater of antiproduction from within the plenum of the working day. And yet, as Shakespeare and others recognized, producing this ongoing holiday was a laborious task. Prince Hal inadvertently captured the predicament of the early modern player when he proclaimed that "If all the year were playing holidays, / To sport would be as tedious as to work."[2]

Insofar as playing could be imagined as a form of work, it was as the work of servants, not craftsmen. Hence early modern players wore the liveries of the lords who acted as their patrons. Perhaps the traditional association of players with the service economy of the aristocratic household later prompted Adam Smith to include them in the ranks of unproductive laborers, along with other kinds of menial servants. The troubling economic situation of professional theater in early modern England may have predated political economy, then, but it participated in certain primordial forms of economic thought, anxiety, and prejudice that political economy would later crystallize out as theoretical categories. Certainly the notions of productive and unproductive activity—work, play, and idleness—occupied a central role in parsing the social status of professional theater.

In the early sixteenth century, "playing" was the most commonly used term for what theater people did when they put on a performance. As Louis Montrose notes, it associates theater with the "hodgepodge of popular entertainments—juggling and clowning, singing and miming, dancing and fencing, cockfighting and bearbeating—from which it was still in the process of separating itself."[3] As the century progressed, however, another term—"acting"—came to supplement, though not replace, the older one.[4] By the time of Shakespeare's *Hamlet*, the two are used interchangeably, if not quite synonymously. (Adam Smith employs both terms in his catalog of unproductive laborers.) "Acting" was, as Andrew Gurr points out, "originally used to describe the 'action' of the orator, his art of gesture."[5] The term thus originates in the political realm, of which oratory was a crucial part. Acting is a counterfeiting of the act understood in an ethical-political sense. Playing, by contrast, is the negation of labor, or rather it is a strange sort of labor that recalls idleness. Acting orients theater on a political axis, playing on an economic one. Their intersection situates theater in relation to both the act and its antithesis, (productive) activity.

I

Hamlet's crisis of the act can be mapped against this crossroad. I would apply a somewhat Lacanian locution to this crisis by saying that the play concerns an act that cannot find its hour.[6] It is not just that Hamlet's famous delay turns on problems of how to time the execution of Claudius, though that is sometimes the case. The play's impediments to action are various: theological, ethical, political, practical, philosophical, psychological. All, however, can be articulated with a time that is famously out of joint.[7] *Hamlet*'s crisis of the act is also a crisis of temporality, conceived in part as the simultaneous "too soon" and "too late" that afflicts the play's hero.

A counterpart to this crisis of the act that cannot ever take place are forms of activity that take place ceaselessly. The most conspicuous of these occupy the realm of death. I am thinking of the worms that dine on Polonius, the king going a progress through the guts of a beggar, Alexander turning into a cork, the sun breeding maggots in a dead dog, the old mole burrowing underground, violets springing from the fair and unpolluted flesh of Ophelia. All of these are acts of consumption that are simultaneously acts of production, the ceaselessly destructive and creative work of nature as it fashions new forms and new lives out of old ones.[8] This background activity offers, as I say, a counterpoint to Hamlet's crisis of the act.[9] Like Hamlet's act, the work of nature "cannot find its hour," but in a very different sense. It churns on without end or interruption, oblivious to the hour, to the difference between day and night, to ethical circumstance or political exigency. Hamlet imagines an act that will bring things to a definitive conclusion, that will fulfill an ethical mandate, right a wrong, reinstate a political dynasty, and end a play. The activity of nature proceeds, by contrast, to no purpose or goal and with no end in sight. While Hamlet's crisis of the act precipitates out the most individuated character in the history of drama, nature's productive activity is anonymous, activity without a subject. Hamlet's crisis of the act is, in short, individuating, decisional, ethico-political. The activity of nature is anonymous, ongoing, productive—much like labor in Smith's *Wealth of Nations*.

But it is not only nature that engages in ceaseless productive activity. The play begins in a bustle of human labor as Danish workers rush to fashion implements of war:

> MARCELLUS: Good now, sit down and tell me he that knows,
> Why this same strict and most observant watch
> So nightly toils the subject of the land,
> And why such daily cast of brazen cannon
> And foreign mart for implements of war,
> Why such impress of shipwrights, whose sore task
> Does not divide the Sunday from the week.
> What might be toward that this sweaty haste
> Doth make the night joint-labourer with the day,
> Who is't that can inform me?
> (1.1.73–81)[10]

These nameless laborers are no less anonymous than the maggots, worms, and violets that perform nature's work—and theirs too proceeds without interruption, eradicating the distinctions between Sabbath and workweek, night and day.[11] Perhaps this is in part what it means to say that time is out of joint: that time's jointures—its natural, divine, and cultural divisions—are violated. In any case, this anonymous background bustle, this ongoing productive turmoil, this "post-haste and rummage in the land" (1.1.110) serves as both foil for and mockery of Hamlet's paralysis of the act.

That this laboring multitude makes armaments seems not at all random. What they produce are means of destruction meant to decompose bodies politic, much as worms decompose the body of Polonius. The industry of warfare overthrows states in order to reconfigure them, to produce new political entities, just as the work of nature dissolves old bodies in order to create fresh ones. Of course, these particular weapons are intended to save Denmark from dissolution. But that is not the way history works in this play. Armies, destructive multitudes, sweep across Europe—ejecting dynasties, reapportioning land, reconfiguring the political order. States are no more immune to a process of continual production/consumption than are our individual human bodies. But the anonymous laborers who produce these weapons are not the ones who order their use. One class makes, another decides. Labor and action occupy separate realms. Indeed, the anonymous workers are consigned to a perpetual theatrical background, never appearing on stage, which is a space reserved for those who act, not for those who make. At least, the *tragic* stage has traditionally been so reserved.

The play's separation of politics and labor is not quite absolute, however. It is the Danish state that has pressed its workers into uninterrupted service as its response to "a state of military alert, if not full-blown emergency."[12] But the political role of the anonymous, laboring multitudes is not exhausted by this instrumental function, for they are both objects of political solicitude and agents of political change in *Hamlet*.[13] Seconding Claudius's decision to send Hamlet abroad, Guildenstern advises him: "Most holy and religious fear it is / To keep those many many bodies safe / That live and feed upon your Majesty" (3.3.8–10). The "many many" feeding bodies of the multitude disturbingly foreshadow the swarming, "politic" worms that will dine upon Polonius's corpse. But in this case Guildenstern imagines the king's body politic perpetually nourishing the people without ever being depleted or transformed.[14] Consumption is therefore divorced from production, since the king is neither decomposed nor remade into something new by the mouths that batten on him. This is because his—now merely parasitic—multitudes feed not on the limited physical substance of the king but on his inexhaustible political substance, his "Majesty." Guildenstern's conservative, optimistic image of political consumption reduces the multitudes to a purely passive political role.

His vision gives way to a more radical one, however, when Laertes leads a popular mob in revolt against Claudius:

> MESSENGER: Save yourself, my lord.
> The ocean, overpeering of his list,
> Eats not the flats with more impetuous haste
> Than the young Laertes, in a riotous head,
> O'erbears your officers. The rabble call him lord,
> And, as the world were now but to begin,
> Antiquity forgot, custom not known,
> The ratifiers and props of every word,
> They cry, "Choose we! Laertes shall be king."
> Caps, hands, and tongues applaud it to the clouds,
> "Laertes shall be king, Laertes king."
> (4.5.98–108)

Now the language of "eating" figures not political dependence but revolution, the consuming of a traditional order so as to produce a novel one. Political upheaval, like the economic production it echoes, proceeds in indifference to time, the swarming multitudes having forgotten "antiquity" and "custom" as they rush to disassemble the state, just as the workers in Act I labor without respect for day and night, Sabbath and workday.

Their political production is, moreover, simultaneously a decision. The crowd *chooses* Laertes for their king, and thus the spuming sea of their activity wondrously crystallizes into a political act. In its oceanic force, therefore, the multitude knocks down not only the barriers of rule and custom but also the very distinction between the economic and political. The line "And, as the world were now but to begin" imparts to this human tide something of the decreative/creative force of Noah's flood. Appropriating to itself the power of God, the multitude both effects a miracle and establishes a new political covenant. Sovereign are they who decide the state of exception— though, like the workers in Act I, they have the good manners to do so offstage.

Marx described labor as the conscious modification and mediation of "man's metabolism with nature," meaning that labor is the process by means of which man converts nature's substance to his own uses and nourishment. The laboring multitudes in *Hamlet* embody not only man's metabolism with nature but also the economic's metabolism with the political. The Danish state appropriates labor (when it impresses munitions workers) and labor, in its turn, appropriates the state (when the multitudes engage in revolt). The economic and the political are linked not only through metaphoric resemblance but through mutual acts of subordination as well—an ongoing and dialectical process that fashions the play's economy into a *political* economy.

By asserting (inaccurately) that Marx *defined* labor as "man's metabolism with nature," Hannah Arendt reinforced her claim that labor occupies the merely natural realm of the *"animal laborans,"* as opposed to a characteristically human world.[15] The laborer, in this view, metabolizes nature only so that nature may in turn metabolize him. Or, as Hamlet puts it, "[W]e fat all creatures else to fat us, and we fat ourselves for maggots" (4.3.21–23). These interlocking cycles of consumption define man's natural existence as an essentially transient one. *Hamlet*'s sustained if implicit analogy between human labor and nature's, the work of shipwrights and the work of maggots, anticipates certain aspects of Arendt's way of thinking. But in extending this continuum to include the realm of the state, *Hamlet* threatens to erode a distinction fundamental to Arendt. If the state is like a body that can be eaten, like metal that can be melted and then forged into cannon, like a shoreline that can be reconfigured by the sea, then production and consumption do not confine themselves entirely to a darkened or veiled space against which the publicity of the political contrasts itself but rather erupt into the very conceptual terrain of politics. By entering into a metabolism with the economic, moreover, the political simultaneously enters into a metabolism with nature. Hence to describe revolution as a flood is something more than mere analogy. It betokens a fundamental transformation of the political itself when the multitudes seize hold of it. (Arendt might be tempted to note, wryly, that the multitude's one political act is to choose a new king, thus abrogating the space of their freedom in the very moment they assert it.)

Earlier I noted that the tragic stage is reserved for those who act, not for those who make. That is true for the ancient Greeks but not for Renaissance tragedy, which often admits comic/productive characters on a limited basis. Workers have some famous cameos in *Hamlet*. The players are one such group, and Hamlet's recourse to animal metaphors when describing them ("a cry of players" [3.2.271–72], "an eyrie of children, little eyases" [2.2.337]) emphasizes their connection with the pack or multitude. But the most notable of these onstage workers is of course the gravedigger—or, as he would describe himself, the grave maker. The second clown, who may or may not be himself a grave maker, even addresses him at one point by name, or something like a name: "Goodman Delver" (5.1.14). At once surname and profession, the word "delver" grants the grave maker something just short of individuation. He is an allegorical embodiment of his own labor, not quite deserving of a name as such. He teeters precariously between identity and anonymity, emerging from his own activity only so as to disappear back into it, just as he transfers the corpses of individuated persons to the mass anonymity of the grave.

He nevertheless possesses enough dramaturgical solidity to speak for himself and even to spar verbally with Hamlet. The living embodiment of activity thus crosses paths with the living embodiment of the act—or rather, of the failure to act. The results of this encounter are complex and in some ways obscure. But before trying to assess them, we should consider more closely the character of the grave maker and the nature of his labor.[16] A simple man, the grave maker is nevertheless not without social and even metaphysical pretensions, though of a leveling sort. He brags that "there is no ancient gentlemen but gardeners, ditchers, and grave-makers" (5.1.29-31), and then goes on to claim that the grave maker "builds stronger than a mason, a shipwright, or a carpenter," since "the houses he makes lasts till doomsday" (5.1.50-51, 59). There is both a temporal and a social dimension to this latter claim, since the grave maker is comparing his lowly, unskilled labor favorably to the work of highly trained guildsmen. Indeed, in calling himself a grave *maker*, he claims an element of *poiesis* for his activity comparable to that of the shipwright, mason, or carpenter. In fact, however, what the grave maker makes is not a thing at all but rather a vacancy—a hole or void. His work is not like that of a craftsman but rather closer to the digging of the peasant farmer, except that no crops result from his exertions. A service worker, he would find himself classed among Adam Smith's unproductive laborers, whose exertions fix themselves in nothing. The physical emptiness of the grave emblematizes the economic emptiness of his sterile, un/productive activity. Nature will produce new things from the bodies the grave maker inters, but he himself makes a thing of nothing.

As if to compensate for this, the grave maker stresses the durability of his endeavors, comparing it favorably with that of skilled guildsmen. It is that which elevates his activity to what Hannah Arendt would call work. Of course, the grave maker exaggerates this durability. Even as he claims that his graves last until doomsday, he is evicting the current tenants of one of them in order to make room for Ophelia. The turnover of graves is slow, but turnover it is nonetheless. And yet the grave maker himself seems to possess the immemorial character he claims for his product, despite his ability to remember his first day on the job. The very name "Goodman Delver" grants him the immortality of an allegorical abstraction. A Hamlet or a Polonius or an Ophelia might cease to be, but not a Goodman Delver. He digs and digs, endlessly, like the old mole, indifferent to change and history—the human counterpart to nature's patient, unceasing labor. His business is mortality, and yet he seems on the verge of transcending it. This accords with his role as informal archivist of the graveyard, the one person who can still identify Yorick's skull and distinguish it from the others, attaching a name and thus a life beyond life to this otherwise anonymous, meaningless bone.

In several respects, the grave maker's work bears an odd resemblance to the work of theater. At least, it shares the paradox of being at once unproductive and enduring. The grave maker's grave is, after all, literally the stage trap, the hole in the stage that comes to represent both the metaphysical and the economic emptiness of the stage itself, that void scooped out of the productive workday. It is not by accident, I think, that the only other workers to appear in *Hamlet* are the players. Their profession is unlike that of the grave maker in that it is subject to "late innovations." (Of this, more later.) But it is equally unproductive, and equally memorializing. Troy may fall, but the dramatic story of Troy's fall lasts till doomsday, like the grave. Theater, in subjecting living action to the dead letter, both mortifies it and preserves it indefinitely.

Players and grave maker hold the mirror up to Hamlet. The Danish prince has been forced to substitute acting in the theatrical sense—feigning, and sometimes clowning—for real action, and in this sense resembles the players. His relations with the grave maker are, if anything, even more rich and complex. Hamlet frequently compares himself to lower-class characters: a "rogue and peasant slave," a scull, a drab. He repeatedly engages in witty, clownish verbal antics resembling those of the grave maker. He even adopts at one point the metaphorical persona of the digger or delver, thus declaring his kinship with both the grave maker and the old mole:

> For 'tis the sport to have the enginer
> Hoist with his own petard, and 't shall go hard
> But I will delve one yard below their mines
> And blow them at the moon.
> (3.4.208–11)[17]

And the grave maker, for his part, is a philosopher of action like Hamlet: "If I drown myself wittingly," he states, discussing Ophelia, "it argues an act, and an act hath three branches—it is to act, to do, to perform" (5.1.10–12). This mirror relation is all the more surprising in that Hamlet and the grave maker embody incompatible principles: making or production on the part of the laborious grave maker, action or doing on the part of the Danish prince. Yet this is not quite right either, and in order to situate Hamlet properly with respect to the grave maker, we must invoke the third of Aristotle's great categories of human action: thinking.

A. W. Schlegel characterized *Hamlet* as a "tragedy of thought," thus suggesting that tragedy had shifted its ground from external action to Hamlet's consciousness.[18] But perhaps we should take the phrase "tragedy of thought" to indicate not only a tragedy that occurs in the realm of thinking but a tragedy that happens to thinking as well, a tragedy afflicting thought. Coleridge understood the play in this sense and so did Freud, who first publicly presented his analysis of *Hamlet* in *The Interpretation of Dreams* (1900). Indeed, Freud's reading of *Hamlet* against Sophocles's *Oedipus* offers a historical narrative of the movement from tragedy of action to tragedy of thought.

Freud treats Sophocles's play in a strictly Aristotelian manner insofar as he emphasizes plot over character. What matters to Freud is not what Oedipus is or wants but what Oedipus does. In killing his father and marrying his mother, Oedipus acts out a foundational incestuous fantasy, but not necessarily *his* fantasy. Paradoxically, Freud's reading does not assume that Oedipus suffers from the Oedipus complex. Freud is not interested in Oedipus's character but rather in the way his actions affect the audience and bring to light *their* Oedipal guilt. Moreover, Oedipal desire can assume the form of action in Greek tragedy because, in this early stage of the history of repression, it is also accessible to thought. Greek guilt is still conscious guilt; hence, it can be both thought and acted out. Things are different when we come to the era of *Hamlet*: "In the *Oedipus* the child's wishful fantasy that underlies it is brought into the open and realized as it would be in a dream. In *Hamlet* it remains repressed; and—just as in the case of a neurosis—we only learn of its existence from its inhibiting consequences."[19] Now it is Hamlet as character who harbors an unconscious Oedipal longing. Hamlet's repressed identification with Claudius inhibits action; thus does Freud claim to solve the mystery of Hamlet's famous delay. But it inhibits thought as well, insofar as Hamlet's essential truth remains hidden from him. It is not that thought stops; rather, it runs on endlessly, albeit along certain obsessive pathways, without really accomplishing anything. This is the tragedy of thought: to be reduced to an ongoing but essentially empty process. Hamlet's thoughts, despite his immense intellectual gifts, circle something to which they cannot gain access but from whose gravitational pull they cannot escape.

It is thus in his thought, which is reduced to an unproductive productivity, that Hamlet mimics the activity of the grave maker. Hamlet's endless, fruitless thinking is the counterpart to the grave maker's endless, fruitless digging. And here we should finally note that most of the play's images of nature's destructive productivity—the old mole, the worms dining on Polonius, the sun breeding maggots in a dead dog, the king going a progress through the guts of a beggar, Alexander turning into a cork—occur only in Hamlet's imagination. (In the source stories, by contrast, they inhabit the real world.)[20] Such images constitute not merely the content of Hamlet's thought, his obsession with death and rot, but also and more importantly the *form* of his thought. These processes of endless but ultimately pointless production capture, in other words, the dilemma of Hamlet's meditations, which likewise churn on to no purpose or resolution. In Hamlet, thought has become detached from the act and thus devolves into mere activity. Reduced to symptom, its sole function is to reveal Hamlet's diseased state, having been unfitted for any other kind of work. No longer an organon or instrument of action, Hamlet's thought is in some sense no longer even his; it is an autonomous, self-driving motion.

Freud's *Interpretation of Dreams*, which first publicly presents his reading of *Hamlet*, also, as it happens, offers a counterpart to Hamlet's mental activity: the dream work or *Traumarbeit*, those unconscious, automatic processes of condensation and displacement that generate the manifest content of dreams. The dream work, like all unconscious processes, operates uninterruptedly, oblivious to time, change, space, and the external world. Its "work" is recombinatory and essentially pointless. While it serves the purpose of evading the ego's sensory mechanisms, this is not its intention, for it has none. As Freud famously remarks, "the dream work does not think."[21] It mimics thought, in that its raw materials are representations, but it endlessly works these into temporary configurations, which it then dismantles and reconfigures again. It is thus not really "work" in the Arendtian sense but rather the mental equivalent to "labor," which is how Arendt would translate the German word *Arbeit*.

We can perhaps clarify the nature of this mental labor by returning to the difference between Aristotle's concept of *poiesis* or making and political economy's concept of production as expounded in my first chapter. For Aristotle, *poiesis* is always the making or crafting of a specific thing, be it a shoe, a house, or a poem. The final product is the goal, or *telos*, of the productive process, the thing that both grants it its reason and brings it to an end. Political economy, by contrast, is concerned with production as such—

not the production of this or that particular thing, but with production as an ongoing and uninterrupted process that leads to ever-increasing accumulations of wealth. It is both atelic and impersonal, neither beginning in the conscious intention of an artificer nor ending in the finished perfection of a product.

For Aristotle, thought is often teleological in a way analogous to making. *Techne* aims at creating something; it is the mental process behind *poiesis* or making itself, and finds its goal in the object or practice it directs. Deliberative thinking, or *phronesis*, aims at reaching a practical decision, and is finally discharged in the act. Hamlet's thought mostly combines philosophical and deliberative elements. But he is neither able to lay out a consistent, practical course of action nor arrive at a satisfying philosophical grasp of his condition. Instead, he comes increasingly to view his own thought as both dilatory and inessential. Like political economy's concept of production, Hamlet's thought—insofar as it is merely symptom—lacks any goal or telos. It simply churns on, producing ever new yet increasingly repetitive material. In this sense, *the symptom is the characteristic thought-form of the age of political economy*—the mental counterpart to production as such. Yet this formulation is not quite correct, for the symptom, like the dream work, does not think. Rather, it is to thought what activity is to the act. Hamlet's "thinking" is ultimately like the labor of the worms as they transform Polonius's body, or a king's body, or Alexander's body, or the body of a dead dog into new and seemingly arbitrary forms. It is like the endless zigzag of the old mole as it burrows underground, or the digging of the grave maker as he repeatedly inters and exhumes bodies. This substitution of mental activity for the mental act, of the symptom for thought, is what makes Hamlet a hero for the age of political economy.

The status of symptom in *Hamlet* is complicated by an aspect of thought I have not yet addressed, however. It is true that for Aristotle, practical and productive modes of thought are end-directed. But a third mode, *nous* or intelligence, is contemplative and pursued as an end in itself—an aimless and pleasurable activity released from the teleology of production or the act.[22] Arendt goes so far as to classify all other forms of thought as "knowledge," and to reserve the more dignified term "thinking" for this pure mental activity alone.[23] Hamlet's penchant for speculative boldness and evident enjoyment in intellection pursued for its own sake would seem to align him with the atelic mode of thought described by Aristotle and Arendt. Yet it is also true that Hamlet increasingly comes to see this activity as a delaying tactic, a way of fending off his unwelcome task. Thought and the symptom collude, something they are able to do all the more effectively because they resemble each other in superficial ways. For, like thinking, symptom detaches itself from all external finalities—in this case, however, not as a gesture of freedom but rather, inversely, because it inhibits thought and thus disables it for any practical use. Thinking transcends practical ends and symptom finds itself cut off from them, but this shared condition of autonomy allows them to embellish and play off each other. It is not just that Hamlet's activity of thought finds itself returning obsessively to the same symptomatic nodes; it is that thinking itself has become as much a mode of avoidance as anything else, and thus even its apparent freedom can be seen, from another perspective, as a kind of symptom.[24]

As it happens, the tradition of viewing Hamlet as symptomatic begins not with Freud or Coleridge or even Schlegel but in the intellectual and cultural circles of the Scottish Enlightenment. Henry Mackenzie, the novelist and editor of the Edinburgh *Mirror*, was the first critic to attribute Hamlet's famous delay to internal fragility. Mackenzie's Hamlet was "endowed with feelings so delicate as to border on weakness, and sensibility too exquisite to allow of determined action."[25] William Richardson—a student of Adam Smith's, a cofounder with Smith of the Royal Academy of Edinburgh, and Professor of Humanity at the University of Glasgow—developed Mackenzie's reading in even more suggestive directions. Richardson argued that the reasons Hamlet gives for not slaying Claudius at the altar constitute "self-deceit," though of an "amiable" sort. He thus attributes Hamlet's action (or inaction) to something inaccessible to thought, and he characterizes Hamlet's bursts of indecorous jocularity as "a symptom, too unambiguous, of his affliction."[26] As far as I can tell, this is the very first time that the word *symptom* is applied to Hamlet. The "modern" or psychoanalytic Hamlet—a Hamlet inhibited from action because of motives of which he is not conscious—thus first takes form within the intellectual milieu of Adam Smith.

Smith himself was no great admirer of *Hamlet*. He liked to quote Voltaire to the effect that the play was "the dream of a drunken savage," and he cites it to illustrate faults of dramatic composition:[27] "But in no part should any thing appear to have a contrary tendency to that of the whole piece. For this reason the . . . scene in . . . and the Scene of the Gravediggers in Hamlet tho very good scenes in their Sort had better been away as they have no share in bringing about the main design of the piece and are somewhat contrary to the temper of the rest of the Scenes."[28] Mixed in with Aristotelian principles of decorum and dramatic unity one detects a rather Hamlet-like impatience with clownish dilation, which "set[s] on some quantity of barren spectators to laugh . . . though in the meantime some necessary question of the play be then to be considered" (3.2.41–43). The graveyard scene offends Smith because it does not advance the principal business of the play. It is a kind of idleness or interruption within the dramatic plot—good in its sort (just as menial servants are good in their sort) but ultimately unproductive, contributing nothing of significance to the design of the whole. Neither aesthetic act nor productively aesthetic activity, it constitutes a kind of empty dithering, an unannounced holiday in which the serious work of dramatic *poiesis* is suspended. Perhaps it is no accident that the father of political economy, who lumps actors in among the unproductive laborers, should likewise be impatient with unproductive stretches of *Hamlet*. And perhaps it is also no accident that among the many dilatory scenes and speeches in Shakespeare, he happens upon one that highlights conspicuously unproductive labor. Form and content thus converge in the graveyard scene, which both is and depicts empty activity. Like the luxuries of having one's tie adjusted or one's dinner cooked—or one's grave dug—it had therefore "better been away" despite the pleasures it affords. Smith was, of course, the opposite of a philistine, and one must be careful in transposing the principles of political economy directly to his literary thought. Nevertheless, *Hamlet*'s grave makers seem to represent a kind of irresistible "quilting point" for Smith in which one discourse momentarily buttons onto the other. But it has been the burden of this book that tragedy is precisely the place where such quilting points occur—where literature and political economy most strikingly and meaningfully intersect.

II

As I argued in chapter 1, Aristotle's definition of tragedy as a *poiesis* or making that imitates a *praxis* or action implies, without quite acknowledging, a conceptual tension between these two terms. In looking at the plot of *Hamlet*, I have attempted to show how production erodes the coherence of action: Hamlet's desire to enact tragic vengeance gets bogged down in death's endlessly productive activity. *Hamlet* thereby takes the merely potential conflict between making and doing that inhabits Aristotle's understanding of tragedy and blows it up into a full-fledged problem. The conflicts that rive Hamlet as character redound upon the structure of *Hamlet* as tragic play. Hamlet's tragedy projects a dilemma for tragedy as such in the modern era.

Here I wish to explore this metadramatic dimension of the problem more fully. In the previous section, my reflections on the work of death found their definitive embodiment in a particular kind of labor: that of the grave maker. But he is not the only plebeian, and therefore laboring, presence in the play. The wandering actors are another, and they supplement the grave maker's work with another kind, this one more directly connected with Shakespeare's own productive activity as playwright. While the activities of grave maker and actor are not obviously alike, they do enfold some deep similarities. From the perspective of political economy, both are unproductive "services" rather than value-producing manufactures. Had he thought to do so, Adam Smith would have lumped grave makers along with actors and buffoons (and kings and queens) in the ranks of the unproductive. But Shakespeare's depiction of the actors, particularly in Act 2 Scene 2, brings the world of theater into still closer connection with that of the graveyard.

The two parts of the scene present two different and complementary faces of theater. Discussion of the arriving players addresses the vagaries of acting as profession. The players, Hamlet is told, have left the city owing to the "late innovation" (2.2.331), a phrase that may refer to (inter alia) the rise of the children's companies in London and subsequent War of the Theaters or else to Essex's abortive rebellion of 1601.[29] The phrase, that is, ambiguously allows of either a political or an economic interpretation—a treasonous if heroic act or everyday business activity. The effect, in either case, is the same: the company leaves the city to go on tour, a common enough event in the England of Shakespeare's day.

The key to the whole exchange is the phrase "late innovation." London's theater business is subject to abrupt changes in fashion. New companies and styles of acting emerge, displacing the old ones. This landscape of commercial mutability echoes the rise and fall of political bodies in warfare. It is also tied to changes in the human body. Signs of physical growth and alteration in the players fascinate Hamlet. He remarks that one lately sports a beard, thus announcing the transition from boy player to adult, and that another boy player "is nearer to heaven than when I saw you last by the altitude of a chopine" (2.2.422–23). The boy is taller but also, in a slightly more covert sense, nearer to his demise. For Hamlet, growth is always a prelude to decay. Just as new styles and acting companies dislodge the old, so new ranks of boy players arrive to take the place of those who are past their prime. The world of commercial theater is in a constant ferment, at once cultural and physiological, as if struck with the ephemerality of performance itself. It is a world of empty activity, afflicted with activity's characteristic impermanence. It is also, not unrelatedly, the space of the multitude and its endless capacity for transformation. The very fact that this company is on tour embodies their essentially nomadic, unstable condition.

The First Player's long speech, by contrast, emphasizes drama's capacity for fixity and endurance. When asking to hear it recited, Hamlet is careful to detach it from the capricious worlds of commerce and the multitude: "it was never acted, or if it was, not above once—for the play, I remember, pleased not the million, 'twas caviare to the general" (2.2.430–33). This is drama as art, as carefully crafted form, as "work." It has implanted itself so ineradicably in Hamlet's memory that he is able to recite its opening lines by heart. The content of the speech likewise transcends time: the actor re-vivifies events of millennia past, despite the fact that Hecuba is nothing to him and he nothing to Hecuba. Empires fall but art endures. Like "Mars's armour, forg'd for proof eterne" (2.2.488), dramatic poetry proves immune to the ravages of time.

Shakespeare's art thus exhibits two very different temporalities depending on whether it is grasped as theater or as drama. In this it resembles the grave maker's work. While the grave maker jokingly insists that his product proves superior to that of the mason or shipwright because of its endless durability ("The houses he makes lasts til doomsday" [5.1.59], a demotic counterpart to "Mars's armour, forg'd for proof eterne"), yet this claim to eternity is belied by the actual nature of his work, which consists of continually burying and unburying bodies. In effect, Shakespeare divides these incompatible temporalities of death between drama, understood as enduring text, and theater, understood as ephemeral performance.

What exactly does Hamlet encounter in the graveyard? The obvious answer is "death"—death as reality rather than as Hamlet tends to imagine it. But what is the difference between the two? When Hamlet contemplates death, he invariably thinks of the flesh alone. It is the flesh upon which worms dine, and from which the sun breeds maggots. It is the flesh that transmogrifies into a cork or goes a progress through the guts of a beggar. The productivity of death feeds on the soft, consumable (and, not incidentally, maternal) tissues of life. When Hamlet comes to the graveyard, he confronts for the first time that which remains when transient flesh disappears: bone. Bone does not last forever; it is not quite Mars's metallic armor, "forg'd for proof eterne." But it lasts for a long time—far longer than the flesh that dissolves around it. The considerable if ultimately limited durability of bone contrasts with the extravagant transience of flesh.

What Hamlet learns in the graveyard, then, is that the body retains a certain skeletal integrity even after the flesh has gone. This bony remnant is anonymous; it requires the grave maker's narration, or Hamlet's imagining, to assume a living identity. (The relation between graveyard and theater thus emerges once more.) But it persists for generations—far beyond the span of an individual human life. Encountering bone seems to offer Hamlet an expanded temporal perspective from which he can perceive his own dilemma with greater equanimity. It is as if he comes to see himself from the place of the bones—their imperturbable *longue durée*. What Hamlet takes away from this experience is a new conception of the act and of its temporality: "If it be now, 'tis not to come; if it be not to come, it will be now; if it be not now, yet it will come. The readiness is all" (5.2.216–18). Hamlet speaks directly of his death, but also, if indirectly, of the act that will precipitate it. He understands for the first time that the act has its own temporality, which is not that of the agent. It is not simply (though this was never simple for Hamlet) a matter of choosing when to act. Rather, the act defines its moment, for which one must be prepared when it comes. Like bone, the act is not soft or pliable; it has its own consistency and structure; it cannot simply be bent to suit its instigator.

Death is not a unitary thing in *Hamlet*. In fact, the play slices it up in more than one fashion. The more traditional divides mortal body from immortal soul. Even here, the dead are delivered to a state that is less eternal rest than eternal restlessness. King Hamlet, tortured by day in the fires of purgatory, is driven by memories of his murder to haunt the world at night. Hamlet too imagines the sleep of death to be perturbed by dreams. Death does not offer the soul escape from the temporal experience of life; it rather extends that experience forever.

But the distinction between immortal soul and mortal body is additionally reproduced within the mortal body itself through the different temporal arcs of bone and flesh. Bone does not last indefinitely, but it does endure for a long time. It intimates the eternal from within the transient face of creation, though (like the tortured souls of the play) it cannot finally free itself from temporal change. It petrifies time but does not finally escape it. Yet the slow dissolution of bone does contrast with the manic transformations of flesh.

The temporality of bone is to that of flesh what the temporality of work (in Arendt's terms) is to that of labor. Of course, bone is not a human artifact and thus does not define a human world. It is nature's (or God's) work, not man's. But, like human work, it gestures toward immortality in its limited way. Moreover, *Hamlet* does depict a human, artifactual counterpart to bone:

writing. Writing is the artificial preservative of memory—a solid, skeletal container of speech's fleshy impermanence.

While it appears at several points in the play, writing is first considered at length in Act 1, Scene 5, immediately following Hamlet's interview with the ghost:

> Remember thee?
> Ay, thou poor ghost, whiles memory holds a seat
> In this distracted globe. Remember thee?
> Yea, from the table of my memory
> I'll wipe away all trivial fond records,
> All saws of books, all forms, all pressures past
> That youth and observation copied there,
> And thy commandment all alone shall live
> Within the book and volume of my brain,
> Unmix'd with baser matter.
>
> (1.5.95–104)

Writing is here both a supplement to memory and a metaphor for it. Hamlet uses it to figure memory of a particularly solid and imperishable kind, though he soon then calls for his "tables" and actually writes his thoughts down. In fact, Hamlet distinguishes between two kinds of writing. One is what he calls "baser matter," the "trivial fond records" of youthful reading and observation that must make way for a more exalted, ideal, and apparently ineradicable kind of writing: his father's commandment. One writing is temporary and disposable, the other not—at least as Hamlet first conceives it. Yet in the event, the father's commandment is not quite as durable as Hamlet imagines, and so the ghost must return in Act 3, Scene 4 to remind his son: "Do not forget. This visitation / Is but to whet thy almost blunted purpose" (3.4.110–11).

Hamlet's speech in Act 1, Scene 5 establishes a template for the play: no writing takes place on a completely virginal surface. The space of writing is always-already written upon, and hence any act of writing must first erase what's there. Hamlet blots out Claudius's original letter to the English king in order to substitute his own message calling for the execution of Rosencrantz and Guildenstern. And he similarly alters the original text of *The Murder of Gonzago* by adding a speech of his own. The space of writing is therefore like the grave, where the bones of the predecessors must be removed to make room for new occupants. The permanence of the grave is compromised by this slow process of interment and disinterment, despite the grave maker's claim that "the houses he makes lasts till doomsday"

(5.1.59), and similarly the permanence of writing is limited by the prospect of future erasure and re- or overwriting.

Commenting on Hamlet's revisions to *The Murder of Gonzago*, William Empson observes that "the character does what the author is doing—altering an old play to fit an immediate political purpose."[30] The rule that, in *Hamlet*, every act of writing is an act of rewriting thus applies to the writing of the play itself. Or as E. E. Stoll put it, Shakespeare "did not write a play but rewrote one; and not once but twice at least did he rewrite it."[31] What the graveyard in *Hamlet* offers is not merely an allegory of writing, then, but above all an allegory of the writing of *Hamlet*. Like the grave maker unearthing the skulls of the dead, Shakespeare digs up the ur-*Hamlet*, Kyd, Belleforest, Seneca, and many others, reworking the substance of their works into his new creation. Playwriting, particularly in the early modern period, involves creating in a space that is previously inscribed, plundering graves that are already occupied. Literary composition depends and thrives upon decomposition.

Let me push this allegory further—as I think Shakespeare did. The body, as Hamlet conceives it, consists of flesh and bone. Flesh, soft and malleable, is subject to a rapid process of transfiguration; bone, hard and durable, to a much slower one. Flesh may then correspond to the play in performance: a merely momentary thing composed of speech and movement, mutating from day to day, incorporating improvisation, reacting to immediate circumstance. Bone corresponds to the play as text: more stable and permanent, but by no means infinitely so. The printed *Hamlet* varied its shape several times in the course of its initial two decades, from the first to the second quarto and then to the Folio editions. A classic like *Hamlet* has remarkably strong bones, but, as Shakespeare surely knew, even these were not completely immune to future modification, nor should they be.

The work of death in *Hamlet* constructs a vast literary ecology in which the play meditates on its own processes of coming to be and passing away—except that nothing really passes away but is rather recycled and made into something new. For Shakespeare, the dead letter participates in the ongoing genesis of death. He is by no means uninterested in literary immortality, or in the monumentalizing capacity of art—particularly in the Sonnets. But in *Hamlet*, his most abiding creation, he understands literary afterlife as at least in part a process of slow recomposition. What ultimately survives is not the work but the process of working and reworking.

For all that, *Hamlet* endures. It has come as close to achieving immortality as any human creation can. Despite the many reworkings it has undergone, it has not metamorphosed into something unrecognizable. Its bones have been carefully tended and preserved, like a saint's relics, even as it is continually thought and imagined anew. It is not "base matter" destined for erasure but something closer to "Mars's armor, forg'd for proof eterne." Somehow the play's metaphorical assimilation of writing to nature or *physis* accounts only imperfectly for its own destiny.

I have thus far assimilated *Hamlet* to the Arendtian temporalities of labor and work, and I have assigned these in turn to the play in its double life as dramatic text and theatrical performance. For Arendt, the durability of work rescues us from the transience of labor and of our own biological limits. Cities endure beyond the individual lifespans of its inhabitants. Yet they too end. The sole source of immortality is therefore the act. The deeds of heroes echo even beyond the end of the cities—and cultures—they inhabit. Because of Homer, the story of Achilles lives on even today. Yet the temporality of the act in Arendt is as complex, and perhaps as paradoxical, as that of the grave maker in *Hamlet*. The extraordinary act is defined by a *megethos* or amplitude that lifts it beyond the ordinary flow of events and imprints it permanently in the memory. The singularity of the act crystallizes it and thereby delivers it from temporal change. In some respects, the act is culture's counterpart to the Freudian trauma that remains unmetabolizable by the psyche and thus repeats itself indefinitely.

But if the memorable act hardens into a kind of stony (or bony) permanence, it is simultaneously (and perhaps contradictorily) subject to constant reworking by the "web of human relationships" in which it is inevitably caught. This process consigns the act to failure as far as its aim is concerned, and thus imparts a tragic dimension to it; yet the peripeties generated by the endless reworking of the act are what make for good, memorable, stories. The act thus obeys a double temporality rather like that of the work of death in *Hamlet*. It has a bony consistency but also undergoes constant, fleshly metamorphosis. It is the conjunction of these two that makes for the greatness of tragic drama in Arendt's view.

Arendt, following Aristotle, understands tragedy as the mimesis of a memorable act possessed of *megethos* or amplitude. That this act is catastrophic only imprints it more powerfully on the memory. Oddly, though, such an act seems to be missing from *Hamlet*. Certainly, it is difficult to ascribe Aristotelian greatness to any *action* of Hamlet's. His revenge against Claudius, when it finally comes, seems almost accidental. It lacks the memorably premeditated atrociousness characteristic of Senecan tragedy—installed in the English tradition by Thomas Kyd in *The Spanish Tragedy* and

Shakespeare himself in *Titus Andronicus*.[32] Shakespeare's *Hamlet* seems self-consciously to have muted the expected climax of revenge tragedy. Hence if *Hamlet* is made great by the magnitude of an act, that act is not Hamlet's but Shakespeare's.

The innovation of *Hamlet*, its own particular greatness, has been variously construed as the substitution of thought for action, or of character for plot. I would put this differently by saying that what Shakespeare imitates in *Hamlet* is not action but the eclipse of action by activity. The paradox of *Hamlet* is that its immortal act is to depict the obsolescence of action. It thereby decisively shifts the very ground of dramatic art. In the great silence created when action reaches its impasse, faint sounds of shoveling can be heard.

CHAPTER FIVE

The Same Old Grind

Milton's Samson as Subtragic Hero

In *Samson or Holy Revenge,* a Dutch Trauerspiel published in 1660, the Hebrew Chorus complains at one point: "O what a shame / To trample on a
conquered hero thus, / To make him toil! 'Tis unjust and past reason."[1]
Making Samson labor at the mill violates the ethical norms for treating a
conquered warrior of his stature, but it also violates the literary norms for
treating the protagonist of a tragic drama. Tragic heroes traditionally love
or kill, suffer and die; at the outer limits they can even—as in the case of
Aeschylus's Prometheus—be clapped in chains. But they do not, almost by
definition, work—much less engage in the kind of repetitive, sweaty, and
mindless toil engaged in by the captured Samson. By depicting a hero who
labors at the mill, Joost Van den Vondel, the author of this Trauerspiel, thus
repeats, in an aesthetic dimension, the crime of Samson's Philistine captors.
Nor is this doubling accidental. The Philistine Prince and Princess in Van
den Vondel's play engage in a long conversation about the social and religious virtues of theater, and their plans for Samson involve not merely displaying his strength for a Philistine audience but having him play himself
in an allegorical masque about his seduction and capture by Delilah. That
the Philistines are playwrights reminds us that the playwright is also a metaphorical Philistine, entrapping the Hebrew hero within a gentile literary
form and, moreover, subjecting him to a laborious degradation not undergone by other tragic heroes.

My point in invoking Van den Vondel, however, is not to explore the by-
ways of authorial sadism. It is rather to point out that Samson is not just
one tragic hero among others. He is a hero who descends to levels of human

experience not undergone by any classical predecessors and, as such, he exerts a reciprocally transformative effect on tragic drama. The Samson story was a popular theme for early modern playwrights; over forty Samson plays were composed in Latin and the vernacular languages during the sixteenth and seventeenth centuries. Among these, Milton's *Samson Agonistes* exhibits a particularly subtle and searching awareness of what it means to inject a laboring hero into the form of classical tragedy.

I

The interest of Samson is not just that he begins as "a person separate to God, / Designed for great exploits" (31–32),[2] and ends up "eyeless in *Gaza* at the Mill with slaves" (41). More than a reversal of fortune is involved. Why, Samson asks in his opening soliloquy, was he set apart if his fate is "To grind in Brazen Fetters under task / With this Heav'n-gifted strength? O glorious strength, / Put to the labour of a Beast, debased / Lower than bondslave!" (35–38). It is not just that Samson once acted and now toils. Rather, the bodily strength that enabled heroic deeds—in a sense, the very physical substance of heroic action itself—has now been converted into labor power. And alienated labor power at that, enriching the enemies of his people. If we take Samson's grammar seriously, it is not he but his strength that has been debased—not he but his strength, which can now be apostrophized as if it were an independent agent, which has been put to bestial toil. But this rechanneling of heroic force into labor power, and the resulting substitution of productive activity for the heroic act, presents in a condensed and catastrophic form the very transition this book has attempted to trace. In this respect *Samson Agonistes* is emblematic of the predicament of modern drama as I understand it.

To be fair, we never actually see Milton's Samson labor, just as we never directly see him die. *Samson Agonistes* takes place on a holiday devoted to the god Dagon; the space for its tragic action is cleared by temporarily releasing Samson from his daily round of milling. Moreover, Milton does not invoke the physical effects of this labor as vividly as does Van den Vondel, who depicts his hero as dusty with flour and as giving off an unbearable stench. For Milton, Samson's toil remains largely in the background. Indeed, Samson's redemption or regeneration (if such it is) might well be described not only as his escape from a state of spiritual despair to become once again God's favorite but also as an escape from labor to the higher realm of tragic action. Pulling down the Philistine Temple is Samson's answer to his enforced toil—a return, as it were, from the improper activity of work to his proper activity of killing. If a tragic hero has anything to do with heavy stones, they should be used not to crush grain but rather to crush the heads of his enemies. And yet the notion of Samson's spiritual regeneration has been subjected to a good deal of critical skepticism in recent decades, and I shall likewise argue here that his tragic act does not really separate itself from the realm of labor, either. Samson's milling, though kept in the background, fundamentally twists the norms of tragic drama. Samson may leave the mill, but the mill, for its part, won't let go of Samson.

If one turns to Milton's prefatory essay, "Of That Sort of Dramatic Poem which Is call'd Tragedy," looking for signs of his revisionary intentions, one will come away disappointed. For there he declares his strict adherence to the example set by "*Aeschylus, Sophocles,* and *Euripides,* the three Tragic Poets unequall'd yet by any and the best rule to all who endeavour to write Tragedy" (62-65). By submitting himself to the "rule" set by his classical predecessors, Milton undertakes a form of literary discipline comparable to Samson's Nazarite vow. Accordingly, he promises to redeem the purity of classical tragedy by purging the debased innovations introduced by Renaissance playwrights—specifically, the use of comic relief. "This is mention'd to vindicate Tragedy from the small esteem, or rather infamy, which in the account of many it undergoes at this day with other common Interludes; happening through the Poets' error of intermixing Comic stuff with Tragic sadness and gravity; or introducing trivial and vulgar persons, which by all judicious hath been counted absurd; and brought in without discretion, corruptly to gratify the people" (29-37).

By "trivial and vulgar persons," Milton means characters such as the grave maker in *Hamlet* or the porter in *Macbeth* who introduce both laughter and labor into an otherwise aristocratic milieu. The space of *Samson Agonistes* will be kept ritually pure of such intermixture. And yet Samson's debased condition at the beginning of the play sounds rather like that of Renaissance tragedy as Milton describes it. Placed in a "common Prison" (6), surrounded by slaves and asses, Samson resembles those "common Interludes" that mix comic and tragic matter. Indeed, for the climax of the play, Samson is brought to the Philistine temple as just such a common interlude or popular entertainment.

> Have they not Sword-players, and ev'ry sort
> Of Gymnic Artists, Wrestlers, Riders, Runners,
> Jugglers and Dancers, Antics, Mummers, Mimics,

> But they must pick me out with shackles tired,
> And over-labour'd at their public Mill,
> To make them sport with blind activity?
>
> (1323–28)

"Although their drudge," insists Samson, he will not be the Philistines' "fool or jester" (1338). And yet "fool" is Samson's favorite derogatory epithet for himself, used from the beginning of the play to the end. "Inferior to the vilest" (77), engaged in "servile toil" (5), dressed "In slavish habit, ill-fitted weeds / O'erworn and soiled" (122–23), in need of "much washing to be touched" (1107), Samson is to all appearances just the kind of "trivial and vulgar person" who would be played by the Shakespearean clown and who, in Milton's opinion, ought therefore to be excluded from tragedy. Samson's descent and bearing invest him with dignity despite his debased circumstances, and Milton is careful not to extract from him the kind of uncomfortable laughter in which Shakespeare, for instance, occasionally indulges at the expense of King Lear—another noble reduced to wretched circumstances. Nevertheless, Samson is split between tragic dignity and a base condition that potentially threatens to reduce him to "Comic stuff." Milton avoids adding low-comic characters to his tragedy, but at the cost of introjecting clownish elements into his tragic hero.

King Lear's degraded condition provides an illuminating contrast with Samson's. Lear finds himself reduced to a limit state. Exposed on the stormy heath, bereft of shelter, food, and reason, he comes face to face with "unaccommodated man," the degree zero of the human condition—"a poor, bare, forked animal" (3.4.105–6).[3] By contrast, Samson is fed, housed, and clothed by his captors, though in a shabby fashion. He is overworked, but not to an unendurable pitch. His physical discomfort does not match that of Philoctetes in Sophocles's play, nor do his chains constrain him to the degree that Prometheus's do in Aeschylus. Samson's dilemma, we might say, is his inability to reach such a limit state—his suspension at a debased but supportable level of existence that denies even his suffering a genuinely tragic grandeur. Debasement, more than physical pain, *is* Samson's punishment. The Philistines aim more at the reduction of his status than at causing excruciating bodily harm. Putting Samson to work at the mill prevents him from achieving the status of triumphant *or* tragic hero.

As Samson reveals, moreover, economic motives are also at play:

> Much more affliction than already felt
> They cannot well impose, nor I sustain,

If they intend advantage of my labours,
The work of many hands, which earns my keeping
With no small profit daily to my owners.

(1257–61)

It is tempting to offer this passage as a privileged point of revelation in the play, a tearing away of the veil to expose the hidden production of surplus value as the startling economic "secret" behind Samson's confinement. And yet Samson offers alternative explanations for his labor, sometimes describing it as a punishment imposed by God (448–49), at other times depicting it as at least somewhat voluntarily undertaken—a way for him to maintain self-respect by earning his keep (573, 1365–67). Samson's milling has in any case an exhibition value for the Philistines as well as an economic one, though we may want to regard this as simply a different kind of surplus extracted from his labors—this time as performance rather than production. The point is that Samson's milling exhibits a frightening logical efficiency, since labor power is both the debased thing into which his heroic strength is converted *and* a motive to maintain him indefinitely in this state of perpetual drudgery.

For present-day readers, Samson's divinely inspired ability to do "the work of many hands" at the Philistine mill looks backward to the old folktale motif of the magic mill and forward to the miracle of machinery, praised by the political economists for its ability to combine and amplify the efforts of individual laborers so that one does the work of many.[4] Samson's mill is thus at once primitive and oddly modern. Certainly, with Samson as engine the Philistines have managed to put together a kind of black-box "factory" that produces ample grain and profits.

Another way of stating this is that neither Samson nor the mill remains unchanged by their encounter. The mill degrades Samson's heroic strength into labor power, while Samson elevates the mill into a miraculously productive device. Really, then, a third thing—Samson-at-the-mill—is born from their conjunction. This assemblage of man and mill is moreover embedded in other assemblages such as the Philistine economy and Samson's relationship with God. Despite beginning the play in a state of apparent isolation, Samson is in fact always and from the beginning plugged into mechanisms of more than one kind. His work is never conducted solely with the inert object that is the millstone but always in relation to others who benefit from the grain he produces or the spectacle he provides. Despite being its enemy, Samson is integrated to a remarkable degree with the Philistine state, which is why he appropriately wears the state livery when entering the temple of Dagon. To revert momentarily to a Lacanian register, we might say that Samson exists in a state of extimacy with respect to the Philistines—that he is both lodged within their world yet irreducibly exterior to it and, in this sense, is the Philistines' privileged *symptom*.

Samson is also plugged into various theological and literary assemblages, of which the typological ones have garnered most attention from recent critics. Likewise noticed but given less emphasis are Samson's conspicuous parallels to the protagonist of Aeschylus's play *Prometheus Bound*. Both Samson and Prometheus spend their respective plays in chains; both therefore remain stationary and are addressed by various visitors, some friendly, some not; both call on the sun; both are undone by secrets, Samson for revealing his and Prometheus for refusing to reveal his; and both end their respective plays overwhelmed by violent force—the difference being that Prometheus, unlike Samson, cannot die.[5] These Promethean references interact complexly with the Christian typologies of Milton's play. On the one hand, Prometheus's act of self-sacrifice on behalf of mankind evokes parallels to Christ.[6] On the other, the Titans, of whom Prometheus was one, revolted against the Olympian gods and were defeated by them. The critic William Riley Parker goes so far as to call Samson a "Hebrew Titan," an epithet supported not only by the play's implicit parallels between Samson and Prometheus but also by the Hebrew Chorus's explicit comparison between Samson and another Titan: Atlas.[7] Celebrating his exploits, the Chorus recalls how Samson

> by main force pull'd up, and on his shoulders bore
> The gates of *Azza*, Post, and massy Bar
> Up to the Hill by *Hebron*, seat of Giants old,
> No journey of a Sabbath day, and loaded so;
> Like whom the Gentiles feign to bear up Heav'n.
> (146–50)

Samson is both an Atlas figure in bearing the gates of Azza upon his shoulders and, proleptically, an anti-Atlas figure who will bring down the Philistines' world. But what is interesting about the Chorus's allusion is that Atlas was forced to bear up heaven after he led the unsuccessful revolt of the Titans against the Olympians. He thus carries a Satanic as well as a divine potential. Moreover, by mentioning Atlas just two lines after an allusion to the pre-Noachide Giants, the Chorus suggestively synchronizes Greek and Hebrew myths of enormous, rebellious races felled by deity. Here we may want to recall that some seventeenth-century commentators saw Samson not as a parallel to, and prefiguration of, Christ but rather as Christ's violent, sinful antithesis—which would render the Atlas reference not entirely benign.[8]

I want to read Parker's phrase "Hebrew Titan" to mean not only that Samson is both things, but also that Hebrews and Titans occupy analogous positions with respect to the reigning orders that "replace" them; in short, that just as the Old Testament is supposedly both fulfilled and canceled by the New, so the Titans must be overthrown and enslaved in order for the Olympian regime to begin. Connecting the two blurs the distinction between antecedent realms that are simply outmoded and those that are positively hostile. Instead of being typologically fulfilled by the new order, the old Greek one is violently suppressed and rejected, and it in turn rejects the new—as Prometheus does when he declares Zeus a tyrant.

In the case of Prometheus, however, these two "orders" have additional significance that redounds upon the Samson story. Aeschylus's Prometheus brings mankind not only fire but also the various arts or *techne* that make human life worth living: carpentry, masonry, metallurgy, and so forth (in Plato's *Protagoras* 321 c these are classed as "arts of Hephaestus") as well as medicine, literacy, and prophecy (classed in Plato as "arts of Athena"). The one thing that Prometheus cannot give man in Plato's version is the "civic art," or *politikos techne*, that only Zeus can furnish. Prometheus's mechanical arts provide physical comfort, but only Zeus allows men to organize themselves into the higher life of the city. In a kind of ironic contrapasso, Prometheus is chained up using the same arts of Hephaestus that he taught to mankind. Associating Samson with Prometheus and Atlas therefore strengthens his connection with manual crafts and labor.[9]

The Prometheus myth, especially as interpreted by Plato, associates the Titan with a realm of *techne* that is located temporally prior to the political, Olympian one. The needs of life are antecedent to judicial or political concerns and must be fulfilled before the latter can come into being. Production precedes action. Of course this temporal priority does not necessarily translate into conceptual priority. Aristotle, as we saw in an earlier chapter, acknowledges that the *polis* relies on the productive activity of the *oikos* but still privileges the *polis* as the teleological fulfillment that transcends its preconditions. The *polis* depends materially on the *oikos* but overgoes it. Prometheus can provide only the technical means of life that will later be completed by Olympian justice.

These Promethean elements in Samson resonate complexly with the Hebrew ones. As an Israelite, Samson predates the Christian era of grace, and as a Titan he predates the Olympian era of the political. As Hebrew as well he would be associated with "carnal Israel," the realm of the flesh as opposed to spirit; as Prometheus he would likewise be associated with those arts that promote "mere life," that of the body as opposed to civic life.[10] Samson's work at the mill does produce grain and thus sustains the flesh, thereby reinforcing both Hebrew and Greek "typologies."

But Samson's Promethean echoes do not just situate him within the realm of mere life; they point to his entrapment by it. In Aeschylus's play, Zeus cannot kill Prometheus, both because the Titan is immortal and because Zeus cannot afford to lose the possibility of learning his secret. He therefore subjects his foe to the prospect of endless imprisonment, chained to a remote mountaintop so that he can neither move nor die. Alive, but isolated and deprived of any social context, Prometheus is forced to live the subpolitical existence he provided for mankind, and to do so endlessly. His kinsman Atlas is likewise ceaselessly constrained, alone and subjected to a laborious task he can never finish.

Milton's Samson finds himself in a Promethean predicament, at once punished and sustained by enemies who cannot afford to kill or even severely harm him because of the profit he produces. Sequestered from the fields of the divine and of the political, Samson is deprived of the possibility of action and condemned to a seemingly interminable state of mere life. The mill wheel, whose circular turning knows neither beginning nor end, becomes therefore an emblem of Samson's predicament, which in some respects is even worse than that of Prometheus. Because the Titan could end his suffering in a moment by agreeing to Zeus's demands, his refusal to do so invests even his powerlessness with heroic stature. Unable to move, he is paradoxically still able to act, if only in a negative fashion, by maintaining his willful defiance of what he regards as tyrannical authority. Samson lacks even this baleful option. Not only is he not defying his foes; he is, through his productive activity, enriching them on a daily basis, as both Manoa and the Chorus are only too happy to remind him. Even his attempts to assume moral responsibility for his predicament have struck critics as both masochistic and megalomaniacal.[11] Unlike his Titanic predecessor, Samson lacks all possibilities for meaningful action.

By play's end, Samson seems to break out of this state of suspension to achieve one final, violent, and cataclysmic act. And yet it is unclear whether Samson's pulling down of the Temple is an escape from his productive activity of milling or merely a perverse extension of it. Samson's mill has already demonstrated a capacity to extend its dominion beyond the merely literal, as when the Chorus observes to Samson that "This Idol's day hath been to thee no day of rest, / Labouring thy mind / More than the working day thy hands" (1297–99). "Labouring thy mind" is less a periphrasis for "thinking" than it is a name for a different kind of mental activity: what happens instead of thought when the mind's motions are captured by those of the mill.[12] Having dominated Samson's body, his *res extensa*, the mill proceeds to colonize his *res cogitans* as well. We might be justified in overlooking the Chorus's figuration of thinking as milling if it did not return, less directly but still unmistakably, in the final moments before Samson's cataclysmic act: "[W]ith head awhile inclined, / And eyes fast fix'd he stood, as one who pray'd, / Or some great matter in his mind revolved" (1637–40). The "great matter" that Samson revolves in his mind punningly invokes the enormous millstone he revolved in the prison house. It may be that the echo is meant to signal how Samson's final act transcends and negates his productive activity, but it may also reduce his final act to a mere continuation of it. In any case, the pun rings oddly in context.

That Samson's pulling down of the Temple can be seen as just more milling is an idea developed explicitly by Van den Vondel:

> My strength, that in its weakness ground their corn,
> If but once more it may repeat its power,
> Shall grind a grist of skulls and human bones
> And so regard the past as richly paid for.[13]

Here, grinding the skulls of his enemies is both a repetition *and* a negation of his earlier activity—figuratively, payback. Milton is far more allusive and less direct than Van den Vondel, but his pun makes Samson's final act into an unmistakable repetition of his earlier activity, and thus raises the question of whether there is any possible escape from the mill. Samson "grinds" himself along with his foes under the massive stones of the Temple, and if this puts an end to his milling, it does so only by converting him from the grinder into the ground. There is an old German saying: "When the mill has no more corn to grind, it grinds itself." Milton's version of this would seem to be: "When the Miller has no more corn to grind, he grinds *him*self." Samson's final act is not so much an escape from the mill as a merging with it, resulting in a mangled heap of stone, blood, and flesh.

Some seventeenth-century biblical commentators were dismayed by Samson's pulling down of the Philistine Temple, a murderous act that struck them as the very opposite of Christ's self-sacrifice.[14] Joseph Wittreich, who catalogs these responses, also notes how Milton's allusion to the play

Christ Suffering in the preface to *Samson Agonistes* draws attention to "the enormous difference between the avenging Samson and the patient Christ, the one delivering his enemies and himself to death and the other dying so that his enemies might be saved."[15] Other modern critics of Milton's poem have likewise expressed doubt about whether there is anything redemptive about its violent climax. Some are troubled by the fact that the generous-minded Philistines ready to ransom Samson are killed along with the rest; others, by the sheer scale of the bloodbath; others, by the fact that all this violence does nothing to liberate the captive Israelites; and others still, by the fact that Samson's "rousing motions," which spur him on to the deed, may be mere bodily impulse rather than divine inspiration.[16] These doubts have been summed up and inflated by recent debates over whether Milton's Samson is a religious terrorist.[17]

The question is how understanding his act as an extension of Samson's milling activity can either add to or clarify the swarm of doubts that already hover about it. My answer would be: not by contributing any new layers of significance to it. On the contrary, the essence of Samson's milling is precisely its meaninglessness, its futile circularity. Milling produces grain, not meaning. It is true that milling has picked up various forms of figurative significance through rabbinical and Christian commentary. For the rabbis, milling could be a metaphor for the sexual act, and for both Talmudic and Christian interpreters, milling could be a figure for scriptural interpretation.[18] While I wouldn't want to deny that the sexual overtones of milling play a role in Samson's pulling down of the Temple, especially given the imagery of childbirth that also occurs there, I think that the brute, meaningless materiality of the process is foremost. The pun that reduces "great matter" from an exalted topic of thought to a large stone is emblematic of the way in which Samson's milling drains significance from his final act, reducing it to what John Guillory has called a "labor of destruction."[19]

Other critics have noted the images of circularity that attend the poem's end. Of the final simile comparing Samson to the phoenix, for instance, Joseph Wittreich remarks that the image of the phoenix "may be of history rolling back into its former self."[20] Even Mary Ann Radzinowicz, on the whole an optimistic and affirmative reader of *Samson Agonistes*, observes that "history moves in circles, like the Philistine mill."[21] Here we may note another, final figurative meaning that attaches to the mill: that of apocalypse. *This* one, at least, is surely invoked by Samson's pulling down of the Temple, but only to be disappointed, since Samson's bloodbath not only fails to end history—it does not advance it an inch. Neglecting to seize the mo-

ment, the Israelites remain justifiably in bondage in the wake of the tragedy visited upon their Philistine enemies. (Indeed, if there is a tragedy to be
found in *Samson Agonistes*, a good case could be made for viewing the Philistines, and not Samson or the Israelites, as the protagonists of it.)

A circular history—that is, a history captured by Samson's mill—is no
history at all. It is a temporal continuum deprived of the transformative
or redemptive potential of the event. Another way to say this is that the
temporality of tragedy cedes to that of *Trauerspiel*. What Walter Benjamin
calls "natural history" results when time petrifies into an unchanging landscape.[22] Accordingly, Samson himself retreats into a creaturely existence,
the zone of mere life that is sustained indefinitely but prevented from acting. This is the ambiguous triumph of labor as Milton portrays it. Production is not, as it will later be for Karl Marx, the engine of historical development. It is rather an incessant round that colonizes and neutralizes the very
possibility of the historical act and, with it, the possibility of the tragic as
well.

II

I have thus far been exploring the notion that labor drags Samson into an
ambiguous zone beneath that of the tragic hero. But it could also be argued
that the apparent meaninglessness or opacity that attaches to Samson's final
action elevates him above the tragic. In Kierkegaard's *Fear and Trembling*, the
figure known as the knight of faith transcends the tragic hero by means of
"an absolute relation to the absolute."[23] Adopting a Hegelian perspective on
classical tragedy, Kierkegaard argues that the tragic hero's action always has
reference to the universal realm of ethics. His paradigm here is Agamemnon, who sacrifices his daughter Iphigenia for the Greek nation as a whole,
thus undergoing personal loss for a higher good. The act of the tragic hero
attempts to sacrifice or dissolve his individuality into the universal of ethics.
By contrast, the knight of faith elevates his particularity above the general,
entering into an individual relation with the absolute that is not mediated
by the universal, and thus appears absurd or meaningless. The paradigm
here is Abraham, whose faith in offering to sacrifice his son simply cannot
be made comprehensible to others. While the tragic hero speaks, because
language opens his action onto the universal of meaning, the knight of faith
remains silent, because his unmediated faith cannot intelligibly be spoken.

Now it can be, and has been, argued that Milton's Samson is just such a
Kierkegaardian knight of faith. Or rather, the one critic who has taken up

this theme maintains that we cannot know whether Samson is one, because his silence remains resolutely uninterpretable.[24] In particular, the content of Samson's notorious "rousing motions" are unknown to us. Are they a silently delivered command from God, a falsely imagined command, or mere impulse from Samson's melancholic body? Certainly Samson's final act does not accord with any obviously universalizable ethical mandate. If it has meaning, its meaning is particular to him alone. The rest of us should not be pulling down temples and killing thousands, even if we could. What Kierkegaard says of Abraham, that "though [he] rouses my admiration, he at the same time appalls me," could be said of Milton's Samson as well.[25]

And yet what is interesting about *Samson Agonistes* from a Kierkegaardian perspective is that it pulls, impossibly, in two directions at once. Samson's absolute relation to the absolute does not absolve him of a simultaneous relation to the ethical. He is at once a priori in the right, given his allegiance to Jehovah, and at the same time subjected to moral scrutiny. The Hebrew dimension of the play embraces the Kierkegaardian absurd insofar as Samson's final act is in some sense unintelligible, beyond explanation or justification. Nevertheless, Samson paradoxically retains a relation to Greek heroism—that is, to the universal. Exploring the issue of universality will initially take us somewhat afield from the topic of labor, but will eventually allow a return to it from a different angle.

The problem of the universal in *Samson Agonistes* is encountered above all in the national or tribal divisions that constitute its world. While it is relatively easy to contrast Dagon as an idol or false god to Jehovah as the true one, things become much murkier in the realm of ethics. Both of his Philistine interlocutors, Dalila and Harapha, are simultaneously foes and mirror images of Samson, which makes ethical adjudication between them frustratingly difficult. John Rumrich voices an increasingly widespread perspective in pointing out the ethical contradictions and inconsistencies that riddle Samson's encounter with Dalila:

> Samson blames Dalila for violating the sanctity of marriage in betraying him, but he himself "still watching to oppress / *Israel*'s oppressors," shows the way, betrothing Philistine women as a provocative tactic and so subordinating the proper ends of marriage to his political and religious agenda: "I . . . / . . . therefore urg'd the marriage on," he admits, "that by occasion hence/I might begin *Israel*'s Deliverance." (232–33, 222–25)[26]

Rumrich describes Samson and Dalila as "opposite numbers, champions of their respective nations, more alike than different."[27] They both regard

THE SAME OLD GRIND 171

themselves as justified in defending their respective nations and gods, even if this involves falsifying the bonds of marriage and betraying a spouse. And the play can offer no universal ethical framework that would decide between these conflicting tribal claims.[28]

Of course, this dilemma may be precisely Milton's point: *Samson Agonistes* takes place prior to the advent of Christian universalism, the absence of which results in the dizzying mirror effects of Samson's encounters with Dalila and Harapha. Lacking access to the universal, Samson's actions are not tragic in a Hegelian sense. Indeed, one critic regards Samson's predating of Christian universalism as precisely his Aristotelian *hamartia*—not an ethical flaw, exactly, but a historically determined ignorance that fuels a blindly tribal form of aggression.[29]

Thinkers as different as Alain Badiou and Daniel Boyarin have identified the *locus classicus* of Christian universalism in the following verse from Paul's epistle to the Galatians: "There is neither Jew nor Greek, there is neither bond nor free, there is neither male nor female: for ye are all one in Jesus Christ" (3:28).[30] Samson is the point-by-point refutation of this verse. Not only is he a Jew, but as a Nazarite, God's covenant with Israel has been redoubled for him personally. Set apart even from the rest of his tribe, he is a kind of Jew to the second power. Not only is Samson male, he also is possessed of an almost parodic hypermasculinity, just as Dalila embodies an explicitly Cleopatra-like hyperfemininity. Samson may be no more a slave than his fellow grinders at the prison house, but his enslaved condition is felt all the more keenly because of his former religious and social eminence. Samson not only embodies all the forms of difference that the Christian covenant will supposedly cancel, according to the famous verse from Galatians, he also drives these differences to their outer limit. In his person he condenses and exaggerates every mode of particularity that Christian universalism will take it upon itself to dissolve. All that being said, Samson nevertheless exhibits certain obscure and primordial impulses toward the universal, but they either fall short of their aim or else achieve a universalism that is itself failed or tragic. These impulses center on two fundamental human activities: sex and labor.

To start with the first of these: despite the hostile maneuvering on both sides, Samson's marriages with Philistine women do threaten to breach the barrier separating Jew and gentile. Samson, of course, insists that he undertook these marriages only so "that by occasion hence / I might begin *Israel*'s Deliverance" (224–25) and that he was "still watching to oppress / *Israel*'s oppressors" (232–33). Yet his father Manoa is openly skeptical of this explanation (420–24), and Samson himself later gives a somewhat different account, claiming that "swoll'n with pride into the snare I fell / Of fair fallacious looks, venereal trains, / Soften'd with pleasure and voluptuous life" (532–34). His insistence that he married solely for political or military advantage clearly covers up, at least in part, for an uncontrollable libido that is attracted to forbidden, Philistine women. Yet Samson's roving eye does indeed prompt him to "love his enemies," if not quite in the sense that Jesus intended, and thus tends to erase the line between Jew and gentile. As Samson remarks to Harapha, "Among the Daughters of the *Philistines* / I chose a Wife, which argued me no foe; / And in your City held my Nuptial Feast" (1192–94). Something like Pauline universalism can be glimpsed here, but because it takes place under the aegis of eros rather than of agape, it allows hatred, jealousy, and aggression to mingle with love. Another way to put this is that Samson's sexual impulses produce a bodily—and thus fallen—counterpart to a Christian universalism that in Saint Paul relies instead on spirit. For Paul, the body—and particularly the penis—is the site of difference, bearing the marks of both circumcision and sexual morphology.[31] It is a site on which two of the three forms of difference mentioned in Galatians 3:28 come to bear. But ironically, Samson's penis, though carrying the mark of Jewish particularity, is a kind of divining rod that leads him against his will into foreign liaisons. Philo of Alexandria interpreted circumcision as a mortification of the sexual passions, but if this is so, the operation has spectacularly failed to "take" in Samson's case.[32] Cutting his hair may temporarily sap his strength, but cutting his foreskin does not apparently dampen his sexual enthusiasms.

But what would happen—to pose a counterfactual—if Samson's marriage with Dalila had worked out? What if they had had a child together? Would this mixing of blood have begun to repair the rift between Hebrew and Philistine? Milton's play does not explore this possibility directly. But I think it does so in a kind of negative fashion. For in the play's catastrophic denouement, Samson achieves a deathly version of precisely this union with his enemies. He is described as "tangled in the fold / Of dire necessity, whose law *conjoin'd* / *Thee* with thy slaughter'd foes" (1665–67, my emphasis). Here the verb "conjoined" manages faintly to evoke marriage even in the context of slaughter. Again, "*Samson with these inmix'd*, inevitably / Pull'd down the same destruction on himself" (1657–58, my emphasis—except for *Samson*). Manoa urges the Chorus: "Let us go find the body where it lies, / Soak'd in his enemies' blood, and from the stream / With lavers pure and cleansing herbs wash off / The clotted gore" (1725–28). Here the mixture of blood that would have taken place with Dalila alone has been extended to the entire Philistine nation, whose bloods now run together with Samson's. These mangled but therefore united bodies offer a grotesquely inverted image of the Pauline universality achievable through love. That images of both child-birth and abortion suffuse the play's catastrophe only underlines the fact that it substitutes for the child that Samson and Dalila never conceived.[33] In place of that life born of love, and the universality it might have foretold, is one founded upon what Paul in the Epistle to the Romans calls "this body of death."

If Samson's erotic desire gestures toward the undoing of national or tribal divisions, it does something similar with gender division. Once con-joined with Dalila, the formerly virile Samson describes himself as "Ef-feminately vanquish'd" and "shor[n] . . . Like a tame Wether" (562, 537–38), while Dalila leaves their interview bearing a phallic if merely metaphorical "sting / Discover'd in the end, till now concealed" (997–98). Both enemies, former paragons of their respective sexes, end up in an ambiguously gen-dered state, neither fully male nor female—just as their marital union ren-ders them neither fully Hebrew nor Philistine. And finally, Dalila promises Samson that if he returns to her,

> I to the Lords will intercede, not doubting
> Their favourable ear, that I may fetch thee
> From forth this loathsome prison-house, to abide
> With me, where my redoubled love and care
> With nursing diligence, to me glad office,
> May ever tend about thee to old age.
>   (920–25)

Released from prison but confined to a kind of pleasurable house arrest, Samson would find himself once again in an ambiguous state, neither fully enslaved nor fully free. His marriage to Dalila thus gestures at undoing all three forms of particularity listed in Galatians 3:28. Yet this undoing is not so much a cancellation or sublation of antithetical states as their endless confusion. It is not as though Jew and gentile, male and female, slave and free would cease to exist; it is simply that they would lose their sharp out-lines in Samson's condition. What Samson can achieve is only the typologi-cal prefiguring of the universal or, rather, the universality of man's fallen state, not of the redeemed one. This is a universality that regresses to a time before the covenant with Israel, not one that overgoes it. It is the universal-ity of wayward sexual desire—that is, of the shared but fallen condition of humanity. Sex, we may therefore say, is a failed universal. While desire is experienced by all, it cannot provide the encompassing ethical framework that both Hegel and Kierkegaard find requisite for tragedy. And by absorbing or contaminating love, it likewise forecloses the Christian universalism Paul announced.

These issues have a literary as well as a thematic dimension. For what is *Samson Agonistes* if not an exogamous "marriage" of Hebraic content and Greek form?[34] In this respect the play invokes Renaissance humanist efforts to combine Greek and Hebrew studies into a unified field of knowledge. But *Samson Agonistes* does not accomplish—nor does it really attempt—a Pauline sublation of Hebrew and Greek strains. Rather, it remains a conspicuously and, I think, an intentionally failed effort at synthesis—a bad marriage of incompatible elements that works out no more amicably than Samson's union with Dalila. The play registers the absence of a globalizing framework in its very form.

If we now turn back to labor, we find that it, like sex, prefigures Christian universalism. For as with his sexual appetites, Samson's labor crosses the line separating tribes or nations. Just as he married a Philistine, Samson labors on behalf the Philistines, and his countrymen exhibit similar forms of discomfort with both activities. When Samson objects to using his God-given strength to honor Dagon at the Philistine temple, the Hebrew Chorus retorts: "Yet with this strength thou serv'st the *Philistines,* / Idolatrous, uncircumcised, unclean" (1363–64). Manoa likewise asks his son: "Wilt thou then serve the *Philistines* with that gift / Which was expressly giv'n thee to annoy them?" (577–78). Manoa essentially accuses Samson of regifting; he takes the strength given him by God and in turn gives it freely to the Philistines. Interestingly, both Manoa and the Chorus seem to view Samson's labor for the Philistines as being at least to some degree voluntary. If Samson truly had no alternative, there would be little point in criticizing his exertions. An ambiguous space between enslavement and freedom, comparable to that which emerges in Samson's debate with Dalila, therefore opens up here as well. Indeed, Samson goes so far as to defend his milling for the Philistines, describing it as "labour / Honest and lawful to deserve my food / Of those who have me in their civil power" (1365–67). He does not, in other words, dispute the semivoluntary quality of his labor but instead explains and justifies his willingness to cooperate with his captors. Moreover, his explanation is itself somewhat suspect. Samson suggests that he works solely in order to earn his keep, with the implication that he does not wish to be beholden to the Philistines. But Samson does more than "deserve his food";

his immense strength generates a significant surplus over and above this. Samson admits as much earlier when he surmises that the Philistines will not punish him past a certain point in order not to endanger the profits he produces for them.

What bothers both Manoa and the Chorus is that Samson treats his foes as friends, aiding the cause of the Philistines by doing prodigious quantities of milling for them. Once again Samson loves his enemies, engaging in unintentional (or is it semi-intentional?) efforts do good to those who harm him. Just as his eros did, Samson's labor crosses enemy lines in a way that both parodies and prefigures Christian charity, limning the possibility of a Pauline universalism even in the midst of ongoing war. But again, just as with eros, Samson's labor resembles charity only to the degree that will allow it to fall conspicuously short of charity's ideal.

For all that, Samson's milling does manage to invoke a universalism, though not a redemptive one. This is the curse laid upon Adam and Eve following the fall that they must henceforth earn their bread by the sweat of their brow. The curse of labor is one shared by all of postlapsarian humanity, uniting them in a condition that is painful but not, in the technical sense of the term, tragic. As did eros, then, labor engages with a precovenantal universalism.[35] What binds mankind together is not a redemptive future but a fallen past—not spirit, but a shared fleshly condition. Sex and labor have more in common than merely being bodily experiences, moreover; together they perpetuate biological existence by conceiving and nourishing it. In a sense, they sustain the zone of mere life to which Samson has been condemned in this play, and which, as we have seen, prevents him from rising to the level of the tragic. Universalizing *this* condition puts tragedy itself in the predicament of Samson, trapped in a realm without access to the ethical and political orders that render tragedy—and tragic action—meaningful. This is not a case of the "death of tragedy," as George Steiner would have it. We should rather say that tragedy, like Samson at the beginning of the play, *cannot die*. It is itself its sepulcher, persisting in a kind of twilight state that resists a definitive end.

Now it could be argued that a Hegelian concern with the universal isn't so much an interpretation as a domestication of tragedy—a way of injecting dialectical optimism that makes tragic loss acceptable to philosophy. For every Agamemnon sacrificing to the ethical whole, there is a suicidal Ajax whose ethical commitments are much less clear. And this is even assuming that an "ethical" interpretation of Agamemnon holds water. One could argue with perhaps greater precision that Agamemnon is every bit as much an incomprehensible knight of faith as Abraham, his sacrifice of Iphigenia just as absurd and repellent. In this sense Samson's final act would be perfectly tragic even without broader justification. But as I hope I have shown, the action of *Samson Agonistes* does blindly grope toward the universal. The play explicitly problematizes the lack of a global ethical framework, establishing it as a desideratum that it manages to anticipate only in failed or fallen form. In this sense *Samson Agonistes* not only is but builds its own sepulcher.

III

At the risk of descending into cliché, I want to situate Milton's universalism of labor in *Samson Agonistes* with respect to a later and even more famous statement of this universalism. I am thinking of course of the best-known line from the *Communist Manifesto*: "Workers of the world, unite! You have nothing to lose but your chains." Certainly the curse on Adam and Eve in Genesis hangs heavily in the background of this phrase. The workers of the world can unite only because this is a world in which most—though not quite all—are condemned to work. I would argue as well that Prometheus, whom Marx pronounced the "most eminent saint and martyr in the philosophical calendar," is invoked by the imagery of the chains.[36] Marx's phrase thus conjoins biblical and Promethean traditions in a way strikingly comparable to what Milton does in *Samson Agonistes*. In Marx's view, to be sure, neither Jehovah nor Zeus is responsible for man's laborious condition. Both capital and the state pinion us, but so too does the twin rule of scarcity and necessity, which in Marx's view can be overthrown only when a certain level of the productive forces is reached under capitalism. Work enchains us insofar as surplus value, absconded with by capitalists, reproduces and expands the repressive apparatus. But that same apparatus, the product of work, also provides the necessary if merely potential precondition for freeing workers from their chains.

It is worth noting as well that work is not for Marx merely the content of a universal condition; it is, rather, that which enables a "world" to be constituted in the first place. A global proletariat can be formed only when a world market has connected the various nations of the planet and slowly eroded both the local traditions and the uneven development that have hitherto separated them. For Marx, as for Saint Paul, there is neither Jew nor Greek, but merely a worldwide proletariat on the cusp of transforming their shared condition into a self-consciously united one.

To do so, however, will require the leap from production to action—from being a worker to being a doer or agent. While it is true that global capitalism has created the preconditions for revolution in Marx's view, the workers themselves must seize those conditions. Not only the hortatory mode but also the heroic cadences of Marx's statement attempt to provoke the proletariat into action, with the aim of creating a world in which both free productive activity and free political action will henceforth be routinely available. This leap from production to action is precisely the one that Milton's Samson finds so bedeviling. For Marx to think his way beyond the same dilemma requires formulating a whole new kind of agent or heroic subject, one that is collective rather than individual—a self-conscious social class. This agent not only bears a universalizing mission on its shoulders, but to do so must also become aware of itself *as* a universal. Only thus can its actions achieve a high-tragic pitch.

Of course, the proletariat does not respond to Marx's clarion call in exactly the way he expects; the apocalyptic fervor of the *Communist Manifesto*, published in the revolutionary year 1848, thus gives way to the more circumspect views of the *Eighteenth Brumaire of Louis Bonaparte*, published in 1852, a work in which the world-historical tragedy is always doubled by farce. *Samson Agonistes* articulates a similar disappointment. After Samson pulls down the Temple of Dagon, thus annihilating the entire leadership of the Philistines, the Hebrews inexplicably fail to seize the moment and instead remain in bondage. Manoa, for one, grasps the liberatory potential of the catastrophe: "to *Israel*," Samson has left "honour . . . and freedom, let but them / Find courage to lay hold on this occasion" (715–16). But his optative serves merely to remind the reader that Manoa's countrymen will not lay hold on the occasion. Hence the deafening crash of the Philistine Temple is ultimately answered by the deafening silence of the Israelites. Moreover, it is this collective silence that retroactively empties out Samson's individual action. If his pulling down of the Temple had actually freed his country, it might have risen to the standards of tragedy as Hegel and Kierkegaard understand it. The meaninglessness of the event, its inability to escape from the circularity of the mill, is enforced by the failure of the nation to heed Samson's call.

Nor is this the first time they have done so. Early in the play, while recalling one of his victories over the Philistines, Samson bitterly surmises:

> Had *Judah* that day join'd, or one whole Tribe,
> They had by this possess'd the Towers of *Gath*,
> And lorded over them whom now they serve;

But what more oft in Nations grown corrupt,
And by their vices brought to servitude,
Than to love Bondage more than Liberty,
Bondage with ease than strenuous Liberty;
And to despise, or envy, or suspect
Whom God hath of his special favour raised
As their Deliverer?
                    (265–74)

More than anything else, *Samson Agonistes* is Milton's great meditation on the problem of voluntary servitude, manifested collectively by Israel's relations with the Philistines and individually by Samson's relations with Dalila. What keeps Israel in chains is its unacknowledged collusion with its captors, its choice of easy bondage over strenuous liberty. The concept of "ease" here is intriguing. Certainly the Israelites don't seem to suffer stark material deprivations as a result of their captivity; while none of them exhibits the sartorial extravagance of a Dalila, they seem to be comfortable enough, and Manoa can even manage to collect the presumably ample funds needed to try to ransom his son. Part of their "ease" involves adapting to a zone of biological sufficiency that they do not wish to risk losing. But in addition, bondage is its own form of ease, relieving the Israelites of the burden of decision and action—or, as Samson puts it (sounding more than a little like Hannah Arendt), "strenuous liberty." What Samson diagnoses here is not a mere failure to act but a positive revulsion toward action as such, the feeling that to be deprived of liberty is preferable to the burden of wielding it. It is one thing to carry the gates of Azza on one's back, as Samson does, or the whole world on one's back, as does Atlas. It is something far more difficult to bear the infinite weight of one's own freedom, if that means not having simply the formal liberty to act but the obligation and the disciplinary vigor to actually do so. Even Samson chooses to turn a mill endlessly rather than exercise or even recognize the full degree of his liberty.

The situation depicted in *Samson Agonistes* is thus a good deal more complex, in some ways, than that explored by Aeschylus. Like Prometheus, Samson is in chains. His capacity to act is in that sense physically constrained. But the other Israelites are not, and even Samson comes to recognize that his own iron shackles are as nothing compared to his mind-forged manacles. It is as if Paul's announcement that "there is neither bond nor free" now signals not the redemptive cancellation of those two states but rather the birth of a new, terrifying condition that is neither bond nor free but rather a hopeless confusion of the two.

Earlier I jokingly compared Milton to Hannah Arendt, but I now wish to take the resemblance somewhat more seriously for a moment. What *Samson Agonistes* shares with Arendt is an apparent sense that labor and action are largely antithetical. Samson's labors not only represent a distinctly subtragic form of suffering for Samson himself; they also perpetuate the zone of mere life that seduces from the hard responsibilities of action; and finally they infect action with the very quality of labor, so that grinding skulls and grinding grain become indistinguishable.

For Marx, by contrast, labor and action are by no means opposed. This is not only because labor creates the material preconditions for revolutionary action but also because the very forms of cooperation required by large-scale capitalist production train the proletariat in working together as a unit, and thus prepare them to act collectively. The factory is thus in some sense a rehearsal space for revolution. And yet, the leap from production to action still remains; if it did not, Marx would have no reason to utter his stirring call. For Milton, by contrast, the notion of productive labor as a historically progressive force is dimly felt, if at all. Labor is rather the primal curse uttered on humankind, the universality of failure. The leap from labor to meaningful action occurs not across a gap but across a chasm, paradoxically rendered even wider by the fact that Samson's final action is conceived as just another form of labor, which tends to empty out its meaning.

Another way of putting this is that labor can serve as historical cause in Marx while it remains primarily consequence in Milton. Labor, for Milton, does not make things happen. It is rather a punishment that follows upon things done wrongly. In the case of Samson, sexual indiscretion causes his fall, and labor is merely the result of it. Hence the implied universal in Milton's play emerges with much greater clarity and thoroughness with respect to sex. It is legible in labor as well, but less obviously and in a way that "leans" on the sexual for its coherence, which is why a detour through the sexual is necessary to grasp it in the first place. Even if it is true, as I have argued, that Samson's labor at the mill colonizes much of the play's world, this is accomplished through the adherence of metaphor, not through a causal logic. Labor in *Samson Agonistes* merely imposes resemblances, and these tend toward the encumbering or emptying out of action, not toward its completion. It should not be surprising, then, that the gap between production and action is largely unbridgeable in Milton.

Pessimistic readings of *Samson Agonistes* have become increasingly common in recent decades, though mine may be darker than most. Certainly, Milton had good cause for despair when he composed his play. The collapse of the Commonwealth and the restoration of monarchy, the defeat of the Good Old Cause to which he had devoted his life, and Milton's parlous personal situation have all been much discussed in this context. But economic factors may also play a role. Blair Hoxby has illuminatingly read *Samson Agonistes* as a response to "an ideology of productivity that was proving an effective means for Anglican Royalists and their allies in the City to counter the iconoclastic rhetoric of their opponents, to consolidate the position of the restored monarchy, and to steer public discourse away from divisive issues of political or church organization toward an ideal of prosperity and productivity that promised to provide a new ground for social consensus."[37]

The challenge posed by post-Restoration prosperity is not just to Milton's particular religious and political beliefs but to political action as such, which gets displaced by economic production and the goods it provides. It simultaneously poses a challenge to tragic drama, which likewise relies on action in the political or ethical sense for its meaning. In Hoxby's view, *Samson Agonistes* is Milton's attempt to resist this productivist ideology and its pacifying effects. "By re-inscribing desire, tragic conflict, the claims of conscience, and iconoclastic violence into the realm of public discourse," he claims, Milton "attempted to prevent the public sphere from being reduced to the world of goods."[38] I find Hoxby's reading so impressive that I wish I could believe in its elements of hope. Certainly the image of a Milton who retains his revolutionary principles even in the context of what Christopher Hill has called "the experience of defeat" is an appealing one.[39] But I find it difficult to see how a tragic protagonist who moves abruptly from a state of paralysis to a spasm of indiscriminate, murderous violence can provide a meaningful model of political resistance. At the same time, I don't want to reject Hoxby's arguments so much as suggest that by infecting action with the quality of labor, *Samson Agonistes* takes a deeper—and, yes, more pessimistic—sounding of the possibilities of action in a novel and alien landscape. The dominant force in this landscape is not the Philistines, Samson's political and religious foes, but rather the mill, to which he is inescapably bound and which conditions and absorbs everything around it. Resistance to *this*, whatever form it may take, will look very different from political resistance as classically conceived. In any case, these possibilities cannot be imagined without first surveying the new landscape in its starkest and most demanding terms. Milton's response to the conditions of Restoration society, above all its choice of prosperity over principle, is to fashion a new kind of dramatic agent: a subtragic hero, suspended beneath the zone of tragic action and deprived of a universal framework that could render action meaningful. Milton has thereby exposed, in an inchoate form, the dilemma facing modern tragedy; it may be asking a bit much to expect him to resolve that dilemma as well.

CHAPTER SIX

Hegel, Marx, and the
Novelization of Tragedy

It seems more than coincidental and perhaps more than a little convenient for the purposes of this book that the arrival of a fully fledged commercial society coincided with (dare we say "caused"?) a hiatus of almost two centuries on the part of major tragic drama. Of course, one must be careful when speaking of this hiatus, which is both geographically uneven and merely relative. The period in question did produce a few tragic playwrights of note, mostly German: Schiller, Kleist, Büchner. But in England and France, which had nurtured tragic playwrights of renown during the early modern period, no comparable figures emerged. Such tragic drama as was written remains of interest mainly to period specialists. In part, this had to do with theatrical energies being deflected into other dramatic forms. In England, the comic stage predominated in the early eighteenth century, followed by the birth of melodrama and the rise of the Music Hall. But for the most part, the tragic stage was simply eclipsed by the novel, which attracted a higher grade of literary talent and produced more brilliant formal innovations.[1] The novel largely displaced tragedy as the vehicle for the age's narrative energies.

Wherever its fictional setting may happen to be, tragedy is originally and essentially an urban form. In some sense theater constitutes a *polis* wherever it occurs, but it is also most at home in the actual city. The novel, by contrast, is a national form, read in relative and dispersed isolation. Tragedy is attended by an urban public; the novel is consumed by something between a public and a population, and it caters to the new forms of sociality described by political economy.[2] Whereas the audience is *subjected* to tragic drama in the presence of others, the novel is itself a companionable form, offering a phantom or asocial sociability. It does so less through the actions of its characters than through the sensibilities of the narrator. In contrast with the "two hours' traffic of the stage," the novel requires an extended stay in the narrator's company, resulting in a fundamental attunement of mind that can develop only over time. When I call the novel a "companionable" form, I mean that it prompts something akin to friendship or even domestic companionability between reader and narrator, yet without *acts of friendship* to sustain it. What remains is simply a shared perspective, the feeling that one is at home in the presence of the narrator's moral, psychological, and aesthetic sensibilities—that the narrator is a trustworthy guide through the complications of plot. When one exits a novel by Austen, Dickens, Eliot, or James it is less the characters than the framing narrative voice of which one takes one's leave. Moreover, while tragedy lacks such a framing voice and thereby throws the viewer back perforce on his or her own critical capacities, the classical novel's narrator more generally performs the act of ethical judgment *for* the reader. We are refined by responding to the narrator's more highly developed powers of observation and judgment. The novel teaches us not how to act, exactly, but rather how to observe and judge action correctly; the novel, therefore, rather than the tragic drama, is the true pedagogical medium for a Smithian ethics as described in this book's first chapter.[3]

The English novel was not, in its first phases, primarily a tragic form, and by the time a tragic strain made itself felt in Hardy and later in Conrad, significant tragedy had already returned to the stage. Conversely, the rebirth of important tragic drama through figures such as Strindberg and Ibsen clearly internalized some of the norms of the realist novel.[4] What began as displacement thus ended as mutual colonization. We need not wait until the late nineteenth century to see the results of this process, however. For the novelizing of the tragic stage is laid out in theoretical fashion through tragic drama's other "other" in the eighteenth and nineteenth centuries: philosophy. Just as Aristotle first subjected tragedy to philosophical treatment after the great fifth-century flourishing of tragedy had passed, so the advent of philosophical aesthetics celebrates tragic form just when it had largely stopped being practiced. As I shall argue in what follows, moreover, there is something distinctly "novelistic" in the treatment of tragedy by aesthetic philosophy. My test cases in this chapter will be Hegel's *Lectures on Aesthetics* and Marx's *Eighteenth Brumaire of Louis Bonaparte*—an odd pairing, admittedly. The latter is not itself a work of philosophical aesthetics, of course, but it does undertake a reading of that tradition as it goes about a very different task.

Now, while it is surely courteous of philosophy to fill in while tragedy goes on extended break, my chapter's project of tracing the novelization of drama through philosophy rather than through plays and novels themselves might seem like a gratuitously, indeed perversely, mediated enterprise—a kind of contortionist's trick. Why follow the process as reflected through philosophy's mirror when we can directly observe the thing itself? The answer—apart from the fact that I would rather occupy my time with good philosophy than with bad tragedies—is that the Hegelian mirror in particular introduces a crucial element: political economy. Hegel was the first philosopher to absorb the lessons of political economy in a truly systematic way—not directly into his treatment of tragedy, of course, but rather in his *Philosophy of Right* and its description of capitalism's "system of needs." I shall argue in what follows that Hegel's understanding of tragedy and its slow novelization, a topic taken up at length in his *Aesthetics*, can and indeed ought to be read in relation to *The Philosophy of Right* and its meditations on civil society and its system of needs. When one does so, what seems to be a purely aesthetic process of evolution turns out to be implicated in the most intimate ways with the development of capitalist modernity. This is an insight, moreover, that Hegel passes on to his recalcitrant and revisionary student, Marx.

I

It isn't certain exactly when Hegel did his reading in Adam Smith, though he clearly knew *The Wealth of Nations* as well as James Steuart's *An Inquiry into the Principles of Political Economy* (1767) by the Jena period.[5] Hegel's knowledge of political economy emerges most directly in the *Elements of the Philosophy of Right* (1821) and its discussion of the "system of needs." I want to begin here and move slowly toward the treatment of tragedy in Hegel's *Lectures on Aesthetics*, a work that oddly seems almost never to be discussed in conjunction with the *Philosophy of Right* despite the facts that the two are roughly contemporary and share important themes.[6]

Hegel expounds the system of needs in the final part of the *Philosophy of Right*, titled "Ethical Life." Ethics is distinguished for Hegel from morality, its abstract (Kantian) counterpart, because it is a system of behavior grounded not in abstract reason alone but in *Sittlichkeit*—the state of being customary or conventional. Ethics receives its substance from the particular institutions that give form to social and ethical life. In the *Philosophy of Right*, Hegel identifies three of these: the family, civil society, and the state. While the family and the state have origins that extend back at least as far as classical antiquity (their conflict informs the plot of *Antigone*, as Hegel claims), civil society is a product of modernity, and specifically of commercial society and its system of needs.

By "system of needs," Hegel means the way that the individual's wants, both biological and cultural, give rise to an overarching market system of production and exchange. Through the division of labor, one fulfills one's own needs by supplying commodities to fulfill the different needs of others. The division of labor not only satisfies existing demands, moreover, but also refines and multiplies them as the supply of commodities becomes ever more variegated and abundant. For Hegel, the main result of this process is particularization: the development of individual differences of taste and interest.[7] Not only does the division of labor encourage diversification within the realm of consumption, moreover, but it also multiplies the forms of production and labor and thus diversifies a population in that way as well, magnifying innate differences of capacity through specialized crafts (*Elements of the Philosophy of Right*, 233). It is through this process of diversification and particularization, Hegel claims, that genuinely human need, as opposed to basic animal needs, comes into existence (228). Moreover, "The right of the subject's *particularity* to find satisfaction, or—to put it differently—the right of *subjective freedom*, is the pivotal and focal point in the difference between *antiquity* and the *modern* age" (151). The system of needs thus completes a characteristically modern form of freedom in which individual predilections and differences are given full rein.

In developing the particularities of individuals, and thus multiplying differences among them, the system of needs would seem to have an antisocial force, ensconcing each of us within our own private nooks. Yet: "In this dependence and reciprocity of work and the satisfaction of needs, subjective selfishness turns into a contribution towards the satisfaction of the needs of everyone else. By a dialectical movement, the particular is mediated by the universal so that each individual, in earning, producing, and enjoying on his own account, thereby earns and produces for the enjoyment of others" (233). The more particularized we become, the more dependent we become on the system of needs to supply our wants, and thus the more dependent we become on each other. Selfishness dialectically reverses into helpfulness, particularity into universality. Hegel's version of the invisible hand thereby reasserts community even as it carries out the process of subjective particularization.

All of this sounds distinctly Smithian, and in some ways it is, and yet Hegel fundamentally shifts the most basic premises of political economy. As Lisa Herzog observes:

> Unlike Smith, Hegel cannot—and indeed, never attempts to—argue for the market from its beneficial consequences. History, for Hegel, is not the "progress of opulence," but the progress of the consciousness of freedom; and this is also the light in which he sees the market. He endorses it for the sake of the realization of subjective freedom, the form of freedom specific to modern societies. It provides individuals with the sphere in which they can act as they like: as separate individuals, unbound by rules and regulations, but also by social expectations and pressures.[8]

Like Arendt, whom he influences, Hegel values freedom over happiness—certainly over the kind of happiness supplied by commodities. The market matters for Hegel not because it provides for material needs but because it actualizes freedom, taking "actualize" in the specifically Hegelian sense wherein the universal realizes itself through the particular. Full freedom is possible only when the universal ends of the modern state are endorsed by the particularized, subjective wills of its individual citizens (*Elements of the Philosophy of Right*, 302). The diversification of tastes and interests is thus not, for Hegel, a mere side-effect of the way in which the market satisfies material needs; it is rather the very point of the market, which does the work of actualizing freedom by individuating the subjectivities of its participants—pushing them toward maximum difference so that these differences can then be gathered up again in a universalizing movement by the invisible hand.[9] It is not as if the material prosperity fostered by the market does not matter—Hegel has a great deal to say about wealth and poverty, as we shall see—but it matters in a way that is subordinate to the question of freedom.

The dialectical reversal effected by the invisible hand is a paradigmatic—perhaps *the* paradigmatic—instance of the cunning of reason. But its effects are complex. From a subjective point of view, all that matters is individual interest and its satisfaction. The recollectivizing movement effected by the division of labor, by contrast, is purely objective. Its participants *are* mutually dependent, but not consciously so; they do not understand or feel the universalizing effect of their particularized wants. As a result, in civil society, ethical life becomes "lost in the extremes," without for all that lacking dialectical connection: "Although particularity and universality have become separated in civil society, they are nevertheless bound up with and conditioned by each other. Although each appears to do precisely the opposite of the other and imagines that it can exist by keeping the other at a distance, each nevertheless has the other as its condition" (*Elements of the Philosophy of Right*, 221). The trick will be to bring the subjective and objective poles into a conscious relation, and that is primarily the work of the state, which embodies objective, universal reason in a way that can be willingly embraced by its citizens, thereby converting the unconscious bonds generated by the system of needs into a self-conscious, rational collectivity of particularized selves. Moreover, the system of needs is not the whole of civil society, which itself contains necessary elements that begin the work completed by the state.

We can get a clearer idea of civil society, and begin to glimpse some connections with tragedy, if we step back and place it within Part III of *The Philosophy of Right* as a whole. There Hegel isolates three ethical institutions—the family, civil society, and the state—with civil society mediating between the other two. The family as an institution is primarily ethical in nature, despite the elements of sexuality, reproduction, and material support that it also involves. But in the family, the ethical relation assumes its most natural, substantial form, that of love, whereas in the state it takes the form of reason and law (*Philosophy of Right*, 199). The family, moreover, makes little to no room for individuality: "the substantial basis of the family relationship is . . . the surrender of personality" (71), with the result that "one is present not as an independent person [*ein person für sich*] but as a *member*" (199). It is as independent persons, however, that citizens form a state, and so the substantial unity of the family must be dissolved. This is the work of civil society. "Civil society . . . is the immense power which draws people to itself and requires them to work for it, to owe everything to it, and to do everything by its means" (263). With its immense productivity and its complex division of labor, civil society takes over the functions of material sustenance previously provided by the family, even as its particularizing function turns the members of the family into autonomous, differentiated individuals. "But civil society tears the individual [*Individuum*] away from family ties, alienates the members of the family from one another, and recognizes them as self-sufficient persons. . . . Thus, the individual [*Individuum*] becomes a *son of civil society*, which has as many claims upon him as he has rights in relation to it" (263). Civil society effects both an atomization and a rebaptism of family members.

If the system of needs were all there was to civil society, however, the individual would be handed over solely to the anarchic realm of particularized desires. Moreover, while the satisfaction of needs provided by a commercial society helps detach the individual from the family, this immediate autonomy is not itself a form of freedom; rather, freedom consists of being liberated *from* the unchosen givenness of individual drives and wants and thus enabled to follow the promptings of reason.[10] Civil society provides two remedies in this regard. One is education, "the art of making human beings ethical" (195), which turns subjectivity toward the universal (225). The other is what Raymond Plant calls "partial communities of the system of needs."[11] These include corporations, which are professional associations akin to medieval guilds or trade unions, and estates (roughly, social classes). Membership in such corporate bodies provides a conscious sense of social belonging, solidarity, and identity. But in contrast to the family, into which one is merely born, here membership is (at least so Hegel claims) voluntary, and hence based on individual preferences, thus reconciling the particular with a social whole (*Philosophy of Right*, 237). These partial communities invest the subject with what one might call, taking a cue from Plant, a "partial universality," and thus mediate between the particularized individual formed by the system of needs and the objective universality of the state.

At the risk of seeming whimsical, one might describe civil society as modernity's vast attempt to prevent future *Antigone*s. At least, the transitional mechanisms provided by civil society seem designed to separate the modern individual from the family and then integrate him with the state through a series of mediating institutions such that family and state can no longer come into conflict, or even direct contact. Of course, Hegel assumes a male political subject, so woman might continue to be the irony even of modern forms of community. Nevertheless, Hegel's model of civil society seems in some respects to have imported a Smithian optimism along with a Smithian model of political economy.

A different Hegelian approach to tragedy, one that Hegel himself did not pursue, could be derived from what Merold Westphal calls the "radical idealism" of the *Philosophy of Right*: "In the order of explanation radical idealism denies that family and state can be accounted for in terms of sexual or economic needs as their basis, while in order of evaluation it denies that these needs are the definitive standards by which family and state should be judged."[12] As Westphal shows, family and state are for Hegel fundamentally *ethical* forms of community that accommodate sexuality and economy as subordinate factors but pursue other aims and arise on a different basis. "Just as sex for reproduction and pleasure does not belong to the essence of family life (though they get included in family life), so economics as production and consumption does not belong to the essence of the state (though they get included in political and cultural life)."[13] Indeed, as we have seen, even the economy does not strictly speaking have an economic basis for Hegel; its "essence" is to particularize the ethical subject, not to satisfy material needs (though it also does the latter). And the subordination of material factors to ethics in Hegel's political philosophy seems analogous to the way in which, in his aesthetic philosophy, the material substrate of art is an integrated part of the artwork but always subordinate to the informing Idea.

When I say that Hegel's radical idealism provides another possible approach to tragedy, I mean that tragedy can be seen as resulting from instances in which the ideally subordinate material stratum becomes insubordinate and thereby upsets the balance of the ethical system. *Antigone* would thus stage not the confrontation between family and state as opposing but substantial ethical unities but rather the undermining of the family's ideal unity by, for instance, the deadly competition between brothers in the name of political self-interest as well as by Antigone's suspiciously sexualized attachment to her fallen brother—an attachment that may invest her otherwise perfectly ethical defense of family bonds with a perverse intensity.[14] Of course, such a reading would undermine the possibility of reconciling opposed ethical spheres that Hegel sees as fundamental to tragedy, which is probably one reason he does not pursue the idea. Undermine, but perhaps not render impossible. Tragic reconciliation would in this case result from mutual recognition of the internally conflicted status of the supposed ethical unities each side is defending. Such a reading seems to do better justice to *Antigone*, which is at least as much about divergences between ethical claims and their material realities as it is about reconciling those claims. The point is that Hegel's system, if read differently, could provide a nondialectical yet still in some sense Hegelian reading of tragedy.

Indeed, it could provide a nondialectical yet still Hegelian reading of the political and social orders as well because the system of the *Philosophy of Right* suffers from some of the very imbalances just enumerated in relation to tragedy. Despite the account I've given of it thus far, things are not all rosy in the system of needs. By the time Hegel composed the *Philosophy of Right* in the second decade of the nineteenth century, the problems of industrial capitalism had become far more evident than they were to Smith. Particularly troubling to Hegel is the issue of poverty and the creation of a rabble (*Pöbel*).

The very quality that allows the system of needs to cater to individual tastes and caprices renders the whole mechanism somewhat capricious.

Commercial society is subject to crises of overproduction (*Philosophy of Right*, 267). The invention of new machinery or a sudden shift in tastes can, in addition, throw large numbers of people out of work. And the specialization of skills required by a complex division of labor makes it difficult for the unemployed to find new jobs. As a result, the commercial economy regularly casts workers into unemployment and poverty. "Despite an *excess of wealth*, civil society is *not wealthy enough*—i.e., its own distinct resources are not sufficient—to prevent an excess of poverty and the creation of a rabble" (267). That capitalism will inevitably produce poverty amidst its wealth is the tragic counterpart to the happy cunning of reason embodied by the invisible hand. The question of poverty is "one which agitates and torments modern societies especially" (267). Civil society possesses means to ameliorate this insoluble problem—regulation of the economy by "the police" to reduce its periodic crises, and colonialism to provide an export market for overproduced commodities—but ultimately these do not suffice.

Especially troubling for Hegel is the production of a "rabble" (*Pöbel*).[15] "Poverty in itself does not reduce people to a rabble; a rabble is created only by the disposition associated with poverty, by inward rebellion against the rich, against society, government, etc." (*Philosophy of Right*, 266). Not material deprivation as such, but alienation from society is the mark of the rabble. Nor is this merely a subjective problem. Because they are deprived of work, the rabble are also excluded from those partial communities, the corporations and estates, which mediate between individuals and the universal reason of the state (344).[16] Hence they lack both political recognition and a political disposition. They are not a social class but a motley, atomized mass—the precursor not of Marx's proletariat but of his *lumpenproletariat*, as we shall see.[17]

The rabble is the tragedy of commercial society. As an unassimilable remainder, it gives the lie to modern society's promise to provide a meaningful ethical and political community for all its members. Yet the creation of a rabble has less to do with a flaw in society's ethical institutions than it does with the contingent, uncontrollable movements of the market. The rabble is what occurs because the capitalist economic mechanism is both prone to contradiction and upheaval and not fully manageable by the institutions through which civil society hopes to control it. In the Jena manuscripts, Hegel describes the market economy as a "monstrous system . . . which requires strict dominance and taming like a wild beast."[18] Signaling the insubordination of the economy as material substrate of modern society, the rabble is a troubling exception to the radical idealism that governs Hegel's political system, which it tears apart just as the uncontrollable forces of sexuality and self-interest do to family and state in *Antigone*.

As we can now see, the transition from Hegel's *Philosophy of Right* to the *Lectures on Aesthetics* is not necessarily as abrupt as one might have expected—leaving aside the fact that Hegel does discuss tragic drama in the *Philosophy of Right* itself (144–46, 181, 201–2), and conversely considers the state in his *Lectures on Aesthetics* (e.g., 182–84). In fact, the treatment of tragedy in the latter work repeats and reconfigures some fundamental issues in the former. The Hegelian rabble will return, surprisingly, as the audience for modern tragedy.

Hegel regards poetry as the highest form of art. This is in part because language is the form of materiality closest to spirit, and in part because it is able to particularize spirit more fully than other media, and thus to actualize it more completely. Art, including poetic art, is the "product of free imagination," by which Hegel means that art is not subject to a means-end rationality.[19] In terms of its goal, art aims at "the production and enjoyment of beauty; in its case aim and development lie directly in the work itself" (*Aesthetics: Lectures on Fine Art*, 992). This autotelic character distinguishes free poetic art from say, oratory, in which artfulness is subjected to practical ends (990–92). But freedom marks not just the aim of art but also its internal structure, which grants a degree of aesthetic and conceptual autonomy to the artwork's internal components. Hegel insists on "the particularization of [the artwork's] individual parts, which to be able to enter into an organic unity, must appear developed on their own account" (981). Indeed, "its particular parts become *independent*" (982) yet still participate in an organic unity: "Everything must be related to this united whole and connected together with this whole concretely and freely" (979). "Freely" means that the parts are not predetermined by, and subordinated to, some preexisting concept that they abstractly serve (allegory might be what Hegel has in mind here), and that would introduce a means-end rationality into the very internal structure of the artwork (983). Instead, the particularized parts participate "freely" in a whole that in some sense arises from them rather than masters them.

This movement of particularization and subsequent unification is characteristic of speculative thought in general (Hegel regards art, in fact, as a less abstract version of speculative reason [*Aesthetics: Lectures on Fine Art*, 984–85]), but Hegel's descriptive language particularly resembles his treatment of modern society, in which subjects particularized by the system of needs freely participate in, and thus endorse, the universal reason embodied in the state. The freedom of the artwork is thus the aesthetic correlate of the freedom of modernity writ large. One might expect this to mean that the modern artwork is supreme for Hegel, but in the case of tragedy this turns out not quite to be the case.

Hegel divides poetry according to the three classical genres, with drama mediating between the other two: "In general we may define the relations of drama to epic and lyric by saying that it stands more or less in the middle between the extensive spread of epic and the concentratedness of lyric" (*Aesthetics: Lectures on Fine Art*, 1168). Epic presents a substantial, external totality at once national and universal; lyric develops an inner, subjective world; and drama becomes the highest form of poetry by encompassing both the objective and the subjective: "This objectivity which proceeds from the subject together with this subjectivity which gains portrayal in its objective realization and validity, is the spirit in its wholeness, and by being *action* provides the form and content of *dramatic* poetry" (1039).

While mediating between epic and lyric may grant drama a more complete grasp of spirit in its totality, it also saddles it with certain representational burdens: "But this conciliation of epic with the inner life of the person who is acting in front of us does not permit drama to describe, as epic does, the external aspect of the locality and the environment, as well as of what happens and is done, and it therefore demands a complete scenic production in order to give real life to the whole work of art" (*Aesthetics: Lectures on Fine Art*, 1158). Trying to jam the expansive totality of epic into dramatic form just will not work, and so drama is forced to represent scenically what epic can describe poetically. In addition, the very nature of action, which externalizes will and character, requires the physical body of the actor to express it (1181). Theatrical production is therefore not optional for drama but demanded by its very nature. Of the three genres of poetry, only drama is tied in this fashion to the material world. In some respects this is a good thing, since it allows drama to incorporate other arts such as music, dance, acting, even architecture. And while poetry must remain predominant, these ancillary arts can also become ends in themselves and strive for beauty, thus enabling a more capacious aesthetic totality to emerge (1182). Drama allots materiality a respected but subordinate place in accord with the radical idealism we have already seen at work in the *Philosophy of Right*.

On the other hand, theatrical embodiment exposes drama to the public, and here things become trickier. While lyric poetry assumes a specialized, cultivated audience, dramatic productions cannot be so choosy:

They are confronted by a specific public for which they are supposedly written, and the author is beholden to it. It has a right to bestow praise or blame
because, as an assembled audience, it is in the presence of a work which is intended to arouse a lively sympathy and give pleasure in this place at this time.
Now such a public, brought together haphazardly for the purpose of pronounc-
ing judgment, is extremely mixed in character: its members differ in education,
interests, habitual tastes, predilections, etc., so that now and again, in order to
please everybody, the author may even need a talent for the bad as well as a certain shamelessness in disregarding the pure demands of genuine art. (*Aesthetics:
Lectures on Fine Art*, 1175)

Hegel clearly has a modern public in mind. These are not the ranked tribes
installed by Cleisthenes that attended Greek theater but a messily heterogeneous audience. We seem to find ourselves squarely in the system of needs,
which has produced irreconcilable differences of taste, outlook, and sophistication, not all of which can be satisfied. Moreover, while Hegel does not
directly invoke the category, it is clear that this modern audience regards the
play not as artwork but as commodity. They have paid their fee and expect a
product that will please them. Not only does the drama not succeed in either
unifying or elevating its audience; their demands rather pull the playwright
down so as to violate the standards of art.

If the structure of the dramatic artwork echoes that of the idealized
Hegelian polity, in the audience it seems to confront an aesthetic counterpart to the "crowd" or "mass" or "rabble"—that is, to the particularized subjectivities produced by the system of needs, but now without the unifying
force exerted by education or partial communities, which would turn them
back toward the universal. (It is worth noting here that in the *Philosophy of
Right*, Hegel invokes a "rich rabble" as well as a poor one.)[20] While Hegel
regards "a healthy and artistically educated public" as "the supreme tribu-
nal" of art (*Aesthetics: Lectures on Fine Art*, 1184), large portions of this public
seem to have skipped class. A well-trained theatrical audience may be found
overseas, but not at home: "In France there is an established artistic taste,
while in Germany anarchy reigns. Here everyone pronounces judgment
out of his own head, and approves or condemns just as the accident of his
own personal views, feelings, or caprices dictates" (1175). It would be one
thing (though not, for all that, a good thing) if the ragtag theatrical public
simply failed to appreciate true art. But as Hegel suggests, their influence
tempts the playwright to abandon the highest artistic standards. This is part
of a larger argument about modernity and the decline of tragedy in the *Aesthetics*, and it is one that brings tragic drama and political economy into
close—if largely implicit—proximity.

As Hegel understands it, tragedy sets not only characters but also their ethical allegiances in conflict; the tragic resolution, however, results not in the defeat of either conflicting principle but in their reconciliation and the realization that their apparent opposition was only superficial:

> The general reason for the necessity of these conflicts I have touched upon already. The substance of ethical life, as a concrete unity, is an ensemble of *different* relations and powers which only in a situation of inactivity, like that of the blessed gods, accomplish the work of the spirit in the enjoyment of an undisturbed life. But the very nature of this ensemble implies its transfer from its first purely abstract *ideality* into its actualization in *reality* and its appearance in the mundane sphere. Owing to the nature of the real world, the mere *difference* of the constituents of this ensemble becomes perverted into *opposition* and collision, once individual characters seize upon them on the territory of specific circumstances. . . . In this way however, an unresolved contradiction is set up; it does appear in the real world but cannot maintain itself there as the substance of reality and what is genuinely true; its proper claim is satisfied only when it is annulled as a contradiction. However justified the tragic character and his aim, however necessary the tragic collision, the third thing required is the tragic resolution of this conflict. By this means eternal justice is exercised on individuals and their aims in the sense that it restores the substance and unity of ethical life with the downfall of the individual who has disturbed its peace. For although the characters have a purpose which is valid in itself, they can carry it out in tragedy only by pursuing it one-sidedly and so contradicting and infringing someone else's purpose. The truly substantial thing which has to be actualized, however, is not the battle between particular aims or characters, although this too has its essential ground in the nature of the real world and human action, but the reconciliation in which the specific individuals and their aims work together harmoniously without opposition and without infringing on one another. Therefore what is superseded in the tragic dénouement is only the one-sided particular which had not been able to adapt itself to this harmony, and now (and this is the tragic thing in its action), unable to renounce itself and its intention, finds itself condemned to total destruction, or, at the very least, forced to abandon, if it can, the accomplishment of its aim. (*Aesthetics: Lectures on Fine Art*, 1196–97)

This is a decidedly comic reading of tragedy, the essence of which turns out be not conflict and irreparable loss but unification and reconciliation. Yes, the actualizing of the ethical order in reality can turn differences into apparent oppositions, and thus can set characters, who identify wholly with only one element of the ethical ensemble, against each other. But their defeat or loss brings the ethical unity once more into view. While the death of the tragic hero is not quite reduced to collateral damage, the viewer is nevertheless reconciled to the ethical order at the end. From conflict a larger, harmonious whole becomes visible. It is owing to this element of reconciliation that the tragic catastrophe is not, for Hegel, merely horrifying.

In order for this process of reconciliation to be intelligible, the characters of tragedy must be visibly identified with a single ethical principle, and this requires a simplification of dramatic character compared to that found in both epic and lyric:

> Genuinely tragic *characters* . . . are what they can and must be in accordance with their essential nature, not an ensemble of qualities separately developed epically in various ways; on the contrary, even if they are living and individual themselves, they are simply the *one* power dominating their own specific character; for, in accordance with their own individuality, they have inseparably identified themselves with some single particular aspect of those solid interests we have enumerated above, and are prepared to answer for that identification. Standing on this height, where the mere accidents of the individual's purely personal life disappear, the tragic heroes of dramatic art have risen to become, as it were, works of sculpture. (*Aesthetics: Lectures on Fine Art*, 1194–95)

As the final reference to statues may suggest, by "genuine" tragic characters Hegel means *Greek* tragic characters. The masks worn by Greek actors, Hegel opines, manifested the "fixed and universal 'pathos'" of the characters they embodied, and he contrasts these with the more fully individualized characters of modern tragedy. Hegel holds with Aristotle that in Greek drama "individuals did not act to display their characters but that these were included for the sake of the action," which was the essential thing (*Aesthetics: Lectures on Fine Art*, 1178).

For Hegel, the Greeks represent "the stage at which tragedy proper, and comedy too, had their highest intrinsic worth" (1208). But this worth cannot be fully appreciated by modern audiences, who demand a different kind of art. Greek drama is not staged today because "it is so foreign to our modern way of looking at things" (1183). We would rank the Greek playwrights with Shakespeare if only "we did not demand a greater depth of subjective inner life and a breadth of individual characterization" (1177). The curtain that falls between us moderns and the Greeks is the one Hegel explores in the *Philosophy of Right*: the fact that modern freedom, as opposed to Greek, is premised on the cultivation of the individual—encouraged first by Protestantism but perfected by commercial society and its system of needs. And it results in an aesthetic that demands fully developed characters.

The results of this transition are manifold. Characters in modern tragedy are driven by subjective motives such as love or personal honor rather than by ethical principle (*Aesthetic: Lectures on Fine Art*, 1223–24). Shakespearean heroes are "without ethical justification, but upheld solely by the formal inevitability of their personality" (1230). There follows from this a multiplication of details concerning both the characters' individual lives and the external world, a larger dramatis personae, the introduction of subplots, and so forth (1206–7). More fundamentally, the detachment of characters from ethical principle (which they still can, but need not, embody [1126]) fundamentally transforms the nature of tragic plot: "Modern tragedy adopts into its own sphere from the start the principle of subjectivity. It takes for its proper subject matter and content the subjective inner life of the character who is not, as in classical tragedy, a purely individual embodiment of ethical powers and, keeping to the same type, it makes actions come into collision with each other as the chance of external circumstances dictates, and makes similar accidents decide, or seem to decide, the outcome" (1223).

Just as character increasingly comes to embody purely subjective qualities and motives, so the collision between characters becomes increasingly unmotivated and random. Chance or accident thus replaces destiny as the deciding factor that drives plot to its conclusion. (*Hamlet* serves Hegel as a privileged example here as throughout his consideration of modern drama.) And as a result, in such plays "what is truly substantial can often glimmer through them in only a very dim way" (*Aesthetics: Lectures on Fine Art*, 1223). Because the conflicts between characters are not determined by the ethical forces they embody, the tragic resolution cannot reveal the deeper justice of an objective spirit that enfolds both opposing principles. But this is not all. Since the accidental circumstances of modern drama can just as easily turn out happily as tragically, this encourages the production of plays that are midway between the tragic and the comic. And it is this blurring or mixing of modes that is particularly portentous for Hegel:

But the deeper harmonization of tragic and comic treatment into a new whole does not consist in juxtaposing or upsetting these opposites [i.e., substance and subject] but in blunting both sides and reconciling their opposition. Instead of acting with comical perversity, the individual is filled with the seriousness characteristic of solid concerns and stable characters, while the tragic fixity of will is so far weakened, and the depth of the collisions involved so far reduced, that there can emerge a reconciliation of interests and a harmonious unification of individuals and their aims. It is in a conception like this that particularly our modern plays and dramas have the basis of their origin. The heart of this principle is the view that, despite all differences and conflicts of charac-

> ters and their interests and passions, human action can nevertheless produce a really fully harmonious situation. . . . Moreover this kind of drama almost runs the risk of departing from the genuine type of drama altogether or of lapsing into prose. . . . The result is that the poet is easily induced to devote the whole force of his production to the inner life of the dramatis personae and to make the course of the situations a mere means to the sketching of character; or alternatively he allows preponderating scope to externals, i.e., to situations and customs of the period. (*Aesthetics: Lectures on Fine Art*, 1203–4)

Tragedy achieves a harmony of ethical spheres, but at the cost of the tragic hero. This new kind of drama holds that "despite all differences and conflicts of characters and their interests and passions, human action can nevertheless produce a really fully harmonious situation." Ethical harmony is now achieved without tragic loss or indeed any real harm to its participants, despite their differences. On the one hand, this harmonizing of tragedy and comedy points to a dramatic form that may be superior to either. Certainly, Hegel praises classical plays such as *Philoctetes* and *The Eumenides* that achieve ethical seriousness without tragic loss, as well as modern works such as Goethe's *Iphigenia*. At the same time, this form runs the danger of degenerating into the pedestrian and thus into something that is no longer art.

Let us look more closely at the qualities of this third dramatic type. Its characters are serious and solid; its plot is likewise serious but not tragic, and it ends happily; it privileges character and waxes expansive over local custom and detail; and it threatens to lapse into prose. If Hegel hadn't tipped his hand already, he does so with this final detail. What is this new genre if not the novel? Or rather a novelized tragedy? Significantly, Hegel has relatively little to say about the novel in his *Lectures on Aesthetics*. While he sometimes comments approvingly on individual novels—Goethe's *Wilhelm Meister*, for example—he does not really define the novel as a genre or assign it any specified place within his system of arts.[21] His few remarks on the topic tend to be parenthetical and dismissive, as when he observes that medieval romance eventually turns into "something like a novel, though here [i.e., in medieval romance] the incidents do not move on the foundation of a fixedly regulated civil organization and prosaic march of events" (*Aesthetics: Lectures on Fine Art*, 1105). Hegel's almost complete silence on the novel as such in his otherwise encyclopedic treatise on the arts can hardly be an oversight, especially since Friedrich Schlegel had crowned the novel as the modern art form par excellence. Hegel concurs—with the small difference that he does not really view the novel as art. Or rather, he situates it as neither art nor nonart—banished to the liminal space of the prosaic, where the aesthetic shades off into the quotidian. In the novel, art is permanently frozen in the process of disappearing.

Indeed, what I have been trying to extract somewhat laboriously from Hegel is stated quite explicitly by Schlegel: "Having made this allowance [that drama is viewed while the novel is read], there is otherwise so little contrast between the drama and the novel that it is rather the drama [and not epic], treated thoroughly and historically, as for instance by Shakespeare, which is the true foundation of the novel."[22] In a related if less approving vein, Goethe opined that, "unfortunately, many dramas are but novels, that proceed by dialogue."[23] That modern drama and the novel were akin was no secret to German Romantic criticism; indeed, Schlegel's coining of the term "romantic" intended to capture the mixing of genres that characterized modern drama and poetry but was exemplified above all by the novel (*Roman*). Hegel's relative silence seems an attempt to stuff the generally acknowledged process of novelization back into the aesthetic box. Or rather, that is not quite the case, since Hegel describes this very process and moreover makes liberal use of the term "romantic" as a synonym for "modern." It is the novel as such that occupies a gaping, resounding hole in the *Lectures on Aesthetics*.

Instead of fully addressing the novel, Hegel somewhat obliquely bewails the novelization of tragedy. This is what modern theater audiences—their tastes rendered diverse and chaotic by the system of needs—appear to demand. In answering every taste and generic preference, a hybrid dramatic form actually embodies none. And it casts an interesting light on the "end of art" to which Hegel alludes, somewhat enigmatically, in the very final pages of the book. On the one hand—we might say, officially—art "ends" with comedy, a still higher form than tragedy, though granted far less extensive consideration by Hegel. Comedy is the end of art because art cannot pass beyond this point, and so absolute spirit must proceed to assume other forms. But the tragicomic drama offers another, less dialectically uplifting "end" for art, one in which tragedy degenerates into the purely prosaic state of the novel. Here artistic forms do not array themselves into edifying historical sequences but simply blend into each other, producing tragedy-comedy-novel, a hybridized, unhappy remainder of what had until then been a dialectically developing process. Not just art, but art history comes to an end. While civil society and the state prove capable of mastering the problems engendered by the market economy (except for poverty, which may unravel the whole thing), tragic drama falls prey to the individualizing,

subjectivizing tendencies of the system of needs. Deprived of ethical orientation, tragic action becomes random and loses its generic orientation as
well, leading, apparently, nowhere in particular. The only thing Hegel didn't
reckon on was the fact that this situation could itself become a theme for
dramatic treatment, and that tragicomedy, in the hands of playwrights such
as Samuel Beckett, would become the perfect medium for exploring this dilemma, as we shall see in the following chapter.

II

The Eighteenth Brumaire of Louis Bonaparte has suffered from no lack of
critical attention.[24] One of Marx's wittiest and most rhetorically exuberant
works, it combines incisive dialectical analysis with a punchy, epigrammati-
cal, and allusive style that has proven irresistible to political theorists and
literary critics alike. The *Eighteenth Brumaire* not only employs tragedy, comedy, and farce as analytical categories but also clearly absorbs elements of
these modes into its own generic makeup, even as it adopts an ambiguous
relationship to the novel.[25] In this it is not without precedent. Hegel's *Phenomenology of Spirit* likewise combines elements of comedy, tragedy, and
Bildungsroman.[26] Friedrich Schlegel conceived of the Romantic novel as a
genre that would not only mix literary kinds but also cross the boundaries
between literature and theory. Perhaps Hegel and Marx can thus be viewed
as the authors of very different kinds of Romantic novel.[27] For what it is
worth, the young Marx began a satirical novel titled *Scorpion and Felix*,
modeled in part on Sterne. He also worked on an unfinished fate-tragedy,
Oulanem.[28]

  In my exposition of Hegel, I attempted to show how the fate of modern
tragedy can be read against the rise of the system of needs. The "idealist"
Hegel thus surprisingly (if implicitly) encourages us to connect the history
of aesthetics to history understood in at least a somewhat more material
sense. To some degree, and just as surprisingly, the "materialist" Marx's ex-
positional method in the *Eighteenth Brumaire* inverts Hegel's: he attempts to
understand a historical event (revolution) at least in part through the aesthetic categories of tragedy and farce. And just as in Hegel, it is the fate of
classical tragedy to become novelized in modern times, so in the *Eighteenth
Brumaire*, the tragic coherence of revolution likewise becomes "novelized"
in ways that no longer allow for clear-cut conclusions. Hegel's account of
the novelization of tragedy redounds in Marx upon history itself, for which
it provides an organizing (or disorganizing) paradigm in the *Eighteenth*

Brumaire. The fate of tragedy thus becomes the fate of modern society. Such at least will be my argument in what follows, though a good deal of more local exposition will be required before the shape of the larger claims looms into view.

What follows is an extended commentary on the famous, first sentences of Marx's work: "Hegel remarks somewhere that all facts and personages of great importance in world history occur, as it were, twice. He forgot to add: the first time as tragedy, the second as farce."[29] This is not, at this point, a particularly novel approach to the *Eighteenth Brumaire*.[30] In adopting it, however, I want to focus on Marx's Hegelian legacy. To what degree is Marx's conception of dramatic genre a Hegelian one? How does this question bear on Marx's distinctive (if sometimes maligned) concept of action? And how does this concept of action respond in turn to the challenge posed by political economy?—a challenge already at work in Hegel, as we have seen. Marx was certainly familiar with both of the Hegelian titles discussed in the previous section. His *Critique of Hegel's Philosophy of Right* is an important early writing. And Marx likewise studied the *Lectures on Aesthetics* carefully, probably in the summer of 1837.[31] While Marx's early writings devote themselves in large part to critiquing the Hegelian legacy, Marx's relation to Hegel is obviously more complex than this fact alone would suggest.

Hegel's theory of action, as developed in the *Philosophy of Right*, focuses largely on the concept of ethical freedom. How is right reconciled with duty and responsibility? More specifically, how is the free choice of a selfhood individuated by the system of needs compatible with the collectively shared, objective reason embodied in the state? How, in short, is freedom available under the conditions of modern civic and political life? Squaring this circle depends for Hegel on *Sittlichkeit*, the necessary embeddedness of ethical choice in concrete, existing institutions and customs. Now at the deepest level, Marx rejects this entire approach to freedom, something that for him can be truly available only when the three bases of Hegelian *Sittlichkeit*—family, marketplace, and state—have been destroyed. Absolute Marxist freedom is unconditioned, and it becomes available only when the era of material and political necessity that marks class society has been brought to its revolutionary close. The realm of freedom is to come, not something in the here and now, as it is for Hegel.

For all that, of course, a more constrained version of freedom marks all times. As Marx puts it in the *Eighteenth Brumaire*, "Men make their own history, but they do not make it just as they please; they do not make it under circumstances chosen by themselves, but under circumstances directly encountered, given, and transmitted from the past" (15). As described here, acting is a form of making—something comparable to production. The English "just as they please" does not quite capture the effect of the German "aus freien Stücken," "out of free pieces," a phrase that reinforces the sense of building something. Marx's concept of *praxis* spans both action and production in the classical sense. In the wake of Adam Smith's displacement of action *by* production, Marx attempts to reformulate an understanding of action that rescues its transformative power by assimilating it (in part) *to*, and modeling it *upon*, production. Production destroys or consumes its raw materials in order to make something new from it; every act of production is in this sense a microrevolution. Likewise, every action negates the existent to some degree and replaces it with a new situation imprinted with itself.

Moreover, the "Stücken," or pieces from which action/production attempts to form something new are themselves nothing but previous actions that have become reified into institutions or historical situations. The raw material of *praxis* is just prior *praxis* that has congealed into social reality, just as, for both Smith and Marx, the commodity is just congealed labor. The difference being that this congealed *praxis* is *not* available as *free* pieces but rather forms something more like a web (or "nightmare" [*Eighteenth Brumaire*, 15]) against and within which the historical agent is forced to struggle.[32] The potentially tragic dimensions of this situation hardly need expounding.

What Marx's productive/active agents are "making" is "their own history," a statement that raises two questions: first, how does one make something as nebulous and gargantuan as "history," and, second, how does one make it so that it is one's "own"? Here again, Marx responds to Smith, for whom men do indeed make history, but unconsciously. What we might call the "deep" movement of Smithian history, as opposed to the surface ruffle of events, results from "the uniform, constant, and uninterrupted effort of every man to better his condition." These isolated efforts form both a spontaneous order and a historical current, though one of which the individual contributors are unaware. In this sense it is not "their" history, and indeed lacks a ruling subject altogether. For Hegel, following Smith, "the history of spirit is its own *deed*; for spirit is only what it does" (*Philosophy of Right*, 372). History is the sequence of actions that constitutes it, but these are not ordered according to the intentions of individual agents. History is the history of *Geist*, not of "men." Marx too understands history as, at one level, the unconscious or unplanned sum of actions of individual agents, but he attributes this Smithian or Hegelian process to alienation, the fact that human actions get taken out of the agents' hands in class society and confront them as an apparently autonomous force.

At the same time, Marx leaves a space for intentional, conscious action. Only, in the wake of Smith and Hegel, and given the vast dimensions of the historical process in which everyone is embedded, such agency must necessarily be collective. The post-Smithian agent is the social *class*. Part of the originality of the *Eighteenth Brumaire* is that its (tragic, or comic, or novelistic) plot involves agents that are primarily classes or class fractions. It is the agonistic struggle among these that constitutes history. Men effectively make "their" history—a history they will or intend, as opposed to one that goes on behind their backs—only as members of a self-conscious social class. And even then, they are pushing against the accumulated weight of alienated past *praxis* frozen into already-existing history.

Marx's theory of *praxis* has come under criticism, notably by Hannah Arendt, for reducing action to production. And yet it seems to me that no one has tried to think through the problem of action in a post-Smithian landscape as thoroughly as Marx. One of the points of interest of the *Eighteenth Brumaire*, in particular, is that it theorizes class agency in relation to something that looks in some ways like, but is not identical to, a social class: the political party. Moreover, it considers class agency in relation to individual agency. In the political coup, Bonaparte *as an individual* appears to have collected in himself the historical agency normally possessed only by a class, and moreover to have discharged it in a decisive, transformative blow. In the preface to the second edition, Marx criticizes Hugo's *Napoleon le Petit* for unintentionally enforcing the "great man" theory of history that the coup would seem to embody. Hugo "does not notice that he makes" Bonaparte "big instead of little by ascribing to him a personal power of initiative such as would be without parallel in world history" (*Eighteenth Brumaire*, 8). Conversely, Proudhon's *Coup d'État* makes the coup into the inevitable result of historical forces without noticing that in doing so it becomes a historical apologia for Bonaparte (8). (Writing a book, like making history, is apparently subject to ironic reversals of aim.) Marx, by contrast, will "demonstrate how the *class struggle* in France created circumstances and relationships that made it possible for a grotesque mediocrity to play a hero's part" (8). It is not that Marx does not believe in individual agency. But a post-Smithian conception of history is simply too big a stone to be pushed along by a single ant—even one sporting an imperial mantle—though extraordinary circumstances can create the false impression that this is happening. Bonaparte's historical mission is to be farcically disproportionate to his historical moment, and thus to parody the "great man" theory of history at the very moment when he seems to embody it. This negative, satirical work, of course, leaves much still undone. If it dismantles the illusion that an individual can leverage the historical force of a social class, it still does not explain how the individual member fits into the active assemblage that is the class, and how his or her agency is articulated with that of the others such that each one can feel part of the "they" that claims history as "their own." It is not as if such questions are never addressed by Marx, but they are not addressed here.

In any case, when we turn to the 1848 revolution as Marx described it, social classes don't appear to be negotiating the field of history any more successfully than individuals would. Virtually every class or class fraction that enters into battle finds its aims somehow frustrated or ironically reversed. For instance, the "pure" republican bourgeoisie manages to gain control of the Constituent National Assembly and the important ministerial posts for a time after the revolution, but only after a proletarian uprising has been put down in bloody fashion:

> The republican bourgeois faction, which had long regarded itself as the legitimate heir of the July Monarchy, thus found its fondest hopes exceeded; it attained power, however, not as it had dreamed under Louis Philippe, through a liberal revolt of the bourgeoisie against the throne, but through a rising of the proletariat against capital, a rising laid low with grape-shot. What it had conceived as the *most revolutionary* event turned out in reality to be the *most counterrevolutionary*. The fruit fell into its lap, but it fell from the tree of knowledge, not from the tree of life. (*Eighteenth Brumaire*, 29)

Still affixed to the conceptual categories of 1789, the pure republicans imagine that the bourgeois republic is the most revolutionary and historically progressive form of government. Half a century later, however, it is achieved not through an uprising against feudal monarchy, but through massacring workers. Instead of displacing the old ruling class, the bourgeois republic assures its existence by defeating the new revolutionary class; it thus unexpectedly finds itself embodying the forces of historical reaction. Moreover, the very conceptual categories that give its struggle meaning have outlived their usefulness, since the sides in this new struggle are defined not by political institutions (republic, monarchy) but by places within the mode of economic production (bourgeoisie, proletariat). While the pure republicans "achieve their ends," that is, political power, its meaning has been so completely inverted as to empty out the achievement. It is as if Oedipus were to congratulate himself over the fact that he did, after all, find a wife.

This brand of irony is not the exception within the *Eighteenth Brumaire* but rather the rule. Here again is a passage in which the high industrial and landed bourgeoisie, having crushed the rights of all lower classes in the name of social order, finds its own weapons turned against it after Bonaparte's coup: "It apotheosized the sword; the sword rules it. It destroyed the revolutionary press; its own press has been destroyed. It placed popular meetings under police supervision; its salons are under the supervision of the police. It disbanded the Democratic national guards; its own National Guard is disbanded. It imposed a state of siege; a state of siege is imposed upon it. It supplanted the juries by military commissions; it stories are supplanted by military commissions" (118). Marx has frequent recourse to chiasmic constructions of this kind throughout the *Eighteenth Brumaire*, and they are invariably used, as here, to signal some dialectical reversal.[33] Political action by just about any agent, when injected into the diabolical machine that is the Revolution of 1848 (and, in a larger sense, history as such), ends up backfiring, usually in a way that delivers some well-deserved *contrapasso* to the offending party.

The systematically ironic reversals produced by the political space of the *Eighteenth Brumaire* recall Hegel's cunning of reason in some respects (or a farcical version thereof), but their sheer number suggests instead the Smithian market economy. Just as every stratagem employed by merchants (or governments swayed by mercantile ideology) to thwart the "natural liberty" of the market goes awry, so do the political machinations of the various class fractions fighting for supremacy in post-1848 France. Of course, in Smith's case, these reversals all result from a single, well-defined economic mechanism. Marx has extended the field of irony to cover society as a whole. Moreover, the specific causal mechanisms at play are heterogeneous, and in many cases do not appear particularly dialectical—or even causal— upon closer examination. Sometimes nothing more is involved than a satisfying comeuppance. In the end it is unclear whether Marx's chiasmic formulations capture a real dialectical process or attempt to create—or at least intensify—the effect of one.

In any case, the cascade of ironic failures that characterize the revolution contribute in no small part to its farcical appearance. Which raises the question of what might constitute a genuinely "tragic" historical mode. Contrasting the French Revolution of 1789 with that of 1848, Marx observes of the former:

And in the classically austere traditions of the Roman Republic its gladiators found the ideals and the art forms, the self-deception that they needed in order to conceal from themselves the bourgeois limitations of the content of their struggles and to keep their enthusiasm on the high plane of the great historical tragedy. . . . Thus the awakening of the dead in those revolutions served the purpose of glorifying new struggles, not of parodying the old; of magnifying the given task in imagination, not a fleeing from its solution in reality; of finding once more the spirit of revolution, not of making its ghost walk about again. (*Eighteenth Brumaire*, 16–17)

In the context of 1789, the republic has genuine historical meaning, not just on a political plane but because it is the state form ushered in by a new bourgeois ruling class and with it a new set of economic and social relations. The French revolution achieved "the task of unchaining and setting up modern *bourgeois* society" (16). It is serious because its social content is serious. By effecting the transition from feudal to bourgeois society, it furthers historical progress toward the eventual overthrow of class society altogether, and thus rises to the level of the "great historical tragedy." At the same time, as Marx points out, there is some self-deception involved here. Once brought into being, bourgeois society does not answer to its heroic origins but busies itself entirely in the sordid pursuit of wealth. There is something inflationary, and thus potentially farcical, even about an event that Marx characterizes as authentically tragic. Yet this misrecognition also allows the revolutionary forces to imagine that they are acting on behalf of the people as a whole, rather than in their own class interest. It thus invests their efforts with a kind of heroic if somewhat misguided magnanimity. In any case, the bourgeois revolution does achieve something great, even though not as great as it imagines. Bourgeois society is a genuine historical advance over the feudal order it replaces.

In order to qualify as possessing tragic dignity then, a revolution must (a) lead to a transformation of the underlying social order, not merely the political one, (b) exert a historically progressive force, and (c) act, or at least believe it is acting, on behalf of mankind as a whole and not of particular class interests. The class that acts as tragic protagonist embodies a principle at once ethical and historical, as in Hegel. However, this principle is embodied not, as with Hegelian *Sittlichkeit*, in existing institutions but rather in those that the revolution will bring into being for the first time. The only revolution that fulfills all three criteria perfectly would seem to be the proletarian revolution to come. All others approximate it more (1848) or less (1789) imperfectly. Yet, as Marx makes clear, the proletarian revolution "cannot draw its poetry from the past, but only from the future" (*Eighteenth Brumaire*, 18) and its conduct will be more methodical than grand; such revolutions "criticize themselves constantly, interrupt themselves continually in their own course, come back to the apparently unfinished to begin it afresh, deride with unmerciful thoroughness the inadequacies, weaknesses, and paltriness of their first attempts" (19). Eminently *practical*, the proletarian revolution has no time for tragic grandeur. The bourgeois revolutionaries of 1789 were therefore the last to fulfill a tragic role; what remains is the deterioration of bourgeois tragedy into comedy/farce. The categories of tragedy and comedy are historical, as in Hegel, and both are destined to pass.

I have been arguing that in response to the crisis of individual action inaugurated by Smith, Marx forges a new kind of collective historical agent: the social class. And yet, in the course of the *Eighteenth Brumaire*, it is unclear that any class or class fraction manages to exert agency more successfully, or in a way less subject to the law of unintended consequences, than the kind at work in Smith. In the end, despite their best efforts, "*all classes . . .* lie prostrate" before a victorious Louis Bonaparte (*Eighteenth Brumaire*, 24), a situation somehow tragic and farcical at once. History as class struggle seems to have ground to a halt. Or it would have, had not Marx formulated yet another form of historical agency, this time invested not in a revolutionary class, but in the revolution itself:

> But the revolution is thoroughgoing. It is still journeying through purgatory. It does its work methodically. By December 2, 1851, it had completed one half of its preparatory work; it is now completing the other half. First it perfected the parliamentary power, in order to be able to overthrow it. Now that it has attained this, it perfects the executive power, reduces it to its purest expression, isolates it, sets it up against itself as the sole target, in order to concentrate all its forces of destruction against it. And when it has done this second half of its preliminary work, Europe will leap from its seat and exultantly exclaim: Well grubbed, old mole! (121)

Marx might simply have decided that the Revolution of 1848 failed because it was premature—because France's relatively early stage of industrialization meant that the proletariat was not numerically large enough, or had not attained a sufficient degree of organization, or that the peasantry had not yet discovered that the smallholding economy was ruinous for them. He does, with varying degrees of explicitness, make all of these claims. But this is not enough. The Revolution of 1848 cannot be merely mistimed or a failure pure and simple, no matter how good the reasons; it must do positive historical work, and it must bring its final triumph closer even when it seems to have stalled or regressed. As odd as it sounds, then, the revolution partakes in some ways of the qualities of Smith's Invisible Hand, a self-organizing process that redeems the actions of its individual participants without their knowledge or intention. Or again, it is something like Hegel's cunning of reason, a concept that likewise derives at least in part from Smith.

Here we might recall a passage from Engels that serves as the unacknowledged source of Marx's opening lines:

> But, after what we saw yesterday, there can be no counting on the *peuple*, and it really seems as though old Hegel, in the guise of the World Spirit, were directing history from the grave and, with the greatest conscientiousness, causing everything to be reenacted twice over, once as grand tragedy and the second time as rotten farce, Casussidière for Danton, L. Blanc for Robespierre, Barthélémy for Saint-Just, Flocon for Carnot, and the moon-calf together with the first available dozen debt-encumbered lieutenants for the little corporal and his band of marshals. Thus the 18th Brumaire would already be upon us.[34]

What Marx attributes to "the revolution," Engels attributes to "old Hegel, in the guise of the World Spirit," who exhibits even the methodical nature that Marx attributes to proletarian revolt. It would thus seem that Marx's invocation of King Hamlet's ghost in the latter passage (which is, after all, about subterranean influences) reanimates Engels's figure of Hegel directing history "from the grave," a reference that drops out of Marx's borrowing in the opening lines of the *Eighteenth Brumaire*.[35] While Marx certainly subjects Hegel and his followers to no small degree of ridicule, especially in his early writings, there seems to be nothing farcical about the Hegelianism of Marx's passages on "the revolution," where he engages in the very same maneuvers he rejects in (for instance) the *Critique of Hegel's Philosophy of Right*. There he takes Hegel to task for hypostasizing predicates and turning them into autonomous entities, then making the subjects to which those predicates really attach into manifestations of the mysteriously autonomous predicates. For instance, instead of human beings displaying subjectivity as a predicate, subjectivity is raised (in somewhat Platonic fashion) into an independent essence of which real, individual human subjects are mere incarnations or instances.[36] One result of this process is to alienate human activity, which now "appears as the activity and product of something other than" actual men.[37] If we turn this critique of Hegel back onto Marx, revolutionary action, the product of individuals and social classes, gets raised into an autonomous, ghostly entity ("the revolution"), which both appropriates and redeems the actions of real agents. Jean-Paul Riquelme rightly notes that Marx's revolution, which is "not a normal actor but the play's controlling presence and its teleology," reduces Louis Bonaparte to "the level of a functionary" of the historical process, thus puncturing his apparent grandeur.[38] This is certainly right, but Bonaparte's demotion is not unique to him; it attaches by implication to every other agent in Marx's work. Revolution is no longer what revolutionary agents engage in and create but rather a hypostasized entity that assigns to those agents their revolutionary roles and that redeems even their apparent failures, making them historically productive. Faced with the disquieting possibility of pure revolutionary failure, Marx responds with a Smithian/Hegelian form of agency, which enacts an ironic reversal upon the ironic reversals of the political field. If every agent's actions go awry, as the *Eighteenth Brumaire* tirelessly demonstrates, those very misfires are collected, redeemed, and rendered historically productive by the revolution.

Its Hegelian attributes further clarify the relationship between "the revolution" and Hegel's view of tragedy. The revolution sets two contending class protagonists against each other, one of which defends the existing social order and the other of which espouses a social order to come. Each embodies a historically valid principle, and the revolution assures that the more universal of the two ultimately triumphs. While it is not true that the contending principles are finally reconciled, as in Hegel, or that their apparent opposition veils a more fundamental harmony, tragic conflict does ultimately trace a dialectically redemptive path. Hegelian tragedy is, at a deep level, comic, although the damage caused in resolving conflict is not to be discounted. Marx's "long view" of the revolution likewise absorbs local, apparent losses into the productivity of the historical process.

The Revolution of 1848 has an additionally theatrical dimension in that it is played out largely in the realm of parliamentary politics, before the public. In the political arena, the direct conflict of social classes is replaced by the contest of political parties, each of which represents a particular class fraction. Here political *representation* allows individuals to stand in for a single class or class fraction in a way analogous to that in which the Hegelian tragic hero embodies and espouses a single ethical principle. For the bourgeois parties, moreover, parliamentary form is not merely a revolutionary means but rather an end, since the establishment of republican government is their political goal. This is particularly true of the "pure" republicans, a grouping that does not represent a well-defined class interest but rather a set of political principles, and that plays an initially leading role in the founding and conduct of the Constituent Assembly after the revolt of February 1848. The pure republicans for the most part embody what Marx calls "parliamentary cretinism" (*Eighteenth Brumaire*, 93): the delusion on the part of parliamentarians that their legislative body is the sole governing force in the social world. Parliamentary cretins hold the magical belief that receiving "a constitutional uniform" makes bourgeois rights "invulnerable" (30), a belief punctured by Bonaparte's coup of 1852. Prior to that, however, the bourgeois parliamentarians believe that "the constitutional existence of liberty remained intact, inviolate, no matter how mortal the blows dealt to its existence in *actual life*" (31). Hence they become increasingly detached from material reality as they labor on "their great legislative work of art" (33). The ethical one-sidedness of the Hegelian tragic hero takes the form of risible blindness to anything outside of purely legislative realities.

One of the principle functions of theatrical metaphor in the *Eighteenth Brumaire* is to insist on the vacuousness of the political—to depict it as a public display that is little more than empty appearance cast up by more fundamental socioeconomic realities. As Engels puts it in his preface to the third edition: "It was precisely Marx who had discovered the great law of motion of history, the law according to which all historical struggles, whether they proceed in the political, religious, philosophical or some other ideological domain, are in fact only the more or less clear expression of struggles of social classes" (in *Eighteenth Brumaire*, 14). Engels is quite clear here—the political is a merely epiphenomenal "ideological domain" expressing or rendering visible the real processes of class struggle. It has been argued that the *Eighteenth Brumaire* is more nuanced in its approach to the political than Engels grasps, but I think he gets it basically right.[39] As far as I can tell, nothing grants the political any significant role in class formation or assigns it any independent force that would react dialectically upon the socioeconomic. Marx himself states that "if one looks at the [political] situation and the parties more closely, . . . this superficial appearance, which veils the *class struggle* and the particular physiognomy of this period, disappears" (46).

A merely epiphenomenal view of politics assigns it a status (paradoxically) not unlike that described by Hannah Arendt: its practical effectivity bracketed, it serves mainly as a stage for disclosure of its participants. Only in this case they cover themselves in public shame rather than glory. "While the Assembly constantly performs on the boards and is exposed to daily public criticism, [Bonaparte] leads a secluded life in the Elysian Fields"

(32). The only thing accomplished by the parliamentary wrangling of the various political parties is the slow erosion of the Assembly's legitimacy, which helps ripen the conditions for Bonaparte's coup. One of the extended motifs of the *Eighteenth Brumaire* is the collapse of parliamentary authority, prompted in part by Bonaparte's maneuvering and in part by the venality and fecklessness of the political parties themselves.

Marx's narrative strategy is to reinforce the illusions of the political even while critiquing them—in effect, to induce a version of parliamentary cretinism in the reader. Thus the opening five chapters focus almost exclusively on Paris and the battles among the parliamentary parties and between the legislative and executive branches of government. Beginning with the sixth chapter, however, Marx initiates a series of "zoom outs" that place these political struggles within a wider social and geographical context. In the sixth chapter, for instance, he details the political effects of an industrial crisis in 1851. Although the crisis extended beyond France and was simply the result of a periodic cycle of overproduction, the French bourgeoisie misattributes it to uncertainty caused by political wrangling in Paris. This causes the extraparliamentary bourgeoisie to break with their own parliamentary representatives and begin to long for a strong executive power and the stability it would bring, further encouraging Bonaparte's coup plans. The economic thus exerts an effect on the political, but only as refracted through French sensibilities, which interpret everything through political categories. Politics is the French ideology, just as philosophy is the German one. Where the English, whose favored discourse is political economy, see the periodic trade crisis for exactly what it is, the French mind conjures up political melodrama:

> Now picture to yourself the French bourgeois, how in the throes of this business panic his trade-crazy brain is tortured, set in a whirl and stunned by rumors of *coup d'état* and the restoration of universal suffrage, by the struggle between parliament and the executive power, by the Fronde war between Orleanists and Legitimists, by the communist conspiracies in the south of France, by alleged *jacqueries* in the departments of Nièvre and Cher, by the advertisements of the different candidates for the presidency, by the cheapjack solutions offered by the journals, by the threats of the republicans to uphold the Constitution and universal suffrage by force of arms, by the gospel preaching émigré heroes *in partibus*, who announced that the world would come to an end on the second Sunday in May 1852—think of all this and you will comprehend why in this unspeakable, deafening chaos of fusion, revision, prorogation, constitution, conspiration, coalition, emigration, usurpation and revolution, the bourgeois

madly snorts at his parliamentary republic: *"Rather an end with terror than terror without end!"* (*Eighteenth Brumaire*, 110)

Thus do the private business interests of the French bourgeoisie impel them to break their own political power. But even this is driven by political illusion. Marx's narrative technique works to enhance this illusion, to focus the reader's gaze solely on the political stage of Paris, in order then to undermine it. In a fine essay on the *Eighteenth Brumaire*, Dermot Ryan argues that "Marx's stated goal in the preface to the second addition to the *Eighteenth Brumaire* is to get beneath the distracting theater and reveal that, in spite of appearances it is indeed class war in France that has thrown up a figure like Louis (144). The revolution, Marx writes, is *gründlich*: foundational. It works on the foundations, in the ground [*gründ*], as it were: offstage and out of sight. We should recognize that the real revolution happens underground and not get distracted by the empty performance on the surface of things (141–42)."[40]

Ryan goes on to complicate this schema, showing that the *poiesis* of imagination serves revolutionary as well as ideological purposes in the *Eighteenth Brumaire*. But the antithesis between politics as stage of pure appearance and the subterranean revolution as that which cannot be visualized gets at a crucial dimension of Marx's method in the *Eighteenth Brumaire*. When Marx begins to "zoom out" in the sixth chapter, it is not to broaden the stage but to examine that which cannot be staged, which resists the visual imperative of the stage or somehow exists "under" it. Now it is true that in the very passage on the revolution in which Marx invokes the subterranean work of the mole, he does so through a theatrical allusion. Moreover, the work done by the revolution in delegitimizing the executive branch of government is demonstrative—hence, in some sense displayed to a certain public. The apparent opposition between the visible and the subterranean is not absolute. It may therefore not be visibility itself that Marx is critiquing. What his metaphors of theatricality address is not the political as such but rather bourgeois republican politics and the forms of visibility endemic to it. For instance, the delegitimizing of the executive carried out by the revolution has as its principal audience the smallholding peasantry, a real social class that (for material reasons Marx explains) is drawn to the executive figure for leadership. The political visibility of this demystifying process is therefore benign. By contrast, the audience for bourgeois politics is "the people," a purely invented grouping that answers to no class categories but is rather produced by republicanist ideology as its imagined constituency. The theater of bourgeois politics is not merely the space for empty appearance, then. The theater itself is illusory—constructed from ideological categories designed to produce a particular kind of political visibility. If the revolutionary bourgeoisie of 1789 is the last "tragic" political class, this is in part because it is the last theatrical one.

Marx's "zoom out" from Parisian politics reaches its apex in chapter 7, where he considers the smallholding peasantry. This is numerically the largest social class in France, still primarily an agricultural economy. And yet the peasantry makes almost no appearance prior to chapter 7, because Marx has until now intentionally reproduced both the focus and the blind spots of the political classes battling it out in the capital. Before chapter 7, that is to say, Paris is the world—or the only part of it that matters. Now it finally appears as the tiny spot it is in the vast stretches of the French countryside, its spatial insignificance echoing to some degree its minor economic status. Only in the political realm does the capital city matter. Even the workers who lead the June 1848 uprising are "the *Paris* proletariat" ([23], my emphasis). The class struggle as we have seen it thus far has been conducted largely in miniature. Chapter 7's brilliant *Verfremdungseffekt* jars us into recognizing that we have shared the ideological horizons of the political even as we thought we were engaged in a critique of it. As a result, we now finally see Paris in context. Political theater appears against its ground—both the actual soil of the countryside and the *gründlich* or foundational against which this theater is defined.

The smallholding peasants enter to solve a theoretical conundrum. In conquering every social class, the state under Bonaparte appears no longer to represent the interests of any. "And yet," Marx reassures us, "the state power is not suspended in mid-air. Bonaparte represents a class, and the most numerous class of French society at that, the *small-holding* [Parzellen] peasant" (123). The peasantry "grounds" not only the theater of politics, then, but the state even in its material existence as bureaucratic apparatus. In addition, they provide the votes to ratify Bonaparte's coup in a subsequent election. But who are these peasants? Marx's portrait of them is colorful if condescending. I shall quote it at length because it brings up a number of important points for analysis:

> The small-holding peasants form a vast mass, the members of which live in similar conditions but without entering into manifold relations with one another. Their mode of production isolates them from one another instead of bringing them into mutual intercourse. The isolation is increased by France's

bad means of communication and by the poverty of the peasants. Their field of production, the small holding, admits of no division of labor in its cultivation, no application of science and, therefore, no diversity of development, no variety of talent, no wealth of social relationships. Each individual peasant family is almost self-sufficient; it itself directly produces the major part of its consumption and thus acquires its means of life more through exchange with nature than in intercourse with society. A smallholding, a peasant and his family; alongside them another smallholding, another peasant and another family. A few score of these make up a village, and a few score of villages make up a department. In this way, the great mass of the French nation is formed by simple addition of homologous magnitudes, much as potatoes in a sack form a sack of potatoes. Insofar as millions of families live under economic conditions of existence that separate their mode of life, their interests and their culture from those of the other classes, and put them in hostile opposition to the latter, they form a class. Insofar as there is merely a local interconnection among the smallholding peasants, and the identity of their interests begets no community, no national bond and no political organization among them, they do not form a class. They are consequently incapable of enforcing their class interest in their own name, whether through a parliament or through a convention. They cannot represent themselves, they must be represented. Their representative must at the same time appear as their master, as an authority over them, as an unlimited governmental power that protects them against the other classes and sends them rain and sunshine from above. The political influence of the smallholding peasants, therefore, finds its final expression in the executive power subordinating society to itself. (*Eighteenth Brumaire*, 123–24)

If the social classes of Paris are obsessed with politics, the smallholding peasants are the paradigmatic antipolitical class. Indeed, it is not clear to Marx that they even are a class. They form a class "in itself" in that their objective interests are defined by their place in the system of production and are therefore objectively opposed to the interests of other classes, but they are not a class "for itself" in that their isolation prevents them from organizing in their own political interest. Hence they remain a "mass." A little further on, Marx observes: "Small holding property . . . has transformed the mass of the French nation into troglodytes. Sixteen million peasants (including women and children) dwell in hovels, a large number of which have but one opening, others only two and the most favored only three. And windows are to a house what the five senses are to the head" (127–28). The windowless hovels of the peasantry suggest so many missing senses. The peasants are metaphorically blind and deaf, deprived of the visual and aural fields that convey both the theatrical and the political. Likewise, the depiction of them as potatoes suggests not only similarity but insensibility; the peasants' only "eyes" are potato eyes. Digging blindly in their isolated plots, they recall the mole of *Hamlet* but (up to this point) display no revolutionary potential.

Marx claims that the similarity among peasants results from their economic self-sufficiency, which encourages no interconnection, no division of labor, no variety of talent. This point clearly harks back to Hegel's treatment in the *Philosophy of Right* of the "system of needs" under capitalism and the way in which it cultivates a rich, individualized form of subjectivity. But while they are not individuated, the smallholding peasants also know no collective form of life. They do not participate in the "partial communities" that according to Hegel bind individuals to the state. They are thus in some respects the rural counterpart to Hegel's "rabble," something whose significance will appear only later.

For all their potato-like simplicity, then, Marx's peasants are actually rather complex social entities. On the one hand, they own their plots of land and are thus closer to the petite bourgeoisie than to the proletariat. This accounts in part for their conservative nature. And yet as they become increasingly impoverished, they take on a revolutionary potential (*Eighteenth Brumaire*, 125). Not yet fully a class, the peasantry nevertheless has a role in Marx's vision of a revolutionary France to come. Once pushed out of their windowless hovels, the peasantry will emerge into the light of political day. And yet their destiny is to play a subordinate role: "The interests of the peasants, therefore, are no longer, as under Napoleon, in accord with, but in opposition to the interests of the bourgeoisie, to capital. Hence the peasants find their natural ally and leader in the *urban proletariat*, whose task is the overthrow of the bourgeois order" (128). The proletariat is the natural ally *and leader* of the immiserated peasantry, who may outnumber them but who lack the political sophistication to lead a revolution. As Marx put it in the 1852 edition: "When he is disappointed in the Napoleonic Restoration, the French peasant will part with his belief in his smallholding, the entire state edifice erected on the small holding will fall to the ground and *the proletarian revolution will obtain that chorus without which its solo song becomes the swansong in all peasant countries*" (148n53). Numerous yet homogeneous, conservative yet radical, neither collectivized nor individuated, petit bourgeois yet rabble, a class yet not a class, the peasantry never becomes a well-defined or leading character in the revolution but rather supplies the chorus to its lead singer. And in the meantime they form the passive base on which Bonaparte builds his political power.

The role of the peasantry will become clearer when they are juxtaposed to their antithesis and counterpart: the *lumpenproletariat*. Marx's treatment of this group has proven irresistible to literary critics writing on the *Eighteenth Brumaire*.[41] If the peasantry constitutes Bonaparte's support in France as a whole, the lumpenproletariat, organized into the Society of December 10, provides Bonaparte's private muscle and popular support in Paris. Marx describes the lumpenproletariat in a justly famous passage:

> On the pretext of founding a benevolent society, the *lumpenproletariat* of Paris had been organized into secret sections, each section being led by Bonapartist agents, with a Bonapartist general at the head of the whole. Alongside decayed *roués* with dubious means of subsistence and of dubious origin, alongside ruined and adventurous offshoots of the bourgeoisie, were vagabonds, discharged soldiers, discharged jailbirds, escaped galley slaves, swindlers, mountebanks, *lazzaroni*, pickpockets, tricksters, gamblers, *maquereaus*, brothel keepers, porters, *literati*, organ grinders, rag pickers, knife grinders, tinkers, beggars—in short, the whole indefinite, disintegrated mass, thrown hither and thither, which the French term *la bohème*; from this kindred element Bonaparte formed the core of the Society of December 10. A "benevolent society"—in so far as, like Bonaparte, all its members felt the need of benefiting themselves at the expense of the labouring nation. This Bonaparte, who constitutes himself *chief of the lumpenproletariat*, who here alone rediscovers in mass form the interests which he personally pursues, who recognizes in this scum, offal, refuse of all classes the only class upon which he can base himself unconditionally, is the real Bonaparte, the Bonaparte *san phrase*. (75)

The lumpenproletariat is a kind of quasi-class, defined paradoxically by the *lack* of a defined place within the dominant relations of production. They are not an inherently organized group with shared material interests but a collection of disreputable and independently operating individuals existing on the margins of society. The only thing that provisionally unifies them is the prospect of material gain. Marx's Rabelaisian and polyvocal catalog emphasizes the heterogeneity of the lumpenproletariat, as well as their excremental status with relation to the class system from which they have been expelled. Unbound from the system of economic production, they are free-floating parasites with no sense of social or class solidarity, willing to serve the interests of whoever lines their pockets.

The lumpenproletariat is, within the symbolic order of the *Eighteenth Brumaire*, both the antithesis and the counterpart of the peasantry. Antithesis: if the peasants are pure homogeneity (indistinguishable potatoes in a sack), the lumpenproletariat is pure heterogeneity. If the "blind" peasants are the negation of political theater and its visual register, the lumpen-proletariat is in some sense a purely theatrical phenomenon in that they "play the part of the people, as Nick Bottom that of the lion" (75). The peasantry is rural, the lumpenproletariat urban. The peasantry is productive (indeed, the Physiocrats had regarded them as the only truly productive class in society), the lumpenproletariat parasitical and unproductive. The peasantry is naive, the lumpenproletariat are cunning swindlers. Counterpart: despite these obvious differences, peasantry and lumpenproletariat have a good deal in common. They form the urban and rural bases, respectively, of Louis Bonaparte. And both serve this function because they regard him as a source of material benefits. The economic isolation of the smallholding parcel causes the peasantry to atomize, and thus they do not fully cohere as a class, much as the lumpenproletariat is a gathering of purely self-interested individuals. More precisely, as we have seen, the peasantry is a class "in itself" but not a class "for itself"; the lumpenproletariat, by contrast, is a class "for itself" (in the basest sense of the phrase) but not a class "in itself" since it is not materially unified by any defined role within the relations of production. Both lumpenproletariat and peasantry occupy a liminal space between mere agglomeration and class. Finally, each has a relationship to the proletariat: one as its revolutionary "chorus" and the other as its debased, uncanny double.

As we shall see, the peasantry is not the only social class that will find a troubling mirror in the lumpenproletariat. We can grasp this fact more fully if we look to the intellectual origins of the lumpenproletariat in Hegel's *Pöbel* or rabble. In his important study on Hegel's rabble, Frank Ruda argues that the "rich" and "poor" rabble in Hegel serve as models for bourgeoisie and proletariat respectively in Marx's earliest works, including his *Critique of Hegel's Philosophy of Right*.[42] This is correct, but by the time of the *Eighteenth Brumaire* rich and poor rabble serve as models for more specialized groupings: the finance aristocracy and the lumpenproletariat, respectively. In any case, a closer look at Hegel's rabble (and at Ruda's study) has much to tell us about Marx's lumpenproletariat and its role in the *Eighteenth Brumaire*.

To recall: the "poor" rabble in Hegel are essentially the unemployed—those who have been deprived of their livelihoods by the irreducible caprice of market society. Having lost their professions, they are not only cast into want; they are also excluded from the "partial communities" of corporation and estate that grant individuals a place in the state and bind them to its ethical structures. The rabble are defined not only by their material condition, however, but also by a subjective choice or act: "Poverty in itself does not reduce people to a rabble; a rabble is created only by the disposition associated with poverty, by inward rebellion against the rich, against society, the government, etc. It also follows that those who are dependent on contingency become frivolous and lazy, like the *lazzaroni* of Naples, for example. This in turn gives rise to the evil that the rabble do not have sufficient honour to gain their livelihood through their own work, yet claim that they have a right to receive their livelihood."[43] The essence of the rabble, as expounded by Ruda, is an act of *unbinding* from the rights and duties that define society's ethical order. "*The true rebellion of the rabble is the unbinding*."[44] The rabble do not, in the manner of revolutionaries, seek to remake the social system but rather to unhook themselves from the existing one. At the same time, they feel they have a right to financial support in compensation for their misfortunes. But they claim this solely for themselves rather than for everyone, and hence assert (as Ruda puts it) a "right without right,"[45] since it lacks universality.

The rabble represent not only an unbound social group, but the disquieting possibility that such an unbinding can become generalized. As Ruda declares (extrapolating, admittedly, from Hegel), "*Anyone at all is latently rabble*."[46] Moreover, "with the emergence of the rabble, civil society becomes more and more rabble-like. Civil society becomes the society of the permanent-rabble in which poor and rich rabble unbind themselves in different ways from the ethical community by claiming their *right without right*."[47] The rabble are the tragedy of civil society not only because they are both its unhappy product and its unassimilable remainder but also because they embody the entropic force endemic to the system of needs itself, a force that may not be contained by the communities of order described by Hegel. In the end, the rabble are nothing more than the principle of "every man for himself" that is the hallmark of commercial society.

That the Hegelian rabble underlies Marx's lumpenproletariat is signaled by Marx's inclusion of the *lazzaroni* in his catalog of *lumpen*. Conversely, Engels refers to the lumpenproletariat as a "rabble."[48] Marx's list emphasizes the unbound quality of the lumpen elements both from society ("discharged" [*entlassene*] soldiers and jailbirds are emblematic) and from each other. The different subspecies of lumpen are merely "alongside" (*neben*) each other, unarticulated into any organic whole, an "indefinite, disintegrated mass," not a social class but an unstable aggregate of the unbound.

As odd as this may seem, Hegel's rabble can also be thought in relation to the categories of tragedy and comedy, and can therefore help illuminate the parts these genres play in the *Eighteenth Brumaire*. Recall that the tragic hero is defined for Hegel through his or her complete identification with one of the ethical institutions of society (family or state in the case of *Antigone*) and as such is conspicuously bound to that institution, to the point of being willing to perish in its defense. The rabble, while in some sense "tragic," are in this specific regard the very antithesis of the tragic, since they are by definition unbound to the ethical order and pursue only their own self-interest. Their services can be bought, but they would never sacrifice themselves to an ethical ideal. In unbinding the ethical order, the rabble unbinds the tragic one as well.

The rabble has a more complicated relation to comedy, of which it is not the negation but the debasement. Comedy, for Hegel, begins where tragedy ends. The comic hero takes for granted the fact that his aims will conclude in failure, but he accepts this fact with a stoic yet lighthearted detachment:

> An individual is only portrayed as laughable when it is obvious that he is not serious at all about the seriousness of his aim and will, so that the seriousness always carries with it, in the eyes of the individual himself, its own destruction, because from beginning to end he cannot devote himself to any higher and universally valid interest which would bring him into a conflict of substance [i.e., with another such interest]. Even if he really does so devote himself, he can only exhibit a character which, owing to what it directly and presently is, has already annihilated what it apparently wanted to accomplish, and we can see at once that the substantial interest has never had a real hold on him.[49]

The comic hero's attachment to an ethical ideal is not entirely serious; it unbinds itself from within, and he can therefore observe its failure with amused detachment. He would never wreck himself through devotion to such an ideal. In a sense, his unseriousness allows him to see already the one-sidedness of tragic conviction, which is why comedy is philosophically superior to tragedy even if it is not aesthetically superior. Laughter, for Hegel, *dissolves*;[50] specifically, it dissolves ethical binding into free self-consciousness. At the same time, comedy must itself remain devoted to presenting the rational. The laughable as such cannot be its aim. Characters merely sunk in vice are unbound from the ethical order, but not in a way that leads to a higher consciousness of that order. We might say that "the laughable," a lower and disreputable category for Hegel (equivalent, I would argue, to Marx's category of "farce"), is what happens when comedy unbinds itself from the rational, a "rabble" form of comedy, or that which absolutizes the rabble element of unbinding already present within comedy. Comedy is haunted by the merely laughable (that is, pure dissolution) in the way that civil society is haunted by the rabble. These two threats come together in an odd and unexpected passage in Hegel's *Aesthetics*: "The general ground for comedy is therefore a world in which man as subject or person has made himself completely master of everything that counts to him otherwise as the essence of what he wills and accomplishes, a world whose aims are therefore self-destructive because they are unsubstantial. Nothing can be done, for example, to help a democratic nation where the citizens are self-seeking, quarrelsome, frivolous, bumptious, without faith or knowledge, garrulous, boastful, and ineffectual: such a nation destroys itself by its own folly."[51] This comic world is not a world of "poor rabble," deprived of everything, but a world of "rich rabble" who have everything already and therefore lack serious content. Not only the aims of such a people but also the people themselves are unsubstantial, and the society therefore undergoes a general unbinding, an uncontrollable movement of becoming-rabble. If comedy dissolves the tragic into a higher consciousness, the laughable just dissolves it, period, along with the ethical and social order to which it attaches.

The following passage from the *Eighteenth Brumaire* occurs right after Marx's catalog of the lumpenproletariat:

> An old crafty *roué*, he [Bonaparte] conceives the historical life of the nations and their performances of state as comedy in the most vulgar sense, as a masquerade where the grand costumes, words and postures serve to mask the pettiest knavery. Thus on his expedition to Strasbourg, where a trained Swiss vulture had played the part of the Napoleonic eagle. For his irruption into Bologna he puts some London lackeys in French uniforms. They represent the army. In his Society of December 10, he assembles ten thousand rascally fellows, who are to play the part of the people, as Nick Bottom that of the lion. At a moment when the bourgeoisie itself played the most complete comedy, but in the most serious matter in the world, without infringing any of the pedantic conditions of French dramatic etiquette, and was itself half deceived, half convinced of the solemnity of its own performance of state, the adventurer, who took the comedy as plain comedy, was bound to win. Only when he has eliminated his solemn opponent, when he himself now takes his imperial role seriously and under the Napoleonic mask imagines he is the real Napoleon, does he become the victim of his own conception of the world, the serious buffoon who no longer takes world history for comedy but his comedy for world history. (75–76)

The bourgeoisie performs a comedy not only in a pedantic and French style, but in a Hegelian one as well. They are "half-convinced of the solemnity of their performances of state." They exhibit, that is, the Hegelian comic hero's unserious seriousness, which attaches itself weakly to aims but in a way that undoes itself. By contrast, Bonaparte, the rabble hero, embodies the laughable. He "unbinds" himself entirely from belief in political forms not through a detached, lighthearted consciousness that rises above the world, as in the case of the comic hero, but through cynical self-interest and Machiavellian ruthlessness. Because he grasps performances of state as mere farce, he always gets the better of his opponents, until he finally achieves his aim and falls into a "tragic" attachment to his own Napoleonic ideas, which he then unconsciously ridicules. For Marx, as for Hegel, farce is the rabble form of comedy. And Bonaparte is its master.

But how exactly does Bonaparte defeat all social classes, including the ruling bourgeoisie, with a ragtag band of lumpenproletarians and the (at best) passive acquiescence of the peasantry? One would have to repeat the entire *Eighteenth Brumaire* to give a fully adequate answer. An important part of it, though, has to do with the bourgeoisie's willing abdication of political rule. Having misinterpreted the commercial crisis of 1851 as a response to political instability in France, the bourgeoisie decides that parliamentary debate is bad for business, and they are therefore willing to jettison republican government—the characteristic political form of their own rule—in order to safeguard their private profits. The political and therefore financial stability offered by a strong, even dictatorial executive power means more to them than their own political power. "The bourgeoisie confesses that its own interests dictate that it should be delivered from the danger of its *own rule*; that, in order to restore tranquility in the country, its bourgeois parliament must, first of all, be given its quietus; that in order to preserve its social power intact, its political power must be broken; that the individual bourgeois can continue to exploit the other classes and to enjoy undisturbed property, family, religion and order only on condition that their class be condemned along with the other classes to like political nullity" (67). The bourgeoisie, in other words, abandons political class solidarity for the principle of "every man for himself." "This bourgeoisie, which every moment sacrificed its general class interests, that is, its political interests, to the narrowest and most sordid private interests" (107). Unbinding himself from the political forms that enable his class to cohere, what is the bourgeois but rich rabble? And if this is the case, which class is *not* rabble? As we have seen, the peasantry's smallholdings induce an isolated and antisocial condition that makes them unable to act as a political class—just like the bourgeoisie. They too contain a rabble element.

And what of the proletariat? As Peter Stallybrass points out in an important article, the term itself was initially indistinguishable from others used to describe rabble or lumpen elements at the bottom of society. "Whereas

[Marx and Engels] found it as the mark of a 'passively rotting mass,' they made it into the label of a collective agency. Moreover, they inverted the meaning of the term, so that it meant not a parasite upon the social body but the body upon which the rest of society was parasitic."[52] The proletariat is the very opposite of the lumpenproletariat: productive rather than parasitical, and committed to a struggle destined to liberate not only themselves but humanity as a whole. They therefore embody a truly universal ethicopolitical principle. And yet following their defeat in the June uprising of 1848, the Paris proletariat abandons their world-historical calling: "forgetting the revolutionary interest of their class for momentary ease and class comfort, they renounced the honour of being a conquering power" (71). In the case of the proletariat, the "ease and comfort" pursued are still those of a class rather than of individuals. In that respect, among many others, they differ from the bourgeoisie and the lumpenproletarians. And yet even they have undergone a partial unbinding from their revolutionary commitments. Hence their class too, for the moment, is "reduced to a political nullity."

All of which raises an important question about the apparent victory of the lumpenproletariat. Is it merely the freak result of an exceptional conjuncture, or does it bespeak a deeper becoming-rabble on the part of society as a whole, one that threatens to render social classes incoherent and thus unable to exert the class agency that Marx formulated as a response to political economy? And if this is the case, what happens to the historical dialectic that underlies Marx's revolutionary hopes? "France," according to Marx, "is the land where, more than any other, the historical class struggles were each time fought out to a decision" (18). And yet the Revolution of 1848 introduces a new and troubling historical dynamic, or rather historical stasis:

> The period that we have before us comprises the most motley mixture of crying contradictions: ... struggles whose first law is indecision; ... passions without truths, truths without passion; heroes without heroic deeds, history without events; development, whose sole driving force seems to be the calendar, wearying with constant repetition of the same tensions and relaxations; antagonisms that periodically seem to work themselves up to a climax only to lose their sharpness and fall away without being able to resolve themselves; ... If any section of history has been painted grey on grey, it is this. Men and events appear as inverted Schlemihls, as shadows that have lost their bodies. (43–44)

Is this, again, an exceptional quality of one limited period, or does it convey something distinctive about capitalist modernity? The becoming-rabble that afflicts all social classes appears to blunt their conflicts, and thus to deprive society of the dialectical momentum required to resolve its contradictions in any crisp or definitive way. Ongoing muddle replaces revolution, or threatens to. Perhaps the most fundamental struggle with the *Eighteenth Brumaire*, then, is not that between social classes, but that between class and (its own internal) rabble, between dialectic and muddle, between history with a well-formed dramatic plot, whether tragic or comic, and one with novelistic "unfinalizability" (to borrow a term from Bakhtin).[53]

It is in the context of the rabble, and of the becoming-rabble of society, that we can finally approach the topic of farce—something we have merely glanced at thus far, though I have identified it with the merely "laughable" in Hegel and thus with a kind of rabble-comedy, unbound from the imperatives of the rational. As Jessica Milner Davis puts it in a study of the genre, "farce is comedy with *self-awareness* left out"—the very thing that defines the comic for Hegel.[54] Farce has always occupied the position of low cousin to high comedy, lacking high comedy's adherence to coherent characters and meaningful plot, and tending to devolve into mere madcap or burlesque. Yet the generic coordinates of farce are historically more complex than that. Davis notes that patrons at the Renaissance courts of France and Italy "demanded for their entertainment a refined, literary comedy which would observe the neo-classical rules of structure and decorum. In Italy, where this kind of comedy was called the *commedia erudite* ('learned comedy'), *farsa* was the recognized term for a loose genre, neither tragedy nor comedy nor pastoral, which could be easy-going precisely because it lacked classical antecedents."[55] Davis quotes from the prologue to Giovan-Maria Cecchi's play *La Romanescu* (*The Roman Girl*, 1585): "The *Farsa* is the third new species between tragedy and comedy. It enjoys the liberties of both, and shuns their limitations. . . . It is not restricted to certain motives; for it accepts all subjects—grave and gay, profane and sacred, urbane and rude, sad and pleasant. It does not care for time or place."[56] Farce "unbinds" itself from the classical system of genres to become a kind of free-floating, parasitic term capable of attaching or rebinding itself to any of the others or of mixing them. As such it blunts the contrasts among established genres, much as the becoming-rabble of social classes blunts class conflict. When Marx contrasts tragedy with farce at the beginning of the *Eighteenth Brumaire*, then, the opposition is an unstable one since farce is a kind of hybrid genre that can contain or mimic tragedy as well as oppose it.

This in turn raises the question of the dialectical function of dramatic genres in Marx's work. An important predecessor to Marx's opening of the *Eighteenth Brumaire* occurs in the *Critique of Hegel's Philosophy of Right. Introduction*:

The modern *ancient régime* is merely the *clown* of the world order whose *real heroes* are dead. History is thorough and passes through many stages while bearing an ancient form to its grave. The last stage of a world historical form is its *comedy*. The Greek gods, who already died once of their wounds in Aeschylus's tragedy *Prometheus Bound*, were forced to die a second death—this time a comic one—in Lucian's dialogues. Why does history take this course? So that mankind may part *happily* from its past. We lay claim to this *happy* historical destiny for the political powers of Germany.[57]

As the reference to Lucian makes clear, Marx understands comedy as satire and, perhaps surprisingly, he regards tragedy as possessing a similar critical function. Whereas for Hegel, tragedy ultimately reconciles apparently competing ethic institutions with each other—and thereby reconciles us to them—for Marx it begins a work of detachment or dissolution that is completed by comedy. Comedy, including farce, renders the given historical world risible so that we can happily rid ourselves of it.[58] In the case of the *Eighteenth Brumaire*, the farcical Bonaparte "strip[s] its halo from the state machine, profanes it and makes it at once loathsome and ridiculous" (135), thereby preparing the state for its ultimate overthrow.

None of this is particularly Hegelian. What *is* Hegelian is the sequence leading from tragedy to comedy to "the end of . . . ," whether that missing term be art or the social order. For Marx, the transition from tragedy to comedy not only signifies the dialectical progress of history, it is also a *means* toward that progress, since the critical work of comedy/satire/farce helps to unbind us from the historically given. Of course, this view is premised on a rather optimistic view of satire or farce in particular and of demystification in general. Bonaparte's ineptitude is supposed to undermine the sanctity of the state, thereby contributing to the radicalization of French society. And the satirical vein of Marx's *Eighteenth Brumaire* clearly intends to help that process along. What Marx does not anticipate is the emergence of modern forms of cynical consciousness that can assume a critical stance and nevertheless continue to acquiesce to the demystified institution.[59]

In a sense, farce embodies this cynical consciousness. Marx wants farce to engage in a historically productive form of unbinding. But in fact it engages in unproductive or parasitical forms of rebinding as well. The word *farce* itself originally referred to interpolated passages "stuffed" into the liturgy, and it continued to be associated with satyr plays, intermezzi, and other short forms parasitical upon more major kinds of drama. In other words, despite its sometimes satirical content, farce remains attached to the very conventions it mocks. Marx's comparison of the lumpenproletariat to

Nick Bottom is instructive here. Bottom and the other mechanicals repeat tragedy (the tale of Pyramus and Thisbe) as farce, and in so doing stage a vicious send-up (whether intended or not) of the aristocratic ideals of the play's main characters. At the same time, their main hope is that their performance will win them a pension of sixpence a day from Duke Theseus, not his overthrow. Or take as another example the opening lines of the *Eighteenth Brumaire*. Does Marx's farcical repetition of Hegel undermine Hegel's authority or reinforce it? Is Marx producing something new from his Hegelian raw materials or attaching himself parasitically to the thing he mocks? Farce can produce a critical consciousness, but typically one that accommodates itself to the object of criticism.

Farce's generic indeterminacy likewise tugs against any clear dialectical succession of genres. Indeed, its capacity to mix different modes anticipates the novel, or rather, like tragicomedy in Hegel, it represents the novelization of drama. And given Marx's habit of mapping dramatic genres onto historical progress, farce points to the possibility of an endless novelization of history as well. None of this, of course, is acknowledged within the official argument of the *Eighteenth Brumaire*, which predicts imminent revolutionary triumph despite (indeed, because of) the temporary setback of Bonaparte's coup. What I am arguing for is a counterplot within the *Eighteenth Brumaire*, one that obliquely acknowledges the possibility of a seemingly interminable capitalist future. Just as Hegel's *Aesthetics* projects two different "ends of art"—one ascending dialectically to philosophy, the other grinding to a halt in the prosaic—so, I would claim, Marx's vision of the class struggle projects both the revolutionary triumph of the proletariat and a slow becoming-rabble of society that forecloses any such definitive conclusion. The proper form for telling this tale is the one Marx has chosen: the tragedy/comedy/novel.

III

When significant tragic drama reemerges in the late nineteenth and early twentieth centuries, the effects of novelization are both unmistakable and varied, from the psychological (and domestic) realism of Ibsen and Chekhov to the widespread use of tragicomic modes in Chekhov, Beckett, and many others. (Marx would have been interested to note that Ionesco labeled his play *Les Chaises* a "farce tragique.") One question perhaps left hanging by this chapter is what contribution Marx's *Eighteenth Brumaire* can make to an understanding of these developments that is not already anticipated by

Hegel. Stage tragedy, after all, does not often share Marx's interest in collective as opposed to individual action, except in the case of overtly political drama such as Hauptmann's *The Weavers* and some of the works of Brecht.

One respect in which the *Eighteenth Brumaire* makes an original theoretical contribution, I think, is in its use of perspectival effects: the initial focus on the Parisian political scene that then zooms out into a series of broader social and geographical landscapes. This returns us to a point I made at the beginning of the chapter: drama is performed for a *public* while the novel is consumed by something between a public and a population. Drama is essentially an urban form, the novel a national one. (It is worth noting here that Hegel conceives of drama from a national perspective, and this is another sign of his novelization of the genre.) One of the things that the *Eighteenth Brumaire* demonstrates is that the city does not contain—either geographically or otherwise—the entire set of economic and social phenomena that informs life within it. Because it can no longer account for itself fully on its own terms, it cannot make sense of urban/political/theatrical experience. (I am not assuming that modern drama is necessarily "about" urban life or that it necessarily takes the city as its mis-en-scène. I am discussing the more fundamental conditions that structure drama as an urban performance no matter what its subject matter.) To borrow a phrase from Fredric Jameson, the city can no longer undertake its own cognitive mapping.[60] The novel would be in this sense a response to the cognitive failure on the part of tragic drama as an urban form—a recognition of the pressure placed by the presence of a national population on the coherence of an urban public. Moreover, as Marx shows, even national boundaries succumb to a version of the same problem, as when the French bourgeoisie misinterpret a continent-wide commercial crisis as caused by purely domestic political uncertainties. One of the conditions for the reemergence of serious tragic drama at the end of the nineteenth century, then, might well be the transformation of urban life by means of its imbrication in national and international flows of capital: in short, the transformation of the city from self-sufficient republican enclave to cities that are either imperialist metropoles themselves or aware of themselves as peripheral (Oslo, Moscow, Stockholm, Dublin), and the reorganization of experience this entails.[61] Such a transformation poses fundamental questions for the possibility of meaningful individual action, a situation to which the rise of "absurdist" theater in the twentieth century is only the most obvious response. Under these circumstances, the novelization of tragedy is not its death knell. It poses deep, perhaps even insoluble, problems. At the same time it allows tragic drama to survive, even to thrive. But this new terrain demands evolutionary adaptions that may render such drama strange, even to itself. Above all it is faced with the challenge of constituting a public within the becoming-rabble that is both its deadly adversary and its very condition of existence. For Hegel, the tragic protagonist is by definition the representative of an extant ethical institution or form of community. Modern tragedy must work without such supports, "suspended in mid-air." Marx employs this phrase to describe the mere appearance of the Bonapartist state in the *Eighteenth Brumaire*, but it is the actual condition of modern drama, challenged as it is to constitute its own public by means of its own resources, finding less and less support in this task from a capitalist modernity dedicated to reproducing populations, not founding publics.

CHAPTER SEVEN

Beckett's Tragic Pantry

Samuel Beckett is the playwright Hegel at once foretold and never could have imagined. Hegel regarded tragicomedy as potentially perfecting tragedy, yet also as a form that threatened to reduce tragedy to the prosaic. Beckett made straight for the catastrophe that Hegel dreaded, employing tragicomedy to achieve an unprecedentedly prosaic form of drama. Yet from this he managed to squeeze out a miraculous poetry. Hegel held that at the end of art, Geist would pass the baton to philosophy. Beckett seized that baton and held onto it, producing a dialogue with philosophy as fraught and rich as his engagement with literature. Indeed, he showed that the playwright could "do" philosophy as brilliantly as any philosopher without sacrificing its theatrical vitality. In these and other ways, Beckett instinctively sought the various endpoints Hegel demarcated—of art, of history, of the history of art. Indeed, his plays paradoxically located themselves after the end, adopted the space of the after as their peculiar homeland, and by so doing scrambled the Hegelian narrative of history by proving that it was possible to "go on" without thereby diluting the definitively terminal nature of the end.

Beckett is, I am suggesting, a post-Hegelian playwright—granted that his project throws the concept of the "post-" into some disarray. To be genuinely post-Hegelian, one must be self-consciously so, and I hold that Beckett is this as well. Indeed, among the things I shall attempt to show in this chapter is that Beckett is seriously, if irreverently, engaged with the Hegelian legacy in French thought, and that this legacy helps him to think through the dilemmas and the possibilities of meaningful action at the end of history.

In so doing, Beckett engages with a new and specific crisis of action with which these French post-Hegelians were also concerned in their different ways. One mark of this crisis is that action's counterpart and antagonist—the thing that at once complements and threatens to displace it—is no longer production, as it had been in classic political economy, but rather consumption. Economic theory had largely abandoned questions of production starting with the marginalist revolution of the 1870s, focusing on consumer demand, rather than labor, as the origin of value. Beckett criticism has on the whole devoted relatively little attention to issues of consumption, and when it has, the emphasis has tended to fall on the scarcities of the immediate postwar situation as background to Beckett's famously resource-deprived landscapes. But as we shall see, this grasps just one pole of a more complex situation.

My readings of *Waiting for Godot* and *Endgame* will pair each play with a post-Hegelian thinker contemporary to Beckett: Alexandre Kojève in the case of *Godot* and Georges Bataille in the case of *Endgame*. For the most part I see Beckett as reacting to and against these figures rather than somehow "illustrating" their philosophical positions. But this very antagonism sometimes locks Beckett in a fairly close embrace, particularly in the case of Kojève. Moreover, while I do attempt to make a case for direct influence, I also invoke Kojève and Bataille as intellectual foils that cast a reflected but illuminating light on Beckett's work, and I will therefore allow myself, particularly in the case of Kojève, to invoke works that Beckett could not himself have read during the period in question. But since Beckett himself was almost perversely inclined to deny philosophical and even literary references in his work, I can console myself with the fact that even the most legitimate arguments for influence would probably elicit the same dour response from him as my more speculative constructions.

I

There is no evidence that Beckett ever attended the fabled seminars on Hegel that Alexandre Kojève offered at the École Practique des Hautes Études from 1933 to 1939. But he could hardly have been ignorant of an event that so prominently shaped Parisian intellectual life, drawing the likes of Georges Bataille, Maurice Merleau-Ponty, Jacques Lacan, Raymond Aron, and many others. It was owing to Kojève that Hegel's master-slave dialectic became a virtual obsession among French thinkers. One of Kojève's most important lectures appeared in the journal *Mésures* in 1939, two others appeared in 1946, and the first edition of the *Introduction à la Lecture de Hegel* was published by Gallimard in 1947, just as Beckett was at work on *Waiting for Godot*. So the work would have been at least partly accessible in written form. Beckett was, moreover, an acquaintance of Raymond Queneau, who edited Kojève's volume. It was perfectly clear to the play's original audiences that the figures of Pozzo and Lucky spoofed the master-slave dialectic in Hegel that Kojève had done so much to popularize.[1]

My initial focus, however, will be on a passage in Kojève that Beckett could not possibly have known or read while composing *Waiting for Godot*. I refer to the notorious footnote on the end of history attached to the second edition of the *Introduction* published in 1962. In that footnote—begun in the first edition but augmented considerably in the second—Kojève meditates on the fate of mankind at the conclusion of history as Hegel understands it. Initially, Kojève argues that man will revert to an animal condition and thus essentially vanish as a distinctive species: "What disappears is Man properly so-called—that is Action negating the given, and Error, or in general, the Subject opposed to the Object. In point of fact, the End of Human Time or History—that is, the definitive annihilation of Man properly so-called or of the free and historical individual—means quite simply the cessation of Action in the full sense of the term. Practically, this means: the cessation of wars and bloody revolutions."[2] For Kojève, man is not simply a being capable of action. Action—defined in Hegelian terms as the negating of the given—is rather constitutive of the human as such. The origin of man occurs in the battle to the death that defines master and slave, a battle in which the desire for recognition prompts the risk of man's biological being and thereby brings the human into existence as the transcendence of that merely biological or animal being. "Man will risk his biological *life* to satisfy his *non-biological* Desire" (*Introduction*, 41; emphasis in original). When man ceases to act (and action is defined here restrictively as a fight to the death), he sinks back into his merely biological existence, seeking only natural objects of desire in the manner of the other animals. At the end of history—the temporal arena of human action—human beings will therefore devolve into "post-historical animals of the species *Homo sapiens*" (159).

All of this is strange enough, but in the first edition it is merely a possibility reserved for an unknown future date when an anticipated Communist revolution will bring about—or rather complete—the slow reversal of positions between master and slave. When Kojève continues the footnote in the second edition, however, he notoriously announces the revelation (a series of revelations, actually) that the end of history has already occurred:

"At the period when I write the above note (1946), Man's return to animality did not appear unthinkable to me as a prospect for the future (more or less near). But shortly afterwards (1948) I understood that the Hegelian-Marxist end of History was not yet to come, but was already a present, here and now" (160). (Before proceeding, I must at least remark on the coincidence that Kojève's change of heart occurs just during the years when Beckett is at work on *Waiting for Godot.*) In effect, Kojève now accepts Hegel's claim that history ended in 1806 at the battle of Jena, which cemented Napoleon's establishment of the universal homogeneous State. Everything that follows, including World War II, is a kind of mopping-up operation that universalizes and perfects the end of history, but is not history itself. Part of this mopping-up operation involves the achievement of a degree of material prosperity that will complete mankind's release from the realm of necessity. Formerly Kojève had adhered to Marx's belief that only a Communist revolution would bring this about, but now he realizes that American consumer culture is the true end of history:

> Already, moreover, this process of elimination [of the residues of History] is more advanced in the North American extensions of Europe than in Europe itself. One can even say that, from a certain point of view, the United States has already obtained the final stage of Marxist "communism," seeing that, practically, all the members of a "classless society" can from now on appropriate for themselves everything that seems good to them, without thereby working any more than their heart dictates.
>
> Now, several voyages of comparison made (between 1948 and 1958) to the United States and the U.S.S.R. gave me the impression that if the Americans give the appearance of rich Sino-Soviets, it is because the Russians and the Chinese are only Americans who are still poor but are rapidly proceeding to get richer. I was led to conclude from this that the "American way of life" was the type of life specific to the post-historical period, the actual presence of United States in the World prefiguring the "eternal present" future of all of humanity. Thus, Man's return to animality appeared no longer as a possibility that was yet to come, but as a certainty that was already present. (160–61)

It has been difficult for commentators to decide exactly how serious Kojève is being here. Certainly, some degree of irony must be involved, since a society of fat Americans stuffing themselves in kitchens full of shiny new appliances hardly seems like a suitably majestic end to history as Kojève understands it.[3] It is worth noting, in any case, the degree to which Kojève's description of consumer culture converges with that of Hannah Arendt, for whom consumption rather than revolutionary action is the fate of the working classes in modern society, reducing Man to the *animal laborans* and progressively closing off any space for political action. As his correspondence with Carl Schmitt reveals, moreover, Kojève sees the replacement of politics by administration as a mark of the posthistorical period—another parallel to Arendt.[4] For Kojève, the individual violence of the original master-slave encounter eventually gives way to collective—ultimately national—forms of violence, which is why the disappearance of "wars and bloody revolutions" marks the end of history. I shall comment on these convergences at greater length in this chapter's second part.

Crucial to the American posthistorical Utopia is not merely the disappearance of war and class struggle but also the virtual disappearance of work. For Kojève, as for Hegel, labor is a form of action—the slave's way of negating the naturally given object—that proves even more historically productive than the master's risking of life in battle. That Americans can "appropriate for themselves everything that seems good to them, without thereby working any more than their heart dictates," eliminates this final form of humanizing action not merely because the time spent working is minimized but because for Kojève the humanizing form of work can be performed only under threat of death and at the behest of another (the master). Hence working as one's own heart dictates neutralizes the very essence of work.

Kojève's first revelation that Americans are the true "post-historical animals of the species *Homo sapiens*" was succeeded, he goes onto tell us, by a second one, prompted by a 1959 trip to Japan. The Japanese, who in Kojève's view have been posthistorical for some time, have managed to sustain their status as human, he claims, by means of a gratuitous, formalized "snobbery." Modes of the Japanese dedication to formalized acts include Noh theater, the tea ceremony, flower arrangement—even kamikaze flights, which Kojève sees not as conducted for military ends but as gratuitous acts of suicide. Because Kojève understands such formalized activities as the negation of any (historicized) content, they count as posthistorical modes of action and hence maintain the requisite distance between human and animal. Henceforth, "posthistorical Man must continue to *detach* 'form' from 'content,' doing so no longer in order actively to transform the latter, but so that he may *oppose* himself as a pure 'form' to himself and to others taken as 'content' of any sort" (162). Unlike labor, formalized snobbery "negates" content not by transforming it but by abandoning it altogether so as to parade itself before others.

Peeling back the layers of orientalist fantasy at work here, we may notice that the Japanese begin to sound a lot like European modernists. Not only did Noh theater influence a wide array of modernist playwrights and directors, but also the separation of form from content that Kojève extols suggests the project of the abstract expressionists who dominated the art world in the late 1940s and early 1950s. As it happens, Kojève's uncle was Wassily Kandinsky, and in 1936 Kojève wrote an essay on his work that emphasized the negation of content by form.[5] The Japanese, in effect, take modernist aesthetics and expand them into an entire way of life. Kamikaze pilots aside, the forms of snobbery that Kojève mentions are all harmless pastimes, suitable for filling up one's day in a calm, posthistorical world.

I think that both of these posthistorical "paths"—the American and the Japanese—have something to contribute to an understanding of *Waiting for Godot*. I want to begin with the American path, which may seem the more counterintuitive of the two since nothing appears more unlike the empty landscape of Godot than Kojève's fantasy of a culture bursting with modern appliances and consumer goods. Indeed, as critics have recently affirmed, Beckett's spare world seems indebted to memories of the food shortages and other deprivations experienced during World War II.[6] While the Marshall Plan (the purpose of which was to transform Europe into precisely the kind of Americanized consumer paradise Kojève envisioned) was formally in place, its effects were negligible during the period when Beckett was writing his play. Things would look somewhat different by 1953, when *Godot* premiered in Paris. In the meantime, though, food rations persisted during the years immediately following the war.[7] Correspondingly, the world of Godot is hungry, lean, shabby, and generally resource-poor. If this is a posthistorical landscape, it is one in which some cataclysm—surely World War II, but more broadly history itself—has returned things to a pseudo-primitive state. Godot's world suffers from a posthistorical penury that somehow suggests the prehistoric—a world in which root vegetables are Vladimir and Estragon's main foodstuffs.

Nevertheless, the play's persistent dearth is oddly shadowed by cornucopia. While Vladimir and Estragon sometimes seem caught in a Hobbesian state of nature—Estragon's nightly beatings and his gnawing on bones come to mind—other details point to a prelapsarian, paradisical scene. Vladimir identifies himself as "Adam" at one point (28),[8] and the tree at center stage recalls not only the cross on Golgotha but also its typological precedent, the Tree of Life in Eden. While it might be argued that these references are meant to invoke the Fall and the expulsion from the Garden (Estragon's reference to Cain and Abel in Act 2 would suggest such a fallen state), the

fact remains that Vladimir and Estragon (the "Adam and Steve" of the ho-
mophobic witticism) are exempt from the injunction to labor that marks
fallen mankind.[9] They spend their days in leisurely—sometimes, playful,
sometimes tense—conversation while attempting to ward off boredom. Ap-
proaching the question from an anthropological rather than theological
perspective, Eric Gans notes that the pair "reproduce the relatively harmonious and peaceful equilibrium of primitive egalitarian society."[10]

To return to the question of hunger: while Estragon displays a yearning
for carrots and a ravenous, unseemly appetite in the presence of Pozzo's
chicken bones, Vladimir doesn't eat at all, or show any interest in food. The
carrots he occasionally dispenses to Estragon seem to function more as a
narcotic or pacifier or a token of paternal love than a serious form of nourishment ("He will tell me about the blows he received and I will give him
a carrot"; 81). Indeed, the one time Estragon announces his hunger and demands a carrot, it is unclear whether what he is really demanding is food or
Vladimir's attention and care. Lucky, who has spent his day lugging a heavy
bag filled with sand, shows no interest in Pozzo's chicken bones, which is
how they find their way to Estragon. Alys Moody shrewdly observes that
hunger in Beckett is usually objectless—something more akin to anorexia.[11]
But before it reaches its advanced stages, real hunger induces an active
search for nourishment, whereas Vladimir and Estragon display very little
interest in eating. If in some respects they are hungry, in others they are
clearly not.

Moreover, the nature of their food supply is paradoxical. While in characteristically Beckettian fashion Vladimir and Estragon have only carrots
and turnips to eat—and soon only turnips—this growing scarcity is balanced by a somewhat magical quality to Vladimir's store. Where did these
roots come from, anyway? Vladimir makes no reference to foraging or theft
or purchase or agriculture. They are simply "there" and in some sense can
be said to originate from his pocket. I make this point because miraculous
if meager provision is not an unusual thing in Beckett. Think of the periodic replenishing of Winnie's lipstick and toothpaste in *Happy Days*, or the
anonymous hand that provides a daily bowl of soup in *Malone Dies*, or the
unidentified deity who supplies endless sacks of tinned sardines to the inhabitants of *How It Is*.

The motif of miraculous provision (Estragon's too-tight boots are replaced in Act 2 with better-fitting ones) renders visible an entire subterranean world of material sustenance that usually serves as the unstated
premise of fiction, and exposes the necessary undergirding of animal exis-

tence that generally goes unremarked. It also makes that world ambivalently charged, at once starving and supersufficient. Turnips are manna, or the root vegetable counterparts to the luscious fruits hanging ripe for the plucking in Eden.

If we now turn from prehistory to posthistory, we find the same division between dearth and abundance, as captured in the very first line of the play: "Nothing to be done." While it applies specifically to Estragon's inability to remove his boot, it also tends to detach itself from its immediate context to become an emblematic utterance. "Nothing to be done" means "the situation is hopeless; nothing can be done to improve it." But at the same time, the French "Rien à faire" can express boredom rather than despair, a more abstract absence of anything to do, which alerts us to the possibility that "nothing to be done" might also mean "Everything has already been done; the situation is so perfect or complete that nothing remains to do." At least, Vladimir's later statement that "we've nothing more to do here" (43) suggests as much, not to mention Estragon's "What do we do now, now that we are happy?" (50). The sterile emptiness of Godot's world is the photographic negative of a perfectly happy and abundant state that nevertheless manages to shine dimly through. Indeed, the business of modern capitalism seems to be humming along somewhere just offstage, since Vladimir and Estragon refer to Godot's "agents," "correspondents," and "bank account" (10–11), while Pozzo is able to procure such creature comforts as roasted chicken, wine, and of course servant. All of which suggests that Beckett's posthistorical scene is not entirely unrelated to Kojève's. Or rather, it holds present-day postwar scarcity and (soon to come) postwar abundance in a complicated and contradictory balance. In any case, "History" is over. It was the unnamed cataclysm that produced this at once pre- and posthistorical landscape.

For Kojève, of course, posthistory (American style) is defined by the absence of possibilities for action and hence the descent into the subhuman. "What do we do, now that we are happy?" is the persistent question of the posthuman animal, provided with consumables but deprived for that reason of anything to *do*. We have yet to address the nature of action in the play, but one thing we can say about it immediately is that it is not work. Lucky engages in a kind of labor that will merit closer scrutiny, and Pozzo at least moves across the stage, toward (he says) the auction where he will try to dispose of his slave. But Vladimir and Estragon devote their existence to conversation alone, and to a brief bout of halfhearted calisthenics meant to release the physical energy not expended in labor. They are far more idle even than the "master," Pozzo.

What possibilities for action remain in this posthistorical landscape? As Vivian Mercier observed of the play, "Nothing happens—twice."[12] Vladimir and Estragon do ponder suicide, and Estragon considers leaving Vladimir, and both consider abandoning their wait for Godot, but none of these things comes to pass. There is a moment in Act 2 when the now-blind Pozzo, having been knocked to the ground, cries out piteously for help. In response, Vladimir exhorts Estragon: "Let us do something while we have the chance! It is not every day that we are needed" (70). What follows, though, is not action but a monologue delivered by Vladimir on the ethics of the decision, the call of the other, and so on, which clearly spoofs the fashionable language of existentialism and its exaltation of the act.

All of which may seem somewhat beside the point, since what Vladimir and Estragon do, obviously, is wait—and this is apparently the great innovation of the play. I say "apparently" because waiting as such isn't as radical or novel a dramatic action as it might at first seem. Just to take the plays treated in this book: Clytemnestra spends most of *Agamemnon* waiting for her husband to return from Troy; Faustus spends his play waiting (implicitly) for his contract with Mephastophilis to expire; Hamlet waits for just the right time to kill Claudius; and Samson awaits some divine message to rouse him from his lethargy. Accomplished waiters though they are, Vladimir and Estragon can't hold a candle to Aeschylus's Prometheus, who spends his play completely immobilized, waiting (he knows it will be eons) for Zeus to come crawling to him for help. Moreover, Hamlet and Faustus, like Vladimir and Estragon, engage in frivolous activities meant to fill the intervening time as they wait. The difference, of course, is that in all these other plays, the waiting eventually comes to an end, generally in a climactic spasm of violence. In Godot the waiting is ill-defined and endless.

Sometimes Vladimir and Estragon feel the burden of waiting, and sometimes they are obviously distracting themselves from this burden, which is only another way of waiting, but sometimes too their activities and conversation take on a life of their own, and then they are not waiting in anything but the most formal sense. In effect, they have momentarily—but only momentarily—forgotten to wait. In any case, waiting does not merely take the place of a more classically "unified" dramatic action. It prevents anything unified from forming, since that would put an end to the wait, and this condemns Vladimir and Estragon to falling back on disconnected "bits" and diversions that fill the time but lead nowhere. Indeed, the play so scrupulously observes the other Aristotelian unities so as to deny us the unity of action—which happens to be the reason for all the others—in a conspicuous way. The unified time of dramatic action, we might say, is replaced on the one hand by the isolated instant and on the other by endlessness. Without developing the point at length right now, I will simply mention that this temporality is also that of Kojève's posthistory, composed as it is of momentary acts of consumption that go on ceaselessly and to no larger purpose.

The primary consequence of this particular temporality is, of course, boredom—the fundamental problem of the play.[13]

VLADIMIR: We wait. We are bored. [*He throws up his hand.*] No, don't protest, we are bored to death, there's no denying it. Good. A diversion comes along and what do we do? We let it go to waste. (71)

It is not enough to say that Vladimir and Estragon feel bored, however. After all, they feel many things: hope, despair, dread, longing, happiness, and so forth. Boredom is something more essential and less subjective than a feeling: a situation, orientation, or, as Heidegger would have it, a *Stimmung* or attunement between self and world.[14] Boredom is the consequence of a world in which there is "nothing to be done," a world without action. As Kojève has it: "Not to *act*, therefore, is not to be as a truly *human* being; it is to be as *Sein*, as given, natural being. Hence it is to fall into decay, to become brutish, and this metaphysical truth is revealed to Man through the phenomenon of boredom: the man who—like a thing, like an animal, like an angel—remains identical to himself—does not negate—does not negate himself—i.e., does not act, is *bored*. And only man can be bored" (54).

Speaking of the Stoics, Kojève remarks that their philosophy "prevents man from acting: it obliges him to remain content with talking. Now, says Hegel, all discourse that remains discourse ends in *boring* man" (53; emphasis in original). This is not only a good description of Vladimir and Estragon's dilemma but also—though Kojève doesn't say so—a good description of his posthistorical world, which is stuffed with goods but devoid of occasions to act. Indeed, its very abundance contributes to the problem. A world devoid of the need to act—a utopian or posthistorical world—falls prey to boredom. It is above all Vladimir and Estragon's boredom, then, that points to the economy of abundance showing through their apparent scarcity. Boredom marks the play's world as posthistorical, but this must be understood in light of the fact that boredom signals the irruption of the posthistorical whenever it occurs, even within the realm of history. No matter the era when one falls prey to boredom, one is already in some sense posthistorical. Boredom arises when the very possibility of action retreats behind an inaccessible horizon. This is the case with posthistory, and it is in part what distinguishes Vladimir and Estragon's waiting from those of the other tragic protagonists I invoked earlier. It is not just that those plays finally bring waiting and inaction to an end; it is that the prospect of that final action, held always in sight, gives the interval a shape and meaning for the tragic protagonist, no matter how long deferred. This is why the tragic avenger (to take an exemplary instance) is never bored with waiting. In *Waiting for Godot*, by contrast, all that remains are pastimes that cannot shape or give meaning to time but merely postpone it or provide momentary distraction from an overwhelming boredom. It is largely because of boredom that "everything oozes" (51), rendering viscous and slow the Heraclitean flow of time. Time in posthistory creeps along like the discharge from a pustulant wound.

Now, the attentive reader will have noticed a major problem with my argument thus far. I am claiming that Godot depicts something like Kojève's vision of posthistory. But the end of history for Kojève is defined by the disappearance of master and slave, who in Beckett's play are apparently alive (if not entirely well) in the persons of Pozzo and Lucky. Indeed, those critics who have argued for a direct influence of Kojève on Beckett—something I have not thus far done—have focused on the Pozzo and Lucky plot, which does bear some striking if not quite systematic parallels to the master-slave dialectic as Kojève describes it. I shall look at some of these shortly. But first I want to point to an important difference. For Hegel and Kojève, the slave's essential activity is work, by which they mean the artisanal fashioning of raw materials into durable, finished forms that are destined to be enjoyed by the master. Work is the slave's action, which means his way of negating the natural given by transforming it: leather into shoe, clay into pot, and so on. But there is no indication that Lucky engages in any work of this kind—the sort that Adam Smith would have recognized as productive labor. Rather, he performs personal services for Pozzo: carrying a picnic basket, handing him items when called for, and above all lugging a large, heavy bag. For Kojève, the relative permanence of the slave's artifacts contrasts with the ephemeral pleasures of the master's consumption, and makes the slave into the engine of long-term historical development. But Lucky's acts of personal service are every bit as transient as Pozzo's whims, and leave no lasting trace behind. They are the disappearing counterparts to Vladimir's and Estragon's always-aborted pastimes.

This is not without precedent. As we have seen, Shakespearean laborers— gravediggers, porters, actors—are more often than not deliverers of personal services, the emptiness of whose exertions sometimes (as in Hamlet) becomes a matter of thematic interest. In *Godot*, the only fashioned objects of sustained attention—hats and boots—are conspicuously empty, as Vladimir and Estragon peer into their depths and try in vain to see if something can be shaken out of them. In essence, all made things are holes, and thereby reminiscent of the work of Shakespeare's gravediggers. (As Vladimir observes at one point: "There's no lack of void" [73].) Moreover, Lucky's most strenuous effort—lugging that heavy bag around—turns out to be utterly pointless when Pozzo reveals in Act 2 that the suitcase is filled with sand. Lucky carries it just so that he can be burdened with something heavy to carry—so that, in other words, he can play the part of the slave. Unlike Kojève's slave who works, Lucky's sole work is to be a slave, to perform his subjection to Pozzo. Lacking any content, Pozzo's mastery has become purely formal: a "Japanese" element of pure "snobbery" in the posthistorical world, though even this constantly teeters on clownish bombast.

As Adorno observes, "Waiting for Godot revolves around the theme of lordship-and-bondage grown senile and demented in an era when exploitation of human labor persists although it could well be abolished."[15] Adorno speaks to the gratuitous lateness of Beckett's master-slave pair, historical remnants doddering about with no real purpose in posthistory. The fact that Pozzo and Lucky move across the stage, in contrast with the perpetual stasis of Vladimir and Estragon, seems designed to evoke in the weakest possible fashion the vector of historical progress. Far from working to free himself from subjection, however, Lucky hopes to tie himself to Pozzo for as long as possible. The only change the pair achieves involves deterioration: Pozzo's going blind and Lucky dumb in Act 2. A senile dialectic indeed, in which repetition under ever-worse conditions replaces historical movement.

One of the most conspicuous Hegelian motifs in this subplot involves Lucky's name—which, besides the more obvious joke, encodes a more specific philosophical one. Kojève observes that "the future and History . . . belong not to the warlike Master, who either dies or preserves himself indefinitely in identity to himself, but to the working Slave" (23). Despite his initial defeat and laborious subjection, then, the slave finds himself the inheritor of history—a "lucky" turn indeed. The story of this volte-face involves both subjective and objective elements. While the master lives a life of pure enjoyment, consuming the products of the slave, the deferred gratification of work forms and educates the slave, subjecting him to an extended *Bildung* that civilizes and cultivates him. As a result, "understanding, abstract thought, science, technique, the arts—all these . . . have their origin in the forced work of the Slave" (49). From this perspective, history is the objective counterpart to or product of the slave's *Bildung*, to which the slave gives further material support by producing advanced means of production and not only consumables. The slave makes not only objects but also history, which in the end he arises and claims for his own.

In this, as in most other respects, Beckett spurns the optimistic contours of Hegelian history. To be sure, Pozzo invokes the Hegelian concept of the slave as bearer of culture:

POZZO: Guess who taught me all these beautiful things. [*Pause. Pointing to Lucky.*] My Lucky! . . . But for him all my thoughts, all my feelings, would have been of common things. [*Pause. With extraordinary vehemence.*] Professional worries! [*Calmer.*] Beauty, grace, truth of the first water, I knew they were all beyond me. So I took a knook. (24–25)

Beckett sees what Hegel and Kojève both miss—that the master can appropriate the slave's culture like any other good, although culture is then in turn transformed by the master's habits of transient enjoyment into a mere entertainment or pastime. (Where theater itself falls in this process is an interesting question.)

Lucky's speech, when it does come, is both the longest in the play and the most incoherent. Bookish, paratactic, multilingual, punctuated by childish puns on bodily functions, it is in some ways a classically if unwittingly high-modernist performance. (Lucky sounds sometimes like a demented Joyce, sometimes like an Eliot shoring fragments against his ruin.) What interests me is his monologue's capacity to depict not only an individual mind but also an intellectual culture in decay. References to "the labors unfinished of Testew and Cunard" (34) and "the labors lost of Steinweg and Peterman" (35) manage to suggest a vast intellectual edifice crumbling in on itself, and not only within Lucky's skull. Lucky himself resembles a broken tape recorder, stuttering and reeling off names, references, and topics with no clear pattern. He is, in a sense, the collapse of *Bildung*, insofar as he has not internalized culture but merely memorized its components, and insofar as the lack of clear progression within the speech speaks to the corresponding lack of a larger, organic narrative of learning and growth. Moreover, as we have seen, for Hegel and Kojève the slave's *Bildung* is both image and engine of historical progress. In Lucky's word salad, then, we can hear the collapse of the temporal coherence and symmetry that in Hegel's view allows historical and philosophical development to proceed in tandem. Perhaps Lucky is the image of the posthistorical intellect, its project at an end and its materials slowly disintegrating

Lucky's monologue offers a dense, inward microcosm of the play as a whole, his disconnected syntactical and phonemic fragments standing in for the serial language games engaged in by Vladimir and Estragon. Once his hat is on, the command to "Think, pig!" (33) sets Lucky's mechanism in motion, and nothing stops it but grabbing the hat from his head. Otherwise the monologue would run on indefinitely, just as Vladimir and Estragon's dialogue does under the impulsion of boredom. This reflection of inner and outer, or subjective and objective, engages with yet another Hegelian theme, again in a parodic register. States Kojève:

> One can *understand* an historical World only because it is *historical*—that is, temporal and consequently finite or mortal. For one only understands it truly— that is, conceptually or philosophically—only in *"Erinnerung"*: it is the *memory (Erinnerung)* of a past real which is the *internalization (Er-innerung)* of this real—i.e., the passing of its "meaning" (or "essence") from the *external* reality into the Concept which is *in* me, inside of the "Subject." And if the totality of History can be so understood (in and by the *Phenomenology*), only at the end *of* History, a particular historical World can be understood only after its end or death in History. (162–63)

Kojève's point is not only the familiar Hegelian one that philosophical understanding is retrospective—that the owl of Minerva flies at dusk. Rather, a sequence of events does not become historical until Spirit internalizes them and accords them the meaningful progression that turns events into history. Events do not become history until they are remembered and understood. "For Understanding or Knowledge of the Past is what, when it is integrated into the Present, transforms this Present into an historical Present, that is, into a Present that realizes a progress in relation to its Past" (164). For Hegel, then, philosophy is not merely the after-the-fact interpretation of history but that which history needs to complete itself. Napoleon's victory at Jena in 1806 would not have been able to bring history to a close had Hegel not simultaneously brought the *Phenomenology* to a close. But this language of historical progress—of history as progress—is precisely the Hegelian premise that *Waiting for Godot* ridicules most mercilessly. It does this in part by jettisoning the kind of unified dramatic "action" that grants not only the play but also the larger historical world its coherence. Hence, posthistory and history can meet up in a confused jumble. And then it caps this failure of progress (literalized in Vladimir and Estragon's failed determination to move) by having it processed in the disordered mind of Lucky, where memory is not an organically unifying internalization or *Er-innerung* but mere mechanical repetition and disgorgement.[16] Lucky, that is to say, is the farcical "Hegel" whose mind reflects and completes the nonprogression of Godot's world.[17]

The Hegelian theme of *Erinnerung* or memory is crucial because forgetting—the failure of memory—is one of the main elements that prevents Beckett's play from constructing a coherent action. When Act 2 begins, Estragon has forgotten pretty much everything that happened in Act 1, including the encounter with Pozzo and Lucky. Pozzo forgets what he says as soon as he says it ("You see, my memory is defective" [30]) and likewise does not recall in Act 2 the events of Act 1. While the loss of memory is potentially liberating ("We could start all over again perhaps" [54], suggests Vladimir), it is also the main entropic force that prevents the play's plot from progressing. Of course, plays are like that. The actors recommence the next day as if they had not already enacted the play's events the day before.[18] Beckett's innovation is to internalize this theatrical amnesia within the plot of the play itself, thereby fending off the possibility of action or history.

The play's final image of history, or of its absence, is the song that Vladimir enters singing at the beginning of Act 2:

A dog came in the kitchen,
And stole a crust of bread.
Then cook up with a ladle
And beat him till he was dead

Then all the dogs came running
And dug the dog a tomb—
[*He stops, broods, resumes*]

Then all the dogs came running
And dug the dog a tomb
And wrote upon the tombstone
For the eyes of dogs to come:

A dog came in the kitchen
And stole a crust of bread . . .
(47–48)

The song depicts the one successful act of historical recording in the poem, as the dogs memorialize their fallen comrade with an act of inscription "for the eyes of dogs to come." Past, present, and future are finally organized into a coherent whole. And yet the dialectical progression of Hegelian history has here become a vicious circle, spiraling into an endlessly repetitive mis en abyme. Like Lucky's speech, this is a self-reflexive emblem of the play, capturing the lack of progress that Act II will represent with respect to Act I. And perhaps these dogs who have attained the human capacities for speech and history even present an inverting specter of the animalization that haunts Vladimir and Estragon as posthistorical men. In any case, the song depicts a form of memory that, no less than forgetting, negates any possibility of historical progress. Whether this is the sign of escape into a posthistorical condition or of endless entrapment within history the song does not quite decide. Nor does the play.

I have yet to discuss Beckett's labeling of his play as a "tragicomedy," and I shall do so now to bring this consideration of history's end to an end. In one sense, of course, tragicomedy invokes Hegel's (itself tragicomic) end of art. But it looks back still further, I think, to the Renaissance plays that begin this "romantic" degeneration for Hegel. One of the great innovations of Renaissance tragedy was to include comic elements within it: the gravediggers in Hamlet, for example. As I have argued in earlier chapters, this innovation allows the previously excluded world of production to confront what had been a realm of pure, aristocratic action, and the mixed genre that results anticipates in some respects the space of political economy itself.

Beckett's tramp-heroes, Vladimir and Estragon, owe a debt not only to the more recent traditions of cinema and the Music Hall but also to the figure of the Shakespearean clown. Indeed, they clearly in some respects reincarnate Hamlet's gravediggers. Vladimir enters Act 2 singing a song of tomb-making, just as Shakespeare's grave maker enters singing while he works. "Where did all these corpses come from?" (54), Vladimir asks later in the act. Shakespeare's grave maker compares his profession to Adam's, and Vladimir likewise takes on that name. *Waiting for Godot* is in some sense an extended act of Shakespearean whistling (or wisecracking) in the graveyard.[19]

And yet Vladimir and Estragon are not digging graves or engaging in any form of labor whatever. Their relation to mortality is more abstract and philosophical—rather like that of Hamlet, in fact. Like Hamlet, moreover, they are philosophical ruminators incapable of action but tempted by suicide; like him, they are held captive by ethical obligations to a spectral figure. Vladimir even quotes Hamlet at one point.[20] I am suggesting, then, that Vladimir and Estragon are both Hamlet and the gravediggers, both tragic hero and Shakespearean clown, both aristocratic master and working slave.

This paradoxical fact is prepared for to some degree by Shakespeare himself, who establishes mirroring relations between Hamlet and the grave maker (Hamlet is often clownish, the grave maker philosophical). And yet in Shakespeare, these resemblances are balanced by fundamental antagonisms—between social classes and between action and production as principles. As I argued, moreover, the difference between action and production is also a difference between two forms of time: Hamlet's time, the time of action that is punctuated and organized by the event, and grave maker's time, the time of production that goes on ceaselessly without respect to season. Hamlet occupies something like history, and the grave maker a world that looks very much the same from one day to the next. Hamlet is tortured by events that occur too soon or too late, knocking time out of joint; the grave maker has in some sense transcended time (and along with it, mortality) altogether. The grave maker's time looks rather more like that of *Waiting for Godot*, with the fundamental difference that his is organized by the activity of work. He sings and converses to enliven labor, while Vladimir and Estragon discuss and clown about in order to postpone the boredom of a world deprived both of the act and of work: the two forms of negation that, for Hegel and Kojève, constitute the realm of the human.

Shakespearean tragedy is already tragicomedy insofar as its tragic action alternates with and plays off of comic subplots. The antagonism between Hamlet and Claudius is compounded by antagonism of a different kind between Hamlet and the grave maker, or Hamlet and the actors. In Beckett's version of tragicomedy, by contrast, these competing groups are fused into one; the defining differences between them have absolutely collapsed. Or rather, they have in Vladimir and Estragon. Pozzo is still the old aristocratic master though subject to bouts of clownishness, and Lucky the working slave though capable of brief (and broken) philosophical flights. Pozzo and Lucky still carry with them the aroma of history, of antagonism between master and slave. Vladimir and Estragon, posthistorical men, have sublated these differences entirely. Their tragicomical existence goes on eternally, incapable of the dramatic resolutions that brought both tragedy and comedy to a close. *Hamlet*, I argued, is a play in which action is in the process of being eclipsed by production. *Waiting for Godot* is a play in which both principles are eclipsed, leaving only the uneasy leisure time of posthistory. For Hamlet, the rest was silence. For Vladimir and Estragon, the rest is boredom.

Another, complementary approach to tragicomedy is through Hegelian history. The initiating act of that history, the confrontation between master and slave, contains both tragic and comic elements, since death is threatened but averted. After his victory, the master wields the tragic forces of war and death, while the slave builds a comic world of growing cultural refinement and material prosperity. History culminates in the final uprising of the slave against master, the Communist revolution that will be tragic (violent) but also comic, ushering in an era of freedom and prosperity. Such, at least, is the early narrative employed by Kojève. In a sense, history has the structure of a revenge tragedy, since the initial act (defeat of slave by master) is answered by a final act (defeat of master by slave) following an interval that is history itself. Only, this final act is a kind of revenge tragicomedy.

After Kojève's "turn," however, things become more complicated. The longer he looks at the posthistorical era, the more equivocal it becomes. Do consumer goods or flower arrangements supply an appropriately grand consummation for the historical process? History was, in the end, a revenge tragicomedy, but one (we learn too late) that concluded in 1806, leaving us only the pale simulacrum of history since then as Spirit irons out its uneven developments and catches up with itself on a global scale. The fifth act, one might say, occurred some time ago, but we the actors are still milling about on stage, vainly trying to improvise with no end of the performance in sight. We have indeed missed our appointment—with history, with the possibility of meaningful action. Perhaps it will come again if we remain waiting in the same place. No, let's go. [We do not move.]

II

If we step back from Kojève's theory of action as negation and observe it critically, some peculiarities come to the fore. Only two kinds of endeavor count as action: the slave's labor and the master's self-sacrificing bravery. The former negates the object of labor; the latter, biological life itself. The former is patient, anonymous, debased; the latter impulsive, individualizing, grandiose. Action either achieves an exalted, heroic (if momentary) pitch or diminishes into ongoing productive busywork. Missing somehow is that middle realm that defines action in the more ordinary sense of the term. The Aristotelian virtues such as justice, temperance, generosity, and so forth seem better to embody the human than a ferocious assault bearing more than a little resemblance to the animal being it pretends to negate. And yet such virtues can find no place in Kojève's schema. The Hegelian master's action gets ramped up to impossible heights, after which the master must satisfy himself with a lifetime devoted to consumption. Heroic action is at once exalted and emptied out.

Something similar, I would argue, occurs in twentieth-century political theory, where thinkers such as Hannah Arendt and Carl Schmitt subject action to an inflationary treatment. Arendt's Greek *polis*, both successor to and continuation of the Homeric battlefield, is a space where immortal glory is to be won or disastrously lost. Action gets defined not by practical consequences but by unforgettable amplitude or Aristotelian *megethos*. Indeed, the Arendtian political sphere suspends the utilitarian purposes of action in order that a theater of disclosure may come to light. It thus magnifies action while negating the practical end or telos toward which action in the more ordinary sense is thought to aim. This simultaneous amplification and emptying out is what I shall refer to as the "inflation of the act," by way of analogy to currency inflation that results in larger sums but reduced purchasing power. Carl Schmitt's decisionism is another instance of the inflation of the act in modern political theory, a raising of action to a well-nigh transcendental absolute.

The inflation of the act is one of modern political theory's characteristic replies to the crisis of the act instituted by political economy. Arendt and Schmitt respond to this crisis with what Freud would call a "reaction formation": they answer political economy's diminution or dethroning of the act by granting it an unprecedented (or at least impractical) grandeur. Action for Arendt, as well as for Schmitt and Kojève, secures a form of sovereignty, although for Arendt this sovereignty does not disrupt the formal equality among citizens. But at the same time, Arendt (more than Schmitt) acknowledges the diminution that action has undergone at the hands of political economy by isolating political action from its own practical ends, thereby reducing it to a brand of performance, if a dignified one. It is no accident, therefore, that Arendt carefully guards the political sphere from the encroachment of the socioeconomic, or that Schmitt defines the transcendence of the decision in part against the bad immanence of the capitalist economy. Kojève's inflationary notions of the act entail a more complex but not unrelated response to capitalism and particularly the consumerist utopia ushered in by the end of history.

I believe that Beckett's *Endgame* can be understood as a deflationary response to the inflation of the act exhibited by certain strains of modern philosophy and political theory. The inflationary thinker to whom Beckett responds, however, is not one of those discussed hitherto but rather Georges Bataille. Like Arendt and Schmitt, Bataille advances an exalted, sovereign concept of action, but unlike them he does not guard this concept from the encroachment of the economic. Instead he expands the field of the economic so as to include extravagantly aneconomic acts of destructive expenditure. Moreover, while economic consumption in particular is action's antithesis in Arendt and the others, Bataille remakes consumption itself into a sovereign gesture.

Like Kojève, and as the result of a Hegelian influence they shared, Bataille is concerned with master and slave. For Bataille, however, enslavement results not from some primordial battle to the death but from the global system of means and ends that defines the utilitarian worldview. Insofar as something is useful, or has use-value, it is not an end in itself but is always subordinated to some other end. "The paradox of my attitude requires that I show the absurdity of a system in which each thing *serves*, in which nothing is *sovereign*."[21] Any means-end activity, such as work or even action, suffers from this inherent subjugation.

Sovereign existence thus requires a complete break with the logic of the useful. "Life *beyond utility* is the domain of sovereignty."[22] For Bataille, sovereignty can consist only of acts of *dépense* or destructive expenditure—the wasting of resources without regard to profit, prestige, useful effects, or even available reserves. Indeed, the more senseless, profligate, and indifferent to means that the act of expenditure is, the more sovereignty it confers. Sovereignty is defined in part by the sheer *scale* of the consumption or expenditure of wealth, which aligns it with the inflationary modes of thought already discussed.

The defining aspects of *dépense*—its magnitude and pointlessness—are supremely embodied for Bataille in the sun, which prodigiously consumes its fuel, endlessly spending and exhausting itself to no purpose. The heat and light produced thereby are not merely a template for human acts of expenditure but also a means, since it is the overwhelming, excessive abundance of solar energy that impels life, including human life, to discharge that excess as waste. As a result of the sun's constant radiance, "on the surface of the globe, for *living matter in general*, energy is always in excess."[23] For Bataille, then, *dépense* is not merely rendered possible but positively mandated by a cosmic excess of energy that demands discharge, either in useful or useless forms.

In the self-depleting, potentially catastrophic squandering of resources that is *dépense*, it is not difficult to catch a glimpse of the old Hegelian master and his reckless hazarding of life forces, although in this case expenditure bespeaks a continuity with Nature rather than a definitive break from it. "Being at the summit, [man's] sovereignty in the living world . . . destines him, in a privileged way, to that glorious operation, to useless consumption."[24] "Luxury, mourning, war, cults, the construction of sumptuary monuments, games, spectacles, arts, perverse sexual activities (i.e., deflected from genital finality)—all these represent activities which, at least in primitive circumstances, have no end beyond themselves."[25]

All of the passages quoted above are taken from works published prior to Beckett's composition of *Endgame*. They were therefore at least theoretically available to him, although every passage but the last is taken from *The Accursed Share*, which was largely ignored upon publication in 1949 and thus unlikely to have attracted Beckett's attention.[26] Yet Beckett certainly knew of Bataille, who wrote an early, important review of *Molloy* of which the author approved. Moreover, a 1951 notebook entry shows that Beckett read a preface to Sade's *Justine* written by Bataille.[27] While that preface by no means lays out the whole of Bataille's thinking during this period, it does touch on some central themes: pleasure as destruction, sovereignty as negation of utility, the drive to consume and waste resources, the sun as sovereign emblem, and so forth. If this were the only piece by Bataille that Beckett ever read (and this is doubtful), it would at least have the virtue of demonstrating Sade's permeating influence. Bataille's understanding of nature as a source of profligate, destructive energies obviously derives largely from such Sadean sources as Pope Pius VI's discourse on nature in *Juliette*.[28] Beckett's interest in, and admiration for, Sade's work was sufficient that he carefully considered (though ultimately rejected) an offer to do an English translation of *Les 120 jours de Sodome*, and he likewise read seminal critical studies of Sade by Blanchot, Klossowski, and others.[29] It likewise seems not unreasonable to assume that Beckett's enthusiasm for Sade would have prompted further reading in Bataille. While Bataille certainly revised crucial aspects of Sade's thinking, both can be found to have left important traces in *Endgame*.

As we have seen, Beckett's engagement with Kojève was largely antagonistic, even mocking at times. And yet for all that, the Kojèvian paradigm achieves a considerable reach within *Waiting for Godot*. Areas of possible agreement or intellectual sympathy between Beckett and Bataille likewise are not hard to find. Both are drawn to what Bataille calls the heterogeneous—that which is expelled and converted to waste by the dominant system of thought. To say this is not to claim that Beckett wrote a play in sympathy with Bataille's views, however. Indeed, *Endgame*'s stance toward Bataille is largely antithetical, and yet it would be truer to say that the play situates itself not so much against as *after* Bataille. *Endgame* excludes the possibility of tragic, sovereign *dépense* because it represents a world in which *dépense* has already definitively occurred. What remains are merely the crumbs (or, more precisely, the grains) of its aftermath. Let's begin with the setting. Two readings of Hamm and Clov's enclosure are standard: that it is a bomb shelter in which they have managed to survive a nuclear war, and that it is a Noah's ark in which they have survived a second Flood.[30] Beckett, of course, leaves his locales elusively over- and underdetermined at once, so that a given interpretive option can never install itself as definitive. What interests me is that both above-mentioned possibilities depict world annihilation as acts of expenditure. A hydrogen bomb simply *is* a miniature sun that consumes its fuel, and with it the surrounding world, in an instant. More broadly, war is for Bataille a prime means of *dépense*, here brought to fruition in a war conducted with terrestrial suns.

Now a careful student of Bataille will object here that nuclear war constitutes a "bad" form of *dépense*. Modern warfare no longer obeys the ancient drive for pure expenditure but is conducted for strategic, utilitarian ends. Indeed, toward the end of *The Accursed Share*, volume 1, Bataille endorses the (as he sees it) sovereign generosity of the Marshall Plan as a way of expending the excesses of capitalist production in a peaceful manner that avoids the threat of modern warfare.[31] Moreover, the sun's heat and light constitute a paradigm for sovereign expenditure because they offer an unconscious *gift*, fomenting life even as they impart a dangerous excess of vital energies, while nuclear war simply annihilates in the name of a more traditional form of political domination.[32] All that being said, a malign, sterile form of expenditure is expenditure nonetheless. Beckett's interest is in a form of cosmic burn-off that ends rather than fosters life.

The myth of Noah's ark depicts a divine rather than human act of expenditure as God destroys his own creation and thereby asserts his sovereignty over it. In Beckett's version, the Flood has been careful (or so Hamm hopes) to prevent the survival of paired males and females, thus forestalling repopulation of the earth. Atomic war or divine Flood—in either case the result is a planet stripped bare, virtually divested of both life and sustenance and thereby lacking as well the means for further acts of *dépense*.[33] The game that has ended, or is ending, in *Endgame* is in part the game of sovereignty. Even the sun, that Bataillian paradigm and source of expenditure, seems to have disappeared, replaced by a uniform gray light. Devoid of excess, the world of the play operates instead at that minimum limit that is perhaps Beckett's most recognizable modality.

And yet even here, *Endgame* distinguishes itself from the usual scenario. As often in Beckett, supplies are running low. In the course of the play it is announced that there are "no more" bicycle wheels, pap, nature, speech, sugarplums, tide, navigators, rugs, painkiller, and coffins. The situation seems to be reminiscent of that in *Waiting for Godot*, in which there are only carrots and turnips to eat until there are no more carrots. Yet as we have seen, Vladimir's pocket also embodies that miraculous restocking that in Beckett usually allows things to go on indefinitely. Clov's pantry is *Endgame*'s counterpart to Vladimir's pocket. Only in this case there is no miraculous restocking, and things do slowly run out, with tragic consequences. Nell dies in the course of the play—whether from old age or starvation remains unclear. And when Clov finally prepares to depart and Hamm covers himself with his bloody handkerchief, there is every reason to think he does so for the last time, as no one and nothing will remain to sustain him if Clov does in fact walk out the door (on which more later). Then, in addition to being a bomb shelter and Noah's ark, the enclosure of *Endgame* will also become an Antigone's cave, its last inhabitant condemned to a few final, starving days of life. Whether death is more tragic than the indefinite perpetuation of the minimal state depicted in Beckett's other works is debatable. But the prospect of dying does point to something distinct about this play, which departs from Beckett's more usual, asymptotic approach to mortality. And the sealing off of a system that for once does not admit of magical replenishment allows Beckett to explore the economics of the minimum with unusual stringency.

Another way of putting this is to say that *Endgame* is run by its background. In addition to the bunker in which the action occurs there is a second space, Clov's kitchen, which is never shown but which silently modulates everything that happens onstage. While we never see the kitchen and its pantry, they are never far from Hamm's and Clov's minds: the physical existence of both characters depends on them, and for Clov, they are a site of domestic labor. The dramatized space divides into a visible zone of action (the bunker) and an invisible zone of material production/consumption/storage. One result of this situation is that every object onstage is converted into a *resource*—it is grasped quantitatively, and thus economically, in relation to the diminishing reserves of the bunker or of the world at large. A bicycle wheel is never just a bicycle wheel, because there is always one fewer of everything until there is one last and then, inevitably, "no more." Every object is assimilated into a sequence of diminishing disbursements and understood as part of that sequence. When an object is used, referred to, or called for, the immediate if sometimes merely implied question is: are there more in the kitchen? The ongoing contest for mastery between Hamm and Clov is thus also a contest between their respective rooms. Which calls the shots: the bunker as space of (reduced) action or the pantry as the space of (reduced) sustenance?

What is "the action" of the play, anyway? Like *Godot*, *Endgame* doesn't offer anything like a unified Aristotelian *mythos* or plot. It is rather an extended but desultory sparring match between Hamm and Clov, master and servant. Beckett claimed that he began the play with actors Roger Blin and Jean Martin, who had played Pozzo and Lucky in *Waiting for Godot*, in mind for the parts of Hamm and Clov.[34] At the same time, he told Jean Martin that "you must realize that Hamm and Clov are Didi and Gogo at a later date, at the end of their lives."[35] Both of these seemingly contradictory statements are at least partly true. Hamm is at once an older Vladimir and an older Pozzo, the latter now not merely blind but paraplegic as well. But by fusing the two pairs into one, Beckett muddles the master-slave relation of Pozzo and Lucky with the essentially egalitarian, if sometime contentious, friendship of Didi and Gogo, and the result is an uncertain and shifting battle for sovereignty between his two main characters. On the one hand, Hamm and Clov never voice the tones of genuine affection, even love, that we sometimes hear between Vladimir and Estragon. If there ever were such warm feelings, they (like pap and sugar plums) have run out. On the other hand, nothing so obvious as a rope binds Clov to Hamm. Clov is not Hamm's slave but his servant, and a vague mixture of dwindling loyalty, professional duty, deadening habit, and the uncertain possibilities for survival outdoors keep him under Hamm's ill-tempered reign. In the end, Clov himself does not know exactly *why* he stays.

The battle for sovereignty between master and servant is diminished in accordance with their circumstances. Hamm issues peevish, often superfluous orders, and Clov either grumblingly carries them out, bitterly rejoices in some impediment to his doing so, or engages in vicious counterblows. But what kinds of lordship are even available? How can a Bataillian brand of sovereignty possibly assert itself when each antagonist is crushingly dependent on the other and thus unable to assert a convincing mastery, in addition to being deprived of means for substantial acts of *dépense*? It is as if Beckett set out to illustrate a Bataillian premise under the worst possible conditions—conditions that frustrate and indeed invert its most fundamental principles.

Those conditions are illustrated vividly in one of Clov's opening statements: "Grain upon grain, one by one, and one day, suddenly, there's a heap, a little heap, the impossible heap" (8). Clov does not specify what is being

added up day by day: perhaps the days themselves, or the minor indignities he undergoes in each of them. But although he says these words while
Hamm still (seemingly) sleeps under his sheet, Hamm picks up the same figure later in the play: "Moment upon moment, pattering down, like the millet grains of . . . [*he hesitates*] . . . that old Greek, and all life long you wait for
that to mount up to a life" (78). Both Hamm and Clov invoke the paradox
of the grains posed by Eubulides of Miletus, a contemporary of Aristotle.
As the paradox is usually stated in its positive or additive version: "Which
grain by being added makes the heap?" At what limit do individual grains
add up to the entity known as the heap or pile? I will turn to the significance of this version shortly, but first I should note that it was equally well
known in a negative or subtractive form: Which grain by being removed
unmakes the heap? *Endgame* clearly invokes both versions, pairing processes of slow addition with those of slow subtraction, in which pap, sugarplums, and biscuits are used up one by one. The most obvious counterparts
to the "negative" millet grains in this respect are the painkiller pills, raising
the counterparadox: which pill, by being taken, leaves you no longer with
a bottle of pills? And even that point is passed, when Hamm finds himself
having taken, without knowing it, the very last pill. Clov's announcement of
this fact is designed to have the maximum sadistic effect:

HAMM: Is it not time for my pain-killer?
CLOV: Yes.
HAMM: Ah! At last! Give it to me! Quick!
CLOV: There's no more pain-killer. (79–80)

This is the closest Clov comes to a genuinely sovereign, Sadean moment in
the play—excepting, perhaps, his intended departure at the end. And yet it
is achieved, not through the squandering of an excess but rather through
the slow leaking away of a pitiable remnant. Indeed, Clov has done nothing
other than administer the pills on schedule, as required of him in his role
as servant. In a sense, his repeated line, "Something is taking its course," indicates the impersonal nature of this process of slow exhaustion, the third-
person formulation suggesting that no one can really own it as an action.
The best Clov can do is extract a frisson of suffering by manipulating the
timing of a final announcement. But the sovereignty this yields is minor and
transient.

While Clov is the play's most ingenious would-be practitioner of
Bataillian sovereignty, Hamm is its official exponent. As he declares not
long before the painkiller episode: "Then let it end! . . . With a bang . . . Of

Darkness!" (86). Hamm doesn't so much imagine as hopelessly attempt to will a Bataillian conclusion—the explosive expenditure of everything. But he knows that the bang has already occurred—there is no fuel for another. And he knows that his attempts to emulate an old-style heroism are therefore belated as well: "Can there be misery—[*he yawns*] loftier than mine? No doubt. Formerly. But now?" (9). Hamm's yawn belies his stated aspiration to loftiness—something literally as well as figuratively unavailable in the bunker, whose only height is defined by Clov's ladder.

The tragedy of Beckett's *Endgame* is therefore the loss of tragedy itself—that is, the wearing down of those heights from which catastrophic expenditure can occur. Aristotelian *megethos* or loftiness as well as Bataillian sovereignty or *dépense* simply cannot find room within the lower limits where the play situates itself. When reduced to dividing a single biscuit, as Nagg is at one point, the sacrifice involved in giving three-quarters to Nell is touching but not sublime. In a world counted grain by grain, losses of tragic stature cannot occur. And action is therefore recalled from the inflationary heights on which it is placed by some modern political thinkers. This deadening limit is not something that Beckett simply imposes on us as spectators, however, but a condition under which he himself labors as playwright. Beckett can no more dispense with tragic tradition in one grand gesture than Hamm can bring about the explosive end he so desperately desires. Tragedy dies grain by grain. Or perhaps pill by pill.

The paradox of the grain in its subtractive version thus informs *Endgame* at many levels. Yet oddly, given the fact that the negative version feels more Beckettian, the paradox is never enunciated in this form. Hamm and Clov instead give voice to the positive or additive version, the logic of which is no less determinative for the play, if somewhat less obvious in its workings. In the additive version, the impossible heap undergoes a phase change—a threshold at which the increase of one more grain causes a new (agglomerative) grouping to form. The grains are now part of a covering entity—the heap. But the existence of a heap is at best quasi-objective: more a judgment call than a definitive threshold, though the judgment requires some basis in fact. And since it is impossible to say which infinitesimal addition causes the sum to cross the threshold, the heap never begins—it is "impossible." Or rather, the heap can be there already but it cannot form grain by grain.

The additive version of the paradox represents the play itself as "heap," a collection of discursive and theatrical bits that never achieve (or try to achieve) organic form. But at the same time, it also offers a new paradigm for dramatic action—one in which the act as event is precipitated out of infinitesimal microevents. Really, there is only one "act" deserving of the name in the whole play—Clov's apparent decision to leave Hamm and the shared bunker. But what prompts this decision? How many incremental repetitions of the same irritating day trigger the actual departure? What is the difference between (say) the 9,024th performance and the 9,023rd that the decision should occur just then?[36] Clov's act does not require deliberation in the classical Aristotelian sense, but merely registers the fact that a "heap" of misery has already somehow formed out of the grains of individual indignities. The act, like the heap on which it is modeled, is therefore impossible.

The status of Clov's act, moreover, remains irreducibly ambiguous. The play ends with Clov still standing onstage. And yet his final entrance *"dressed for the road. Panama hat, tweed coat, raincoat over his arm, umbrella, bag"* (90) surely cannot be a pantomime for Hamm's benefit, since Hamm is blind and cannot register these facts. I take the ending of the play to depict Clov as extracting a last moment of enjoyment from the spectacle of Hamm's solitude before exiting, though I cannot rule out the possibility of a final hesitation. In any case, Beckett conceives of action not as the decision of a deliberative, rational, volitional subject but as a heap that results from the pure accumulation of impersonal microprocesses ("Something is taking its course"). It is in this sense that, despite obvious differences, *Endgame* looks dimly forward to such later experiments as *Quad*, where characters are essentially moving particles, and questions of motive or meaning do not really arise. And it is worth noting (though here I will readily accept that the matter is far from Beckett's concerns or intentions), that political economy produces a similar theoretical landscape insofar as its focus is on the nation or population rather than the individual, and insofar as it concerns itself with acts of production that matter only in their accumulated sum. Political economy dethroned action not only by elevating production in its stead as prime source of human happiness (or, conversely, misery), but also by shifting attention to the population as mass entity, which retroactively converted the individual into a microcomponent of negligible import.[37]

Population, by the way, is of no small concern in *Endgame*, since the threat of reproduction, and hence of everything's starting up again, haunts Hamm throughout. The stray flea or rat must be killed immediately, lest copulation thrive. This is in part because he wants a definitive ending for the world as well as for himself, and in part, one suspects, because his carefully nurtured singularity would disappear, or at least show to less good effect, in a world crammed with others—that is to say, if he were to become once more part of a "population." Sexual reproduction is a chain reaction no less deadly to Hamm than the atomic one is to other mortals. The only thing worse than addition is multiplication. Let us recall the passage in *Godot*:

VLADIMIR: We have kept out appointment and that's an end to that. We are not saints, but we have kept our appointment. How many people can boast as much?
ESTRAGON: Billions. (70)

For Hamm, the nightmare of nuclear holocaust is balanced by the nightmare of no nuclear holocaust. The deaths of billions is in some sense no more horrifying than the existence of billions. In the former case, nothing would happen because there would be no one to make it happen. In the latter, nothing that happens would matter because it would be lost in the meaningless turmoil of innumerable actions.

If there is one thing that Beckett takes more seriously than perhaps any other modern playwright, it is the Aristotelian unities—along with the pseudo-Aristotelian unity of character. From the five (or is it six?) characters in *Waiting for Godot*, he whittles his way down to four in *Endgame*, two in *Happy Days*, and then as often as not one in *Krapp's Last Tape* and any number of later works. The Beckettian scenario demands intimacy and concentration. Yet it is threatened by the logics of addition and subtraction. How many grains can one subtract and still have a heap? This pertains not only to numbers of characters but also to the multiple attributes that constitute dramatic character, which are progressively stripped away in the search for a limit. But if Beckett is haunted by and drawn to the final term of zero, he is affected in the same way by the specter of multiplication, which is no less fatal for theater as he conceives it. The terrifying counterpart to the empty pantry is Joyce's "Here Comes Everybody." Both are modern dilemmas, and both are articulated in classical form by political economy: the Malthusian nightmare of final resource depletion and the Smithian dream of the quietly productive, burgeoning population.

If the act cannot be saved through being inflated, and Beckett surely suggests that it cannot, the alternative is to labor at the lower limit. We must learn to add and subtract simultaneously, to heap and unheap grains one by one.[38] I do not wish to suggest, however, that Beckett's deflation of the act is an attempt to restore a politically or ethically reasonable concept of action in the face of a hypertrophied, Bataillian one. There is nothing "therapeutic" about Beckett's aims—no wish that inflationary conceptions can be cathartically purged, resulting in a healthy mean. One does not "learn how to act" from Beckett. What distinguishes him from figures such as Bataille, Arendt, and Schmitt is his clear-sighted recognition that the crisis of action is strictly speaking *insoluble*. What Beckett stages is the impasse. Yet this does not mean that action cannot occur. It simply means that when it does occur, it does so in the absence of conditions of possibility. That the heap is "impossible" does not mean that there are no heaps. It just means that such heaps as there are exist despite the fact that you cannot make one. "I can't go on, I'll go on." Think of how saccharine this famous line from *The Unnameable* would become if there were a "yet" or "nevertheless" (even implied) between the phrases. "I'll go on" does not contradict "I can't go on." It forgets it, which is not the same as negating it. "I can't go on, yet I'll go on" would be pseudo-heroic, the kind of line Hamm might utter in one of his more self-pitying moments. The comma splice instead establishes an impassable limit to which the "I'll go on" has no logical relation.[39] Beckettian action is therefore an effect without a cause, indeed an effect in violation of (or better, indifferent to) cause. The Beckettian impasse is not merely that actions cannot occur but that they cannot occur and still sometimes, miraculously, do.

All of which is not to say that action in *Endgame* is devoid of political meaning. The master-slave relation that for Kojève constitutes history is finally resolved, though under terms that Kojève could never have imagined. Even more pointed, perhaps, is the rejection of Bataille's vision of revolutionary violence. Bataille foresees "the revolutionary destruction of the [ruling] classes . . . through a bloody and in no way limited social expenditure" and calls for "the *great night* when their beautiful phrases will be drowned out by death screams in riots."[40] While revolutionary violence is for Marx a necessary means of overthrowing an oppressive system, for Bataille it is an end in itself, an orgiastic act of *dépense* in which the bourgeoisie drowns in buckets of its own blood. In *Endgame*, the only blood is that which seeps slowly from Hamm's nose onto his handkerchief. Tensions between master and slave are resolved not by tragic violence but by Clov's putting on his hat and coat and (almost) walking out the door. His only "act" is to absent himself, to leave the stage and recede once again into the background of drama. From a theatrical perspective, this action is as close to nonaction as one can get. And yet it has a quiet, devastating dignity to which Hamm has no response. Left alone, his face covered with his "old stancher," Hamm is abandoned to that silence in which he can perhaps hear the last millet grains pattering down, one by one.

After Beckett

The story I have told is as follows: action emerges, miraculously, from an ongoing matrix of production. Over time, but particularly with the rise of modern commercial society, production begins to eclipse action's claims to be the principal source of human happiness. Political economy is the moment when this process begins to become conscious of itself—indeed, begins consciously to accelerate. Political economy devalues action, but this process is not uncontested. Compensatory overvaluations of action follow. Tragedy registers this ongoing struggle and also becomes a privileged repository of the hopes invested in action. I have followed this story in selected episodes from Aeschylus through Beckett. This takes us to the middle of the twentieth century but hardly to the present day. To conclude, then, I shall look briefly at some developments from the last half century.

In his book *Grammar of the Multitude*, the Italian philosopher Paolo Virno points to the rise of post-Fordist production as marking an epochal shift in the historical relations between *praxis* and *poiesis*. Whereas capitalist labor through the period of Fordist production had become progressively de-skilled and therefore a predominantly physiological process, so-called post-Fordist production requires workers to participate in decision making, distribution of tasks, and innovation. Its products themselves are often immaterial and composed of information. As a result, "it is the whole person who is subdued, the person's basic communicative and cognitive habits."[1] Capital subsumes intellect as well as body, in a process comparable to the subsumption of affective labor that other theorists have explored in relation to the service economy, often with a specific focus on female workers.[2] In a sense, Fordist labor strikes a Cartesian bargain with the worker: capital has the right to the body or *res extensa* but not the *res cogitans*. Post-Fordist labor, by contrast, is Faustian: it takes the body too but is primarily interested in the soul.

Under post-Fordist production, claims Virno, "the [Aristotelian] boundaries between pure intellectual activity, political action, and labor have dissolved" (50). Like Hannah Arendt, Virno is concerned with a collapse of formerly separate spheres, although "I maintain that things have gone in the opposite direction from what Hannah Arendt seems to believe; it is not that politics has conformed to labor; it is rather that labor has acquired the traditional features of political action[:] . . . the relationship with the presence of others, the beginning of new processes, and the constitutive familiarity with contingency, the unforeseen, and the possible" (51). These "political" elements mean that labor becomes something closer to a performance than to making in the traditional sense. "*Productive* labor, in its totality, appropriates the special characteristics of the performing artist" (54), thus overturning the traditional division, which we have seen operating from the early modern period through Adam Smith, that grouped performers among unproductive laborers. To some degree, all production becomes cultural production, and Virno singles out the culture industry as an anticipatory paradigm for post-Fordist production in general (56–59). Indeed, Virno goes so far as to describe the workplace as a "stage" (59) for "virtuosic labor" (54), thereby applying to production the metaphor of theater, traditionally used to describe the political sphere.

Subsuming elements of political action does not, however, necessarily lead to a politicizing of the workplace in any meaningful sense. Virno does not seem to regard the presence of these elements as potentially destabilizing or as facilitating the political organization of workers. Indeed, the only forms of resistance fomented by this new situation, in Virno's view, are disobedience and "exit"—the latter a withdrawal of these capacities from the workplace, a way of defecting rather than fighting. This rather brief and disappointing menu of options for the post-Fordist "multitude" suggests that the subsumption of doing by making amounts to something close to definitive: a final reabsorption of the act by the productive matrix from which it originally arose, thereby bringing our narrative to a melancholic end.

Subjectively, the post-Fordist regime is less alienating than the Fordist one it replaces, allowing the worker to feel like a collaborator whose expertise and insight are valued. At the same time, these qualities serve to enrich capital alone, and the worker's "input" is never allowed to question either the private ownership of capital or the managerial structure that supports it. The post-Fordist enterprise provides forms of satisfaction unavailable to its predecessor, and may even point in a utopian direction while subsuming the worker to an unprecedented degree.

The use of theatrical language in Virno and others inevitably raises the question: if the post-Fordist workplace is a kind of theater, is contemporary theater post-Fordist? This question has absorbed critics of postdramatic theater in particular. On the one hand, postdramatic theater rejects the "incipient Taylorism" that Nicholas Ridout detects in the director-dominated productions of the late nineteenth and early twentieth centuries.[3] And along with the tyranny of the director, the tyranny of the dramatic text often goes out the window, replaced with a more collaborative organization of the postdramatic performance. As Elinor Fuchs observed, "Never before, also, had the dramatic text been looked upon as the enemy, rather than the vehicle, of theatrical presence. Inspired by Artaud's rejection of the 'masterpiece' and by Grotowski's training, many theaters came to regard the author's script as an element of political oppression in the theatrical process, demanding submission to external authority."[4] This development bespeaks a wider politicization of the internal structures of the theater company, something proscribed to the post-Fordist enterprise in the corporate world. Some postdramatic theater companies were more democratic in their financial and legal organization, which encouraged a more thoroughgoing politicization of the enterprise. At the same time, participants were aware that their expressive and intellectual powers were being commodified, and that they were engaging in forms of affective labor comparable in some respects to those of the service industries.

Critical approaches to postdramatic performance have likewise been divided. In his book *Passionate Amateurs: Theatre, Communism, and Love*, Nicholas Ridout emphasizes the "communist potential" of the theatrical amateur who "acts out of love": "The passionate amateurs of this book's title are those who attempt, 'in this sphere' of capitalism, to realize something that looks and feels like the true realm of freedom—not the 'free time' of capitalist leisure—but knowing, very often, that in that attempt, they risk subsuming their labors of love entirely to the demands of the sphere of necessity in which they must make their living."[5] Conversely, in *Murmuring of the Artistic Multitude: Global Art, Memory, and Subsumption*, Pascal Gielen does not content himself with emphasizing the subordination of art to global capital in an age of post-Fordism. He insists that the art world provided a "laboratory" in which the strategies and techniques of post-Fordism were worked out prior to being transferred to the corporate sphere.[6] Both books, it could be argued, seize on real aspects and potentials of the post-Fordist era but come to different conclusions. Meanwhile, postdramatic theater itself is aware of its status as a form of post-Fordist labor and not infrequently makes this a topic of its performances.[7] If it cannot transcend its post-Fordist condition, postdramatic theater at least attempts to render it critically self-aware.

Although both postdramatic theater and post-Fordism lie beyond the purview of this book, they exert pressure on some of the central categories and concepts I have been employing throughout. Adam Smith's distinction between productive and unproductive labor placed actors on the side of the unproductive—those whose efforts disappear in the moment of their exertion instead of imprinting themselves in enduring (and accumulatable) form in material commodities. But the prominence of "immaterial labor" in the post-Fordist era throws this distinction into disarray. With the rise of the service economy, the actor is now in some sense the paradigm for productive labor, which has jettisoned the imperative to endure. Within postdramatic theater itself, the dethronement of the dramatic text or "work" has far-reaching consequences. The actor, who no longer imitates the actions of a fictional persona, morphs into the performer, whose actions occupy the here-and-now of performance.[8] Action is no longer mediated by fiction but appears in immediate form. Likewise, "the fundamental *shift from work to event* was momentous for theater aesthetics."[9] Instead of presenting the dramatic "work," postdramatic theater stages the event, with its higher potential for contingency and the unexpected. Another way to put this is to say that the status of "the work" is no longer monopolized by the figure of the playwright but is distributed more widely in the company. Of course, the playwright's work was never the only kind in play. Actors, stagehands, set designers, and others contribute to the work of theater in every age. But those other kinds of labor are ephemeral—tied to the temporality of performance, while the dramatic work is that which *lasts*—or at least that which *may* last—and can thus be reperformed indefinitely.[10] The privileging of the playwright's labor thus reflects a metaphysics very much at work in classical political economy but largely outdated in the post-Fordist era. Along with the rest of Aristotelian dramaturgy, the delicate relation between *poiesis* and *praxis* comes under strain in postdramatic theater, if it does not threaten to collapse entirely. Perhaps this is theater's counterpart to the collapse of distinctions between production and the political in the post-Fordist workplace as described by Virno and others.

Despite its fascination with electronic media and mediation, postdramatic theater is a more immediate form than dramatic theater, which always relies on the separation provided by mimesis. Separation is likewise central to Hannah Arendt's conception of the act. Since Arendt is a crucial figure for Virno, we cannot fully grasp the significance of the collapse of separation in the latter unless we appreciate its role in the former—a role that is foundational to politics and to tragedy. Arendt's figure of the table as that which at once relates and separates describes a situation in which a public is brought together by some shared concern and yet maintained in their plurality and thus prevented from collapsing into a One. Only this separation provides a suitable stage for the political act. Unsurprisingly, then, the actual stage likewise depends on separations of various kinds. The Theater of Athens not only enjoyed its own space, apart from both agora and assembly, but also took place during a festival time set off from the secular calendar—a practice continuing into both Roman and medieval theater. Greek theater likewise divided the playing area into *orchestra* and *skene*, and kept both separate from the *theatron* or viewing area, just as medieval theater divided the staging area (under very different principles) into *locus* and *platea*.[11] These forms of physical and temporal separation, moreover, were accompanied by representational and cultural ones of various kinds, all converging to maintain a space apart in which the act could occur. Comedy invites degrees of adjacency and intimacy that put theatrical separation under pressure without quite collapsing it, but tragedy is the form that maximizes distances, and thereby sustains a space for the act.

It is probably not coincidental, then, that Greek tragedy often portrays crises of separation—and none more clearly than Sophocles's *Oedipus the King*. Oedipus, the supposedly foreign hero who saves Thebes by solving the Sphinx's riddle and providing Jocasta with an exogamous spouse, turns out to be Jocasta's own child, and thus the bearer of a forbidden closeness. In truth, the theme of incest simply raises to a higher power the problem of the aristocratic family as such, the clannishness of which interferes with the separation necessary for citizenship—which is why Cleisthenes's great act of dividing family members among unrelated "tribes" was a crucial founding moment for Athenian democracy. Thebes responds to incestuous closeness by expelling Oedipus, thus attempting to establish a definitive separation, but the curse returns via his children, who continue to plague the city. There appears to be no way out of this perpetual crisis of separation—except that it occurs in Thebes, Greek tragedy's disastrous antitype to Athens. Athenian playgoers could therefore view the implosion of Thebes at a secure distance. *Oedipus at Colonus* even celebrates Athens' ability to assimilate the figure of Oedipus safely, through various forms of internal distancing that Thebes cannot manage.

Tragedy explores crises of separation because separation, by its very nature, cannot be completely secure. It involves opposing forces held in balance, and it can therefore collapse and then provoke violent expulsion as a countermeasure. (The Athenian habit of exiling unmanageable or dangerously powerful citizens to protect the coherence of the *polis* is worth considering here.) Arendt herself engages in compensatory theoretical forms of expulsion when she feels the separation of political and economic spheres to be collapsing, a problem initiated by the rise of commercial society.[12] Virno's vision of post-Fordist culture would be the final term of this collapse, a definitive absorption of action's space by production, leaving only exit (but to where, exactly?) as a last resort.

And what of dramatic theater in these circumstances? Postdramatic theater is quite at home in the immediate. But drama is not. What future can there be for drama in an age when the forms of separation that clear its space give way? How can *dramatic* tragedy persist under circumstances that seem inhospitable to it? Despite insisting that postdramatic theater never leaves drama behind but is in a perpetual state of emergence from it, Lehman has a habit of declaring significant aspects of dramatic theater "obsolete." In a way, Beckett can be taken as a transitional figure here, since postdramatic elements occupy the space of drama even in his earlier works for the stage, and become more prominent as his career unfolds. After Beckett, the most significant forms of dramatic theater are not left untouched by the postdramatic. A new, hybrid form of tragic drama/postdrama emerges that is just as critically aware of its social and political status as purely postdramatic theater. My test case here is Sarah Kane's *Blasted* (1995), a play that is self-consciously post-Beckettian and, I would argue, self-consciously post-Fordist as well. I should recognize, before proceeding, that the choice of Kane's play to represent dramatic theater "after Beckett" may strike readers as arbitrary—as would the choice of any one play or playwright. My focus on Kane is meant not to assign aesthetic preeminence or centrality to *Blasted* but rather to recognize the fact that it reflects with unusual clarity and directness some of the themes I am pursuing. I do think, however, that *Blasted* is an interesting and significant play in its own right.

I

Blasted takes place in a nondescript Leeds hotel room, where Ian, a hard-drinking, hard-bitten forty-five-year-old journalist (and *soi-disant* undercover government agent) dying of lung disease meets up with Cate, a twenty-one-year-old former lover afflicted with a stutter and seizures when under stress. The first scene finds the racist, condescending Ian trying to re-ignite a sexual relationship with Cate, who no longer loves him and agrees to see him only out of kindness and concern. His advances rebuffed, Ian rapes Cate in the interval between the first and second scenes. In scene 2, Cate gets revenge of sorts by destroying Ian's leather jacket and later bit-ing his penis savagely during fellatio. She exits into the en suite bathroom, and a series of knocks on the hotel room's door announces the arrival of a soldier participating in an unexplained war that has somehow engulfed Leeds. The soldier disarms Ian and takes control of the hotel room, piss-ing on the bed to signal his dominance. At the end of the scene a mortar shell blasts a hole in the wall of the hotel room. In scene 3, the soldier has been knocked unconscious by the mortar blast, but he quickly recovers and regains control of the situation. He ridicules Ian's pretensions to mascu-line violence, then rapes Ian, shoves a pistol up his anus, and sucks out his eyes and consumes them, in a conscious reenactment of the rape and murder of the soldier's girlfriend Col by other soldiers. In scene 4 the sol-dier has committed suicide with Ian's pistol. Cate returns to the hotel room carrying a baby that someone has given her to care for. The blind Ian begs Cate to give him his gun so that he can commit suicide, but Cate empties it of bullets before handing it over. The baby dies of starvation. In scene 5, Cate buries the baby in a hole in the hotel room floor, then leaves. Time passes, and Ian is shown in brief tableaux masturbating, strangling him-self, shitting, laughing, having a nightmare, crying bloody tears, and lying weak with hunger. He finally digs up the baby, eats it, then crawls into the hole the baby was buried in and dies "with relief" (60).[13] Cate returns to the room with food she has procured by selling her body to soldiers, and offers some to the dead but still somehow conscious Ian, who thanks her. The play ends with rain dripping from the ceiling onto Ian's head, which is the only part of him protruding from the hole in the floor.

Blasted was largely dismissed by theater critics as obscene, pathological, and theatrically inept upon its London premiere in December 1995.[14] The play's abrupt and unexplained switch from relatively realistic modes of rep-resentation to more fragmented and symbolic ones—in part, from dramatic to postdramatic modes—drew as much scorn as its sensational depictions of offensive acts. A 2001 revival following Sarah Kane's suicide in 1999 elic-ited more balanced responses, as critics absorbed the play's fierce moral and political vision as well as its literary indebtedness to Beckett and other canonical authors. Kane herself had in the meantime come to be regarded as a leading figure in a movement of young British playwrights dubbed variously "the New Brutalism" and "In-Yer-Face Theater."[15] Academic critics subsequently did a better job than journalists of grasping the complexities and nuance that were sometimes overshadowed by the play's abrasive surface.[16]

Here I want to treat Kane's play as a response to the collapse of social spaces deplored by Virno. The action of *Blasted* takes place entirely inside a hotel room, described in the stage directions as *"the kind that is so expensive it could be anywhere in the world"* (3). Kane was quite explicit about having observed the Aristotelian unity of space even while violating the others, and yet the play subjects its scene to dislocation of various kinds, beginning with the fact that the style of the hotel room embodies the homogenizing effects of international capital, such that is it at once in Leeds and "anywhere," locally present but globally abstract.[17] The war that eventually erupts was inspired by televised scenes from the Bosnian conflict, and in a draft version of the play the soldier is explicitly Serbian. That is no longer clear in the finished version, but neither is the confident claim on the part of some critics that a civil war has replaced the Bosnian one. The soldier appears at one point to indicate unequivocally that he is not English (41), though he is not otherwise identified and seems to have been cast as English in production. Like the hotel, the conflict is of a kind "that could be anywhere in the world," at once English and Bosnian and generic. The war is preceded by Ian's racist griping about the immigrant staff of the hotel ("Hate this city. Stinks. Wogs and Pakis taking over" [4] and by his calling in a newspaper story about an English tourist murdered while on vacation in 'an isolated New Zealand forest'" [12]). Flows of immigrant labor, capital, and tourism dislocate geographical boundaries in a way that prepares for the violent blasting open of the hotel room's Ibsen-esque integrity.[18] Moreover, Ian's racist resentment at what he perceives as an international invasion of England (despite—or because of—the fact that he himself is Welsh, not English) recalls the ethnic cleansing that marked the Bosnian conflict.

This dialectic of invasion and expulsion afflicts not only geographical but bodily space as well. Cate is distressed when Ian puts his tongue in her mouth during a kiss, and as a vegetarian she is horrified by the smell of the ham sandwiches that Ian orders from room service. (By the end of the play, however, she has no problem eating the sausages she has obtained by selling herself, while Ian has moved on to ingesting human baby.) Both Cate and Ian are raped in the course of the play, and Ian has his eyes sucked out as well. After her rape, Cate violently coughs out a pubic hair stuck in her throat. Likewise, Ian's lung cancer sends him into repeated, violent coughing fits, while Cate's seizures provide a kind of "exit" from violent situations, landing her in an undefined elsewhere from which she just as abruptly returns. Bodily expulsion—of phlegm, urine, feces, sperm, and so on—is the play's countermovement to bodily invasion. It is telling that the hotel room, which clearly echoes the bunker in *Endgame*, has replaced Clov's kitchen with an en suite bathroom.[19] While provision becomes a daunting problem once the war begins, expulsion and elimination are initially the more pressing needs.

At one point, when Cate tries to convince Ian to quit smoking, the following exchange occurs:

CATE: Imagine what your lungs must look like.
IAN: Don't need to imagine. I've seen.
CATE: When?
IAN: Last year. When I came round, surgeon brought in this lump of rotting pork, stank. My lung. (11)

This image of exteriorized interiority (though the lung is also an organ that takes the outside into the inside) condenses the physiological and political pressures under which bodily integrity is placed in the play. Comparing the lung to rotten pork recalls Cate's description of the ham sandwiches ("Dead meat. Blood." [7]), and the "stink" of the diseased lung invokes both the smell that Ian attributes to the "Wogs and Pakis" and the stink he repeatedly tries to shower off from his own body. Uncertainty about his corporeal boundaries causes Ian to confuse personal hygiene and ethnic cleansing.

More broadly, the extracted lung represents the problem of vision in the play: scooped out from the body's interior, it is an unspeakable sight and thus bores its way back inside—but this time inside the psyche rather than the body, thus pointing to another confusion of boundaries that the play provokes. In this case the sensuous immediacy of the lung is enhanced rather than dampened by the fact that, unlike the horrors to come, it is described rather than directly presented. Early reviews suggest that audiences felt assaulted by the play's ongoing pageant of visual and verbal obscenities. Paul Taylor of the *Independent* wrote: "Sitting through *Blasted* is a little like having your face rammed into an overflowing ashtray, just for starters, and then having your whole head held down in a bucket of offal. As a theatrical experience, there is nothing wrong in principle with either of these ordeals. Provided, that is, you can feel something happening in your heart and mind as well as to your nervous system as a result."[20] Taylor's remarks assimilate *Blasted* to its eponymous mortar blast as something that acts directly and traumatically on the nervous system, bypassing mind and heart. If his assessment were correct, this would prove problematic for any aspirations *Blasted* might have as a political play, since it forecloses both the empathy demanded by a naturalist style of drama *and* the critically reflective distance of the Brechtian spectator. Perhaps it is not entirely accidental that Taylor's images of ashtray and bucket of offal evoke Ian's smoking habit and the extracted lung that results. In this view the play itself is like a rotting lung, or fecal matter, the invasive presence of which prompts an expulsive response from the audience: an extreme and vulgarized version of Aristotelian catharsis. Kane herself went further, expressing the view that she would be disappointed if her plays did not cause at least some spectators to leave the theater: "I've seen productions of *Blasted* where there was no reason to walk out because somehow they never connected emotionally, you could completely distance yourself from what was going on."[21] Instead of purging the viewers, her plays wish to purge themselves *of* viewers, to send at least a portion of them fleeing through the exits. The collapse of geographical, bodily, and psychic spaces onstage is complemented by a collapse of the theatrical space itself and the separation required for spectatorship.[22]

None of these attacks on separation correspond precisely to the kind that Virno describes. It is worth noting, though, that the world of employment that *Blasted* projects is a broadly post-Fordist one. The lower-middle-class Cate has applied for a job as personal assistant in an advertising company, a service job that sets her only slightly above the (always unseen) staff of the hotel at which they are staying. (Cate learns the name—Andrew—of one of these hotel employees, much to Ian's disgust, and describes him as "nice" [17], revealing at once her friendly openness and the dexterity with which Andrew performs his affective labor.) But it is Ian whose profession as tabloid journalist places him squarely in the post-Fordist regime that subordinates the intellectual capacities of workers. This would perhaps not matter so much if Ian's profession did not trail him throughout the play. His very first action upon entering the hotel room is to throw a pile of newspapers on the bed, signaling that his work intrudes even on this putatively romantic getaway. (Likewise, Ian carries the pistol that is tool of the trade for his other "job" as secret government agent.) Much later, when Ian defecates in the by then bombed-out hotel room, he wipes himself with those same newspapers.

More to the point, we actually see Ian at work as he dictates a news story over the phone:

IAN: A serial killer slaughtered British tourist Samantha Scrace, S-C-R-A-
C-E, in a sick murder ritual comma, police revealed yesterday point new
par. The bubbly nineteen-year-old from Leeds was among seven victims
buried in identical triangular tombs in an isolated New Zealand forest point new par. Each had been stabbed more than twenty times and
placed face down, comma, hands bound behind their backs point new
par. Caps up ashes at the site showed the maniac had stayed to cook
a meal, caps down point new par. Samantha comma, a beautiful red-
head with dreams of becoming a model comma, was on the trip of a lifetime after finishing her A levels last year point. Samantha's heartbroken
mum said yesterday colon quoting, we pray the police will come up with
something dash, anything comma, soon point still quoting. The sooner
this lunatic is brought to justice the better point end quote new par. The
Foreign Office warned tourists Down Under to take extra care point. A
spokesman said colon quoting, common sense is the best rule point end
quote, copy ends.
   [*He listens. Then he laughs.*]
   Exactly. (12–13)

It is unclear whether this performance is conducted in complete indifference to Cate or in an attempt to impress her. In either case, the story
foreshadows the disturbing violence to come, both to Cate as female victim of Ian and later to Ian himself at the hands of the soldier. Inserting
the typographical codes that will space the story properly on the page reveals the craftsman-like qualities of Ian's work, his ability to filter horrifying content through a purely technical lens. Indeed, it is his professional detachment from the human import of the story—emphasized by his derisive
laughter at the end—that is the most disturbing thing about this episode.
This detachment makes Ian into the counterpart of the story's "maniac"
who can stay and coolly cook up a meal after slaughter. It likewise bespeaks
Ian's alienation from his own intellectual and moral capacities, and thus his
utter (if complicit) subordination to the post-Fordist regime. The spacing
of the story exhibits an ambiguous character. It marks Ian's separation from
the content of his work but, simultaneously, his intellectual subsumption by
the work process. The figure of the hack, who puts his literary talents to use
for trite but remunerative performances, raises the more general dilemma
of the post-Fordist worker to a more cynical and self-conscious level.
   This instance of journalistic *poiesis* is of still greater significance, moreover, because Ian's dictated tabloid story is in some ways a miniaturized
image of the play text. *Blasted* was criticized for presenting sensational-

ized, disturbing content that is of a higher cultural register than tabloid fare (though it includes this and one other snippet of such fare) but not entirely unrelated to it. In addition, *Blasted* draws conspicuous attention to the spacing between scenes, which is filled with the sound of (spring, then summer, then autumn, then heavy winter) rain. Important, violent plot elements— the rape of Cate, the suicide of the soldier—occur in these empty intervals. The fifth scene includes a series of blackouts followed by brief, brightly lit tableaux of Ian in various postures, thereby absorbing the device of spacing between scenes into the scene itself. All of these are conspicuous dramaturgical counterparts to the typographical instructions in Ian's dictated story. Cate's seizures and stutters can be seen as introducing comparable spacings into the fictional plot of the play, and the holes in the hotel room wall and floor dig them into the very fabric of the production.

It might seem surprising that Kane would embody her own artistic production in a character as antipathetic as Ian. And her vocation as independent, avant-garde playwright would seem to have little enough in common with Ian's job as tabloid hack. Kane declared in one interview, though, that "I love Ian."[23] Love him or not, and despite all obvious differences, she appears to claim some degree of kinship to this cynical intellectual worker. (Both Cate's and Ian's names are near or partial homophones for "Kane.") Certainly, as playwright, she is forced to treat the visceral, horrifying material of her play with some critical and technical detachment. The spacings within the play are the privileged signifiers of that detachment, proof that what she has wrought is in fact a work of art and not merely the hysterical outpourings of a disturbed young woman—the counterpart to one of Cate's seizures. (The reviewer Jack Tinker for the *Daily Mail* opined that the grant from the Jerwood Foundation that Kane received to work on the play "might have been better spent on a course of remedial therapy."[24]) If the play tends to annihilate its separation from the audience, it nevertheless maintains these internal spacings. The problem is that the very thing that announces the artistic qualities of Kane's work may also bespeak its status as polished commodity. In an article titled "Lukewarm Britannia," Vera Gottlieb notes of the In-Yer-Face plays of the 1990s: "In effect the plays end up as 'products': the 'themes' of consumerism, drug culture, and sexuality paralyze the plays. . . . [T]he plays of the Nineties seem to have moved even further away from the politically oppositional, and to have given up even an attempt to engage with significant public issues."[25] While this criticism may be more appropriate to a play such as Mark Ravenhill's *Shopping and Fucking* than it is to Kane's *Blasted*, and while Gottlieb's insistence

on direct political content—and thus a clearly defined oppositional stance—
may itself be somewhat constricting, she does point out the way in which
the horrifying thrills of a play such as *Blasted* may provide satisfactions not
entirely unrelated to those on offer from tabloid journalism and other products of the culture industry. Kane's play, at least, takes some cognizance of
this dilemma—whether in a self-critical fashion or with the cynicism of an
Ian we cannot say. In any case, the fact that the "free productive activity" of
the avant-garde playwright cannot definitively separate itself from the work
of the tabloid hack is simply an inescapable condition of the post-Fordist
world in which Kane finds herself—one in which the unassimilable and the
all-too-easily assimilable bear an uneasy kinship.

What I have been calling a crisis of separation in the play manifests itself
in the problem of action. *Blasted* exhibits something like a revenge tragedy
plot, but one that has become hopelessly dislocated. Ian's rape of Cate is
clearly answered by the soldier's rape of Ian. And yet any satisfying sense
of comeuppance is compromised if not entirely negated by the graphic, excessive nature of the sequence in which Ian is raped onstage, has a pistol
jammed up his anus, and then has his eyes sucked out and eaten. (By play's
end he is, like King Lear, more sinned against than sinning.) The soldier's
actions, moreover, which happen to avenge Cate's violation, are a reenactment on the soldier's part of a completely different, prior atrocity carried
out by other soldiers on his own girlfriend—that is, if the soldier's story can
be trusted. Even if it is, his vengeance is carried out not against the offending soldiers but against an innocent party—at least with respect to this particular event. And again—if the soldier can be believed—he has carried out
unprovoked atrocities of rape and murder on his own, so he hardly carries
any ethical mandate as avenger. Revenge tragedy always suffers from dis-
placements and excesses that prevent its ethical ledger from ever quite bal-
ancing out, but in this case the spectator is deprived of any secure ground
from which judgments can even be hazarded.

The elements of revenge tragedy are further complicated by the fact that
the soldier is lonely and horny and wants to "make love" to Ian (42), and,
more suggestively still, by the fact that he wants Ian as journalist to tell the
story of what happened to his girlfriend Col. When Ian demurs, saying that
he doesn't cover international events but only those that have a "personal"
element (48), the soldier obliges, making Col's story quite "personal" for Ian
by inscribing it violently upon his body. He thereby undoes the spacing that
had previously allowed Ian to separate himself from the tragic content of
his work. In at least this one respect, then, the soldier's actions are redemp-

tive, even if exacted at a terrible price, since Ian finally learns to "feel what wretches feel." Something not entirely unrelated happens to Cate. By the end of the play, she is reduced to selling her body to soldiers in exchange for food, thus reenacting in a different key the rape in the hotel room. Of course, the act is now voluntary on Cate's part, if volition can have any real meaning when the only alternative is imminent starvation. But I also think that, in a moment of characteristic black humor on Kane's part, Cate's new form of employment must be seen as fulfilling her earlier hope of becoming a "personal assistant." The logic of the service economy has not entirely disappeared even in the apocalyptic chaos that reigns at play's end, and it manages to insinuate itself into the—already overdetermined—revenge plot.

If there is any action that manages to achieve even a provisional separation from this logic and strike a redemptive note, it is Cate's decision to return at play's end with food for Ian. The same impulse that inspired Cate to accept care of a baby—in a plot element clearly borrowed from Brecht's *The Caucasian Chalk Circle*—also prompts her to care for Ian, now reduced to an infantilized helplessness himself. (He has, of course, earlier consumed the baby that Cate unsuccessfully cared for, and his final position with only bloody head sticking out of a hole in the floor suggests, among other things, an infant emerging from the womb.) Earlier in the play, Ian had derided Cate because she continued to live with her mother and declared that she "couldn't" leave her (6)—whether because she was caring for her mother or being care for by her is unclear, though the fact that her mother gives her money suggests the latter. "When are you going to stand on your own feet?" asks Ian (8), suggesting that Cate's inability to separate herself from maternal care leaves her in a dependent, child-like condition. And yet, Ian's vaunted independence is belied by his subsumption within the newspaper company, as well as by his desperate emotional neediness in Cate's presence. Cate's failure to achieve separation from her mother, by contrast, maintains her in a space where, at least, her personal capacities are not immediately commodified and alienated from her. True, her maternal impulses toward Ian at the end cannot be realized without the prostitution that supplies her with bread, sausages, and gin. But a kind of aneconomic tenderness persists and prompts the play's final words: Ian's "thank you" (61).

In *The Human Condition*, Arendt identifies irreversibility as the central problem afflicting action. What is done cannot be undone, regardless of the consequences. Vengeance is, for Arendt, not a sufficient answer to a wrong committed because vengeance is an automatism, not an action. It repeats the original mistake instead of mending it. Forgiveness is the only form of action through which action's inherent irreversibility can be assuaged.[26] Few plays illustrate the repetition compulsion behind vengeance as starkly as *Blasted*, which posits forgiveness as the sole means of exit from revenge's infernal machine. Vengeance remains entangled in the original act, while forgiveness achieves that separation without which further action cannot occur. Forgiveness is completely misunderstood if it is seen as that which brings hostile parties together. Hatred and revenge bring hostile parties together. Forgiveness is rather that which enables them to detach and resume the separation necessary for life to go on. Never is Cate more distant from Ian than when she feeds her blinded, deceased, but still needy rapist by hand.

II

Earlier I described Kane as both a post-Beckettian and a post-Fordist playwright, and the first of these is still to be explored. Among the various factors that led to a reconsideration of initially hostile responses to *Blasted* was a dawning recognition of its dramatic pedigree, specifically its dense web of allusion to plays by Beckett, Shakespeare, Bond, and others.[27] More successfully than the spacing I discussed earlier, these seemed to bespeak a literary quality that distinguished Kane's work from mere sensation-mongering. The presence of *King Lear* (the play's title, Kane informs us, resonates with Lear's blasted heath, and Ian's enucleation echoes Gloucester's) as well as borrowings from *Waiting for Godot* and *Endgame* are particularly pervasive and unmistakable.

It is a truism to say that British (and not only British) playwriting after Beckett cannot avoid grappling with his work, though that grappling need not take the form of direct allusion as it does in Kane. Beckett, in any case, exerts a by no means entirely benign form of influence, not only because of his towering achievement but also because he so clearly situates himself as the last playwright, imperiously occupying "the end" or even a space after the end, which places putative successors in an awkward position. What could "after Beckett" conceivably mean?

Here I shall focus primarily on some of the ways *Blasted* echoes *Endgame*. The play's final image, with Ian's head protruding from the ground, clearly invokes not only Winnie in the second act of *Happy Days* but also Nagg's and Nell's heads emerging from the trash cans of *Endgame*. More broadly, the hotel room devolves over the course of the play into *Endgame*'s bunker, now presided over by blind Ian rather than blind Hamm. Cate plays

Clov here, perhaps nowhere more clearly than when Ian begs her to hand him his revolver so that he may kill himself, and Cate does so, but only after emptying its chamber of bullets. Those bullets are Kane's grim counterpart to Beckett's painkiller pills (they would serve precisely that function for Ian), and Cate thus presents him with a merciful, but also somewhat sadistic, "no more."

What I described in my seventh chapter as miraculous provision in Beckett has its counterpart here as well, in the trays of sandwiches and breakfasts and bottles of gin waiting at the hotel room door every time it is opened in scenes 1 and 2. In *Blasted*, however, the Beckettian "miracle" is revealed as the labor of immigrant service workers, who remain discreetly invisible themselves. When the war starts and hotel service stops, Cate takes over Clov's task of rustling up provisions, not from a kitchen (which has been replaced by an en suite bathroom) but from the battle-torn world outside. Not only are these provisions not miraculous—they don't prevent Ian from starving to death or finding himself forced to dine on dead baby—but the personal cost to Cate of procuring them is made vividly apparent. And of course, Kane reverses the ending of *Endgame*. Whereas, in my reading, Clov is about to depart at play's end and leave Hamm to death by starvation, Cate returns to feed the already dead but still hungry Ian. In doing so she gives Clov a redemptive turn by melding him with Shakespeare's Cordelia, who returns to care for Lear.

As even these couple of examples suggest, Kane's strategy for appropriating Beckett involves embedding his scenarios in more historically specified contexts. By the end there are still abject bodies in need of provision, but the mechanisms of provisioning are laid bare in ways that no longer allow them to function as mere metaphysical presuppositions. Moreover, while *Endgame* takes place subsequent to some world-ending catastrophe, warfare still rages on in *Blasted*, which therefore draws us back from posthistory into something like the historical present, or a dystopian version thereof. The play even blows a hole into the sealed bunker of *Endgame* to signal the way in which its inescapable present has also been punctured.

In July 1993, while an early draft version of *Blasted* was being staged at Birmingham University's Allardyce Nicoll Studio, Susan Sontag was in Sarajevo directing a production of *Waiting for Godot*, in a theater—indeed a city—without electricity. Rehearsals were interrupted by the sound of exploding shells, and the actors had to lie down during performance breaks because of malnutrition. Sniper fire and the rumble of armored vehicles could be heard at the end of one performance.[28] At around the time that Kane had the insight of dragging Beckett into the historical reality of the Bosnian conflict, the same thing was happening in reality in Bosnia itself. In Sontag's view, "*Waiting for Godot*, written some forty years ago, seems written for, and about, Sarajevo."[29] The extremity of the historical present calls forth, for Sontag, a latent contemporaneity lurking in Beckett's work. In some sense, Sontag's production of *Waiting for Godot* was also the first performance of the *Blasted* that Kane had not yet brought to completion.

Blasted, we might say, undoes *Endgame*'s (and therefore Beckett's) position after-the-end by pulling it back into its presuppositions, both temporal and material. To this list we might add literary presuppositions, since Kane's extensive borrowings from *King Lear* point to one of *Endgame*'s principal sources as well, its status in this regard made vivid by Jan Kott's famous chapter in *Shakespeare Our Contemporary*.[30] Something like a coherent dramatic tradition thus emerges from Kane's allusions and appears to undergird *Blasted*. These literary layerings might well have accentuated the spatial dislocation I traced earlier, since the setting of the play is not only in Leeds and Bosnia and "anywhere" but also on Lear's blasted heath and in Hamm's bunker. But to judge from the pacifying effect that awareness of these borrowings had on critics, one would have to say that they function instead to provide temporal order and spacing to what might otherwise be a collapse of differences, and that they help reestablish the separation required for dramatic theater in the more traditional sense to function, even as they allow *Blasted* to get up In-Yer-Face.

They also provide a way of thinking about Kane's playwriting that distances it from tabloid journalism or post-Fordist labor in general, without quite negating the connections between these that Kane is clearly at pains to point out. For me, the play's final image, with Ian's eyeless head emerging from the floor, allows for yet another if perhaps odd reading. Its resonances are so unmistakably Beckettian that in this closing *pietà*, Ian represents not only Hamm being fed by Clov, and Lear being nursed by Cordelia, but also a zombified Beckett himself being tended to by Kane/Cate. Insofar as Kane's handling of Beckett (et al.) is not merely an attempt at literary respectability but a genuine act of loving care—care made more absurd in that it is for the inaccessible dead—it places her capacities at least provisionally outside of any obvious circuit of post-Fordist or other recuperation.[31] Dramatic lineage grasped as enduring comes to the rescue by supplying the separation-in-relation necessary for tragedy to go on, under ever more challenging conditions. Even if tragedy has died, as George Steiner claims, it still needs to be fed.

Notes

INTRODUCTION

1. Alain Badiou, *Rhapsody for the Theatre*, ed. and trans. Bruno Bosteels (London: Verso, 2013), 86–87. Compare the avant-garde theater director Romeo Castellucci, who declares that for tragedy, "an authentic foundation is impossible today." Claudia Castellucci et al., *The Theatre of Societas Raffaello Sanzio* (London and New York: Routledge, 2007), 30. Cited in Nicholas Ridout, *Passionate Amateurs: Theatre, Communism, and Love* (Ann Arbor: University of Michigan Press, 2014), 3.

2. George Steiner, *The Death of Tragedy* (New Haven, CT: Yale University Press, 1996), 193.

3. Ibid., xi.

4. In Peter Szondi, *Theory of Modern Drama*, trans. Michael Hays (Minneapolis: University of Minnesota Press, 1987), Szondi likewise identifies a crisis in modern drama that specifically dislocates dramatic action. His description of the social context for this crisis differs from mine, however.

5. Aristotle, *On Poetics*, trans. Seth Benardete and Michael Davis (South Bend, IN: St. Augustine's Press, 2002), 17.

6. Ibid., 6.

7. Quoted in Gertrude Stein, *Last Operas and Plays*, ed. and intro. Carl Van Vechten (New York: Rinehart, 1949), x. I take this quotation in turn from Elinor Fuchs, *The Death of Character: Perspectives on Theater after Modernism* (Bloomington: Indiana University Press, 1996), 96.

8. See Fuchs, *Death of Character*, 92–107.

9. Quoted in Hans-Thies Lehmann, *Postdramatic Theatre*, trans. Karen Jürs-Munby (London: Routledge, 2006), 60, who in turn takes it from Peter Szondi. I have corrected the title and date of Sulzer's volume as they appear in Lehmann.

10. Jacques Rancière, *Aisthesis: Scenes from the Aesthetic Regime of Art*, trans. Zakir Paul (London and New York: Verso, 2013), xv–xvi.

11. Lehmann, *Postdramatic Theatre*, 74.

12. Ibid., 37.

13. Ibid., 42.

14. Sigmund Freud, *The Interpretation of Dreams*, in *The Standard Edition of the Complete Psychological Works of Sigmund Freud*, ed. James Strachey et al., 24 vols. (London: Hogarth Press, 1953–74), 4: 264.

15. Ibid., 4: 262.

16. See Lehmann, *Postdramatic Theatre*.

17. Judith Butler, *Antigone's Claim: Kinship between Life and Death* (New York: Columbia University Press, 2000); Martha C. Nussbaum, *The Fragility of Goodness: Luck and Ethics in Greek Tragedy and Philosophy* (Cambridge: Cambridge University Press, 1986); Bonnie Honig, *Antigone, Interrupted* (Cambridge: Cambridge University Press, 2013); J. Peter Euben, *The Tragedy of Political Theory: The Road Not Taken* (Princeton, NJ: Princeton University Press, 1990); Christopher Rocco, *Tragedy and Enlightenment: Athenian Political Thought and the Dilemmas of Modernity* (Berkeley: University of California Press, 1997); David Scott, *Conscripts of Modernity: The Tragedy of Colonial Enlightenment* (Durham, NC: Duke University Press, 2004).

18. For a recent and often incisive Marxist critique of Smith, see Michael Perelman, *The Invention of Capitalism: Classical Political Economy and the Secret History of Primitive Accumulation* (Durham, NC: Duke University Press, 2000).

19. This is not to deny the fact that Smith could be willfully blind to developments in his own era. For a good account, see Perelman, *Invention of Capitalism*.

20. Jean-Pierre Vernant, "The Historical Moment of Tragedy in Greece: Some Social and Psychological Conditions," and "Tensions and Ambiguities in Greek Tragedies," in *Myth and Tragedy in Ancient Greece*, by Jean-Pierre Vernant and Pierre Vidal-Naquet, trans. Janet Lloyd (New York: Zone Books, 1990), 23–48.

21. On the surprising persistence of the figure of the sovereign in modern drama, see Nicole Jerr, "Exit the King? Modern Theater and the Revolution," in *The Scaffolding of Sovereignty: Aesthetic and Global Perspectives on the History of a Concept*, ed. Zvi Ben-Dor Benite, S. Geroulanos, and Nicole Jerr (New York: Columbia University Press, forthcoming).

22. See Arthur Miller, "Tragedy and the Common Man," *New York Times*, February 27, 1949, and *Death of a Salesman* (New York: Penguin, 1976), 56. Quotes are from this edition of *Death of a Salesman*.

23. Peter Szondi raises similar issues in *Theory of Modern Drama*, esp. 35–41.

24. In Bertolt Brecht, *Brecht on Theatre: The Development of an Aesthetic*, ed. and trans. John Willett (New York: Hill and Wang, 1992), 67.

25. Ibid., 183.

26. For the purposes of this argument, sympathy and empathy can be considered synonymous. In fact, I have never encountered an attempt to distinguish between the two that did not strike me as confused and self-contradictory.

27. In his essay "Emotion, Brecht, Empathy vs. Sympathy," *The Brecht Yearbook/Das Brecht Jahrbuch* 33 (2008): 53–68, Darko Suvin argues that Brecht's rejection of empathy (*Einfühlung*) does not banish tragic affect altogether and that he endorses forms of sympathy (*Mitgefühl* or *Mitleidung*) that include an element of critical distance within them. The conceptualizing of sympathy he traces back to "the pioneering Adam Smith" (64). As my treatment of Smithian sympathy will show, this legacy is more ambiguous than Suvin acknowledges. In any case, one must confront a division within Brecht's treatment of empathy. On the one hand, empathetic loss of one's critical faculties prompted by complete identification with another person can encourage the kinds of mass manipulation practiced by the National Socialists. Suvin's notion of "sympathizing distance" would help to counter this danger. On the other hand, Brecht also criticizes empathy, not because it allows us to be manipulated into mindless action but because it robs us of the power to act at all. This, I think, is where the enervating dimension of Smithian sympathy comes into play, despite the fact that it incorporates (as Suvin rightly notes) critical reflection.

28. Immanuel Kant, *Critique of Judgment*, trans. Werner S. Pluhar (Indianapolis: Hackett, 1987), 133.

29. Ibid., 134.

30. Keith A. Dickson, "Brecht: An Aristotelian *Malgré Lui*," *Modern Drama* 11, no. 2 (1968): 111–21. R. Darren Gobert, "Cognitive Catharsis in *The Caucasian Chalk Circle*," *Modern Drama* 49, no. 1 (2006): 12–40.

31. Brecht, *Brecht on Theatre*, 76.

32. Ibid., 34.

33. The pretention of drama to restore to its audience their powers of action is one that Jacques Rancière takes to task in his essay "The Emancipated Spectator." See Rancière, *The Emancipated Spectator*, trans. Gregory Elliott (London: Verso, 2011), 1–24. I don't think the matter can be dismissed as easily (or for the reasons) that Rancière suggests.

34. Raymond Williams, *Modern Tragedy*, ed. Pamela McCallum (Peterborough, ON: Broadview Encore Editions, 2006), 33.

35. Ibid., 108

36. Ibid., 120–21.

37. Ibid., 131.

38. Ibid., 98.

39. See Ridout, *Passionate Amateurs*.

40. I adopt Marlowe's spelling "Mephastophilis" from the A-text in order to identify his character in particular, as opposed to the general figure of Mephistopheles/Mephistophilis.

41. Hegel's *Lectures on Aesthetics*—which is the English translation of the original title in German, *Vorlesungen über die Ästhetik*—is how this work is generally known in English. However, the standard English translation of the work itself is titled *Aesthetics: Lectures on Fine Art*. When citing specific passages in English, I will use the latter title but will in all other instances use the more standard *Lectures on Aesthetics*.

CHAPTER ONE

1. Adam Smith, *An Inquiry into the Nature and Causes of the Wealth of Nations*, ed. Edwin Cannan (New York: Modern Library, 1994), 67, 133. For reference purposes this will sometimes be shortened to WN.

2. Samuel Fleischacker, *On Adam Smith's* Wealth of Nations: *A Philosophical Companion* (Princeton, NJ: Princeton University Press, 2004), 34: "Smith's most famous doctrine about political economy, after all, is the doctrine of unanticipated consequences."

3. In his *Lectures on Rhetoric and Belles Lettres*, Smith advocates a plain, perspicuous, and concise style of writing. See the discussion in Vivienne Brown, *Adam Smith's Discourse: Canonicity, Commerce, and Conscience* (New York and London: Routledge, 1994), 9–22. See also Lisa Herzog, "The Commodity of Commerce: Smith's Rhetoric of Sympathy in the Opening of *The Wealth of Nations*," *Philosophy and Rhetoric* 46, no. 1 (2013): 65–87, esp. 70–71.

4. The claim that *The Wealth of Nations* is "amoral" is made by Vivienne Brown, *Adam Smith's Discourse*, 39 passim. Brown, moreover, insists that "WN stands as a largely single-voiced monologic text, with its expressed certainties and intellectual order" (43), and she distinguishes it from the dialogical structure of *The Theory of Moral Sentiments* in this regard. By contrast, Emma Rothschild emphasizes the heterogeneity of *The Wealth of Nations*—the way it mixes history, theory, policy, and so forth—and regards this as reflecting the messy heterogeneity of the commercial economy itself. Emma Rothschild, *Economic Sentiments: Adam Smith, Condorcet, and the Enlightenment* (Cambridge, MA: Harvard University Press, 2001), 237. Lisa Herzog ("Commodity of Commerce," 78) explicitly contests Brown's claim that *The Wealth of Nations* is monological.

5. Quoted from David Bevington, ed., *The Complete Works of Shakespeare*, 5th ed. (New York: Pearson Macmillan, 2004). The echo was first identified by Martin Harries in *Scare Quotes from Shakespeare: Marx, Keynes, and the Language of Reenchantment* (Stanford, CA: Stanford University Press, 2000), 14–18, and then again (and apparently independently) by Emma Rothschild, who detects a possible reference to Voltaire's *Oedipe* (1718) as well. Rothschild, *Economic Sentiments*, 119.

6. See Catherine Packham, "The Physiology of Political Economy: Vitalism and Adam Smith's *Wealth of Nations*," *Journal of the History of Ideas* 63, no. 3 (2002): 465–81.

7. Pasquale Pasquino, "Theatrum Politicum: The Genealogy of Capital—Police and the State of Prosperity," in *The Foucault Effect: Studies in Governmentality*, ed. Graham Burchell, Colin Gordon, and Peter Miller (Chicago: University of Chicago Press, 1991), 105-18.

8. In his *Lectures on Jurisprudence*, Smith describes government as "desirous of promoting the opulence of the state. This produces what we call police. Whatever regulations are made with respect to the trade, commerce, agriculture, manufactures of the country are considered as belonging to the police" (1.2). Here "police" encompasses matters of material prosperity alone. Adam Smith, *Lectures on Jurisprudence*, ed. R. L. Meek, D. D. Raphael, and P. G. Stein (New York: Oxford University Press, 1978).

9. Brown, *Adam Smith's Discourse*, 214.

10. Adam Ferguson, *An Essay on the History of Civil Society*, ed. Fania Oz-Salzberger (Cambridge: Cambridge University Press, 1995), 59.

11. See Charles L. Griswold Jr., *Adam Smith and the Virtues of Enlightenment* (Cambridge: Cambridge University Press, 1999), 136: "In both of his books Smith is recommending a society devoted to the improvement of the human lot but governed by a systematic self-deception about its own ends. Such a society is therefore inclined to private, though not necessarily public, unhappiness. The failure of the pursuit of happiness on the part of the great mass of individuals in modern commercial society is known to the philosopher at the outset."

12. One way of understanding this problem pertains to the possible discrepancy between the visions of happiness promulgated by *The Wealth of Nations* and by *The Theory of Moral Sentiments*, where tranquility and consciousness of moral rectitude trump material comfort. Another is internal to *The Wealth of Nations*. There, production always aims at (or should aim at) consumption. But the most flourishing societies are not those that direct a large proportion of the national revenue toward immediate consumption, but rather those that frugally reinvest it in production. Hence, there is a self-limiting quality to the material satisfactions offered by commercial activity, which are always in some sense ideally suspended in a perpetual cycle of production rather than finally released for individual enjoyment.

13. Aristotle, *Nicomachean Ethics*, trans. Christopher Rowe (Oxford and New York: Oxford University Press, 2002), 102. That Aristotle is a major influence on Smith has long been recognized. For some recent treatments, see Gloria Vivenza, *Adam Smith and the Classics: The Classical Heritage in Adam Smith's Thought* (Oxford and New York: Oxford University Press, 2001), and Ryan Hanley, *Adam Smith and the Character of Virtue* (New York: Cambridge University Press, 2009).

14. Aristotle, *On Poetics*, trans. Seth Benardete and Michael Davis (South Bend, IN: St. Augustine's Press, 2002), 17.

15. Adam Smith, *The Theory of Moral Sentiments* (New York: Prometheus Books, 2000), 73.

16. This is a point elaborated by Marx but logically implicit in Smith's labor theory of value as well.

17. Michel Foucault, *The Birth of Biopolitics: Lectures at the Collège de France, 1978-1979*, trans. Graham Burchell (New York: Palgrave Macmillan, 2008), 292.

18. Michel Foucault, "Governmentality," in *The Foucault Effect: Studies in Governmentality*, ed. Graham Burchell, Colin Gordon, and Peter Miller (Chicago: University of Chicago Press, 1991), 87-104.

19. Foucault, *Birth of Biopolitics*, 15, 28.

20. Ibid., 279.

21. Ferguson, *An Essay on the History of Civil Society*, 119. Quoted in Ronald Hamowy, *The Scottish Enlightenment and the Theory of Spontaneous Order* (Carbondale: Southern Illinois University Press, 1987), 25.

22. Quoted in Fleischacker, *On Adam Smith's* Wealth of Nations, 248.

23. Griswold, *Adam Smith and the Virtues of Enlightenment*, 206-7.

24. Albert O. Hirschbaum, *The Passions and the Interests: Arguments for Capitalism before Its Triumph* (Princeton, NJ: Princeton University Press, 1977).

25. Actually, quite a few commentators have identified a tragic dimension to Smith's vision of commercial society, but this sense derives principally from the *Theory of Moral Sentiments* and the *Lectures on Jurisprudence*, not from *The Wealth of Nations*. For arguments that Smith recognizes this tragic dimension and attempts to respond to it, see Hanley, *Adam Smith and the Character of Virtue*, and David C. Rasmussen, *The Problems and Promise of Commercial Society: Adam Smith's Response to Rousseau* (University Park: Pennsylvania State University Press, 2008).

26. James R. Otteson, *Adam Smith's Marketplace of Life* (Cambridge and New York: Cambridge University Press, 2002).

27. Ibid., 101.

28. Ibid., 6.

29. There is one additional, brief reprise of Smith's statement on 235 of *Theory of Moral Sentiments*.

30. Griswold, *Adam Smith and the Virtues of Enlightenment*, 46, 196.

31. See Otteson, *Adam Smith's Marketplace*, 114, 199-200. See also Griswold, *Adam Smith and the Virtues of Enlightenment*, 102.

32. Otteson, *Adam Smith's Marketplace*, 199-200.

33. For a clear exposition of active and reactive in Nietzsche, see Gilles Deleuze, *Nietzsche and Philosophy*, trans. Hugh Tomlinson (New York: Columbia University Press, 1983), 39-72.

34. Quoted in Fleischacker, *On Adam Smith's* Wealth of Nations, 248.

35. See, e.g., David Marshall, "Adam Smith and the Theatricality of Moral Sentiments," in David Marshall, *The Figure of Theater: Shaftsbury, Defoe, Adam Smith, and George Eliot* (New York: Columbia University Press, 1986), 167-92. See also David Marshall, *The Surprising Effects of Sympathy: Marivaux, Diderot, Rousseau, and Mary Shelley* (Chicago: University of Chicago Press, 1986). Charles Griswold suggestively connects Smith's use of a theatrical model with his skeptical attention to appearances rather than essences. *Adam Smith and the Virtues of Enlightenment*, 65-70.

36. For a suggestive reading of *Philoctetes* against Smith's *Theory of Moral Sentiments*, see Martha C. Nussbaum, "The 'Morality of Pity': Sophocles' *Philoctetes*," in *Rethinking Tragedy*, ed. Rita Felski (Baltimore: Johns Hopkins University Press, 2008), 148-69.

37. Such an approach is not peculiar to Smith, of course, or even to the eighteenth century. In *What Was Tragedy?: Theory and the Early Modern Canon* (Oxford: Oxford University Press, 2015), Blair Hoxby claims that the early modern period understood tragedy as the representation of passions more than as the imitation of action. He notes, moreover, that this tendency becomes most widespread in the eighteenth century (72). My argument might help to explain why this is so.

38. Jean-Jacques Rousseau, *Politics and the Arts: Letter to M. d'Alembert on the Theatre*, trans. Allan Bloom (Ithaca, NY: Cornell University Press, 1960), 4.

39. Smith's account of attempts to hide tears at the tragic theater may conceivably have been inspired in part by the following passage from Rousseau's *Letter to M. d'Alembert on the Theatre*: "Thus the tyrant of Phera hid himself at the theatre for fear of being seen groaning with Andromache and Priam, while he heard without emotion the cries of so many unfortunate victims slain daily by his orders" (Rousseau, *Politics and the Arts*, 24). Smith, we know, owned a copy of Rousseau's *Letter* (Rasmussen, *Problems and Promise of Commercial Society*, 57). Alexander's hypocritical tears become generalized here as the discrepancy between the theatergoer's sympathy for fictional characters and his disapproval of his fellow spectators.

40. Jean-Pierre Vernant, "The Historical Moment of Tragedy in Greece: Some of the Social and Psychological Conditions," and "Tensions and Ambiguities in Greek Tragedy," in *Myth and Tragedy in Ancient Greece*, by Jean-Pierre Vernant and Pierre Vidal-Naquet, trans. Janet Lloyd (New York: Zone Books, 1990), 23-28, 29-48.

41. I thank Joanna Picciotto for a discussion that inspired this paragraph.

42. See Hanley, *Adam Smith and the Character of Virtue*.

43. See ibid., esp. chap. 5, "Magnanimity, or Classical Virtue," 174. John W. Danford argues, as does Hanley, that commercial society encourages the softer, humane virtues at the expense of

honor and glory. See Danford, "Adam Smith, Equality, and the Wealth of Sympathy," *American Journal of Political Science* 24, no. 4 (1980): 674-95.

44. Hanley, *Adam Smith and the Character of Virtue*, 26, 28, 42, 45, and 134, draws repeated and, in my view, exaggerated connections between Smith and Nietzsche.

45. See Fania Oz-Salzberger, "Ferguson's Theory of Action," in *Adam Ferguson: History, Progress, and Human Nature*, ed. Eugene Heath and Vincenzo Merolle (London: Pickering and Chatto, 2008), 147-56.

46. Ferguson, *Essay on the History of Civil Society*, 28.

47. See Brandon Turner, "Adam Ferguson on 'Action' and the Possibility of Non-Political Participation," *Polity* 44, no. 2 (2012): 212-33.

48. See also Craig Smith, "Ferguson and the Active Genius of Mankind," in *Adam Ferguson: History, Progress, and Human Nature*, ed. Eugene Heath and Vincenzo Merolle (London: Pickering and Chatto, 2008), 157-70.

49. See Dana R. Villa's superb study, *Arendt and Heidegger: The Fate of the Political* (Princeton, NJ: Princeton University Press, 1996).

50. For an extended and usefully skeptical treatment of this theme in Arendt, see Hannah Fenichel Pitkin, *The Attack of the Blob: Hannah Arendt's Concept of the Social* (Chicago: University of Chicago Press, 1998).

51. Hannah Arendt, *The Human Condition*, 2nd ed. (Chicago: University of Chicago Press, 1998), 52.

52. Here I am leaving aside the question of whether Greek politics, which are paradigmatic for Arendt, actually worked in the way she suggests. I take up this issue in "Theater and Democratic Thought: Arendt to Rancière," *Critical Inquiry* 37, no. 3 (2011): 545-72.

53. "Economics widens its horizon and turns into a general science of all and every human action, into praxeology." Ludwig von Mises, *Human Action: A Treatise on Economics* (Auburn, AL: Ludwig von Mises Institute, 1998), 233.

54. Ibid., 220-21.

55. Ibid., 122.

56. "By the same token, the simple fact that Adam Smith needed an 'invisible hand' to guide economic dealings on the exchange market shows plainly that more than sheer economic activity is involved in exchange and that 'economic man,' when he makes his appearance on the market, is an acting being and neither exclusively a producer or trader and barterer" (Arendt, *Human Condition*, 185). Here Arendt misunderstands the invisible hand as something imposed on economic activity from without, in the manner of a benign Providence, rather than as an order arising solely from that activity. Or rather, she seems to regard it as a necessary fiction Smith resorted to in order to make the divergent motives of economic agents appear to harmonize. This reading may derive in part from some equally perplexing remarks in Gunnar Myrdal's book *The Political Element in the Development of Economic Theory* (English trans., 1953), which Arendt cites more than once in the footnotes to *The Human Condition* and praises as "brilliant" (44n6) In any case, Arendt's misconstructions of Smith are as nothing compared to what she inflicts upon Marx.

57. Although my approach to Arendt's take on tragic drama differs from his, I am indebted to Robert C. Pirro, *Hannah Arendt and the Politics of Tragedy* (DeKalb: Northern Illinois University Press, 2001).

58. Paul A. Kottman, *A Politics of the Scene* (Stanford, CA: Stanford University Press, 2008).

CHAPTER TWO

1. Simon Goldhill, "Civic Ideology and the Problem of Difference: The Politics of Aeschylean Tragedy," *Journal of Hellenic Studies* 120 (2000): 34-56. Reference is to p. 45.

2. Isocrates, "On the Peace," in *Isocrates II*, trans. George Norlin (Cambridge, MA: Harvard Uni-

versity Press, 1991), 57–58. Quoted on p. 101 of Simon Goldhill, "The Great Dionysia and Civic Ideology," in *Nothing to Do with Dionysos?: Athenian Drama in Its Social Context*, ed. John J. Winkler and Froma I. Zeitlin (Princeton, NJ: Princeton University Press, 1990), 97–129.

3. *The Frogs*, 1014–17, in *Aristophanes IV*, trans. Jeffrey Henderson, Loeb Classical Library 180 (Cambridge, MA: Harvard University Press, 2002), 162.

4. John J. Winkler, "The Ephebes' Song: *Tragodia* and *Polis*," in *Nothing to Do with Dionysos?* ed. Winkler and Zeitlin, 20–62. Citation from p. 22. Twisting this around somewhat, Nicole Loraux in *The Mourning Voice: An Essay on Greek Tragedy*, trans. Elizabeth Trapnell Rawlings (Ithaca, NY: Cornell University Press, 2002), writes of "*choreutai* constituting a pacifist version of citizen-soldiers," and she cites Aristophanes's *The Frogs*, 1419, to the effect that "the existence of choruses symbolizes peacetime" (19 and n.). Jasper Griffin, "The Social Function of Greek Tragedy," *Classical Quarterly*, n.s., 48, no. 1 (1998), 39–61, criticizes Winkler for exaggerating the military aspects of the Dionysian festival (see 43–50). There is also some unresolved controversy over whether the ephebe yet existed as a formal institution in the fifth century (Goldhill, "Great Dionysia and Civic Ideology," 124–25). The most searching discussion of Winkler's thesis that I can find occurs in Peter Wilson, *The Athenian Institution of the Khoregia: The Chorus, the City, and the Stage* (Cambridge: Cambridge University Press, 2003), 77–79. Wilson makes a couple of pertinent objections yet declares that the ephebic hypothesis "cannot be dismissed out of hand." In any case, as Wilson observes, "the line between festival and 'military' *leitourgia* is not sharply defined. Choral activity itself—including tragedy, with its rectilinear, rank-and-file *khoros*—encouraged skills of orderliness, obedience, and co-ordination as well as of physical fitness, which would serve the hoplite in the phalanx" (46–47). The Winkler thesis is useful to me primarily for condensing a transition to the "field of death" that occurs in any case. My argument does not strictly rely on its correctness.

5. M. I. Finley, *The Ancient Economy*, 2nd ed., updated (Berkeley: University of California Press, 1989), 126, 72.

6. Ellen Meiksins Wood, *Peasant-Citizen and Slave: The Foundations of Athenian Democracy* (New York: Verso, 1988), 124. However, the system of public subsidies (including participation in the Assembly and attendance at the Greater Dionysia) actually expanded in the fourth century after the loss of the Empire. See Josiah Ober, *Mass and Elite in Democratic Athens: Rhetoric, Ideology, and the Power of the People* (Princeton, NJ: Princeton University Press, 1989), 23–24. Ober casts doubt on Athenian democracy's reliance on Empire.

7. On pensions, see William T. Loomis, *Wages, Welfare Costs, and Inflation in Classical Athens* (Ann Arbor: University of Michigan Press, 1998), 220–23.

8. Wood, *Peasant-Citizen and Slave*, 122.

9. Aristotle, *The Politics and the Constitution of Athens*, ed. Stephen Everson (New York: Cambridge University Press, 1996), 229.

10. See, e.g., Thucydides, *The Peloponnesian War*, 6.24.

11. Moses I. Finley has declared that "the ancients . . . lacked the concept of an 'economy,'" because they lacked the thing itself—if by "economy" we mean an autonomous subsystem of society operating according to its own logic and laws. Economy activity was, rather, "embedded" in other social institutions in a way that prevented markets or economic rationality in the modern sense from developing. See Finley, *Ancient Economy*, 21 and passim. See also Finley, "Aristotle and Economic Analysis," in *Studies in Ancient Society*, ed. M. I. Finley (London: Routledge and Kegan Paul, 1971), 26–52. It is not necessary for me to engage in the long-running battle between "primitivists" and "modernists" over the validity of Finley's thesis, though my indebtedness to Finley's account of the Athenian economy will be readily apparent. For some recent statements, see Edmund M. Burke, "The Economy of Athens in the Classical Era: Some Adjustments to the Primitivist Model," *Transactions of the American Philological Association* 122 (1992): 199–226; Jean Andreau, "Twenty Years after Moses Finley's *The Ancient Economy*," and Scott Miekle, "Modernism, Economics, and the Ancient Economy," both in *The Ancient Economy*, ed. Walter Scheidel and Sitta von Reden (New York: Routledge, 2002), 33–49 and 233–50.

12. Finley, *Ancient Economy*, 125.

13. Ibid., 195.

14. Thucydides, *The Peloponnesian War*, trans. Walter Blanco (New York: Norton, 1998), 73. Mark Griffith points out that the Greek text gives *panta*, "everything," for Blanco's "all sorts of merchandise," and that the term doubtless includes cultural as well as material goods.

15. Aristophanes, *The Wasps*, 706-11, *Aristophanes II*, trans. Jeffrey Henderson, Loeb Classical Library 488 (Cambridge, MA: Harvard University Press, 1998), 313.

16. Leo Strauss, *Xenophon's Socratic Discourse: An Interpretation of the Oeconomicus* (South Bend, IN: St. Augustine's Press, 1998), 20. This volume includes a full English translation of the *Oeconomicus*, from which this quotation is taken.

17. See, for instance, Steven Jonstone, "Virtuous Toil, Vicious Work: Xenophon on Aristocratic Style," *Classical Philology* 89, no. 3 (1994): 219-40, esp. 229-32. Farming is an elite form of toil that prepares the body for war and involves administrative reason.

18. Aristotle, *Politics*, 179.

19. Ibid., 68.

20. Ibid., 176.

21. Ibid., 13.

22. Ibid., 70, 97.

23. Ibid., 97.

24. Goldhill, "Great Dionysia and Civic Ideology," 112.

25. Augusto Boal, *Theater of the Oppressed*, trans. Charles A. and Maria-Odilia Leal McBride (New York: Theatre Communications Group, 1985), 12.

26. Stephen Halliwell, *Aristotle's Poetics* (Chicago: University of Chicago Press, 1998), 106.

27. Mark Griffith, "Brilliant Dynasts: Power and Politics in the *Oresteia*," *Classical Antiquity* 14, no. 1 (1995): 62-129. Quotation from p. 73.

28. See Loraux's discussion of *aion* as inexhaustible life in *Mourning Voice*, 26-32.

29. David Rosenbloom, "Myth, History, and Hegemony in Aeschylus," in *History, Tragedy, Theory: Dialogues on Athenian Drama*, ed. Barbara Goff (Austin: University of Texas Press, 1995), 91-130. Quotation from p. 95. See also 95, 106.

30. Aeschylus, *Oresteia*, ed. and trans. Alan H. Sommerstein, Loeb Classical Library 146 (Cambridge, MA: Harvard University Press, 2008). All quotations in English and Greek will be taken from this edition.

31. Ischomachos's lengthy account of his wife's superior competence in managing the household leads Socrates to compliment her "manly understanding." To which Ischomachos responds: "And yet once, Socrates, . . . I saw she had applied a good deal of white lead to her face, that she might seem to be fairer than she was, and some dye, so that she would look more flushed than was the truth, and she also wore high shoes, that she might seem taller than she naturally was" (Xen, *Oec.* 10.2; Strauss, *Xenophon's Socratic Discourse*, 44). It is not coincidental that Socrates's praise for the wife's "manly understanding" should immediately prompt a narrative of feminine deceptiveness from Ischomachos. But this minor peccadillo would resonate for many of Xenophon's original readers, aware as they were that Ischomachos's wife would betray him seriously in later years—taking up sexually with his son-in-law, driving her daughter to near suicide and then expelling her from her husband's house, claiming she was pregnant by the son-in-law but then, when the child was born, denying that it was his. See Andocides, *On the Mysteries*, 124-27.

In *Agamemnon*, the chorus praises Clytemnestra in terms similar to those with which Socrates praises Ischomachos's wife: "Lady, you have spoken wisely, like a sensible man" (351), but she too later deceives her husband and exhibits a tragically dangerous eros.

32. Footnote to *Agamemnon* 49 in Aeschylus, *Oresteia*, ed. Sommerstein, 9.

33. *Aeschylus I: Oresteia*, trans. Richmond Lattimore (Chicago: University of Chicago Press, 1953), 1, 49.

34. In the simile, the Olympians send Furies to avenge the vultures, and in the *Eumenides*, of course, Furies attempt to avenge Clytemnestra.

35. The term used here for offspring, *neossos*, can also mean specifically "nestlings," and is picked up in precisely that sense by Orestes's prayer in *Choephoroi* 256 to denote the orphaned offspring of the father eagle.

36. Two relatively recent examples are Sitta von Reden, *Exchange in Ancient Greece* (London: Duckworth, 1995), 147-68; and Richard Seaford, "Tragic Money," *Journal of Hellenic Studies* 118 (1998): 119-39.

37. Von Reden, *Exchange in Ancient Greece*, insists that "the purple tapestry was certainly not bought with money" (164), a claim contested by Seaford, "Tragic Money," 124n59.

38. Seaford, "Tragic Money," 128.

39. Simon Goldhill, *Language, Sexuality, Narrative: The* Oresteia (Cambridge: Cambridge University Press, 1984), 78.

40. Martin Heidegger, "The Question concerning Technology," in Heidegger, *Basic Writings*, ed. David Farrell Krell (London: Harper Perennial Modern Thought, 2008), 322. I am tempted to take this Heideggerian conceit still further and claim that the fecund breeding of the sea is what Heidegger refers to as *physis*, a blossoming or bringing forth of being that Agamemnon reduces to the standing reserve.

41. Cf. *Choe*. 1010-14: "Did she do it or did she not? This garment [the robe in which Agamemnon was trapped] is my witness to how it was dyed by Aigisthus' sword; and the stain of blood, joining with the lapse of time, has contributed to ruining many of the dyes in the embroidery."

42. Clytemnestra inserts herself into this line of perverse feeding when she exclaims that Agamemnon's blood nourishes her as the rain does the corn (1388-92).

43. When Orestes describes the serpent killing the father eagle "in the twisting coils" (*Choe*. 248) the terms used to describe this can also apply to the twisting of rope or cloth, the plaiting of baskets, and so forth, thus again indirectly associating Clytemnestra and weaving.

44. Clytemnestra's name means literally "famous plotter."

45. Michael Davis, *The Poetry of Philosophy: On Aristotle's* Poetics (Lanham, MD: Rowman and Littlefield, 1992), 91.

46. Ruth Padel, "Making Space Speak," in *Nothing to Do with Dionysos?* ed. Winkler and Zeitlin, 336-65. See p. 346.

47. Ibid., 345.

48. Ibid., 342.

49. Aeschylus, *Oresteia*, ed. Sommerstein, 305n152.

50. Apollo states, among other things, that a father can produce children without a mother but that a mother cannot produce offspring without a father. The fact that he makes this claim in front of an audience composed partly of the Furies, who have a mother but no father, should be quite enough to unsettle his theories.

51. See G. E. R. Lloyd, *Science, Folklore, and Ideology: Studies in the Life Sciences in Ancient Greece* (Cambridge: Cambridge University Press, 1983), 86-94 ("Alternative Theories of the Female Seed"), and esp. 87 and 90.

52. Goldhill, *Language, Sexuality, Narrative*, 170.

53. Conveniently, the members of the chorus attribute their enslavement to the gods and not to Agamemnon (75-77).

54. A. M. Bowie, "Religion and Politics in Aeschylus' *Oresteia*," *Classical Quarterly*, n.s., 43, no. 1 (1993): 10-31, esp. 24-26. See also George Thomson, "Mystical Allusions in the *Oresteia*," *Journal of Hellenic Studies* 55, no. 1 (1935): 20-34, and 55, no. 2 (1935): 228-30.

55. There is of course a considerable literature on Dionysos and Greek drama. Some notable instances from recent decades include Richard Seaford, "Dionysiac Drama and the Dionysiac Mysteries," *Classical Quarterly* 31, no. 2 (1981): 252-75; Charles Segal, *Dionysiac Poetics and Euripides' Bacchae* (Princeton, NJ: Princeton University Press, 1982); E. Easterling, "A Show for Dionysos,"

in *The Cambridge Companion to Greek Tragedy*, ed. E. Easterling (Cambridge: Cambridge University Press, 1997), 36–53; Rainer Friedrich, "Everything to Do with Dionysos? Ritualism, the Dionysiac, and the Tragic," in *Tragedy and the Tragic: Greek Theatre and Beyond*, ed. M. S. Silk (New York: Oxford University Press, 1998), 257–83; Richard Seaford, "Something to Do with Dionysos—Tragedy and the Dionysiac: Responses to Friedrich," in Silk, *Tragedy and the Tragic*, 284–94.

56. Of course, the councilors are soldier-citizens like any others. It is not so much a different breed as a different type of activity at stake here.

57. Emile Benveniste, "Expression indo-européenne de l'éternité," *Bulletin de la societé de Paris* 38 (1937): 103–12.

58. Ibid.

59. Ibid., 111, quoted and translated in Loraux, *Mourning Voice*, 28.

60. See Aeschylus, *Eumenides*, ed. Alan H. Sommerstein (Cambridge: Cambridge University Press, 1989), 6–12.

61. On the logic of the pack, see "1914: One or Several Wolves?," in Gilles Deleuze and Félix Guattari, *A Thousand Plateaus: Capitalism and Schizophrenia*, trans. Brian Massumi (Minneapolis: University of Minnesota Press, 1987), 26–38.

62. Aristotle, *Pol.* 1261a15–31.

63. Griffith, "Brilliant Dynasts," 101.

64. In speaking of the "toil or labor of battle" I would seem to be collapsing the very dichotomy on which this chapter relies, since imperial warfare is regarded in Periclean rhetoric as a form of *action* in contrast with productive labor. And yet the herald's speech in *Ag.* 551ff. depicts warfare as a grimy, exhausting, and distinctly unheroic form of toil. For the common soldier, the (essentially aristocratic) contrast between heroic action and labor simply does not obtain. The herald thus reveals an original, laborious underside to heroic action, just as Cilissa (his counterpart) in the *Choephoroi* reveals the labor required to raise the heroic figure of Orestes. What I have just described as the "centrifugal" movement of the *Oresteia* is repeatedly undercut by a countermovement that erases difference.

65. It might be objected that I am misconstruing the semantics of *ponos*, which denotes voluntary, stylized, and elite forms of exertion as opposed to the enforced, productive labor of the artisanal classes. See Jonstone, "Virtuous Toil, Vicious Work," and Nicole Loraux, "*Ponos*: Sur quelques difficultés de la peine comme nom du travail," *Annali del Seminario di Studi del Mondo Classico* 4 (1982): 171–92. Without venturing to wade in waters far too deep for me, I would nevertheless note that the materials on which Jonstone in particular draws derive largely from the fourth century, and that the contexts in which *ponos* appears in the *Oresteia* do not consistently seem to support the distinctions he draws. Loraux's piece emphasizes the ambiguities surrounding *ponos*, which is used by a speaker in Demosthenes, for instance, to refer to labor in the silver mines (Loraux, "*Ponos*," 178).

66. One result of this is that the very antitheses I attempt to make the Furies support are necessarily compromised. For instance, they represent the rights of the *oikos* in opposition to those of the *polis*, yet at one point they describe themselves as *praktores* or tax collectors (319) in their pursuit of Orestes's blood. See Goldhill, *Language, Narrative, Sexuality*, 228, and Von Reden, *Exchange*, 158, on Aeschylus's use of this term.

67. Goldhill, *Language, Narrative, Sexuality*, 272.

68. I owe this point—among others—to Mark Griffith.

69. Rosenbloom, "Myth, History, and Hegemony in Aeschylus," 97.

70. Bowie, "Religion and Politics in Aeschylus' *Oresteia*," 28.

71. On jury intimidation, see *Eum.* 711–14; and on family connections, see Griffith, "Brilliant Dynasts," 102.

72. See the passage from Wilson, *Athenian Institution of the Khoregia*, 46–47, quoted in note 4, above.

73. J. Peter Euben makes related claims for Greek theater in *The Tragedy of Political Theory: The Road Not Taken* (Princeton, NJ: Princeton University Press, 1990).

74. I recognize that this claim will look strange if not incoherent to students of Arendt, who was nothing if not careful to segregate political action from *poiesis*. But drama is clearly a form of making that acts in many respect like public speech. Indeed, I would insist that even made things can sometimes possess a natality as powerful as that of persons, and that works of art, including plays, are among these.

75. Plutarch, "Life of Pericles" 2.1 in *Lives, III*, trans. Bernadotte Perrin, Loeb Classics (Cambridge, MA: Harvard University Press, 1916).

CHAPTER THREE

1. The historical data for this paragraph come from W. D. Lebek, "Moneymaking on the Roman Stage," in *Roman Theater and Society: E. Togo Solomon Conference Papers*, ed. William J. Slater (Ann Arbor: University of Michigan Press, 1996), 29–48.

2. Walter W. Greg, ed., *Henslowe Papers: Being Documents Supplementary to Henslowe's Diary* (London: A. H. Bullen, 1907), 72.

3. Ibid., 73–74.

4. Ibid., 75.

5. Ibid., 77.

6. Daniel J. Vitkus, ed., *Three Turk Plays from Early Modern England: "Selimus," "A Christian Turned Turk," and "The Renegado"* (New York: Columbia University Press, 2000).

7. John Henry Jones, ed., *The English Faust Book* (New York: Cambridge University Press, 1994), 139–41. This episode leaves a minute textual residue in the B-version, where Mephastophilis declares at the end of scene 8 that "I'll wing myself, and forthwith fly amain / Unto my Faustus, at the Great Turk's court."

8. I shall employ the spelling of the A-text in order to distinguish Marlowe's character from Mephistopheles.

9. F. G. Fleay, *A Chronicle History of the London Stage* (London, 1890), 117.

10. The most vigorous effort to rehabilitate Henslowe and to discredit the older view of him is in Carol Chillington Rutter, *Documents of the Rose Theater* (Manchester: Manchester University Press, 1984), 1–5. See also R. A. Foakes, ed., *Henslowe's Diary*, 2nd ed. (Cambridge: Cambridge University Press, 2002), xxxvi; and Neil Carson, *A Companion to Henslowe's Diary* (Cambridge: Cambridge University Press, 1988).

11. E. K. Chambers, *The Elizabethan Stage*, 4 vols. (Oxford: Clarendon Press, 1923), 1:368. The most patently damning pieces of evidence against Henslowe are a couple of legal documents composed in 1615 on behalf of an acting company under his proprietorship. The "Articles of Grievance" and "Articles of Oppression" tax Henslowe with various misdeeds, such as dissolving acting companies just as they are about to discharge their debts to him, then reconstituting the companies along with their original indebtedness. If this claim is true (and we do not possess Henslowe's response to this document), contractual obligations to Henslowe could sometimes prove interminable. The "Articles" report Henslowe as saying of the players, "should these fellowes Come out of my debt, I should have noe rule with them" (Greg, *Henslowe Papers*, 89).

Rutter dismisses the "Articles" as follows: "One way of evaluating the players' claims is to observe what they accepted in settlement of them, for having itemised £567 in damages against Henslowe they eventually adjusted their claims, agreed that they *owed* him £400 and gratefully accepted an abatement to £200." I find this reading of the matter tendentious. The evidentiary basis for Rutter's claim is apparently the document included as Article 107 in the *Henslowe Papers*, about which several things ought to be said. First, the players' enumerated claims against Henslowe do amount to £567, but these are assessed against Henslowe's prior charge that the players owe him £600. Greg interprets the "Articles" as claiming, therefore, that the players owe Henslowe £33, not that Henslowe owes them £567, and his interpretation of these (admittedly sometimes confusing) documents seems right to me. I would put the result as follows: Henslowe originally claimed that the players owed him £600, but in the end his surviving partners "gratefully" accepted only £200 of the original sum. (My "gratefully" is inserted to echo Rutter's, which is purely and equally supposititious.) To judge the validity of the players' charges by the final disposition of the matter is problematic in any case. We have no idea of whether the dispute ever went to court, or of what effect Henslowe's ensuing death may have had on the determination of either side to press its claims.

In addition, while Article 107 is probably connected to the "Articles," it by no means self-evidently represents a final adjudication of the claims made there. Greg supposes that the players may have incurred additional debts to Henslowe after the matters mentioned in the "Articles" were resolved, and his view is accepted by R. A. Foakes in *Henslowe's Diary*, ix. My point, in any case, is not that the charges in the "Articles" should be taken at face value. It is that they cannot be summarily dismissed, either.

While the "Articles" cast a shadow over Henslowe's later years, the documentary record reveals nothing comparable about his dealings at the Rose Theater. If the Lord Admiral's Men were unhappy with Henslowe's roles as banker and moneylender for the company, their grievances have not survived. As R. A. Foakes states in his edition of *Henslowe's Diary*, "The account-book reveals a friendly and, on the whole, harmonious relationship between Henslowe and the players" (Foakes, *Henslowe's Diary*, xxxvi). The sulfurous Henslowe, assuming he exists, emerged only toward the end of his life, during the period of his dealings with Daborne.

A theatrical landlord better cast than Henslowe for the role of villain may be Francis Langley, whose business practices at the Swan and Boar's Head Theaters were both extortionate and well documented. In a bill of 1597 addressed to the queen, Lord Pembroke's Men vividly depict the stranglehold that Langley had on them after they contracted to perform exclusively at the Swan. The language of the bill is suggestive in our context:

> [And] among the Diverse other Agrementes betwene them [i.e., Langley and Lord Pembroke's Men] in and aboute the same the said Langlie Craftelie and Cunninglye intendinge and goinge aboute to Circumvent and overreache your said Subjectes in and aboute the takinge of the said Howse moved and Required that your said Subjectes woulde become bounde to him the said Langlie in some great penaltye withe Condicioun that they should not absent themselves nor playe els where but in the said plaiehouse Called the Swan as aforesaid whereuppon your highnes said Subjectes (nothing suspectinge the said Langlie his purpose and dishonest dealing and Craftie Complott whiche now Appeareth verie palpable).

And so forth. (The bill is reproduced in its entirely in C. W. Wallace, "The Swan Theatre and the Earl of Pembroke's Servants," *Englische Studien* 43 (1910-11): 340-95. The quoted passage occurs on pages 345-46.) Having become "bound" to the fiendish Langley and only subsequently discovering their peril, Pembroke's Men petition a higher, benign authority for release. One of the players listed in the bill happens to be William Bird, who along with Samuel Rowley composed the 1602 additions to *Doctor Faustus* for which Henslowe advanced payment.

12. All quotations of the play are from Christopher Marlowe, *Dr Faustus*, ed. Roma Gill (New York: W. W. Norton, 1989).

13. Greg, *Henslowe Papers*, 66n.

14. W. W. Greg, ed., *Marlowe's Doctor Faustus, 1604-1616: Parallel Texts* (Oxford: Clarendon Press, 1950), 61-62.

15. For the payment, see Foakes, *Henslowe's Diary*, 206. Whether the additions appear in the B-text is, of course, still a matter of dispute. Greg insisted that they do not. His position on this and other matters is challenged by Eric Rasmussen in *A Textual Companion to* Doctor Faustus (New York: Manchester University Press, 1993). My analysis will focus on the A-text, which is probably more Marlovian and to my mind a better play.

16. Foakes, *Henslowe's Diary*, 319-20, 325. A list of playing apparel in the hand of Edward Alleyn includes "Faustus Jerkin his clok" (Foakes, *Henslowe's Diary*, 293). "Hell mouth" is men-

tioned explicitly only in the B-text, where Mephastophilis also tells Faustus: "First wear this girdle, then appear / Invisible to all are here" (Marlowe, *Dr Faustus*, 77). In the A-text, Faustus's invisibility at the pope's court is not attributed to a "girdel" or gown. Perhaps the additions of the B-text were written partly with a view to employing props that had subsequently come into the company's possession. Or perhaps the B-text formally recognizes staging conventions that were already in effect when the A-text was performed at the Rose in 1594.

17. Exactly where this "dragon" appears in *Doctor Faustus* is a matter of some dispute. Robert K. Root argued in "Two Notes on *Doctor Faustus*" (*Englische Studien* 43 [1910–11]: 144–49) that the dragon is not used to pull Faustus through the sky. Rather, it is the costume that Mephastophilis wears when he first appears to Faustus. If this is true, then my contention that *all* of the listed properties are provided by Mephastophilis to Faustus must be modified, though Mephastophilis himself will become in this case a special effect.

18. Henslowe states he "bought" only the "robe for to goo invisibell." The other items appear on the lists of costumes and stage properties belonging to the Lord Admiral's Men. And the mere fact that the papers were in Henslowe's possession does not mean that he purchased the listed items for the company. He may have had the lists drawn up in order to record the capital stock of his theatrical tenants, or he may, as landlord, simply have found it prudent to keep a list of expensive properties stored in his theater. One essay does, however, suggest that Henslowe may have used his pawn-broking business to provide costumes and properties for plays at the Rose Theater. See Natasha Korda, "Household Property/Stage Property: Henslowe as Pawnbroker," *Theatre Journal* 48 (1996): 181–95.

A further note on the "robe": it is included in a list of costumes that Henslowe bought after April 3, 1598. Greg regards it as "probable" (*Marlowe's Doctor Faustus*, 11–12) and Carol Chillington Rutter simply states as fact (*Documents of the Rose Theater*, 124) that *Doctor Faustus* was withdrawn from the stage after Alleyn's retirement in 1597. If this is the case, then the robe cannot have been purchased for, or even initially employed in, productions of *Faustus*. However, the retirement of the play in 1597 is purely conjectural, since Henslowe stops recording daily receipts, and with it the records of individual play performances, by that time.

Of course, whoever furnished costumes and stage properties for *Doctor Faustus* would have to provide far more than the items I have listed, and not only to the actor (Alleyn) playing Faustus. My point is that the expenses large enough to be recorded—those properties involving what we might call "special effects" designed specifically for the play—correspond to those that, in the text of the play itself, Mephastophilis provides to, or manifests for, Faustus. Lena Cowen Orlin argues that Henslowe's inventory of stage properties "amounts to being a list of theatrical fittings and that there were other, now lost, accountings for moveables." See Orlin, "Things with Little Social Life (Henslowe's Theatrical Properties and Elizabethan Household Fittings)," in *Staged Properties in Early Modern English Drama*, ed. Jonathan Gil Harris and Natasha Korda (New York: Cambridge University Press, 2002), 99–128. Quotation from p. 114.

19. To be more precise: for a playwright such as Marlowe, who was not himself a member of an acting company, it made little difference whether he sold his plays directly to the players or contracted with an intermediary such as Henslowe.

20. T. McAlindon, *Doctor Faustus: Divine in Show* (New York: Twayne, 1994), 13. In his book *Christopher Marlowe* (London: Macmillan, 1991), Roger Sales offers a reading of the play in which Faustus is a playwright and Lucifer is a Renaissance prince (pp. 133–60).

21. See Emily Stockard, "The Soul as Commodity: Materialism in *Doctor Faustus*," *Renaissance Papers* (2012): 21–30.

22. C. B. Macpherson, *The Political Theory of Possessive Individualism, Hobbes to Locke* (Oxford: Oxford University Press, 1962).

23. Cited in Jonathan Gil Harris and Natasha Korda, "Introduction: Towards a Materialist Account of Stage Properties," in Harris and Korda, *Staged Properties in Early Modern English Drama*, 6.

24. See Joseph Loewenstein, *Ben Jonson and Possessive Authorship* (Cambridge: Cambridge University Press, 2002), 177-78. Jonson's "Expostulation with Inigo Jones" develops the mind-body opposition in a way that compares Jones's spectacles to magical conjuration (11, 49-50, and 88-90).

25. See Loewenstein, *Ben Jonson*, 59-61.

26. I by no means intend, of course, to suggest any correlation between the level of a playwright's psychic investment in his or her work and the quality of work produced, or to insinuate that playwrights who wrote at a faster pace than Marlowe produced inferior work.

27. Loewenstein, *Ben Jonson and Possessive Authorship*.

28. For an illuminating, materialist account of the prehistory of copyright, see Joseph Loewenstein, *The Author's Due: Printing and the Prehistory of Copyright* (Chicago: University of Chicago Press, 2002).

29. A partial acknowledgment and amelioration of this fact was the institution of the "benefit" performance, in which the playwright received a certain portion of the receipts from one of the first days' performances. But there is no evidence that this practice yet existed when *Doctor Faustus* was written. I should add that the fact of economic alienation does not necessarily imply that playwrights were indigent, or that they were unhappy with the prices they received for their plays, which could rise to £20 in the early seventeenth century—a tidy sum.

30. On speech acts and magic in *Doctor Faustus*, see Eric Byville, "How to Do Witchcraft Tragedy with Speech Acts," *Comparative Drama* 45, no. 2 (2011): 1-33; Daniel Gates, "Unpardonable Sins: The Hazards of Performative Language in the Tragic Cases of Francesco Spiera and *Doctor Faustus*," *Comparative Drama* 38, no. 1 (2004): 59-81; Genevieve Guenther, "Why Devils Came When Faustus Called Them," *Modern Philology* 109, no. 1 (2011): 46-70; Andrew Sofer, "How to Do Things with Devils: Conjuring Performatives in *Doctor Faustus*," *Theatre Journal* 61 (2009): 1-21; and David Hawkes, *The Faust Myth: Religion and the Rise of Representation* (New York: Palgrave Macmillan, 2007).

31. The literature on *Doctor Faustus* and Protestantism is obviously extensive. For a recent overview, see Kristen Poole, "*Doctor Faustus* and Reformation Theology," in *Early Modern English Drama*, ed. Garrett A. Sullivan Jr., Patrick Cheney, and Andrew Hadfield (Oxford: Oxford University Press, 2005), 96-107. On Marlowe and Luther, see Clifford Davidson, "Doctor Faustus of Wittenberg," *Studies in Philology* 59, no. 3 (1962): 514-23; and Lynne Robertson, "Marlowe and Luther," *American Notes and Queries* 12, no. 4 (1999): 3-6.

32. On Calvinist influences on the play, see Pauline Honderich, "John Calvin and Doctor Faustus," *Modern Language Review* 68, no. 1 (1973): 1-13.

33. J. L. Austin, *How to Do Things with Words*, 2nd ed. (Cambridge, MA: Harvard University Press, 1975), 14.

34. For the text of the act and a discussion of its provenance and meaning, see Hugh Gazzard, "An Act to Restrain Abuses of Players (1606)," *Review of English Studies*, n.s., 61, no. 251 (2009): 495-528.

35. I explore this story and its literary implication at greater length in Richard Halpern, "'Pining Their Maws': Female Readers and the Erotic Ontology of the Text in Shakespeare's *Venus and Adonis*," in *Venus and Adonis: Critical Essays*, ed. Philip C. Kolin (New York: Garland, 1997), 377-88.

36. Harry Levin, *The Overreacher: A Study of Christopher Marlowe* (Cambridge, MA: Harvard University Press, 1952), 120-21.

37. Greg, *Marlowe's Doctor Faustus*, 33, 39.

38. The B-text, which probably incorporates the Bird-Rowley additions of 1602, employs spectacle more generously. Either the authors failed to grasp Marlowe's original intention, or the economic exigencies of theatrical revival demanded new and improved special effects to lure audiences back to an old play.

39. I suspect that this equivocation over whether Faustus's magic can summon up the "real presence" of Alexander also offers a refracted parody of the magic of the Eucharist.

40. See E. K. Chambers, *The Elizabethan Stage*, 4 vols. (Oxford: Clarendon Press, 1923), 3:423-24.

41. Anthony Munday, *A Second and Third Blast of Retrait from Plaies and Theaters* (1580), in *The English Drama and Stage*, ed. W. C. Hazlitt (1869; rpt. New York: Burt Franklin, n.d.), 139.

42. The phrase "theater of night" will inevitably recall the so-called school of night with which Marlowe was associated. See M. C. Bradbrook, *The School of Night: A Study of the Literary Relationships of Sir Walter Raleigh* (New York: Russell and Russell, 1965), esp. 101–24.

43. For another recent approach to ethics in the play, see Lowell Gallagher, "Faustus's Blood and the (Messianic) Question of Ethics," *English Literary History* 73 (2006): 1–29.

44. For his most direct formulation of the matter, see Saint Augustine, *Enchiridion*, translated as *Faith, Hope, and Charity*, trans. Louis A. Arand (New York: Newman Press, 1978), sec. 11, 18–19.

45. See *The "De Malo" of Thomas Aquinas*, trans. Richard Regan (New York: Oxford University Press, 2001), 63–65.

46. *De Malo*, sec. 14, 22.

47. Saint Augustine, *Enchiridion*, sec. 11.

48. Saint Augustine, *The City of God against the Pagans, IV. Books XII–XV*, trans. Philip Levine (Cambridge: Harvard University Press, 1968), XII. vi (23).

49. Saint Augustine, *The City of God against the Pagans, III. Books VII–XI*, trans. Davis S. Wiesen, XI. ix (463).

50. Saint Augustine, *City of God, IV*, XII. ix (39).

51. Saint Augustine, *City of God, IV*, XII, vii (33).

52. Augustine's Aristotelianism will not allow him to imagine an *absolute* void, however. What precedes creation is "not complete and utter nothingness: there was this formless matter entirely without feature . . . an intermediate stage between form and non-existence, some formless thing that was next to being nothing at all." Saint Augustine, *Confessions*, trans. R. S. Pine-Coffin (London: Penguin, 1931), XII, 3 and 6 (pp. 282, 283). On the resistance to imagining nothingness in early Western thought, see Charles Seife, *Zero: The Biography of a Dangerous Idea* (New York: Penguin, 2000), 25–61.

53. See Alain Badiou, *Ethics: An Essay on the Understanding of Evil*, trans. Peter Hallward (New York: Verso, 2001).

54. Norman Austin, *Helen of Troy and Her Shameless Phantom* (Ithaca, NY: Cornell University Press, 1994), 4, 34.

55. Homer, *The Iliad*, trans. Richmond Lattimore (Chicago: University of Chicago Press, 1962), 104. The Greek text is 3.158.

56. I am quoting Austin, *Helen*, 10. The relevant passage in the *Odyssey* is 4.561–69.

57. See Graham Hammill, *Sexuality and Form: Caravaggio, Marlowe, and Bacon* (Chicago: University of Chicago Press, 2000), 119–21. The fact that a boy actor plays the part of Helen naturally comes into play here as well.

58. On Helen as succubus, see Hammill, *Sexuality and Form*, 119–20.

59. Plato, *Complete Works*, ed. John M. Cooper (Indianapolis: Hackett, 1997), 1194.

60. Both works are translated in Michael Gagarin and Paul Woodruff, eds., *Early Greek Political Thought from Homer to the Sophists* (Cambridge: Cambridge University Press, 1995), 190–95 and 206–9.

61. Quoted in Austin, *Helen*, 24n1.

62. Ibid., 144.

63. Euripides, *Helen*, trans. Richmond Lattimore, in *Euripides II*, ed. David Grene and Richmond Lattimore (Chicago: University of Chicago Press, 1956). Greek text from Euripides, *Helen, Phoenician Women, Orestes*, ed. and trans. David Kovacs (Cambridge, MA: Harvard University Press, 2002).

64. Indeed, the phrase itself originates in Gorgias's oration "On Not Being," and is then quoted by Sextus Empiricus, by which path it might have made its way to Marlowe—although a Ramist route is more likely.

65. For an extended discussion, see Charles Segal, "Gorgias and the Psychology of the *Logos*,"

Harvard Studies in Classical Philology 66 (1962): 99-155. Somewhat surprisingly, Gorgias's enco-mium posits Helen as the victim of poetic and rhetorical force rather than its origin.

66. Theodor W. Adorno, *Aesthetic Theory*, trans. Robert Hullot-Kentor (Minneapolis: University of Minnesota Press, 1997), 78.

67. Ibid., 81.

68. Austin, *Helen*, 24-25. For the opposing view of Helen as mere goods, see Matthew Gumpert, *Grafting Helen: The Abduction of the Classical Past* (Madison: University of Wisconsin Press, 2001), 58-68. Both Gumpert's and Austin's books were quite helpful for my discussion of Helen.

69. The connection was made by Hans Meyer in his book *Thomas Mann: Werk und Entwicklung* (Berlin: Volk und Welt, 1950), 370, where he argues that the "middle devil" in the novel's famous twenty-fifth chapter may be based on Adorno. Meyer's claim has been challenged by Michael Maar, who argues that Mann had Mahler, not Adorno, in mind. See Maar, "Teddy and Tommy: The Masks of *Doctor Faustus*," *New Left Review* 20 (March-April 2003): 113-30. What is beyond dispute is that Mann borrowed extensively from Adorno's *Philosophy of Music* for his *Doctor Faustus*.

CHAPTER FOUR

1. The Lord Mayor and Aldermen to the Privy Council, July 28, 1597, in E. K. Chambers, ed., *The Elizabethan Stage*, 4 vols. (Oxford: Clarendon Press, 1923), 4:322.

2. William Shakespeare, *King Henry IV, Part 1*, ed. David Scott Kastan (London: Arden Shake-speare, 2002), 1.2.194-95.

3. Louis Montrose, *The Purpose of Playing: Shakespeare and the Cultural Politics of the Elizabe-than Theater* (Chicago: University of Chicago Press, 1996), 19.

4. Actually, a variety of verbs, such as *keep, use, exercise, practice, play, shew, enact, recite, per-sonate, act,* and *present,* are found in contemporary documents. Some of these emphasize theater's resemblance to craft activity instead of its opposition to it. For a nuanced discussion, see Mary Thomas Crane, "What Was Performance?," *Criticism* 43, no. 2 (2002): 169-87. For more on the re-lation between theater and the *techne* of artisanal and scientific practice, see Henry S. Turner, *The English Renaissance Stage: Geometry, Poetics, and the Practical Spatial Arts, 1580-1630* (New York: Oxford University Press, 2006).

5. Andrew Gurr, *The Shakespearean Stage, 1574-1642*, 3rd ed. (Cambridge: Cambridge University Press, 1992), 99.

6. I am drawing throughout this paragraph on Lacan's seminar on *Hamlet*. See "Hamlet, par Lacan," in *Ornicar?* 24 (1981): 7-31; 25 (1982): 13-35; and 26-27 (1983): 7-44. See also my dis-cussion of this seminar in Richard Halpern, *Shakespeare among the Moderns* (Ithaca, NY: Cornell University Press, 1997), 254-68, and esp. 263.

7. Jacques Derrida takes up the politico-ethical ramifications of Hamlet's "time . . . out of joint" in *Spectres of Marx: The State of the Debt, the Work of Mourning, and the New International,* trans. Peggy Kamuf (New York: Routledge, 1994). I have critiqued Derrida's reading of *Hamlet* and Marx in "An Impure History of Ghosts: Derrida, Marx, Shakespeare," in *Marxist Shakespeares*, ed. Jean Howard and Scott Cutler Shershow (New York: Routledge, 2000), 31-52. The present essay further elaborates certain lines of argument developed in that earlier piece.

8. For political economy, production and consumption are likewise interlinked: "Production is also immediately consumption. Twofold consumption, subjective and objective: the individual not only develops his abilities in production, but also expends them, uses them up in the act of production, just as natural procreation is a consumption of life forces. Secondly: consumption of the means of production, which become worn out through use, and are partly (e.g., in combustion) dissolved into their element again. Likewise, consumption of raw material, which loses its natural form and composition by being used up. The act of production is therefore in all its moments an act of consumption." Karl Marx, *Grundrisse: Foundations of the Critique of Political Economy (Rough Draft)*, trans. Martin Nicolaus (London: Penguin, 1993), 90.

9. While I am reading this theme of physical transformation "forward" toward the language of political economy, I should note that Shakespeare could conceivably have derived it, directly or indirectly, from the works of Giordano Bruno. The notion that Hamlet's meditations on the work of death, in the graveyard scene especially, may originate in Bruno's theme of "cosmic metabolism" was more appealing to nineteenth-century Shakespeare scholars than to subsequent ones. See Hilary Gatti, *The Renaissance Drama of Knowledge: Giordano Bruno in England* (Abington and New York: Routledge, 2013), 153, 168-88. I borrow the term "cosmic metabolism" from Dorothea Waley Singer, *Giordano Bruno: His Life and Thought* (New York: Henry Schuman, 1950), 71-74.

10. All quotations of *Hamlet* are from the Arden edition, ed. Harold Jenkins (New York: Routledge, 1982).

11. As Julia Lupton rightly points out to me, natural creatures in *Hamlet* do observe a "theopolitical temporality" that respects differences between day and night, among others. For example:

> The cock, that is the trumpet of the morn,
> Doth with his lofty and shrill-sounding throat
> Awake the god of day, and at his warning,
> Whether in sea or fire, in earth or air,
> Th'extravagant and erring spirit hies
> To his confine.
>   (1.1.155-60)

Or again:

> The glow-worm shows the matin to be near
> And gins to pale his uneffectual fire.
>   (1.5.89-90)

All that being noted, the worms and grubs that feed on corpses seem to do so day and night. Equally unconscious of time of day is the blind underground burrowing of moles. Nature's work of death, in other words—the processes of rotting, decomposition, and recomposition—occupies an elemental level that in some ways falls "beneath" distinctions of natural time.

12. Julia Reinhard Lupton, "Hamlet among Friends and Enemies: Shakespeare and Schmitt" (unpublished essay), 12.

13. For more on the concept of the multitude, see Paolo Virno, *Grammar of the Multitude*, trans. Isabella Bertoletti et al. (New York: Semiotext(e), 2004); Antonio Negri, *The Savage Anomaly: The Power of Spinoza's Metaphysics and Politics*, trans. Michael Hardt (Minneapolis: University of Minnesota Press, 1991); and Michael Hardt and Antonio Negri, *Multitude: War and Democracy in the Age of Empire* (New York: Penguin, 2004).

14. In this sense, the king's body is also a maternal body, as Hamlet will suggest at 4.3.52-56. Compare *Julius Caesar* 2.2.76-79.

15. "Labour is, first of all, a process between man and nature, a process by which man, through his own actions, mediates, regulates and controls the metabolism between himself and nature." Karl Marx, *Capital: A Critique of Political Economy*, trans. Ben Fowkes (New York: Random House, 1997). Cf. Hannah Arendt, *The Human Condition*, 2nd ed. (Chicago: University of Chicago Press, 1998), 98-100. Arendt's condensation of Marx's statement so that labor simply becomes "man's metabolism with nature" is, however, highly tendentious, since in Marx's formulation, labor subjects the interaction with nature to human intentionality and action. It thereby establishes a break as well as a continuity with natural process, a crucial dialectical subtlety that is misleadingly (and, I think, maliciously) erased in Arendt's treatment.

16. Here as elsewhere in this essay I am deeply indebted to Margreta de Grazia's book *"Hamlet" without Hamlet* (Cambridge: Cambridge University Press, 2007). Not only in her focus on land and in her reading of the role of the grave maker (and his relation to Hamlet) but also in her meditations on anonymity, de Grazia has proven inspirational for my work. I differ from her only in insisting that Hamlet remains the center of *Hamlet*—that his paradigmatic status as modern indi-

vidual is conditioned and contextualized rather than subverted by the play's attention to impersonal process. If, as de Grazia claims, "Hamlet's disengagement from the land-driven plot of the play is the very precondition of the modernity ascribed to him after 1800" (de Grazia, *"Hamlet" without Hamlet*, 4), my essay attempts to provide positive conditions for this in the rise of political economy as symptom of capitalist production rather than merely negative ones (i.e., modernity's disengagement from landed values). Moreover, since the philosophical tradition I discuss here precedes as well as postdates the play, it has its own historical claims, though doubtless less weighty than what de Grazia so meticulously and compellingly details.

17. On *Hamlet* and mining/digging, see Martin Harries, *Scare Quotes from Shakespeare: Marx, Keynes, and the Language of Reenchantment* (Stanford, CA: Stanford University Press, 2000), 93-124.

18. A. W. Schlegel, *Course of Lectures on Dramatic Art and Literature*, trans. John Black (London, 1846; repr., New York: AMS, 1973), 404.

19. Sigmund Freud, *The Interpretation of Dreams*, in *The Standard Edition of the Complete Psychological Works of Sigmund Freud*, ed. James Strachey et al., 24 vols. (London: Hogarth Press, 1953-74), 4:264.

20. In Saxo Grammaticus and Belleforest, Hamlet attends a feast given by the English king and is miraculously able to intuit that the wheat from which the bread was made had been grown in fields drenched in human blood, and that the pigs from which the pork came had fed on cadavers. See Geoffrey Bullough, *Narrative and Dramatic Sources of Shakespeare*, 8 vols. (New York: Columbia University Press, 1973), 7:67-68, 108-9. That Hamlet is able to divine these facts may have suggested to Shakespeare a mind attuned to such transformations. In the sources, Hamlet likewise does not merely imagine a Polonius dined on by worms but cuts the body of the dead Polonius-figure into pieces and feeds them to hogs (Bullough, *Narrative and Dramatic Sources of Shakespeare*, 7:65, 94).

21. The dream work "does not think, calculate or judge in any way at all; it restricts itself to giving things a new form." Freud, *Interpretation of Dreams*, 507.

22. See Aristotle, *Nicomachean Ethics*, trans. Christopher Rowe (New York: Oxford University Press, 2002), 250-54.

23. Hannah Arendt, "Part I: Thinking," in *The Life of the Mind*, one-volume edition (New York: Harcourt, 1978).

24. I should admit that in reading the situation thus I appear to be "siding" with Freud, whose deterministic model of the psyche is inhospitable to Arendt's belief in the freedom of thought. And perhaps this is one reason why Arendt has nothing direct to say about Freud in *The Life of the Mind*—a rather startling omission. (But see 34-36 and 74, where Arendt indirectly disposes of psychoanalysis by compartmentalizing mind from soul and body.) It is beyond the bounds of this chapter—and my own intellectual capacities—to decide this disagreement. I would only remark that it may be precipitous to cast Arendt in the role of idealist. For Freud, the radical force of the unconscious consists in its capacity to interrupt the continuity of thought. For Arendt, the radical force of thinking consists in its capacity to interrupt the continuity of the world.

25. *Mirror* (Edinburgh), April 18, 1780, 394.

26. William Richardson, *Essays on Shakespeare's Dramatic Characters of "Richard the Third," "King Lear," and "Timon of Athens." To which are added, an Essay on the Faults of Shakespeare; and, Additional Observations on the Character of Hamlet* (London, 1784; repr., New York: AMS, 1974), 162, 167-68.

27. *The Bee, or Literary Weekly Intelligencer*, May 11, 1791. Quoted in Smith, *Lectures on Rhetoric and Belles Lettres*, in *The Glasgow Edition of the Works and Correspondence of Adam Smith*, 6 vols. (Oxford: Clarendon Press, 1983), 4:229.

28. Smith, *Lectures on Rhetoric and Belles Lettres*, 121. The ellipses mark blanks in the manuscript, and the editors of the Glasgow Edition surmise that the blanks "probably refer to the Porter Scene in *Macbeth*, II.iii." If so, this comports nicely with the analysis that follows, since the Porter is another unproductive laborer or menial servant.

29. For a discussion of these and other possibilities, see Roslyn Lander Knutson, *Playing Companies and Commerce in Shakespeare's Time* (Cambridge: Cambridge University Press, 2005), 113–23.

30. William Empson, *Essays on Shakespeare*, ed. David B. Pine (Cambridge: Cambridge University Press, 1986), 81.

31. Elmer Edgar Stoll, *Hamlet: An Historical and Comparative Study* (1919; repr., New York: Gordian Press, 1968), 2.

32. Compare Schlegel: "The criminals are at last punished, but, as it were, by an accidental blow, and not in the solemn way requisite to convey to the world a warning example of justice." *Course of Lectures on Dramatic Art and Literature*, 406. By contrast to Shakespeare's, Belleforest's Hamlet does plan a spectacular revenge: "I hope to take such and so great vengeance, that these countreyes shall for ever speake therof." Bullough, *Narrative and Dramatic Sources of Shakespeare*, 7:97.

CHAPTER FIVE

1. A translation appears in Watson Kirkconnell, *That Invincible Samson: The Theme of Samson Agonistes in World Literature with Translations of the Major Analogues* (Toronto: University of Toronto Press, 1966). Quotation from p. 92.

2. All quotations of the play are from [John] Milton, *Samson Agonistes*, ed. F. T. Prince (Oxford: Oxford University Press, 1957).

3. *The Complete Works of Shakespeare*, 5th ed., ed. David Bevington (New York: Pearson Longman, 2005).

4. The motif of the magic mill is 565 in the Aarne-Thompson classification system.

5. For these parallels see William Riley Parker, *Milton's Debt to Greek Tragedy in Samson Agonistes* (Baltimore: Johns Hopkins University Press, 1937), 89, 178, and, more generally, 177–85; Joseph Wittreich, *Shifting Contexts: Interpreting "Samson Agonistes"* (Pittsburgh: Duquesne University Press, 2002), 199; and Derek N. C. Wood, *"Exiled from Light": Divine Law, Morality, and Violence in Milton's* Samson Agonistes (Toronto: University of Toronto Press, 2001), 162. Parallels between Samson and Hercules, another laboring hero, were drawn by early modern commentators. See Wittreich, *Shifting Contexts*, 50–51.

6. These parallels are worked out in the commentary to Thomas Stanley's 1633 edition of Aeschylus. See Margaret Arnold, "Thomas Stanley's *Aeschylus*: Renaissance Practical Criticism of Greek Tragedy," *Illinois Classical Studies* 9, no. 2 (1984): 229–49.

7. Parker, *Milton's Debt*, 88.

8. See Joseph Wittreich, *Interpreting "Samson Agonistes"* (Princeton, NJ: Princeton University Press, 1986), 44–45, 110–12. Wittreich's attempts to demonstrate parallels between Samson and the Antichrist were criticized in reviews by Anthony Low and Philip Gallagher on evidentiary grounds. See Wood, *Exiled from Light*, 9–12. See also Wittreich, *Shifting Contexts*, 108.

9. At the same time, certain elements in Milton's poem work to undo this association. *Techne*, especially metallurgy, gets associated with his foe Harapha rather than with Samson. When challenging Harapha to a fight, Samson mocks his opponent's reliance on (and apparent infatuation with) elaborate armor:

> Then put on all thy gorgeous arms, thy Helmet
> And Brigandine of brass, thy broad Habergeon,
> Vant-brass and Greaves, and Gauntlet, add thy Spear
> A Weaver's beam, and seven-times-folded shield;
> I only with an Oaken staff will meet thee,
>
> (1119–23)

Likewise, Samson had done his slaughter at Rameth-Lechi "with what trivial weapons came to hand, / The Jaw of a dead Ass, his sword of bone" (142–45). In this sense Samson is pretechnological, accomplishing his heroic deeds with natural objects lying about rather than with crafted weapons. His avoidance of the shears perhaps partakes of this general aversion to the metallic. It is as if Milton felt compelled to displace the technological associations inevitably invoked by the figure of Prometheus onto Harapha as Samson's foil. Harapha, of course, gets associated with the classical Giants—who were born fully armored and with spear in hand—rather than with the Titans (1247–49). By threatening to defeat the armored Harapha with his "Oaken staff," Samson (or rather, Milton speaking through him) may allude to Hercules's defeat of the armored Alcyonus, eldest of the Giants, using only his club.

10. The phrase "carnal Israel" comes from Saint Augustine, *Tractatus adversus Judaeos* vii.9. See Daniel Boyarin, *Carnal Israel: Reading Sex in Talmudic Culture* (Berkeley: University of California Press, 1995).

11. See, e.g., Stanley Fish, *How Milton Works* (Cambridge, MA: Harvard University Press, 2001), 408.

12. The connection between this and Hamlet's circular patterns of thought, described in the previous chapter, should be obvious. In this context it is worth noting that the original, Norse version of Hamlet was likewise associated with a mill.

13. Kirkconnell, *That Invincible Samson*, 121.

14. Wittreich, *Interpreting "Samson Agonistes,"* 45.

15. Wittreich, *Shifting Contexts*, 108.

16. For a sampling of such responses, see Wittreich, *Interpreting "Samson Agonistes,"* 79, 283–84; Wood, *Exiled from Light*, 49, 166–91; Mary Ann Radzinowicz, *Toward* Samson Agonistes: *The Growth of the Poet's Mind* (Princeton, NJ: Princeton University Press, 1978), 107–8.

17. This dreary debate was launched in print by John C. Carey, "A Work in Praise of Terrorism? September 11 and *Samson Agonistes*," *Times Literary Supplement*, September 6, 2002, 15–16. See also Feisal G. Mohamed, "Confronting Religious Violence: *Samson Agonistes*," *PMLA* 120, no. 2 (2005): 327–40, and several of the essays in Michael Lieb and Albert C. Labiola, eds., *Milton in the Age of Fish: Essays on Authorship, Text, and Terrorism* (Pittsburgh: Duquesne University Press, 2006). The fact that this debate was inspired by, and continued to revolve around, questions arising from 9/11 testifies to the dispiriting state of political discourse among most Miltonists. Why, I can't help wondering, was an act of Muslim terrorism required to first raise the question of whether Milton's Samson was a terrorist? The necessary political framework was amply supplied as long ago as 1947, when an extensive campaign of terror, including the bombing of schools and hospitals, was undertaken to clear away the resident Palestinian population during the founding of the state of Israel. But the concept of the "Jewish terrorist" is still essentially foreclosed from American political discourse, which is why the figure of the Muslim must always be invoked. Not to mention the rather complex (but of course unaddressed) political questions surrounding the very concept of "terrorism" as presently deployed by government and mainstream media.

18. On sexual associations, see Jeffrey Shoulson, *Milton and the Rabbis: Hebraism, Hellenism, and Christianity* (New York: Columbia University Press, 2001), 254. On the mill and interpretation, see Rodney Delasanta, "The Mill in Chaucer's *Reeve's Tale*," *Chaucer Review* 36, no. 2 (2002): 270–76.

19. John Guillory, "The Father's House: *Samson Agonistes* in Its Historical Moment," in *Re-membering Milton: Essays on the Texts and the Traditions*, ed. Mary Nyquist and Margaret W. Ferguson (New York: Methuen, 1987), 152. "Labor," notes Guillory, "is the shadow cast by all of Samson's actions" (159). Blair Hoxby refers to Samson's "work of destruction" in *Mammon's Music: Literature and Economics in the Age of Milton* (New Haven, CT: Yale University Press, 2002), 228.

20. Wittreich, *Shifting Contexts*, 268.

21. Radzinowicz, *Toward* Samson Agonistes, 100.

22. On the relation between *Samson Agonistes* and Benjamin's *Origins of German Tragic Drama*, see Victoria Kahn, "Aesthetics as Critique: Tragedy and Trauerspiel in *Samson Agonistes*," in *Reading Renaissance Ethics*, ed. Marshall Grossman (New York: Routledge, 2007), 104–30; and Julia Reinhard Lupton, *Citizen-Saints: Shakespeare and Political Theology* (Chicago: University of Chicago Press, 2005), 181–204.

23. Søren Kierkegaard, *Fear and Trembling: A Philosophical Masterpiece* (Radford, VA: Wilder Publications, 2008), 40.

24. Brendan Quigley, "The Distant Hero of *Samson Agonistes*," *English Literary History* 72, no. 3 (2005): 529-51.

25. Kierkegaard, *Fear and Trembling*, 44.

26. John Rumrich, "Milton and the Excluded Middle," in *Altering Eyes: New Perspectives on Samson Agonistes*, ed. Joseph Wittreich (Newark: University of Delaware Press, 2002), 307-32. Quotation from p. 324.

27. Rumrich, "Milton and the Excluded Middle," 323. Wood, *Exiled from Light*, 152-53, discusses Samson and Dalila as mirror images, and John Guillory describes Dalila as "Samson's female double" in "Dalila's House: *Samson Agonistes* and the Sexual Division of Labor," in *Rewriting the Renaissance: The Discourses of Sexual Difference in Early Modern Europe*, ed. Margaret W. Ferguson, Maureen Quilligan, and Nancy Vickers (Chicago: University of Chicago Press, 1986), 111.

28. From a strictly theological standpoint, no such universalizing framework is necessary. God's decision to make Israel his chosen nation is strictly speaking unconditioned and unconditional. It does not depend on or convey upon Israel any ethical superiority compared to other nations but is a pure expression of divine will. Indeed, there is an element of what Kierkegaard would call the absurd in God's decision. At the same time, this fact cannot simply cancel the significance of ethical questions in Milton's play. What appears, then, at first as an oscillation between national perspectives reproduces itself at a higher level as a conflict between theological and ethical perspectives.

29. Wood, *Exiled from Light*, 69.

30. Alain Badiou, *Saint Paul: The Foundation of Universalism*, trans. Ray Brassier (Stanford, CA: Stanford University Press, 2003); Daniel Boyarin, *A Radical Jew: Paul and the Politics of Identity* (Berkeley: University of California Press, 1994).

31. Boyarin, *A Radical Jew*, 7.

32. On Philo, see ibid., 26-27, 80.

33. William Kerrigan hears (correctly, in my view) echoes of childbirth as well as defecation in these lines:

> Thus utter'd, straining all his nerves he bow'd;
> as with the force of the winds and water pent,
> when Mountains tremble, those two massy Pillars
> With horrible convulsion to and fro,
> he tugg'd, he shook, till down they came and drew
> The whole roof after them with burst of thunder
> upon the heads of all who sat beneath.
>   (1646-52)

William Kerrigan, *The Prophetic Milton* (Charlottesville: University Press of Virginia, 1974), 217. Compare Manoa, who laments: "What windy joy this day I had conceived / Hopeful of his Delivery, which now proves / Abortive" (1573-76).

34. On the systematic imitation of Greek tragic form in the structure of *Samson Agonistes*, see Parker, *Milton's Debt*, 17.

35. I should mention yet another precovenantal universalism available to Milton: the so-called Noachide laws. According to rabbinical commentators, God delivered a set of laws to Noah (or to Noah's sons, or to Adam) that would apply to all human beings. The Noachide laws are superseded only for the Hebrews by Mosaic law, but they are enjoined upon the rest of mankind. Milton would have learned of these laws through John Selden's *De Iure Naturali & Gentium, Iuxta Disciplinam Ebraeorum* (1640). Indeed, Samson (or rather, Milton through Samson) "cites" the title of Selden's book while berating Dalila: "If aught against my life / Thy country sought of thee, it sought unjustly, / Against the law of nature, law of nations" (888-90). Despite this, it seems to me that the Noachide laws play little to no role in Milton's poem, and it also seems to me that recent

commentators have considerably exaggerated the supposedly tolerationist dimension of these laws (which is not to deny that their reception may have contributed to the development of religious toleration in Europe). For a discussion of Selden's *De Iure Naturali & Gentium*, see G. J. Toomer, *John Selden: A Life in Scholarship*, 2 vols. (Oxford: Oxford University Press, 2009), 2:490–562. For a discussion of the Noachide laws and religious toleration, see Eric Nelson, *The Hebrew Republic: Jewish Sources and the Transformation of European Political Thought* (Cambridge, MA: Harvard University Press, 2010), 88–137. On Selden and *Samson Agonistes*, see Jason Rosenblatt, *Renaissance England's Chief Rabbi: John Selden* (Oxford: Oxford University Press, 2008), 93–111, 135–57.

36. *Collected Works of Karl Marx and Friedrich Engels*, vol. 1 (New York: International Publishers, 1975–), 30.

37. Hoxby, *Mammon's Music*, 217.

38. Ibid., 232.

39. Christopher Hill, *The Experience of Defeat: Milton and Some Contemporaries* (London: Faber and Faber, 1984).

CHAPTER SIX

1. The problem is more interesting than this, though, since often the *same* literary talents failed on the stage and succeeded at the novel. See David Kurnick, *Empty Houses: Theatrical Failure and the Novel* (Princeton, NJ: Princeton University Press, 2012). Likewise, some of the great lyric poets of the period produced tragic drama of significantly lesser renown. On the problem of action in Romantic drama, see William Jewett, *Fatal Autonomy: Romantic Drama and the Rhetoric of Agency* (Ithaca, NY: Cornell University Press, 1997).

2. On the English novel and political economy, see Catherine Gallagher, *The Body Economic: Life, Death, and Sensation in Political Economy and the Victorian Novel* (Princeton, NJ: Princeton University Press, 2006); James Thompson, *Models of Value: Eighteenth-Century Political Economy and the Novel* (Durham, NC: Duke University Press, 1996); Eleanor Courtmanche, *The "Invisible Hand" and British Fiction, 1818–1860* (London: Palgrave Macmillan, 2011). Of these three books, the concerns of Courtmanche's are closest to my own.

3. For a far more sophisticated account of this relation than the one I am suggesting, see Rae Greiner, *Sympathetic Realism in Nineteenth-Century British Fiction* (Baltimore: Johns Hopkins University Press, 2012).

4. In "Rhapsody for the Theatre," Alain Badiou speaks of "an invasion of theatre by the novel" in the nineteenth century. By this Badiou means that drama begins to display a desire for completeness, for the status of the book, as opposed to the "not-all" of the properly theatrical text. As will be seen, I understand the novelization of the theater in different though not incompatible terms. See Alain Badiou, *Rhapsody for the Theatre*, trans. Bruno Bosteels (London and New York: Verso, 2013), 49.

5. Norbert Wasiask, *The Scottish Enlightenment and Hegel's Account of "Civil Society"* (Dordrecht and Boston: Kluwers, 1988), 112–13. As Wasiak observes, a direct knowledge on Hegel's part of Ricardo and Say is less likely (133).

6. Hegel's *Lectures on Aesthetics*, published posthumously in 1835, draws on lectures that Hegel gave in Heidelberg in 1818 and in Berlin in 1820–21, 1826, and 1828–29. The 1835 edition was based on a lost series of lecture notes compiled by Hegel's student Heinrich Gustav Hotho. There is some critical controversy surrounding the question of whether Hotho's edition distorts Hegel's thought. "Hegel's Aesthetics," *Stanford Encyclopedia of Philosophy*, http://plato.stanford.edu/entries/hegel-aesthetics/.

One study that does attempt to relate the *Lectures on Aesthetics* to the *Philosophy of Right* is Derek W. M. Barker, *Tragedy and Citizenship: Conflict, Reconciliation, and Democracy from Haemon to Hegel* (Albany: State University of New York Press, 2009). Barker is critical of the role of reconciliation in both Hegelian aesthetics and ethics, which he sees as leading to an institutional politics rather than a democratic one. Allen Speight, *Hegel, Literature, and the Problem of Agency* (Cambridge: Cambridge University Press, 2001) takes a somewhat different path, showing how Hegel employs tragedy, comedy, and novel to elucidate a distinctive theory of action in the *Phenomenology of Spirit* and then, in a final chapter, following Hegel's theory of action into the *Philosophy of Right*. Neither relates Hegel's theory of tragedy to his treatment of the system of needs in the *Philosophy of Right*.

7. G. W. F. Hegel, *Elements of the Philosophy of Right*, trans. H. B. Nisbet (Cambridge and New York: Cambridge University Press, 1991), 227.

8. Lisa Herzog, *Inventing the Market: Smith, Hegel, and Political Theory* (Oxford and New York: Oxford University Press, 2013), 59.

9. For Smith the spontaneous order of the market arises from, and is to that degree secondary to, the actions of its individual participants. For Hegel, by contrast, the individual is rather a particularized "moment" of the universal, through which it brings itself to actualization.

10. On this point see Raymond Plant, "Hegel and the Political Economy," in *Hegel on Economics and Freedom*, ed. William Maker (Macon, GA: Mercer University Press, 1987), 108.

11. Raymond Plant, "Economic and Social Integration in Hegel's Political Philosophy," in *Hegel's Social and Political Thought: The Philosophy of Objective Spirit*, ed. Donald Phillip Verene (Atlantic Highlands, NJ: Humanities Press, 1980), 81.

12. Merold Westphal, "Hegel's Radical Idealism: Family and State as Ethical Communities," in *The State and Civil Society: Studies in Hegel's Political Philosophy*, ed. Z. A. Pelczynski (Cambridge and New York: Cambridge University Press, 1984), 77-92. Quotation from p. 77.

13. Ibid., 90.

14. This theme is developed in Judith Butler, *Antigone's Claim* (New York: Columbia University Press, 2002).

15. For the philosophical implications of the rabble, see Frank Ruda, *Hegel's Rabble: An Investigation into Hegel's* Philosophy of Right (London: Continuum 2001); for some historical background to the concept, see Gareth Stedman Jones, "Hegel and the Economics of Civil Society," in *Civil Society: History and Possibilities*, ed. Sudipta Kaviraj and Sunil Khilnani (Cambridge and New York: Cambridge University Press, 2001), 126-30.

16. Hegel is discussing the people as "crowd" (*die Menge*) or "mass" (*die Masse*) that assembles outside of its partial communities. But the problem obviously applies more directly to the rabble, who are by definition permanently excluded from those communities.

17. Hegel mentions the *lazzaroni* of Naples in his discussion of the rabble (266), a category included by Marx in his description of the lumpenproletariat in the *Eighteenth Brumaire*.

18. Quoted in Herzog, *Inventing the Market*, 55. Herzog's book explores the differences between Hegel's relatively chaotic and (as she puts it) "Dionysian" vision of the market and Smith's more orderly and optimistic one, as well as the implications of these differences for political theory.

19. G. W. F. Hegel, *Aesthetics: Lectures on Fine Art*, vol. 2, trans. T. M. Knox (Oxford and New York: Oxford University Press, 1975), 979.

20. Ruda, *Hegel's Rabble*, 35-57.

21. In *Art of the Modern Age* (Princeton, NJ: Princeton University Press, 2000), J. M. Schaefer cryptically declares that Hegel's brief discussion of the novel constitutes "the most dazzling pages in the *Aesthetics*" (155), but he does not explain this judgment, and others have been disinclined to agree. For a more balanced treatment, see Benjamin Rutter, *Hegel on the Modern Arts* (Cambridge: Cambridge University Press, 2010), 154-65.

22. Friedrich Schlegel, "Letter about the Novel," in *German Aesthetic and Literary Criticism: The Romantic Ironists and Goethe*, ed. Kathleen M. Wheeler (Cambridge and New York: Cambridge University Press), 78.

23. Goethe, *Wilhelm Meister's Apprenticeship*, excerpted in Wheeler, *German Aesthetic and Literary Criticism*, 234.

24. Significant studies include Michel Chaouli, "Masking and Unmasking: The Ideological Fantasies of the *Eighteenth Brumaire*," *Qui Parle* 3, no. 1 (1989): 53-71; Martin Harries, *Scare Quotes from Shakespeare: Marx, Keynes, and the Language of Reenchantment* (Stanford, CA: Stanford University Press, 2000), 54-124; Peter Hayes, "Utopia and the Lumpenproletariat: Marx's *The Eighteenth Brumaire of Louis Bonaparte*," *Review of Politics* 50, no. 3 (1988): 445-65; Kojin Karatani, *History and Repetition*, ed. Seiji M. Lippit (New York: Columbia University Press, 2012), 1-26; Dominick LaCapra, *Rethinking Intellectual History: Texts, Contexts, Language* (Ithaca, NY: Cornell University Press, 1983), 268-90; Jeffrey Mehlman, *Revolution and Repetition: Marx / Hugo / Balzac* (Berkeley: University of California Press, 1977); John Paul Riquelme, "*The Eighteenth Brumaire* of Karl Marx as Symbolic Action," *History and Theory* 19, no. 1 (1980): 58-72; Dermot Ryan, "The Future of an Allusion: Poïesis in Karl Marx's *The Eighteenth Brumaire of Louis Bonaparte*," *SubStance* 41, no. 3 (2012): 127-46; Peter Stallybrass, "Marx and Heterogeneity: Thinking the Lumpenproletariat," *Representations* 31 (Summer 1990): 69-75; Peter Stallybrass, "'Well-Grubbed, Old Mole': Marx, Hamlet, and the (Un)fixing of Representation," in *Marxist Shakespeares*, ed. Jean E. Howard and Scott Cutler Shershow (London: Routledge, 2001), 16-130; Massimiliano Tomba, *Marx's Temporalities*, trans. Peter D. Thomas and Sara R. Farris (Leiden and Boston: Brill, 2013), 35-59.

25. For a classic study of tragic and comic paradigms in the *Eighteenth Brumaire*, see Hayden White, *Metahistory: The Historical Imagination in Nineteenth-Century Europe* (Baltimore: Johns Hopkins University Press, 1973), 120-27. On the *Eighteenth Brumaire* and the novel, see Mehlman, *Revolution and Repetition*; and Sandy Petrey, "The Reality of Representation: Between Marx and Balzac," *Critical Inquiry* 14, no. 3 (1988): 448-68.

26. See Speight, *Hegel, Literature, and the Problem of Agency*.

27. Mehlman, *Revolution and Repetition*, describes the *Eighteenth Brumaire* as a "strange theoretical novel" (39).

28. S. S. Prawer, *Karl Marx and World Literature* (Oxford: Oxford University Press, 1976), 25, 16.

29. Karl Marx, *The Eighteenth Brumaire of Louis Bonaparte* (New York: International Publishers, 1961), 15.

30. I am preceded by, above all, Martin Harries's wonderful treatment of this topic in *Scare Quotes*.

31. Prawer, *Karl Marx and World Literature*. 22.

32. "Alp" is a nightmare or incubus, but also, literally, an Alp or mountain—the very opposite of the convenient "freien Stücken" out of which action would ideally proceed. In this context it might also invoke the punishment dealt out to the rebellious Giants by the victorious Olympian gods, who turned their gigantic enemies into mountains through the petrifying gaze of Medusa. The "Alps" of the past that weigh down living brains would then be congealed masses of revolutionary force or energy.

33. See Riquelme, "*The Eighteenth Brumaire*," 60-61, on Marx's use of chiasmus.

34. Friedrich Engels, Letter to Marx, December 3, 1951, in Karl Marx and Friedrich Engels, *Collected Works* (New York: International Publishers, 1975-ca. 2004), 38:505.

35. Martin Harries (*Scare Quotes from Shakespeare*, 83) points out that Hegel uses the "old mole" as a figure for the dialectic.

36. Marx, *Early Writings*, trans. Rodney Livingstone and Gregor Benton (New York: Penguin, 1992), 80.

37. Ibid., 98.

38. Riquelme, "*The Eighteenth Brumaire*," 66.

39. In his important article "Marx and Heterogeneity," Peter Stallybrass claims that "in the *Eighteenth Brumaire* Marx begins to think of bourgeois politics in a quite new way; not as the distorted mirror of social relations but as at least one of the fields in which classes are fashioned. Politics is now seen less as a (superstructural) level than as a formative process" (70). While I find this view appealing, I also find little or no evidence in the *Eighteenth Brumaire* to support it.

40. Ryan, "Future of an Allusion."

41. See, e.g., Mehlman, *Revolution and Repetition*; Stallybrass, "Marx and Heterogeneity"; Hayes, "Utopia and the Lumpenproletariat."

42. Ruda, *Hegel's Rabble*, 169–79.

43. Hegel, *Philosophy of Right*, 266.

44. Ruda, *Hegel's Rabble*, 73.

45. Ibid., 61.

46. Ibid., 47.

47. Ibid., 68.

48. Marx and Engels, *Collected Works* 21:99, cited in Stallybrass, "Marx and Heterogeneity," 88–89.

49. Hegel, *Aesthetics: Lectures on Fine Art*, 1220.

50. Ibid., 1199.

51. Ibid., 1199.

52. Stallybrass, "Marx and Heterogeneity," 85.

53. See Mikhail Bakhtin, *Problems of Dostoyevsky's Poetics*, trans. Caryl Emerson (Minneapolis: University of Minnesota Press, 1984). Allen Speight describes the Romantic project of the novel as "one of irony and essential *incompletion*." Speight, *Hegel*, 110.

54. Jessica Milner Davis, *Farce* (London: Methuen, 1978), 88.

55. Ibid., 13.

56. J. S. Kennard, trans., *The Italian Theatre*, vol. 1 (New York, 1932), quoted in Davis, *Farce*, 14.

57. Marx, *Early Writings*, 247–48.

58. Cf. Harries, *Scare Quotes*, 63.

59. See Peter Sloterdijk, *Critique of Cynical Reason* (Minneapolis: University of Minnesota Press, 1988).

60. See Fredric Jameson, "Cognitive Mapping," in *Marxism and the Interpretation of Culture*, ed. Cary Nelson and Lawrence Grossberg (Urbana: University of Illinois Press, 1988), 347–60; Jameson, "Modernism and Imperialism" in Terry Eagleton, Fredric Jameson, and Edward Said, *Nationalism, Colonialism, and Literature* (Minneapolis: University of Minnesota Press, 1990), 43–66.

61. On the importance of peripheral cities to the reemergence of modern tragedy, see John Orr, *Tragic Drama and Modern Society: Studies in the Social and Literary Theory of Drama from 1880 to the Present* (London: Macmillan, 1981), xvii. Cited in Terry Eagleton, *Sweet Violence: The Idea of the Tragic* (Oxford: Blackwell, 2003), 183.

CHAPTER SEVEN

1. See the discussions in Paul A. Cantor, "*Waiting for Godot* and the End of History: Postmodernism as a Democratic Aesthetic," in *Democracy and the Arts*, ed. Arthur M. Melzer, Jerry Weinberger, and M. Richard Zinman (Ithaca, NY: Cornell University Press, 1999), 172–92; and Angela Moorjani, "Diogenes Lampoons Alexandre Kojève: Cultural Ghosts in Beckett's Early French Plays," in *Drawing on Beckett: Portraits, Performances, and Cultural Contexts*, ed. Linda Ben-Zvi (Tel Aviv: Assaph Books, 2003), 69–88.

2. Alexandre Kojève, *Introduction to the Reading of Hegel: Lectures on the Phenomenology of Spirit*, ed. Allan Bloom (Ithaca, NY: Cornell University Press, 1980), 158–59.

3. On Kojève as possible "postmodern ironist," see James H. Nichols Jr., *Alexandre Kojève: Wisdom at the End of History* (Lanham, MD: Rowman and Littlefield, 2007), 9, 87, 115–18, 120, 130n2; and Shadia B. Drury, *Alexandre Kojève: The Roots of Postmodern Politics* (New York: St. Martin's Press, 1994).

4. Alexandre Kojève and Carl Schmitt, "Correspondence," trans. and ed. Erik de Vries, *Interpretation: A Journal of Political Philosophy* 29, no. 1 (2001): 91–115.

5. Alexandre Kojève, "Les peintures concrètes de Kandinsky," *Revue de Metaphysique et de Morale* 90, no. 2 (1985): 149–71.

6. See Alison Caruth, "War Rations and the Food Politics of Late Modernism," *Modernism/modernity* 16, no. 4 (2009): 767–95; and Marjorie Perloff, "'In Love with Hiding': Samuel Beckett's War," *Iowa Review* 35, no. 1 (2005): 76–103. Alys Moody, "Tasteless Beckett: Towards an Aesthetics of Hunger," *symploke* 19, nos. 1–2 (2011): 55–73, offers a less historical and more theoretical approach to the problem of hunger in Beckett.

7. Caruth, "War Rations," 789.

8. All quotations of the play are taken from Samuel Beckett, *Waiting for Godot: A Tragicomedy in Two Acts* (New York: Grove Press, 1963). In the absence of line numbers, all citations are by page number.

9. As Martin Harries points out to me, however, Vladimir and Estragon seem to be hoping for employment of some kind from Godot. If this reasonable reading of the "vague supplication" they make to him is correct, one wonders whether they are hoping for income or merely something to do.

10. Eric Gans, "Beckett and the Problem of Modern Culture," *SubStance* 11, no. 2 (1982): 3–15. Quotation from p. 14.

11. Moody, "Tasteless Beckett," 56–57.

12. Vivian Mercier, review of *Waiting for Godot, Irish Times*, February 18, 1956, 6.

13. There is a considerable bibliography on the philosophical, literary, and sociological dimensions of boredom that treat the issue with much greater subtlety and depth than I do here. I am concerned only with the problem as it pertains to Kojève's interests. The philosophical *locus classicus* is Martin Heidegger, *The Fundamental Problem of Metaphysics: World, Finitude, Solitude*, trans. William McNeill and Nicholas Walker (Bloomington: Indiana University Press, 1995), 75–167. James Phillips treats boredom in Beckett in relation to both Heidegger and Adorno in "Beckett's Boredom," in *Essays on Boredom and Modernity*, ed. Carla Dalle Pezze (Amsterdam: Rodopi, 2009), 109–26.

14. Heidegger, *Fundamental Problem of Metaphysics*, 74–77 and passim.

15. Theodor W. Adorno, *Aesthetic Theory*, trans. Robert Hullot-Kentor (Minneapolis: University of Minnesota Press, 1998), 354. See also James M. Harding, "Trying to Understand Godot: Adorno, Beckett, and the Senility of Historical Dialectics," *Clio* 23, no. 1 (1993): 1–22.

16. Compare Walter Benjamin's treatment of "shock experience" and memory in "On Some Motifs in Baudelaire," in Benjamin, *Illuminations: Essays and Reflections*, trans. Harry Zohn (New York: Schocken, 1969), 155–200.

17. Hegel's *Phenomenology* is a "slave uprising" insofar as it gathers together those civilizing forces (understanding, arts, sciences, etc.) that are the product of the slave and uses these to "comprehend" (in every sense) the historical process that Napoleon, employing the master's tools of violence and war, could not bring to an end without it. And I would say that Kojève reproduces this slave's uprising in the lecture "In Place of an Introduction," which translates and comments on the section on master and slave from the *Phenomenology*. As any reader of this lecture knows, the commentary soon overwhelms and takes command of the Hegelian "master's" discourse.

18. I am being intentionally literal-minded here. From another perspective, the stage is always "haunted" by past performances. See Marvin Carlson, *The Haunted Stage: The Theater as Memory Machine* (Ann Arbor: University of Michigan Press, 2003). But there is at the same time the fiction that the characters onstage were not saying the very same things the night before, and the night before that.

19. Norman Berlin, "Traffic of Our Stage: Why 'Waiting for Godot'?," *Massachusetts Review* 40, no. 3 (1999): 420–34, offers other parallels on 431.

20. "Words words" (41), which I take to be a partial quotation of Hamlet's "Words, words, words."

21. Georges Bataille, *The Accursed Share: An Essay on General Economy*, vols. 2 and 3: *The History of Eroticism* and *Sovereignty*, trans. Robert Hurley (New York: Zone Books, 1993), 16.

22. Ibid., 198.

23. Ibid., 23.

24. Ibid., 23.

25. Georges Bataille, *Visions of Excess: Selected Writings, 1927-1939*, trans. Alan Stoekl (Minneapolis: University of Minnesota Press, 1985), 118.

26. Alan Stoekl, *Bataille's Peak: Energy, Religion, and Postsustainability* (Minneapolis: University of Minnesota Press, 2007), 36.

27. Sade, *Justine, ou les Malheurs de la Vertu* (Paris: Le Soleil Noir, 1950). For Beckett's notebook entry, and more on Beckett's intellectual relation to Bataille, see Peter Fifield, "'Accursed Progenitor!': *Fin de partie* and Georges Bataille," *Samuel Beckett Today/Aujourd'hui* 22 (2010): 107-21.

28. For Bataille's indebtedness to Sade, whose thinking he nevertheless transforms, see Geoffrey Roche, "Black Sun: Bataille on Sade," *Janus Head* 9, no. 1 (2006): 157-80. See also Stoekl, *Bataille's Peak*, 10-31 and passim.

29. James Knowlson, *Damned to Fame: The Life of Samuel Beckett* (New York: Grove Press, 1996), 269; Samuel Beckett, *The Letters of Samuel Beckett*, vol. 2, *1941-1956*, ed. George Craig et al. (Cambridge: Cambridge University Press, 2011), 210-11, 223-26.

30. Stanley Cavell advances both interpretations in his seminal essay, "Ending the Waiting Game: A Reading of Beckett's *Endgame*," in *Must We Mean What We Say?: A Book of Essays* (Cambridge: Cambridge University Press, 1976), 136-37. Vivian Mercier mentions the atomic option in *Beckett/Beckett* (Oxford: Oxford University Press, 1977), 174, and it has since become a commonplace in both critical and directorial contexts.

31. Bataille, *Accursed Share* 1, 169-90.

32. Bataille writes of "the atomic explosion whose disastrous effects could no doubt prove *much greater* than those of natural cataclysms—but we cannot hope for anything miraculous to come of it except in a negative sense." Bataille, *Accursed Share* 2 and 3, 451n8.

33. My claim that Bataillian expenditure relies on the availability of significant resources runs counter to Alan Stoekl's recent book, *Bataille's Peak: Energy, Religion, and Postsustainability*. Stoekl argues that *dépense* is not only possible under conditions of resource exhaustion but also offers a way out of the wasteful energy consumption on which advanced capitalism has come to rely. While I have benefited from Stoekl's subtle, patient, and often inspired exegesis of Bataille, I do think that it tends to ignore or downplay those elements of *scale* that suffuse Bataille's writings. Yes, the experience of the sacred can be powered by the body alone, in its anguish, ecstasy, and perverse sexuality. But Bataille is not infrequently drawn to images of vast, cataclysmic expenditure as well, not least when depicting political revolution. Or take this description of the Marshall Plan from *The Accursed Share*:

> While it is true that it is hard to imagine the United States prospering for long without the aid of a hecatomb of riches, in the form of airplanes, bombs and other military equipment, one can conceive of an equivalent hecatomb devoted to nonlethal works. In other words, if war is necessary to the American economy, it does not follow that war has to hold to the traditional form. Indeed, one easily imagines, coming from across the Atlantic, a resolute movement refusing to follow the routine: A conflict is not necessarily military; one can envisage a vast economic competition, which, for the competitor with the initiative, would cost sacrifices comparable to those of war, and which, from a budget *of the same scale* as war budgets, would involve expenditure that would not be compensated by any hope of capitalist profit (2 and 3, 172, my emphasis).

The sublimity of Bataille's vision frequently (though not always) relies on a grandness of scale that is not merely incidental.

34. Ruby Cohn, *Just Play: Beckett's Theater* (Princeton, NJ: Princeton University Press, 1980), 173-74.

35. Quoted in S. E. Gontarski, "An End to Endings: Samuel Beckett's Endgame(s)," *Samuel Beckett Today/Aujourd'hui* 19 (2008): 424.

36. I am leaving out of the equation the possibility that Clov's spotting of the boy outside, which indicates life beyond the bunker, is a precipitating event of the more ordinary sort. But this trigger in turn presupposes a threshold already reached via infinitesimal increments.

37. The marginalist revolution of the 1870s took this process one step further by turning even the individual into a "balance" that weighed "indefinitely small" or "infinitesimal" units of pleasure and pain, thus miniaturizing Bentham's utilitarian calculus by reducing the scale of enjoyment to something not entirely alien to that found in Beckett's works. See W. Stanley Jevons, *The Theory of Political Economy* (London: Macmillan, 1871), vii, 11, and 14.

38. A final question: do the collected thematics of the heap (admirably explicated by Gordon Teskey in *Delirious Milton: The Fate of the Poet in Modernity* [Cambridge, MA: Harvard University Press, 2009], 180-202), grain, blindness, and the desperate attempt to end self and world at once, suffice to establish a connection between *Endgame* and *Samson Agonistes*?

39. We might even think of the comma as a diacritical "grain" or minim that cannot, through addition, make up the heap.

40. Bataille, *Visions of Excess*, 121, 128.

POSTSCRIPT

1. Paolo Virno, *A Grammar of the Multitude: For an Analysis of Contemporary Forms of Life*, trans. Isabella Bertoletti, James Cascaito, and Andrea Casson (Los Angeles: Semiotext[e], 2004), 41.

2. See Arlie Russell Hochschild's classic study, *The Managed Heart: The Commercialization of Human Feeling* (Berkeley: University of California Press, 1983), and Kathi Weeks, *The Problem with Work: Feminism, Marxism, Antiwork Politics, and Postwork Imaginaries* (Durham, NC: Duke University Press, 2011).

3. Nicholas Ridout, *Passionate Amateurs: Theatre, Communism, and Love* (Ann Arbor: University of Michigan Press, 2014), 50.

4. Elinor Fuchs, *The Death of Character: Perspectives on Theater after Modernism* (Bloomington: Indiana University Press, 1996), 70.

5. Ridout, *Passionate Amateurs*, 6, 29, 4.

6. Pascal Gielen, *The Murmuring of the Artistic Multitude: Global Art, Memory and Post-Fordism* (Amsterdam: Valiz, 2010), 25.

7. See, for instance, the performances discussed in Shannon Jackson, "Tech Support: Labor in the Global Theatres of the Builder's Association and Rimini Protokoll," in Jackson, *Social Works: Performing Art, Supporting Publics* (London and New York: Routledge, 2011); Shannon Jackson, "Just in Time: Performance and the Aesthetics of Precarity," *TDR: The Drama Review* 56, no. 4 (2012): 10-31; and Michael Shayne Boyle, "'Love Is Colder Than Capital': The Post-Fordist Labor of René Pollesch's Postdramatic Theater," http://www.academia.edu/4287016/Just-in-Time_Precarity_Affect_and_the_Labor_of_Performance.

8. See Hans-Thies Lehmann, *Postdramatic Theatre*, trans. Karen Jürs-Munby (London: Routledge, 2006), 57, 58, 123, 164.

9. Ibid., 61.

10. Performance may, of course, embrace its relation to ephemerality and disappearance. See, e.g., Peggy Phelan, *Unmarked: The Politics of Performance* (London and New York: Routledge, 1993), chap. 7: "The Ontology of Performance: Representation without Reproduction" (146-66), and Rebecca Schneider, *Performing Remains: Art and War in Times of Theatrical Reenactment* (London and New York: Routledge, 2011).

11. See Robert Weimann, *Shakespeare and the Popular Tradition in the Theater: Studies in the Social Dimension of Dramatic Form and Function* (Baltimore: Johns Hopkins University Press, 1978), esp. 73-85.

12. I explore Arendt's (and Jacques Rancière's) tendency to patrol the boundaries of the political in my essay, "Greek Tragedy and Democratic Thought: Arendt to Rancière," *Critical Inquiry* 37, no. 3 (2011): 545-72.

13. All quotations of *Blasted* are taken from Sarah Kane, *Complete Plays* (London: Methuen, 2001). In the absence of line numbers, I cite the play by page number.

14. See, e.g., Jack Tinker, "This Disgusting Feast of Filth," *Daily Mail*, January 19, 1995; and Michael Billington, "The Good Fairies Desert the Court's Theatre of the Absurd," *The Guardian*, January 20, 1995, both reprinted in *Theatre Record* 15, no. 1 (1995): 42-43, 39.

15. See Aleks Siertz, *In-Yer-Face Theatre: British Drama Today* (London: Faber and Faber, 2001).

16. For some especially valuable examples, see Graham Saunders, *"Love Me or Kill Me": Sarah Kane and the Theatre of Extremes* (Manchester: Manchester University Press, 2002), 37-70; several of the essays in Laurens De Vos and Graham Sunders, eds., *Sarah Kane in Context* (Manchester: Manchester University Press, 2010); Helen Iball, *Sarah Kane's* Blasted (London: Continuum, 2008); Kim Solga, *"Blasted's* Hysteria: Rape, Realism, and the Threshold of the Visible," *Modern Drama* 50, no. 3 (2007): 346-74; and Christopher Wixson, "'In Better Places': Space, Identity, and Alienation in Sarah Kane's *Blasted*," *Comparative Drama* 39, no. 1 (2005): 75-91.

17. "In terms of Aristotle's Unities, the time and action are disrupted, while unity of place is maintained." Sarah Kane, quoted in Saunders, *Love Me or Kill Me*, 41.

18. Kane herself cited Ibsen as an influence on scene 1. Quoted in Saunders, *Love Me or Kill Me*, 41.

19. For an acute analysis of the symbolic and material layout of the hotel room, see Helen Iball, "Room Service: En Suite on the *Blasted* Frontline," *Contemporary Theatre Review* 15, no. 3 (2005): 320-29.

20. Paul Taylor, "Courting Disaster," *Independent*, January 20, 1995. Quoted in De Vos and Saunders, *Sarah Kane in Context*, 91.

21. Quoted in Saunders, *Love Me or Kill Me*, 14.

22. Cf. Herbert Blau's dicta that "there is no theater without *separation*" and that "the audience is there as the aggregate body of separation." Herbert Blau, *The Audience* (Baltimore: Johns Hopkins University Press, 1990), 10, 84.

23. Interview quoted in Saunders, *Love Me or Kill Me*, 33.

24. Jack Tinker, "This Disgusting Feast of Filth," *Daily Mail*, January 19, 1995. Reprinted in *Theatre Record* 15, no. 1 (1995): 39.

25. Vera Gottlieb, "Lukewarm Britain," in *Theatre in a Cool Climate*, ed. Vera Gottlieb and Colin Chambers (Oxford: Amber Lane Press, 1999), 201-12. Quotation from p. 212.

26. Hannah Arendt, *The Human Condition*, 2nd ed. (Chicago: University of Chicago Press, 1998), 236-43.

27. See, for instance, Benedict Nightingale's review of the 2001 production for *The Times*, April 5, 2001. Reprinted in *Theatre Record* 21, no. 7 (2001): 421.

28. Susan Sontag, "Godot Comes to Sarajevo," *New York Review of Books* 40, no. 17 (1993): 52-59.

29. Ibid., 52.

30. Jan Kott, "*King Lear* or *Endgame*," in Kott, *Shakespeare Our Contemporary* (New York: Norton, 1974), 127-68. On *Blasted*, Lear, and Beckett, see Graham Saunders, *Love Me or Kill Me*, 54-70. See also Graham Saunders, "The Beckettian World of Sarah Kane," in De Vos and Saunders, *Sarah Kane in Context*, 68-79, and Graham Saunders, "'Out Vile Jelly': Sarah Kane's 'Blasted' and Shakespeare's 'King Lear,'" *New Theatre Quarterly* 20, no. 1 (2004): 69-78.

31. Here I align myself with Nicholas Ridout's emphasis on love as that which exceeds recuperation/subsumption.

Index

Abraham, 169-70, 175-76

abstract expressionism, 231

absurdist theater, 224

Accursed Share, The (Bataille), 246-47, 299n33

Achilles, 34, 131, 157

action, 6, 9, 17, 25, 29, 31, 33-34, 38-41, 43, 45-46, 48, 53, 55, 62, 79-81, 85, 89-90, 92-93, 101, 105-7, 121, 123, 129-30, 140, 142, 146, 148-49, 151, 157, 171, 176, 178, 182, 191, 193-96, 205, 228, 233, 239, 241, 245, 248-52, 258, 262, 267-69; alienation of, 110; concept of, 199, 253; crisis of, 2-5, 7-8, 10-13, 18, 23, 52, 59-60, 138, 227, 254; exchange, as form of, 66-67; fate of, 7; as heroic, 24, 35, 37, 60, 77, 82-84, 160, 243; human essence of, 54; imitation of, 2, 8; and inaction, 138, 150, 236; and intention, 44; and labor, 179-80; as meaningful, 24, 57, 122, 166, 175, 179-80, 224, 226, 243; as political, 13-15, 18-20, 24, 27, 51, 59-61, 63, 70, 73-74, 108, 177, 180, 203, 230, 244, 256; possibility of, 60, 235-36, 240; and production, 8, 26-27, 165, 177, 179, 200-201, 242, 255, 260; as revolutionary, 206-7, 229-30; and speech, 66, 68-70; as states of suffering, 47; as term, 42; as thinking, 147, 158; and tragedy, 2, 49, 110, 120, 160, 169, 175, 180, 198, 242; unity of, 234-35; as "whole," 20-22; and work, 64-65, 71. *See also* crisis of action

Act to Restrain the Abuses of Players (1606), 123

Adam Smith's Marketplace of Life (Otteson), 41

adikéma kema (unjust act), 49

adikon, to (unjust), 49

Adorno, Theodor, 237, 288n69; art, semblance character of, 136-37

Aegisthus, 93, 95

Aeschylus, 11, 25, 74, 76, 81-83, 86-87, 89-90, 92, 97, 99, 102, 107, 159, 161-62, 164-66, 178, 222, 234, 255

Aesopus, 109

aesthetic philosophy, 182, 188

Aesthetics: Lectures on Fine Arts (Hegel). See *Lectures on Aesthetics*

Aesthetic Theory (Adorno), 136

Agamben, Giorgio, 81, 139

Agamemnon, 9, 25, 81-82, 84-90, 91-93, 95-97, 101, 104, 175-76, 281n40, 281n42, 281n53; death of, 88, 90; raptor economy, as exemplifying, 93; sacrifice of, 169, 175

Agamemnon (Aeschylus), 25, 85-92, 95, 99-100, 104, 234; eagles, portent of, 105; mother hare, 105; raptors, invoking of, 84

aigypios, 83-84

Ajax, 175

akrasia, 122

Alexander the Great, 26, 119, 126-27, 134, 141, 148-49

39, 242–46, 254, 298n13; act, inflationary notions of, 244; end of history, 27, 228–30, 236, 239, 244; Japan, visit to, 230; labor, as form of action, 230; master-slave encounter, 228, 230, 236–38, 243, 254; and posthistory, 233, 235–36, 243
Kott, Jan, 271
Kottman, Paul A., 73
Krapp's Last Tape (Beckett), 253
Kyd, Thomas, 156–58

labor theory of value, 34, 62, 66–67
Labour Party, 22
Lacan, Jacques, 51, 130, 140, 164, 227, 288n6
Laertes, 143
Langley, Francis, 283–84n11
Lattimore, Richmond, 83
Lear, King, 50, 96, 162, 267, 269–71
Lectures on Aesthetics (Hegel), 26, 182–83, 190, 192, 196–97, 199, 218, 223, 295n21
Lectures on Jurisprudence (Smith), 276n8, 277n25
Lehmann, Hans-Thies, 4–5, 260
Levin, Harry, 125–26
Libation Bearers, The (Aeschylus), 25
Life of the Mind, The (Arendt), 290n24
Loewenstein, Joseph, 117
Loman, Willy, 15–17
London (England), 139, 152
Loraux, Nicole, 278–79n4, 282n65
Lord Admiral's Men, 110, 113–14, 283–84n11, 285n18
Lord Pembroke's Men, 113, 283–84n11
Lucian, 222
Lucky, 228, 232–33, 236–37, 240–42, 249; name of, 237; speech of, 238–39, 241
Lukács, Georg, 4
Lupton, Julia Reinhard, 289n11
Lutheranism, 122
lyric poetry, 191, 194

Maar, Michael, 288n69
Macbeth, 30–31, 52–53
Macbeth (Shakespeare), 161; invisible hand, 30–31, 52–53
Machiavel and the Devil (Daborne), 111–12, 116
Machiavelli, Niccolò, 60
Mackenzie, Henry, 150
Macpherson, C. B., 116
Maeterlink, Edward, 3

Magnificent Entertainment, The (Dekker), 117
Mahler, Gustav, 288n69
Maledicat, 118, 123
Malone Dies (Beckett), 232
Malthus, Thomas Robert, 16
Mann, Thomas, 137, 288n69
Manoa, 174, 177–78
Marlowe, Christopher, 11, 25, 110–20, 122–26, 128–32, 135, 137, 285n19, 286n26, 287n64. *See also individual works*
Marshall Plan, 231, 247, 299n33
Martin, Jean, 249
Marx, Karl, 11–13, 20, 24, 27, 40, 53, 60, 106, 109–10, 143–44, 169, 176–77, 179, 182–83, 189, 198–25, 254, 278n56, 289n15, 295n17, 296n39; action, problem of, 200–201, 203; agency, 207, 220; class struggle, and becoming-rabble, 223, 225; comedy, as satire, 222; economic alienation, 119; and farce, 219, 221–23; "great man" theory of history, parodying of, 202; Hegelian legacy of, 199; history, understanding of, 200–202, 208, 222, 229; and lumpenproletariat, 189, 214–16, 218, 220, 222–23; parliamentary cretinism, 208; *praxis*, concept of, 200–201; proletarian revolution, 204–7, 213; social class, 201–2, 205; and tragedy, 222
medieval drama, 109
megethos (amplitude), 23, 157
melodrama, 181
Menelaus, 133
Mephastophilis, 112–18, 121–22, 125–28, 130, 133, 135–37, 284–85n16, 284–85n17, 285n18; Faustus, pact with, 25, 114–17, 120–22, 126–28, 133; heaven, banishment from, 133
Mercier, Vivian, 234, 299n30
Merleau-Ponty, Maurice, 227
Mésures (journal), 227
Meyer, Hans, 288n69
Mill, John Stuart, 11–12
Miller, Arthur, 13–15, 17, 21–22
Milton, John, 12, 26, 31, 160–62, 164, 166–72, 176, 178, 180, 292n17; labor, as punishment, 179; Noachide laws, 293–94n35
mimesis, 69, 135–36, 258–59
Mises, Ludwig von, 66–67, 72
modernity, 62, 108, 191–92; crisis of action, 3; and tragedy, 2, 192; tragic drama, 2, 225
Modern Tragedy (Williams), 1, 20–23
Montesquieu, 60